Annotated Catalogue of the

H. Colin Slim
Stravinsky Collection

Donated by him
to The University of British Columbia Library

National Library of Canada Cataloguing in Publication Data
University of British Columbia Library,
Special Collections and University Archives Division.
    Annotated cataloque of the H. Colin Slim Stravinsky collection
    donated by him to the University of British Columbia Library

    ISBN 0-88865-221-6

    1. Stravinsky, Igor, 1882-1971 – Archives – Catalogs. 2. University
of British Columbia Library. Special Collections and University Archives
Division – Catalogs. I. Slim, H. Colin (Harry Colin). II. Title.
ML134.S96S54 2002   016.78'092   C2001-911513X

The Library gratefully acknowledges the financial support and collecting commitment of Dr. H. Colin Slim that made this catalogue possible. This catalogue is not for sale. It is distributed gratis to conservatories of music, scholarly institutions, and to individuals with an interest in Igor Stravinsky. Its intent is to increase an appreciation of the composer's achievements and to stimulate further research about him and his works.

Printed and bound in Canada by Benwell-Atkins
Set in Bembo and Univers by Artegraphica Design Co. Ltd.
Copy editor: Susan Quirk
Designer: Irma Rodriguez, Artegraphica Design Co. Ltd.
Proofreader: Gail Copeland
Indexer: Patricia Buchanan

The University of British Columbia Library
1956 Main Mall
Vancouver, BC V6T 1Z1
Tel.: (604) 822-4879
Fax: (604) 822-9587
spcoll@interchange.ubc.ca
www.library.ubc.ca/spcoll

For

LUCY, MATTIE, GIB, AND GIBSON

and in memory of

HARRY SLIM (1900–72)

and

MARJORIE ANN SLIM (NÉE COLLINS, 1902–57),

loving and beloved parents

I CANNOT, UNDERSTAND ME, CANNOT,

COMPOSE WHAT OTHERS WANT FROM ME — THAT IS,

TO REITERATE: REPEAT ANYBODY YOU LIKE BUT NOT YOURSELF —

BECAUSE THAT IS EXACTLY HOW PEOPLE

WRITE THEMSELVES OUT.

Stravinsky, letter to Benois, 3 October 1913,
I.F. Stravinsky: Perepiska s russkimi korrespondentami: Materalï k biographi,
ed. Viktor Varunts (Moscow: Kompozitor, 2000), vol. 2 (1913-22), pp. 146-7.
Translation provided by Stanislav Shvabrin and Michael Green.

THE LETTERS AND JOURNALS WE LEAVE BEHIND

AND THE IMPRESSIONS WE HAVE MADE ON OUR CONTEMPORARIES

ARE THE MERE HUSK OF OUR ESSENTIAL LIFE.

WHEN WE DIE, THE KERNEL IS BURIED WITH US.

Janet Malcolm,
"Travels with Chekhov," *The New Yorker,* 21 and 28 February 2000: 248

ACKNOWLEDGMENTS

Madame Denise Strawinsky, Fondation Théodore Strawinsky, Geneva, and John Stravinsky, Bellport, New York, have graciously permitted the reproduction of printed, written, and visual materials by and pertaining to Igor Stravinsky in this catalogue.

Regarding the commentary to many of its entries, I am indebted to a modern "Mighty Five," all of them multiple contributors. Their patriarch is Robert Craft, whom I do not know personally (although I once sang *Zvezdolikiy* under his direction). His many publications obligate all admirers of the composer. My colleagues Stephen Walsh and Richard Taruskin have rendered the utmost assistance. Viktor Varunts generously sent me the initial two volumes of his meticulous edition in progress of Stravinsky's Russian correspondence. For this catalogue I did not utilize the riches of the recently published *Stravinsky Inside Out,* by Charles M. Joseph, though several of his earlier publications are cited here. One can only stand in awe of such a collective expertise. Without their extraordinary knowledge of the composer and his works, the catalogue could never have been completed, and I wish to thank them most heartily.

Among those responsible for scholarly collections who have so kindly aided me, I must single out Johanna Blask, Paul Sacher Foundation, Basel; Charlotte B. Brown, Jefferey Rankin, and Octavio Olvera, Special Collections, Charles E. Young Research Library, University of California, Los Angeles; Kate Rivers, Music Division, Library of Congress; John Roberts and (formerly) Judy Tsou, Music Library, University of California, Berkeley; and J. Rigbie Turner, The Morgan Library, New York.

For help with myriad details great and small – too many to explicate here – I gratefully acknowledge the late Frances Marr Adaskin, Gordon Adaskin, Sally Avila, M. Elizabeth Bartlet, Ullrich Bethe, Bonnie J. Blackburn, Richard Boursey, Jeanice Brooks, Malcolm H. Brown, William Theophilus Brown, James Camner, Paul Cary, Lenore Coral, Lisa Cox, Caleb Cushing, Annette Fern, Elliot Forbes, Julio Gonzales, Michael Green, Ralph Grierson, Diane Haskell, Daniel Heartz, Robert Heylmun, Monika Holl, Dell Anne Hollingsworth, the late Dorothy Ellis McQuoid Hopper, Carol S. Jacobs, Owen Jander, Leonard W. Johnson, Charles M. Joseph,

Simon Karlinsky, Patricia Kellogg, Warren Kirkendale, Steven Lacoste, James Lambert, Vladimir and Victorina Lefebvre, Harry Locke, Lewis Lockwood, J. & J. Lubrano, Gibson Mann, Esperanza Martinez, the late Roddy McDowall, Timothy J. McGee, Barbara Meloni, Seymour Menton, Carol Merrill-Mirsky, Ronald L. Milne, Hiroyuki Minamino, Jean Mongrédien, Marcia P. Neville, Linda K. Ogden, Thomas Peattie, Audrey Piggott, Katherine Powers, Jesse Read, Dale Reubart, Richard Romm, Kay Kaufman Shelemay, John Shepard, Stanislav Shvabrin, Martin A. Silver, George Sponhaltz, Dean Carl Trock, Viktor Varunts, Elisabeth Vilatte, Frank Villella, Ronald W. Wakefield, Michael Walensky, James Westby, Ross Whitney, Marianne Wurlitzer, and Gene Bruck.

This catalogue is not for sale. It is distributed gratis to conservatories of music, scholarly institutions, and to individuals with an interest in Igor Stravinsky. Its intent is to increase an appreciation of the composer's achievements and to stimulate further research about him and his works.

Conspectus

ANNOTATED CATALOGUE OF THE

H. Colin Slim
Stravinsky Collection

INTRODUCTION

A few words seem in order to introduce this catalogue, to explain my great interest in the twentieth-century composer, Igor Fyodorovich Stravinsky (1882-1971),[1] and to describe how the collection came to be assembled. Other Stravinsky enthusiasts have offered various degrees of competition. For example, the Foundation in Basle set up in 1973 by Paul Sacher (1906-99) – which, since 1983, houses the largest archive of the composer's music manuscripts, documents, and memorabilia – has had almost unlimited buying power. And during the past thirty years the Pierpont Morgan Library in New York has added significantly to its already outstanding holdings. Obviously, the present collection is not comparable in scope to either of these collections.

Still, it has proved possible over the thirty years since Stravinsky's death to assemble a modest collection, even this slim one. Every period of the composer's extraordinarily rich and varied life is represented here, although his career in Russia is touched on in just two entries.

His Russian period – before he arrived in Paris in June 1910 for the premiere of *The Firebird* – is alluded to in Entry 1 by a reference to his teacher, Nicolai Rimsky-Korsakov (1844-1908). He returned to Russian territory mostly in the summers to his estate in Ustilug until the beginning of the First World War, during which and for a year and a half afterward he lived in Switzerland with his family. For all intents and purposes, by the premiere of *The Firebird,* Stravinsky had emigrated to the West.

Entry 3, however, is much more than an allusion to Stravinsky's Russian career. It is a precious and concrete musical quotation – albeit a miniature one – from *Deux poèmes,* his second-last work to be conceived and completed on Russian soil, during the summer of 1911 at Ustilug. One hopes that the relative paucity of representation of his Russian years in the collection will some day be rectified. Such early items still surface on the market, even if rarely.[2]

Even though this collection has no correspondence dating before 1911, three men who figure in it knew Stravinsky earlier in Russia. His friendship spanning the longest number of years was with Alexis Fyodorovich Kall (1878-1948). In 1940 Kall stated that he had known Stravinsky four decades earlier, that is, during some of their years together at the University of St. Petersburg. And indeed, both men were reported together at Rimsky-Korsakov's home in November of 1903. In this collection, however, Kall first surfaces only in 1935, in a photograph with Stravinsky and the actor Edward G. Robinson taken in Los Angeles (Entry 40), then again in late 1939 at Cambridge, Massachusetts, as mentioned in Stravinsky's letter to Pierre Monteux (Entry 65), and finally in 1940 as a photographer of the composer and his second wife, Vera, aboard ship on their way to Kall's home in Los Angeles (Entry 69).

The second of these figures is Alfredo Casella (1883-1947). Stravinsky first met him in November 1907 at an orchestral rehearsal in St. Petersburg, even though Casella forgot this encounter until Stravinsky reminded him of it four years later in Paris. Relatively early in their relationship, the Stravinsky-Casella correspondence is represented by three postcards in the period 1914-15 (entries 7-9).

Although of the shortest duration, the friendship which exerted by far the greatest influence upon Stravinsky was the one with Sergei Pavlovich Diaghilev (1872-1929). Attending the premiere of the *Scherzo fantastique* (1908) in January 1909, Diaghilev quickly commissioned from the young composer two orchestrations of Chopin for the appearance of the Russian Ballet in Paris that June. By the time Diaghilev's official commission for *The Firebird* (1910) arrived in December 1909, Stravinsky recalled that he had already been composing it for a month.[3] Diaghilev's name is already implicit in the present collection's first item with its mention of *The Firebird* and *Petrushka*; indeed, Stravinsky was with Diaghilev in Rome when he was finishing this second ballet score in May 1911. Diaghilev's name appears explicitly thereafter (entries 4, 6, 8-9, 17, 19, 37, 43, 46, 78, 86, 94).

In respect to my native city, Vancouver, the collection contains four items (entries 91-4) relating to Stravinsky's first visit. Accompanied by his daughter Milène and her husband André Marion, his secretary, Stravinsky rehearsed and conducted the Vancouver Symphony Orchestra, 2-5 October 1952. Additional materials concerning this visit certainly remain in the city.[4]

Sadly, however, there is nothing whatever concerning his second visit in mid-July 1965 to conduct the orchestra at the Vancouver Festival. This time his second wife, Vera, his brilliant associate, the conductor Robert Craft, and his putative biographer, Lawrence Morton, accompanied him. Because I had not lived in Vancouver for ten years and was that very July occupied with moving from Chicago to California, I missed attending Stravinsky's last concerts in Vancouver. Surely mementoes of this 1965 visit still exist in Vancouver?[5] Owners of such memorabilia might well want to consider donating them to the University of British Columbia (UBC), the home of this collection.

Over the years, this collection has grown through the generosity of friends, colleagues, and dealers. To them I extend my thanks as well as appreciation for their tolerance of the peculiar obsession called collecting.

Among the first Stravinsky works I recall hearing in Vancouver – admittedly with considerable perplexity at age sixteen – was the Sunday afternoon broadcast premiere on 27 January 1946 of the *Symphony in Three Movements* (1945) with him conducting the New York Philharmonic. (This performance is now available on CD.) To anticipate a little, a mere fifteen years later at the University of Chicago, its first movement was being taught to freshmen humanities students. Even then, however, this was not without contentious and sometimes bitter debate among that fractious faculty – which included me at the time – about the structure and meaning of this compelling work.

Interest in Stravinsky's music quickened when I discovered *The Rite of Spring* (1913) on a 1948 recording by the Amsterdam Concertgebuow under Edward van Beinum. As an undergraduate in the period 1947-51 pursuing a triple major in English, German, and Music at UBC, I purchased my first miniature score of that very work, soon followed by the miniature score to his 1947 revision of *Petrushka* (1911). Then, as now, scores were expensive. Canada added, moreover, a hefty additional twenty-five percent tariff – not helpful for a college music student in the slowly recovering post-Second World War Canadian economy.

For the record then, before departing Vancouver in September 1953 to enrol in Harvard's graduate school, I had already met Stravinsky and heard him rehearse the Vancouver Symphony Orchestra – but more of that below. By this time, I had acquired seven more scores: in July 1951, the *Concerto per due pianoforti soli* (1935) and, in August, *Les Noces* (1923); in September 1952, the 1919 *Firebird Suite*; in November, the *Symphony of Psalms* (1930); in December, *Apollon Musagète* (1928); and, sometime that year, the *Suite no. 2 for Small Orchestra* (1921). Early in 1953, having heard Stravinsky conduct it in Vancouver the previous season, I bought a miniature score of the symphonic version of *Scherzo à la Russe* (1945). Except for *Apollon Musagète* – which full score, with the *Symphony of Psalms,* I got by joining Boosey and Hawkes's "Score of the Month Club" – his works thus acquired were vital for me to conduct and perform them, first in Vancouver in 1952, then in Concord in 1956, later in Chicago in 1959-65, and, lastly, in Los Angeles in 1966.

Studying in Vancouver during 1952-53 for entrance examinations to graduate school, I took the opportunity that March to become acquainted with Stravinsky's *Poetics of Music* (Cambridge, MA, 1947), a translation (Entry 86) of six lectures he had delivered in French at Harvard in 1939-40 as the Charles Eliot Norton Professor of

Poetry (Entry 78). While journeying shortly thereafter to Ottawa late in April 1953 with co-pianist John Brockington (1929-) to accompany the British Columbia Ballet at the Fifth Canadian Ballet Festival, I bought in a small Montreal bookshop a first edition of his *Chroniques de ma vie* (Paris, 1935) and the Plon re-edition of the *Poétique Musicale* (1952). Inscribed copies of both – the former to his English translator and the latter to the Music Department at UBC – are in this collection (entries 43 and 94).

Stravinsky scores I acquired early in Vancouver and the remainder of his works, bought mostly at Chicago in 1962, formed the basis for teaching courses about his music at the University of Chicago, 1959-65, as well as at the University of California, Irvine, from 1965 until my retirement in 1994, and in a graduate seminar there in the spring of 2001. And although Stravinsky certainly never knew it, several of his scores bought earlier in Vancouver – the *Concerto per due pianoforti soli, Les Noces, The Firebird Suite,* and the *Symphony of Psalms* – were, directly or indirectly, responsible for my two brief encounters with him: one in Vancouver in 1952, the other in Los Angeles fourteen years later.

To tell of the first encounter requires going back to the fall of 1951. With John Brockington as co-pianist, I had begun to practise the *Concerto per due pianoforti soli,* at the same time preparing myself in order to conduct *Les Noces* at UBC. Both works soon had their Canadian premieres at the university, early in April 1952. We were coached in the concerto by our mutual teacher, the distinguished pianist, Frances Marr Adaskin (1900-2001). With her husband, Harry Adaskin (1901-94), the first professor of Music at UBC, she also performed the *Duo Concertant* (1932). She joined Brockington, faculty member the late Barbara Pentland (1912-2000), and student Franklin Fetherstonhaugh (1931-) in playing the four pianos required for *Les Noces*.

Our performance in April 1952 of these three works at UBC (see Entry 90) was ultimately responsible for an invitation to Stravinsky to lead the Vancouver Symphony Orchestra the following October. Even before our concert, Professor Adaskin had written him, on 27 February, inviting him to UBC around 7 April to lecture about his music, an engagement that he was unable to accept. On 8 April he thanked Adaskin for having sent him the program, hoping it had been successful, and enquiring about possibly conducting the Vancouver Symphony Orchestra late in September. Adaskin put the Board of Directors of the Symphony Society in touch with him and, on 25 April the orchestra's business manager C.E. Barraclough tentatively suggested 5 October to Stravinsky. The same day (5 May) that Barraclough mailed a formal invitation, Adaskin wrote too, suggesting that he also conduct a concert of his chamber music at UBC in October for which Adaskin would rehearse the players. He agreed and proposed including his son, Soulima (see Entry 61). Unfortunately, the entire project fell through because Adaskin was unable to raise sufficient funds for what he deemed would necessarily entail a large number of rehearsals, characterizing professional musicians in Vancouver at that time as insufficiently experienced in modern music.[6]

Arriving in Vancouver from Seattle by train on 1 October 1952 with his daughter Milène and her husband André Marion (1909-83) (see entries 6 and 102), Stravinsky rehearsed the orchestra hard on 2 October through 4 October, and on the morning of 5 October.[7] The autographed photograph that he presented to Harry Adaskin on 3 October in his home at UBC and one of Stravinsky taken two days later by Eric Skipsey are in this collection (entries 91-2).

To the final (semi–public) rehearsal on Sunday morning 5 October, Barraclough drove Stravinsky and me, mostly tongue-tied, from the Hotel Vancouver to the Orpheum Theatre. Half a century later, I still cannot fully explain not mentioning to him our performances of his music at UBC the previous April. After being introduced to him, I instinctively remained quiet, sensing that he was concentrating on the coming rehearsal. There, with a Kalmus pirated edition in hand, I followed and annotated in it his quite fluid conducting of the 1919 *Firebird Suite*. Hearing also at this rehearsal for the first time the "Little Russian" symphony by Tchaikovsky (1840-93), I vividly recall him turning his back to the first violins whenever any lyric passage would occur. One of my early teachers in Vancouver, the Viennese-born Dr. Ida Halpern (1910-87), substantiated this recollection. Reviewing the concert, she wrote: "There was none of the over-emotionalism of Tschaikovsky's latest [*recte:* last] symphony in this work."[8] A photograph shows Stravinsky rehearsing the first movement of this symphony at Aspen Colorado at the beginning of August 1950.[9] A decade earlier Edwin and Dorothy Ellis McQuoid had heard Stravinsky lead both the "Little Russian" and the 1919 *Firebird Suite* at the Hollywood Bowl. Their souvenir from him of that occasion, 27 August 1940, is in the present collection (Entry 71).

Mrs. Adaskin published in 1994 a charming anecdote about Stravinsky's 1952 appearance in Vancouver,[10] to which she kindly confided additional details during my summer visits to Vancouver in 1995 and 1997. Playing for Stravinsky his *Divertimento* – arranged by him and Samuel Dushkin [1891-1976], published 1934 in Berlin – on the evening of 3 October in their home at UBC, a work which the Adaskins were then preparing for public performance, they asked his opinion concerning two pitches – A and A-flat. (These notes appear in the piano part of its "Sinfonia" p. 5, mm. 6-7, and her copy contains her inked-in cautionary A-natural sign, m. 6.) Uncertain which note was correct, he tried out on their piano the passage in question both ways several times from the beginning, ultimately declaring that it "could be eizer," though preferring A. Their dilemma was resolved when the

Adaskins indeed heard the cellos play A during his performance of the orchestral *Divertimento* (p. 7, two measures before rehearsal no. **10**) he led with the Vancouver Symphony Orchestra two days later, a work that I had heard him rehearse that very morning. Two autograph pages of it are in the collection (Entry 45).

As a teaching assistant at Harvard in 1956 for Professor Arthur Tillman Merritt (1902-98) in his course, "Form and Analysis," I had the good fortune to study the *Dumbarton Oaks Concerto* (1938) with Merritt and with his undergraduates. He was a former student (1927-28) in Paris of Nadia Boulanger, who conducted the work's premiere at Dumbarton Oaks in 1938, and he was a professor in the Harvard music department at the time of Stravinsky's residence as the Charles Eliot Norton Professor of Poetry. A long-time scholar of his music, Merritt brought an uncommon degree of familiarity with and insight into Stravinsky's music.[11]

During my graduate student years in Cambridge, the nearby Concord Orchestra had appointed me its conductor (1955-58). On 1 February 1956, with these adventurous and well-educated amateur adult musicians I led, for their and for my first time, Stravinsky's *Suite no. 2 for Small Orchestra* (1921). This same suite I programmed again at the University of Chicago on 9 December 1960, during my time as assistant professor and conductor of the university's symphony orchestra (1959-65). Thereafter, his music frequently appeared on our orchestra's concerts: *Scherzo à la Russe* on 27 May 1961, *Circus Polka* (1942), and his arrangement of *The Star-Spangled Banner* (1941) on 1 December 1962, his arrangement of the *Song of the Volga Boatmen* (1917) on 25 May 1963, and the *Symphonies of Wind Instruments* (1920) the following year, 8 and 23 May. At Chicago in the spring quarter of 1963, I also offered undergraduate courses on Stravinsky. With Professor Grosvenor Cooper (1913-84) kindly assisting at piano I, we played the *Concerto per due pianoforti soli* for the students who were at that time studying it, thus bringing an immediacy of experience of this splendid composition to our classroom.

The next summer, on 18 July 1964, I heard Stravinsky conduct his *Orpheus* (1947) at Ravinia Park with the Chicago Symphony Orchestra, a work he recorded two days later with that great ensemble. And shortly before resigning from the University of Chicago the following year to join the new Irvine campus of the University of California, I had the good fortune to hear, in Chicago on 17 April, world premieres of *Variations Aldous Huxley in Memoriam* (1964) and the *Introitus T.S. Eliot in Memoriam* (1965), with Robert Craft conducting and Stravinsky in the audience.

A second and slightly longer conversation than the one I had with him in Vancouver took place in Los Angeles early in 1966, shortly after being appointed associate professor and chairman of the music department at Irvine. Late in the previous fall, one of my adult students, Elizabeth Mason, who then belonged to the Roger Wagner Chorale in Los Angeles, mentioned that additional male singers were being sought for performances of *Zvezdolikiy* (1911), to be conducted by Craft, as well as for the *Symphony of Psalms* and for Stravinsky's arrangement of Bach's Chorale-Variations on *Vom Himmel hoch* (1956). The latter two works he was to lead in 1966 with the Los Angeles Philharmonic, 27-28 January.[12] Though assuredly not an accomplished singer, I felt the opportunity to perform under the eighty-three-year-old composer was too good to pass up. At intermission of the final chorus rehearsal on 26 January which he attended, I made bold to present him a copy of my edition of *Musica nova 1540* (Chicago and London: University of Chicago Press, 1964), together with a brief letter thanking him for the pleasure his works afforded me. Pointing out the volume to Craft, he accepted it and nodded appreciatively in my direction.

While Craft led the *Symphony in C* (1940) on 27 January, I sat backstage reading my miniature score about a metre from Stravinsky who, with his full score, was timing Craft's excellent performance. At its close, I turned to him and said: "Thank you, maestro, for composing such a beautiful work." In his basso profondo and an accent hardly possible even to approximate, he replied: "Zchew know, I like eet myzelf."

As a professor at the Irvine campus (1965-94), I again played his music and several times taught students about it. With my colleague, Arnold Juda (1913-88), we programmed his *Eight Easy Pieces for Piano Duet* (1914-17) at a recital in the early 1970s to raise funds for student scholarships. In the fall of 1968, and during the spring quarters of 1972 and 1978, I offered courses for undergraduates on his music. And for the Music department's required course, "Form and Analysis," I often assigned his 1923 *Octet* (see Entry 56). Our analyses of it helped produce an excellent public performance in 1993 by several undergraduate wind players who had taken this course.

Happily enough, two scores I had bought at Vancouver in the early 1950s, *Les Noces* and the *Scherzo à la Russe,* not only related to my conducting career at Vancouver and Chicago but, more than forty years later, were themselves to enter my collection, though in a different medium. For the *Scherzo* I obtained the autograph of the composer's own earlier arrangement for two pianos as well as some business contracts relating to the sale of his version for jazz band (entries 80-1).

For *Les Noces*, a work particularly close to my heart, I have been even luckier. The collection includes: one page of Stravinsky's sketches for his arrangement early in 1923 for player piano; an inscribed 1923 photograph to George Auric, one of the ballet's four original pianists; a letter from Stravinsky in Monte Carlo mentioning its rehearsals there by the Ballets Russes in April 1923 (two months before its premiere in Paris); a letter of thanks written a month after the premiere to Vasily Fedorovitch Kibalchich, the chorus director; and a brief autograph quotation from its final tableau, copied out in 1937 (entries 21-4, and 55).

That first Sunday morning of October 1952 during which I heard him rehearse compositions by Glinka and Tchaikovsky, as well as four of his own works, remains indelibly printed in my memory. Appropriately enough, Stravinsky autographs – mostly in excerpts – of four works he conducted in Vancouver, as well as references to three of them, are in the collection. In the order of his Vancouver program they are: Tchaikovsky's *Second Symphony* (entries 65, 71), and his own *Scherzo à la Russe* (entries 80-1), *Divertimento* (45), and *The Firebird* (1, 48, 61, and 115).

I did not begin serious collecting of Stravinskiana until 1977 (Entry 10), when I had paid off the mortgage on my house in Laguna Beach and enjoyed a comfortable income as full professor at Irvine. The mania accelerated in 1985 after I became an above-scale professor. And from the time I had attained the income of an emeritus professor in 1994, it raged unchecked until editing this catalogue late in 2000 necessarily put out the conflagration.

A visit in June 1994 to Dorothy Louise Ellis McQuoid Hopper (1911-98),[13] who resided in nearby San Clemente, fanned these flames. I wanted to thank her personally for having donated an autograph postcard by Igor and Vera Stravinsky (Entry 70) to the music department for presentation upon my retirement from the University of California. She had first met Stravinsky in mid-December 1939 detraining from San Francisco, when she drove him and his long-time friend, her piano teacher Alexis Kall (entries 40 and 65), from Union Station in Los Angeles to Kall's home (entries 67-8). She and her first husband, Edwin Kerien McQuoid (1910-50), then a screen projectionist for Paramount Pictures and a professional photographer, subsequently befriended the Stravinskys shortly after their arrival in Hollywood on 26 May 1940 (see entries 69-75). Apparently Mrs. Hopper's closest contacts with the Stravinskys were from December 1939 through the summer of 1942, after which her third child, daughter Alexis – named to honour Kall – born that November, occupied her attention. As late as the 1950s, however, she sent them an invitation to the wedding of one of her sons.

Her recollections of playing the piano for and with Stravinsky in 1940-41 remained vivid. In 1996-97 she sold me half a dozen mementoes of her association with him (entries 68, 71-5). Her charming account of her 1940 "Firebird" hat as well as a recollection in September 1994 by her second son, Cary Ellis McQuoid (1934-97), of a near-disaster backstage for Stravinsky's dress shirt at the Hollywood Bowl on 27 August 1940, are hereby preserved (Entry 71).

Very generously, she allowed me photocopies of other items Stravinsky had inscribed for her and for her first husband during this period. Following her death early in 1998, the originals passed to her first son and daughter. For the record and in chronological order they are: a picture-postcard of Stravinsky on the back of which on 17 December 1939 he set to music his sentence in English praising her (see Entry 67); a small uninscribed photograph of her piano teacher Alexis Kall and Stravinsky at Gerry's Landing, Cambridge, taken 5 May 1940;[14] a small photograph taken by Stravinsky early in June 1940 at the Hollywood Farmers Market of her, Edwin McQuoid, and Vera Stravinsky;[15] a newspaper photograph she clipped from the *Hollywood Citizen-News* of 9 August 1940 depicting the return of the Stravinskys from Mexico that morning, a photograph she recalled taking;[16] a copy inscribed by Stravinsky of Eva vB. Hansel and Helen L. Kaufmann, *Minute Sketches of Great Composers* (New York, NY: Grosset and Dunlap, 1932), which biographical sketch Stravinsky in the summer or fall of 1940 rightly dubbed "perfectly idiotic"; and an undated note from Vera Stravinsky congratulating Dorothy and her husband on the birth, 2 November 1942, of her daughter, Alexis.

Materials in my collection encompass a sixty-year period from *The Firebird* until the composer's funeral in Venice. They fall into nine broad categories:

1   photographs of the composer (many of them signed)
2   portraits – an etching, a drawing, and a pastel (the latter with his inscription and musical quotation)
3   personal and business letters, postcards, handwritten and typed memoranda, and a telegram
4   philatelic items
5   programs (three signed) and a funeral poster
6   publishers' contracts
7   printed music and books: inscribed copies of the composer's arrangement of *The Star-Spangled Banner,* of his *Monumentum,* of his *Chroniques de ma vie* and *Autobiography,* of his *Poétique musicale* and of its translation, *Poetics of Music,* and of two volumes of essays in German celebrating his seventieth and eightieth birthdays
8   a signed autograph drawing of his right hand
9   autograph music – signed quotations, including a miniature manuscript, a page of sketches, a two-page preliminary manuscript orchestral score, and a fourteen-page set of transparencies

Although Stravinsky was an inveterate taker of photographs, according to Mrs. Hopper, he was sometimes a reluctant subject in them. I have avoided purchasing work by such well-known – and expensive – American photographers as Edward

Weston, George Platt Lynes, Arnold Newman, and Richard Avedon whose portraits of him are so often reproduced. Instead, I have sought out photographs less often seen, such as those by Horace Scandlin, Ingi, Roddy McDowall, and Douglas Glass, or those almost never reproduced by Fred Fehl in New York, by Lazaro Sudak in Buenos Aires, and Erio Piccagliani in Milan, and by such amateurs as Edwin and Dorothy Ellis McQuoid in California, and Alexis Kall. Two exceptions are an inscribed photograph by Eric Satie of Debussy and Stravinsky, apparently taken in 1911, and a rephotograph by the well-known French fashion photographer, George Hoyningen-Huené taken in 1934. One anonymous photograph inscribed to Georges Auric of early 1923 shows Stravinsky standing outside an unidentified house; another inscribed anonymous Dutch one of the following year pictures Paul Hindemith, then violist of the Amar Quartet, standing next to a seated Stravinsky.

Only reluctantly have uninscribed rephotographs been included. One of the two exceptions is the 1935 image of Alexis Kall, Stravinsky's friend in Los Angeles (Entry 40). Reasons for including it are not only because of his connection with Stravinsky and Edward G. Robinson. From about 1923 Kall was also the piano teacher of Dorothy Ellis (from 1931–50, Mrs. Edwin McQuoid and, from 1984–88, Mrs. Jerry Hopper) to whom he introduced Stravinsky in December 1939 and from whom I purchased many mementoes inscribed by the composer. The other rephotograph included here is of a photograph of Stravinsky taken during his first visit to Vancouver in 1952 by Eric Skipsey, then resident in the city. To my knowledge, it is the only formal portrait of him taken in Vancouver that year (Entry 92).

An examination of the list of Stravinsky's correspondents in the archives of the Sacher Foundation has disclosed that he wrote to more than 4000 different people![17] Although the composer kept a "Copie des lettres" with an index, 1912-27, Craft notes that some copies are illegible.[18] Thus, several letters in the present collection written during those years will be *unica,* probably the case for many, if not all, of the postcards. Both categories may well increase that already remarkable number of correspondents.

A substantial portion of his correspondence was with the most famous persons of his day. In this collection such persons, mention of, or depictions of them, include Rimsky-Korsakov (Entry 1), Sergei Diaghilev (entries 4, 6, 8-9, 17, 19, 37), Alfredo Casella (entries 7-9), Willem Mengelberg and Sir Henry Wood (Entry 7), Maurice Ravel (Entry 9), Colette (Entry 11), Alexander Sakharoff (Entry 12), Coco Chanel (Entry 16), Léon Bakst (Entry 19), Georges Auric (Entry 22), Ernest Ansermet (entries 23-4, 38), Jean Cocteau (Entry 25), Paul Hindemith (Entry 28), Pablo Picasso (Entry 32), the Princesse de Polignac, Arturo Toscanini, and Claude Debussy (Entry 34), Edward G. Robinson (Entry 40), Vittorio Gui (Entry 63), Victoria

Ocampo, Nadia Boulanger, and Alfred Cortot (Entry 64), Pierre Monteux (Entry 65), Dylan Thomas and Aldous Huxley (Entry 95), Lincoln Kirstein (Entry 103), T.S. Eliot, Stephen Spender, Aldous Huxley, and Victoria Ocampo (Entry 104), Virgil Thomson (Entry 109), J. Robert Oppenheimer (Entry 117), and George Balanchine (Entry 122).

To be noted, especially in the postcards, is his frugal habit of occupying every possible centimetre of space for his message (see Entry 6). His tiny manuscript of most of his 1911 Balmont song is surely a *locus classicus* of this art (Entry 3).

Most correspondents are represented here by only a single item. Seven exceptions, however, each embodying closely proximate communications, deserve mention. They are: two to the critic Michel-Dimitri Calvocoressi (entries 1, 4); three postcards to the composer-conductor Alfredo Casella (entries 7-9); three items to Stravinsky's later literary collaborator, Roland-Manuel (entries 15, 17, and 64); three letters to the singer Vera Janacopulos (entries 23 and 26-7); two to the Russian emigré violinist-teacher, Julian Brodetsky (entries 77 and 79); four to his New York lawyer, Arnold Weissberger (entries 97-9, and 103); and two letters to his lover, Vera Sudeykina (1888-1982) (entries 18-19), who became his mistress in July 1921 and, in March 1940, his wife.

The extraordinarily well-protected inner man reveals himself with every guard down in those two passionate love letters to Vera Sudeykina late in the autumn of 1921. The earlier one, of which just a fragment survives (Entry 18), is unprecedented in acknowledging that he feels little shame in speaking out through music, a process that he subsequently either hedged about or denied outright. Equally fervent, the other love letter (Entry 19) also reveals fear that either his wife, Catherine (1882-1939), or Vera's husband, Sergei Sudeykin, might discover their affair – although apparently by this time Sudeykin well knew what was going on.

Twenty-two autographs include musical quotations (all but three of his own music): entries 3 (1911), 7 (1914, a work by Casella), 48-60 (1937), 62 and 66 (1939), 71 (1940, a work by Tchaikovsky), 76 (1941, the US national anthem), 106 (1959), 115 (1966), and 119 (1967). They strikingly parallel his credo to Benois in 1913 about composing (quoted at the beginning of this essay) and also bear out Craft's observation in 1994 about Stravinsky's originality in autographing.[19]

All of the items formerly belonging to Mrs. Clara Bickford (1903-85) in Cleveland (entries 47-60), to Mrs. Hopper in Los Angeles and San Clemente (entries 67-8 and 70-5), and to Professor and Mrs. Harry Adaskin in Vancouver (entries 91 and 93-4) have a clear provenance. But there is an added satisfaction. Mrs. Bickford's Stravinsky collection has been preserved in its original state, Mrs. Hopper's and the Adaskins' mostly so, away from the grasp of dealers – some of whom eagerly dismember historical collections for the sake of a fast buck. Entry 100 testifies all too eloquently to this barbarous practice.

Stravinsky had a keen instinct for financial and business negotiations. His training in law at St. Petersburg University manifests itself here in five areas. Unashamedly, he extracted a substantial loan in 1923 from the Brazilian singer Vera Janacopulos-Staal. In return he promised to collaborate with her and to support her concert life in the future (Entry 23).

Concerning royalties and music publishing, there is Stravinsky's curt letter in 1917 to the German Institute for Musical Performing Rights (Entry 13), a savvy letter of 1918 to the publisher of the Éditions de la Sirène (Entry 14), and one in 1927 to an editor in the Édition russe de musique (Entry 36), not to speak of the nine-page contract of 1944 with the Blue Network, Associated Music Publishers, and Chappell (Entry 81). This last is of such three-way complexity that it required one further page of a lawyer's services to bring the parties together. Signed in an exceedingly shaky hand, a final letter in 1970 (Entry 120) concerns his possible loss or misplacing of a contract with J. and W. Chester in England.

In the realm of recording there are three letters from the summer of 1954 between him and his New York lawyer, Arnold Weissberger, and one to the producer John McClure in 1967. All deal with Columbia Records (entries 97-9 and 117).

In respect to book publishing, his 1957 letter to Weissberger concerns reprinting his 1936 autobiography (Entry 103). One the next year to Deborah Ishlon (104) seeks publishers in New York, London, and Buenos Aires for his first book of conversations with Craft.

Stravinsky long wanted to tap into Hollywood's pot of gold by writing movie scores. For example, the fourteen pages of autograph transparencies (Entry 80) began life early in 1943 as sketches for film music, a project later aborted. His wish to write for the movies is documented for a final time in 1964 (Entry 113).

The 1956 drawing of his own hand (Entry 100) is chronologically the third one he had made for friends and admirers. The present locations of the first two (1924 and c. 1950) are unknown. The exemplar in this collection, however, has finer details than another (perhaps the last one) he made six years later.

A sketch page for *Les Noces* (Entry 21) shows him at work in 1923 on his arrangement for player piano of the final part of that work's second tableau. It features an accompanimental figure not found in any of the different versions of *Les Noces* he made in 1917 and 1919, and the finished scoring in 1923.

His two-page holograph orchestral score for the *Divertimento* (Entry 45), though lacking a few woodwind chords, is apparently a working draft in the process of selecting materials suitable for his 1934 orchestral suite drawn from its parent ballet, *Le baiser de la fée* (1928). Its two pages are all that survive from this process.

Both the 1911 miniature (Entry 3) and the 1943-44 holograph of the two-piano version of the *Scherzo à la Russe* (Entry 80), fully justify Janet Flanner's observations made in *The New Yorker*: "his manuscripts, which used to be in colors, like liturgies, are now in mere black and white, but museum pieces for meticulousness."[20] Indeed, Stravinsky had chided composer Nicholas Nabokov (1903-78) at their first meeting in 1927 for the sloppiness of Nabokov's music manuscript.[21] He was not shy about his music copying – for example, in a letter of 3 September 1930 to the conductor, Ernest Ansermet about the *Symphony of Psalms*: the orchestra score "which I wrote calligraphically so as to make the best copyists envious(!)";[22] on 30 August 1943, Stravinsky proudly wrote his publisher that "my calligraphic manuscripts resemble those of no other author."[23]

Many others besides Flanner agreed with his own evaluations. Interviewing him at Hollywood in 1946, J. Douglas Cook wrote: "His manuscripts are marvels of beauty and accuracy."[24] Late in life, Nadia Boulanger observed apropos his calligraphy: "il n'y a pas une barre de mesure qui soit moins bien tirée, pas une clé qui soit moins belle que l'autre!"[25] Craft's unrivalled acquaintance with Stravinsky's manuscripts allowed him in 1978 to speak in a similar vein.[26]

Collecting these materials over some twenty years was great fun, with one exception. Negotiations for it dragged over some thirteen months and resulted in some unpleasantness, which I am glad to say was ultimately resolved. As one browses the catalogue entries, one might want to ponder that, if items in the collection have historical value and continuing relevance, it is not only because of who signed them but also for whom Stravinsky did so – the great and the humble alike.

Notes

1 The finest summation of the composer's life and works is by Stephen Walsh, "Stravinsky, Igor," *The New Grove Dictionary of Music and Musicians,* 2nd ed., ed. Stanley Sadie and John Tyrrell (London: Macmillan, 2000). (Regarding the spelling of "Stravinsky," see the commentary for Entry 46.)

2 For example, his manuscript of his unpublished orchestration of Chopin's *Nocturne in A-flat major* (op. 32, no. 2), commissioned by Diaghilev for the ballet *Les Sylphides* and premiered at Paris, 2 June 1909, was auctioned by Sotheby's London on 15-16 May 1997, lot 301 with plate. The Paul Sacher Foundation purchased it for £13,800: see Felix Meyer, ed., *Settling New Scores* (Mainz: Schott, 1998), p. 70, no. 20 with a different plate. See also Albi Rosenthal, "The Paul Sacher Foundation at the Crossroads: The Purchase of the Igor Stravinsky Archive," *Paul Sacher in memoriam* (Basle: Sacher Foundation, 2000), pp. 37-40.

3 Richard Taruskin, *Stravinsky and the Russian Traditions* (Berkeley and Los Angeles, CA: University of California Press, 1996), n. 113 on p. 418, pp. 579-80.

4 For example, he signed his name on 3 October 1952 in the Adaskin's guest book, owned by the late Frances Marr Adaskin. An extensive dossier in the Stravinsky archives of the Paul Sacher Foundation, Basle, includes a letter of 6 November 1952 from Harry Adaskin thanking Stravinsky for "your parcel of autographed books, inscribed so warmly and generously." A letter of 5 December 1952, from A.E. Lord, Honourary Secretary, Board of Governors of University of British Columbia, thanks him for copies of his *Poétique musicale* and of *Musik der Zeit,* both inscribed by him to the Department of Music, on which see entries 93-4. On 16 October 1952, Barbara Pentland (1912-2000) thanked him for sending her a "drawing of him in action by Madame Marion [his married daughter, Milène]," about whom see Entry 6. A copy of the orchestra's program, 5 October 1952, is in the archives of the symphony society. Numerous photographs appear in the three local newspapers 2-6 October 1952 (i.e., *The Vancouver Sun, The Vancouver Daily Province,* and *The News-Herald,* one in the latter taken 3 October by D'Arcy). Another taken at the same occasion is in *Les Cahiers canadiens de musique/The Canada Music Book* 4-5 (1972): 26. For a photograph taken of him after the last rehearsal, see Entry 92.

5 Among them is a signed program of the July 1965 concert held by the Vancouver Symphony Society, as well as photographs from local newspapers; one of the latter, from *The Vancouver Daily Province,* appears with an interview from *The Vancouver Sun* in Robert Craft, *A Stravinsky Scrapbook 1940-1971* (New York, NY: Thames and Hudson, 1983), pp. 130-1. A plate of Stravinsky conducting the Vancouver Symphony Orchestra, reproduced in *Les Cahiers canadiens de musique/The Canada Music Book* 4-5 (1972): 28, erroneously notes the date as June rather than July 1965. The cropped photograph of Igor Stravinsky with the Vancouver Symphony Orchestra in 1965 in Lloyd Dykk's article, "Igor Stravinsky, the five-foot-four-inch giant of contemporary music, visited Vancouver twice," *The Vancouver Sun,* 20-27 July 2000, p. C31, appears in a fuller form in *Festival Vancouver 2000, Program Book,* p. 4.

6 This account is based on documents held by the Paul Sacher Foundation, Stravinsky papers: Vancouver (1952), neither Adaskin nor the symphony society having preserved their records; see also Harry Adaskin, *A Fiddler's Choice, Memoirs 1938 to 1980* (Vancouver, BC: November House, 1982), pp. 132-7.

7 See Wright Balfour, "Igor Stravinsky Arrives for Symphony Concert," *The News-Herald,* 2 October 1952, p. 1 with picture; Jack Delong, "Igor Doesn't Give Hoot, Out They [Visitors] Go," *The Vancouver Sun,* 4 October 1952, p. 6 with picture; and Dr. Ida Halpern, "Rehearsals Start: Stravinsky, Orchestra Happy," *The Vancouver Daily Province,* 3 October 1952, section 2, p. 2 with picture.

8 "Expectations Fulfilled: Stravinsky, Orchestra in Great Concert," *The Vancouver Daily Province,* 6 October 1952, p. 15. In a copy of Halpern's review, now in the Paul Sacher Foundation, Stravinsky underlined (as false, obviously): "Tchaikovsky, *whom he [Stravinsky] heard conducting his*

own works." Nevertheless, he sent her a gift which she acknowledged in November, "thanking you for your delightful book," and again on 6 February 1953.

9 Robert Craft, ed., *Dearest Bubushkin: The correspondence of Vera and Igor Stravinsky, 1921-1954, with excerpts from Vera Stravinsky's diaries, 1922-1971,* trans. Lucia Davidova (New York, NY: Thames and Hudson, 1985), p. 149, pl. 109.

10 Frances Adaskin, "The Evolution of a Musical Vancouver," *The Weekend Sun,* 24 September 1994, Saturday Review section, D10. She is recalling – without acknowledging it – a more detailed account in Harry Adaskin, *A Fiddler's World, Memoirs to 1938* (Vancouver, BC: November House, 1977), p. 174.

11 Merritt is mentioned in Vera Stravinsky's diary, in entries for 29 April 1940 and 22 January 1941 (*Dearest Bubushkin,* ed. Craft, trans. Davidova). A facsimile of a letter in 1943 from Stravinsky in Hollywood to Merritt, "my dear friend," is in Elliot Forbes, *A History of Music at Harvard to 1972* (Cambridge, MA: Harvard University Press, 1988), p. 75.

12 See the *Los Angeles Times Calendar,* Sunday, 23 January 1966, p. 24, and a review, *Los Angeles Times,* 29 January 1966, section 1, p. 20, both with photographs.

13 On her, see Ruth Holmes Hansen, "Dorothy Ellis, the Author," *The Baton of Phi Beta* (March 1939): pp. 21, 26; "Dorothy Louise Ellis (Mrs. Edwin Kerien McQuoid)," *Who's Who in California 1942-1943,* ed. Russell Holmes Fletcher (Los Angeles: Who's Who Publications, 1941 [sic]), vol. 1, pp. 277-8; "Ellis, Dorothy," in *Music and Dance in California and the West,* ed. Richard Drake Saunders (Hollywood: Drake-William, 1948), pp. 198-9 (with photo); and Robin Hinch, "Music Was Theme of Dorothy Hopper's life; Obituary," *The Orange County Register,* 28 February 1998, Metro section, p. 7.

14 Another, virtually identical, version is part of a series of photographs owned by Professor Elliot Forbes of Cambridge, Massachusetts, who kindly allowed Dr. Slim copies of them in 1995.

15 A cropped reproduction is in *Dearest Bubushkin,* ed. Craft, trans. Davidova, p. 113, pl. 90.

16 Reproduced in *Igor and Vera Stravinsky, a photograph album 1921 to 1971,* ed. Robert Craft (New York, NY: Thames and Hudson, 1982), p. 97, pl. 161.

17 Volker Scherliess, "Strawinsky in Amerika," in *Biographische Konstellation und künstlerisches Handeln,* ed. Giselher Schubert (Mainz: Schott, 1997), p. 170.

18 Vera Stravinsky and Robert Craft, *Stravinsky in Pictures and Documents* (New York, NY: Simon and Schuster, 1978), p. 613, n. 146.

19 Robert Craft, *Stravinsky: Chronicle of a Friendship,* 2nd ed. (Nashville, TN, and London: Vanderbilt University Press, 1994), n. on p. 506.

20 Janet Flanner, "Russian Firebird," *The New Yorker* 11 (5 January 1935): 28.

21 Stravinsky and Craft, *Stravinsky in Pictures and Documents,* p. 293.

22 Claude Tappolet, ed., *Correspondance Ernest Ansermet-Igor Strawinsky (1914-1967)* (Geneva: Georg, 1990-92), vol. 2, p. 245, no. 367 (trans. H. Colin Slim); Robert Craft, ed., *Stravinsky Selected Correspondence* (New York, NY: Alfred A. Knopf, 1982-85), vol. 1, pp. 215-16.

23 Craft, ed., *Stravinsky Selected Correspondence,* vol. 3, p. 286.

24 *San Francisco Opera, Concert and Symphony* 11, 10 (1946): 25.

25 See Bruno Monsaingeon, *Mademoiselle. Entretiens avec Nadia Boulanger* (Paris: Van de Velde, 1981), p. 90.

26 Stravinsky and Craft, *Stravinsky in Pictures and Documents,* p. 14.

CATALOGUE

Each entry consists of a detailed transcription and, where necessary, translation. In transcriptions, neither Stravinsky's linguistic errors in French and English nor his frequent omissions of French accents have been rectified. Translation from the Russian is by Stanislav Shvabrin and Michael Green unless otherwise noted. Leonard W. Johnson provided almost all the French translations.

Each entry is preceded by a description, and followed by acquisition information, provenance, commentary, and works consulted. In the description, height precedes width in dimensions. Size of photographs is of the image only, unless otherwise stated. Repairs made to any entry by Linda K. Ogden, Berkeley, California, are described. A date in parentheses following a musical composition is its year of completion. References in the works consulted for each entry are presented in full, even though they may be repeated elsewhere. The *sigla* below are used for the most frequently cited materials on Stravinsky. The following abbreviations are used in the works consulted:

C. concerti

n. note or footnote

no. number

P. programmi

S. scritti

Sigla

JAMS   *Journal of The American Musicological Society.*

MGG   *Die Musik in Geschichte und Gegenwart,* ed. Friedrich Blume. Cassel: Bärenreiter, 1949-86. 17 vols.

NG   *The New Grove Dictionary of Music and Musicians,* ed. Stanley Sadie. London: Macmillan, 1980. 20 vols; rev. 2nd ed. Stanley Sadie and John Tyrrell. London: Macmillan, 2000. 29 vols. References in this catalogue are to the 1980 edition, unless otherwise specified.

SAc   Théodore and Denise Strawinsky. *Au coeur du Foyer. Catherine et Igor Strawinsky 1906-1940.* Bourg-la-Reine, France: ZurfluH, 1998.

SBu   *Dearest Bubushkin: The Correspondence of Vera and Igor Stravinsky, 1921-1954, with excerpts from Vera Stravinsky's diaries 1922-1971,* ed. Robert Craft, trans. Lucia Davidova. New York, NY: Thames and Hudson, 1985.

SChron   Igor Stravinsky. *Chroniques de ma vie.* Paris: Denoël and Steele, 1935. 2 vols.

SConv   Igor Stravinsky and Robert Craft. *Conversations with Igor Stravinsky.* Garden City, NY: Doubleday; London: Faber and Faber, 1959.

SC&I   Théodore Stravinsky. *Catherine & Igor Stravinsky: a family album.* London: Boosey and Hawkes, 1973.

SD   Igor Stravinsky and Robert Craft. *Dialogues.* London: Faber and Faber, 1982.

SD&D   Igor Stravinsky and Robert Craft. *Dialogues and a Diary.* Garden City, NY: Doubleday, 1963.

SE&D   Igor Stravinsky and Robert Craft. *Expositions and Developments.* Garden City, NY: Doubleday, 1962; repr. Berkeley and Los Angeles, CA: University of California Press, 1981.

SI&V   Vera Stravinsky, Rita McCaffrey, and Robert Craft, ed. *Igor and Vera Stravinsky, a photograph album 1921 to 1971.* London and New York, NY: Thames and Hudson, 1982.

SM&C   Igor Stravinsky and Robert Craft. *Memories and Commentaries.* Garden City, NY: Doubleday, 1960; repr. Berkeley and Los Angeles, CA: University of California Press, 1981.

SP&D   Vera Stravinsky and Robert Craft. *Stravinsky in pictures and documents.* New York, NY: Simon and Schuster, 1978.

SP&RK   *I.F. Stravinsky: Perepiska s russkimi korrespondentami. Materiali k biographi.* ed. Viktor Varunts. Moscow: Kompozitor, 1998-2000. 2 vols (1882-1912, 1913-22).

SSC   Igor Stravinsky. *Selected Correspondence,* ed. Robert Craft. New York, NY: Alfred A. Knopf, 1982-85. 3 vols.

SScrbk   Robert Craft. *A Stravinsky Scrapbook 1940-1971.* New York, NY: Thames and Hudson, 1983.

ST&C   Igor Stravinsky and Robert Craft. *Themes and Conclusions.* London: Faber, 1972; repr. Berkeley and Los Angeles, CA: University of California Press, 1982.

ST&E   Igor Stravinsky and Robert Craft. *Themes and Episodes.* New York, NY: Alfred A. Knopf, 1966.

1 (1911). Autograph letter on both sides of a thick card with rounded edges, 11.4 × 8.9 cm, in French in black ink, 22 May 1911, to Michel-Dimitri Calvocoressi (1877-1944) (as ascertained from content):

22-V 1911 Rome

Cher ami,

Merci pour votre charmant envoi, que j'ai eu le plus grand plaisir à lire. Je m'empresse seulement de Vous indiquer une petite erreur de fait: c'est que les paroles de Rimsky ont été prononcées d'une autre oeuvre moderniste (le nom de l'auteur m'echape)

Quant à mon "Oiseau de Feu"– il [crossed out in ink] été a été composé 2 ans après la mort de Rimsky.

Il va sans dire que je serai heureux de vous avoir à la première de "Petrouchka".

Je viendrai à Paris au comencement de juin. Quelle joie de [reverse side] se retrouver de nouveau entre des amis.

Mes respectieux hommages à Madame Calvocoressi ainsi que ceux de ma femme. Pour Vous cher ami mes souvenirs sincères

Affectieusement

votre Igor Strawinsky

Roma

Albergo d'Italia

[Michel-Dimitri Calvocoressi]   Rome

[Paris]   22 May 1911

Dear friend:

Thanks for your delightful enclosure which I've had the greatest pleasure reading. I only hasten to tell you about a small factual error: Rimsky's comments were made about a different modernist work (the name of the composer escapes me)[.]

As for my *Firebird* – it was composed two years after Rimsky's death.

It goes without saying that I shall be happy to have you at the premiere of *Petrushka.*

I'm coming to Paris at the beginning of June. What joy to find oneself again among friends.

My respectful compliments to Mrs. Calvocoressi, as well as those of my wife. For you, dear friend, my sincere regards[.]

Affectionately,

your Igor Strawinsky

Acquisition: H. Colin Slim 8 May 1996 from "Les Autographes" – Thierry Bodin, 45, rue de l'Abbé Grégoire, 75006 Paris, his *Catalogue 67* (July 1995), item 275. The letter is accompanied by a "Certificat pour un bien culturel," dated Paris 17 April 1996, from the Ministère chargé de la culture.

Provenance: Probably from the archive of Calvocoressi, later belonging to Gerald Abraham (1904-88).

Commentary

The letter is unpublished, its envelope missing. The unnamed addressee can readily be deduced from Stravinsky's mention of Madame Calvocoressi, the critic's mother; he married in 1916.

Written four days before Stravinsky completed *Petrushka* at Rome, Entry 1 may well stem from Calvocoressi's archive – administered until 1988 by his colleague in England from the 1930s, Gerald Abraham, his collaborator in *Studies in Russian Music* (London: H. Reeves, 1935). Another letter from Stravinsky to Calvocoressi, the first in their selected correspondence 1912-14, published by Craft, was sold at auction for DM3,200 in 1988, the year of Abraham's death.

Entry 1 is not the earliest extant letter to Calvocoressi: the Pierpont Morgan Library, New York, holds one (acquired in 1975) that Stravinsky wrote him a month earlier, on 20 April, from Beaulieu-sur-Mer commenting favourably on his translation of the *Deux mélodies* (1907-08). In it he is further pleased that Calvocoressi has been requested to write an article about him. In context, the "charmant envoi" of Entry 1 was surely an essay about him by Calvocoressi, and probably the one to which he refers in his April letter held by the Morgan Library.

Born in Marseilles and educated in Paris, Calvocoressi had already by 1907 published a book on Russian music and the following year one on Musorgsky. In May 1907 he assisted Sergei Diaghilev in presenting five concerts of Russian music in Paris. The first one featured Nicolai Rimsky-Korsakov as conductor, the same year Rimsky engaged Calvocoressi for the French translation of *The Golden Cockerell*. Known to Rimsky-Korsakov since 1905, he met Stravinsky at the time of *The Firebird* (1910).

Calvocoressi's two factual errors noted by Stravinsky in Entry 1 – Rimsky-Korsakov speaking about some other work by a modernist composer (not one by Stravinsky), and the correction about composing *The Firebird* two years after his death – are exactly the same two mistakes in Calvocoressi's article which appeared shortly thereafter, on 1 August 1911 in *The Musical Times*. Taruskin characterizes it as "a milestone: the first critical article devoted entirely to the new composer to be published anywhere." Calvocoressi nonetheless went astray when he reported in it: "Rimsky-Korsakov appears to have found his young pupil's independence and daring rather startling, but not repellent; and when he heard for the first time the music of *The Bird of Fire* he is said to have tersely given vent to his feelings in this sentence; 'Look here, stop playing this horrid thing, otherwise I might begin to enjoy it.' " This erroneous anecdote, which Taruskin suggests went the rounds in St. Petersburg, was perpetuated, for example, in 1915 by Carl Van Vechten and persisted in the 1925 Chicago Symphony Program Notes when Stravinsky conducted *The Firebird* there on 20-21 February.

Rimsky, of course, never heard a note of *The Firebird*. And Stravinsky is correct. Rimsky apparently passed his remark not about him but, as Steven Baur shows, about a "moderniste" work by Ravel which both he and Rimsky heard in St. Petersburg at one of the 'Evenings of Contemporary Music' in November 1907. In his *Chroniques de ma vie,* Stravinsky later wrongly identified the "moderniste" composer as Debussy. Taruskin observes: "fairly hilarious is Calvocoressi's garbling of an anecdote."

To judge by the first sentence in Entry 1, the essay apparently pleased Stravinsky, even though Calvocoressi also incorrectly mentions: "*Petrushka,* finished last winter." As he penned Entry 1 to Calvocoressi,

Stravinsky still had four more days' work in order to complete his score. By the time his corrections reached Calvocoressi, apparently it was too late to alter the essay submitted to *The Musical Times,* for these mistakes do not appear in his essay a month earlier about *Petrushka* in *The Monthly Musical Record.* (The same mistakes may occur in an article by Calvocoressi about *The Firebird* published at Moscow in a June 1911 issue of *Muzika,* but only excerpts from it appear in Taruskin's source, a study by Valery Smirnov.)

Although Calvocoressi had first met him during the final eight rehearsals of *The Firebird,* which had brought the composer to Paris on 7 June 1910, he did not become a friend until the following winter at Beaulieu-sur-Mer (near Nice), where Stravinsky lived with his family from November 1910 until 6 May 1911, except for a brief excursion to St. Petersburg late in December 1910. At Beaulieu, Stravinsky played him parts of *Petrushka,* which, by 26 January 1911, he had already finished composing into the latter half of the fourth tableau.

Quarrelling in 1910 with Diaghilev, Calvocoressi resigned at the close of that season featuring the premiere on 25 June of *The Firebird.* In November of the following year Calvocoressi signed his French translation of V. Svétlov [V.I. Ivchenko], *Le ballet contemporain* (1912). Although Stravinsky knew its original Russian version, he did not like the book. In it, Calvocoressi himself discusses both *The Firebird* and *Petrushka.* From 1911-14 he made translations into various languages of vocal works by Stravinsky for publication. The closeness of their friendship can be gauged from the gift he made to Calvocoressi on 6 July 1913 of a notebook containing the sketches of his arrangement (April 1913) of the final chorus of *Khovanshchina* (now owned by Oliver Neighbour, London).

Much of Calvocoressi's music criticism during this period appeared in *Comoedia illustré* and some of it was about Stravinsky. For example, "Aux concerts" of December 1910 contains a photograph of him and a discussion of *Fireworks* and *The Firebird,* preceding the discussions of the latter in the Russian and English press cited by Taruskin. At the outbreak of the First World War, Calvocoressi settled in England, where he worked as a music historian until his unexpected demise.

Leaving the Ballets Russes at Monte Carlo and returning to Beaulieu late in April 1911, Stravinsky joined Diaghilev in Rome on 6 May and also Alexandre Benois (1870-1960), the author of the scenario and the designer of *Petrushka*. He and Benois stayed at the Albergo d'Italia, near the Quattro Fontane. There, with the Barberini Gardens near their hotel, he worked on the last pages of his ballet, finishing it on 26 May. A drawing by Benois, reproduced by Vera Stravinsky and Craft, shows him composing *Petrushka* at the piano in shirtsleeves in the basement of the Teatro Costanzi. Choreographed by Michel Fokine (1880-1942) in Rome before Stravinsky and the company left for Paris on 31 May, the ballet received its premiere on 13 June and Calvocoressi did indeed attend. For a 1913 postcard from Stravinsky to the critic, see Entry 4.

For photographs of Stravinsky rehearsing *The Firebird* in 1962, see Entry 111 and for autograph quotations from its "Introduction," and "Berceuse," see entries 115 and 48. For discussions about *Petrushka,* see entries 6-9, for an inscribed printed copy, Entry 68, and for autograph quotations from its "Magic Trick" and "Russian Dance," see entries 49 and 119.

Works Consulted

Abraham, Gerald. "Calvocoressi." NG. vol. 3, pp. 633-4.

Argonautes sale. Paris, 1975, lot 72.

Baur, Steven. "Ravel's 'Russian' Period: Octatonicism in the Early Works, 1893-1908." JAMS 52 (1999): 561-8, 590.

Buckle, Richard. *Diaghilev*. New York, NY: Atheneum, 1979. pp. 96-101, 178, 195-202.

Calvocoressi, Michel-Dimitri. "A Russian Composer of To-Day: Igor Stravinsky." *The Musical Times* 52 (1 August 1911): 511-12.

—. "Aux concerts," *Comoedia illustré* 3, 6 (December 1910): 180.

—. "Ballet Russes: Deuxième Série: *Petrouchka, Schéhérazade,*" *Comoedia illustré* 3, 19 (July 1911): 614-21.

—. "Petrouchka," *The Monthly Musical Record* 41 (1 July 1911): 171.

—. *Music and Ballet. Recollections*. London: Faber and Faber, 1934; repr. New York, NY: AMS Press, 1978. pp. 178, 221.

Chicago Symphony Program Notes. 20-21 February 1925. p. 193.

Music Letters in the Pierpont Morgan Library. A Catalogue. December 1993. p. 394: Koch 400 (Box 66).

Rimsky-Korsakov, Nicolai Andreyevich. *Polnoye sobraniye sochineiy: literaturniye proizvedeniya i perepiska*. [Literary Production and Correspondence: Complete Collected Writings.] Moscow: Muzgiz/Muzïka, 1970. vol. 7. p. 312.

Schouvaloff, Alexander. *The Art of Ballets Russes: The Serge Lifar Collection of Theater Designs, Costumes, and Paintings at the Wadsworth Atheneum, Hartford, Connecticut.* New Haven, CT and London: Yale University Press, 1997. pp. 117-27.

Smirnov, Valery. *Tvorcheskoye formirovaniye I.F. Stravinskogo.* [I.F. Stravinsky's Creative Process.] Leningrad: Muzïka, 1970. n. 1, p. 9.

Stargardt, J.A. *Autographen aus allen Gebieten. Katalog 641.* Marburg, 9–10 March 1988, lot 1068. p. 356.

SChron. vol. 1, p. 41.

SP&D. p. 69. pl. on p. 71.

SP&RK. vol. 1, pp. 315–16 (trans. Stanislav Shvabrin and Michael Green), p. 521 (index: Calvocoressi); vol. 2, p. 748 (index: Calvocoressi).

SSC. vol. 2, p. 98.

Svétlov, Valerian. [V.I. Ivchenko], *Le ballet contemporain,* trans. Calvocoressi. Paris: de Brunoff, 1912. pp. 115–16, 128–9.

Taruskin, Richard. *Stravinsky and the Russian Traditions.* Berkeley and Los Angeles, CA: University of California Press, 1996. 2 vols. n. 17 on p. 376, pp. 639–41, 683, 686–7, fig. 13.1 on p. 979, n. 48 on p. 1053.

–. "Stravinsky's *Petrushka,*" *Petrushka. Sources and Contents.* ed. Andrew Wachtel. Evanston, IL: Northwestern University Press, 1998. p. 111.

Van Vechten, Carl. *Music after the Great War and other studies.* 2nd ed. New York, NY: Schirmer, 1915. p. 104.

Walsh, Stephen. *Stravinsky, A Creative Spring: Russia and France, 1882-1934.* New York, NY: Alfred A. Knopf, 1999. pp. 160-2.

White, Eric Walter. *Stravinsky: The Composer and His Works.* 2nd ed. Berkeley and Los Angeles, CA: University of California Press, 1979; repr. 1984. p. 545.

2

(1911). Original, unsigned Russian picture postcard, 13.6 × 8.6 cm, depicting "Igor Strawinsky" with his name in Cyrillic characters above left and numbered "55" at lower left; on reverse side (in Russian): "Music Store of Russian Music. Published Moscow. 1911."

Acquisition: H. Colin Slim in New York on 22 April 1995 from Wurlitzer-Bruck (60 Riverside Drive / New York).

Provenance: Unidentified elderly ballet dancer in New York, c. 1995.

Commentary

The photograph itself in this postcard dates from around the time of the premiere of *Petrushka*, 13 June 1911, when the composer was living mostly in France and Switzerland. The same image, captioned and printed in Russian: "Kompozitor Igor Stravinsky / (Cm. 'Peterburgskiy Listok' No. 266)," i.e., "Composer Igor Stravinsky / (see the 'Petersburg [News-]Sheet' No. 266)," appears in a newspaper clipping he inscribed and dated in ink: "Pesrg. Listok 27 Sept. 1912," in one of his photograph albums. On another copy of this picture postcard he wrote a note of 23 February 1912 to Florent Schmitt. A modern image of the postcard, slightly enlarged to 14.7 × 9.5 cm but cropped a little, was reproduced c. 1989 from the New York Public Library of the Performing Arts by Crossing Cards (Crossing Press / Box 1048 / Freedom, CA / 95019), no. 122. Entry 2 is framed (right) with Entry 5.

Works Consulted

Lesure, François. *Igor Stravinsky. La carrière européenne.* Paris: Musée d'Art Moderne, 1980. p. 19, no. 44.

SE&D. 1962. pl. 7 btn pp. 72 and 73; 1981. pl. 4 facing p. 32.

3   **(1911). Autograph signed and dated miniature manuscript (on the reverse of the right side of an unevenly cut-down photograph of Stravinsky's villa at Ustilug), 8.85 × c. 6.35 cm, of the last twelve bars of his song "Myosotis" [Forget-me-not] from *Deux poèmes* (1911) on Russian texts by Konstantin Dimitriyevich Balmont (1867-1942), copied (without poem), in French, in black ink on nine hand-ruled staves, Ustilug, [July] 1911, to an unnamed correspondent, probably in France:**

[heading] chansons de "myosotis" / que je vien de composer.
[above top four staves] Chant. Lento
[middle pair] Encore plus lent [and sideways at extreme left]
Chant et piano
[below last three staves] Oustilog 1911 / tout à vous Igor /
Strawinsky.

Songs [sic] of "Forget-me-not" which I have just composed.
[above top four staves] Voice. Slowly
[middle pair] Yet more slowly [and sideways at extreme left] Voice
and piano
Ustilug 1911. Yours, Igor Strawinsky.

Acquisition: H. Colin Slim in Los Angeles on 11 February 2000 from La
Scala Autographs, Inc. (Pennington, NJ).
Provenance: Sotheby's, *Printed and Manuscript Music* (London: 9 December,
1999), lot 243, p. 125 (unsold), with ill. of music.

Commentary

In its complete form, Entry 3 was the second Russian song dedicated to
his mother, Anna, in the composer's manuscript copy (pp. 6-8) sent to
the printer (auctioned by Christie's in 1996, both songs are now in the
Pierpont Morgan Library, Lehman Deposit). In 1912, it was published
by the Russischer Musik Verlag (no. 130) as the first of the pair, both
reprinted by Boosey and Hawkes in 1947. In 1954 he revised both
songs, adding a chamber ensemble, the 1956 published version for
voice and piano reflecting these revisions.

Basing its observations only on the 1954 revision, Sotheby's catalogue therefore speaks incorrectly of divergences in the bass, mm. 2-3, of Entry 3. The only note difference between it and the autograph song, on the one hand, and all the printed editions, on the other, occurs in the left hand of the piano's final bar of the central section. There Entry 3 and the autograph of the song read B for the second eighth note, whereas all printed versions have D.

For whomever this tiny, remarkable calligraphic manuscript was intended, it was probably sent in an envelope – and perhaps accompanied by a letter – not to a Russian, but to a Frenchman, probably a composer or a critic. Entry 3, or rather the *Deux poèmes,* bears the distinction of being the penultimate work Stravinsky was to initiate and to finish on Russian soil.

On 18 June 1911, after the final performances of *Petrushka,* Stravinsky and his wife, Ekaterina [Catherine], had left Paris for their villa at Ustilug in Volhynia, southwest Ukraine (on the border between present-day Poland and Russia). There, from late June to mid-July, he set two poems by Balmont: "Nezabudochka-tsvetochek" [The Little Flower Forget-me-not] and "Golub" [The Dove] for high voice and piano. By 20 July he seems to have finished them for, on that day, he wrote Florent Schmitt (1870-1958) in Paris that he had begun setting Balmont's "Zvezdolikiy" [The Star-Faced One] for male chorus and orchestra. His heading in Entry 3: "the song 'myosotis' which I have just composed" suggests the song is very recent (i.e., no later than mid-July).

In reviewing the two songs on 22 August 1912, Nikolai Miaskovsky wrote of their "harmonious combination of French grace and subtlety with a genuinely Slavic sincerity and profound tenderness" (Brown, p. 41). They received their premiere that year at St. Petersburg on 11 December, having been published with translations in French, German, and English, the French one being the work of Calvocoressi. In view of this, of his having pleased Stravinsky in April 1911 with his translation of the composer's *Deux mélodies* (see Entry 1), and of his later hopes in 1913 for translating *The Nightingale* – which were, in fact, fulfilled (see Entry 4) – it seems possible that Calvocoressi in Paris was the intended recipient of Entry 3.

Equally feasible candidates would have been Florent Schmitt or Maurice Delage (1879-1961), composer-friends with whom Stravinsky frequently corresponded. For example, that 1911 summer at Ustilug produced the celebrated – and carefully posed – snapshot of the nude composer standing on the east bank of the Luga River (tributary of the River Bug) on the other side of which grazes a white horse. He sent copies to both Delage and Schmitt. (On Delage, see Entry 4.)

Using the back of a photograph of his Ustilug home – finished in 1908 – for Entry 3 and inscribing its location below his music seem particularly felicitous. We know that he enjoyed the area for many a summer from 1890 to 1914. This fragmentary photograph is probably one of the few contemporary views extant of the rear of his villa. The Stravinsky estate there was ravaged by the Austro-German army in the summer of 1915 and his house damaged. Remodelled, it survived the 1941 invasion, losing only a chimney, although in 1994 Walsh reports that it had been turned into a museum with a not very good bust of him outside.

Works Consulted

Brown, Malcolm Hamrick. "Stravinsky and Prokofiev: Sizing Up the Competition." *Confronting Stravinsky: Man, Musician, and Modernist.* ed. Jann Pasler. Berkeley and Los Angeles, CA, and London: University of California Press, 1986. p. 41.

Christie's, *Valuable Printed Books, Music and Manuscripts.* London, 26 June 1996, lot 290. pp. 228-9, with ills.

Craft, Robert. *Stravinsky: Chronicle of a Friendship.* 2nd ed. Nashville, TN, and London: Vanderbilt University Press, 1994. p. 524: 18 July 1970.

Hucher, Yves. *Florent Schmitt.* Paris: Plon, 1953. p. 163: letter of 2 February 1912; misdated as 2 November 1912.

Lesure, François. *Igor Stravinsky. La carrière européenne.* Paris: Musée d'Art Moderne, 1980. p. 19, no. 41.

Lesure, François, ed. *Stravinsky. Études et temoignages.* Paris: Jean Claude Lattès, 1982. p. 231.

SC&I. pl. [22]: front view of Ustilug villa.

SI&V. pl. 85 on p. 69 (misdated as 1912).

SP&D. pp. 38-9.

SP&RK. vol. 1. n. 4 on p. 281; p. 497, no. 24.

SSC. vol. 2. p. 104: 2 February 1912; misdated as 2 November 1911.

SScrbk. pl. 90, p. 43.

Taruskin, Richard. *Stravinsky and the Russian Traditions.* Berkeley and Los Angeles, CA: University of California Press, 1996. pl. 9.5b (misdated as 1912) on p. 651, pp. 779-807.

Walsh, Stephen. *The Music of Stravinsky*. Oxford: Oxford University Press, 1988. pp. 35-9, n. 11 on p. 278.

—. *Stravinsky, A Creative Spring: Russia and France, 1882-1934*. New York, NY: Alfred A. Knopf, 1999. pp. 115-16, 168-72, pl. [5, lower: Ustilug villa] btn pp. 172-3, p. 178, n. 45 on p. 592.

4

(1913). Autograph pre-stamped Swiss postcard, 9.0 × 14.0 cm, announcing the Schweizer. Landesaustellung, 15.Mai-15.Okt. 1914 BERN, three times postmarked Clarens 19 X.13.XII [a.m.], with a *Par exprès* sticker and circular stamp, Hotel des Crêtes, Clarens-Montreux, written in French, in brown ink on both sides, 19 October 1913, to [Michel-Dimitri] Calvocoressi:

Monsieur Calvocoressi
164 Rue de Courcelles
Paris
EXPRES

[postscript lower left] Donnez moi s.v.p. des nouvelles de Delage je vous en supplie!

[reverse]   Clarens 19 X 1913

Vieux! Merci d'avoir penser à mon Rossignol. Certainement que cela m'arrangerai mais je suis obligé moralement de demander d'abord Diaghilew car il avais l'intention de le jouer ce printemps à Paris. Je ne suis pas encore sur si il le fera. Je m'en vais lui télégraphier instantanement et vous repondrai ce qu'il dira.
        A vous toujours IStrawinsky

Michel-Dimitri Calvocoressi   Clarens
Paris   19 October 1913

Old pal!
Thanks for having considered my *Nightingale*. Certainly that would
suit me, but I am morally obliged to ask Diaghilev first because he
intends to perform it this spring in Paris. I am still not certain that he
will do so. I'm going to telegraph him about it immediately and shall
tell you what he says.

    Yours as ever, I Strawinsky
p.s. Please give me news about [Maurice] Delage, I *beseech you!*

Acquisition: H. Colin Slim in Los Angeles on 11 February 2000 from La
Scala Autographs.
Provenance: Private collector, Paris, December 1999.

Commentary

Entry 4 is written on a postcard bearing the stamp of the hotel in which
Ravel lived while working with Stravinsky at Clarens the previous
March and April. The hotel stamp points to a life-long habit of using
stationery at hand; other examples are entries 17, 23, 30-31, 47, 71, and 74.

    The postcard responds to Calvocoressi's enquiry from Paris of 16
October 1913 as to whether anyone had yet been chosen to make the
English translation of his opera, *Le Rossignol* (1909; 1914), upon which
Stravinsky was then still working. As promised, the composer did
indeed cable Diaghilev who telegraphed him at Clarens on 20 October
1913: "Yes, I am planning to mount *The Nightingale* [in] Paris and
London." It was premiered by Diaghilev at the Paris Opéra on 26 May
1914.

    At its publication in 1923, the opera had a French translation by
Calvocoressi; there was not one in English until Robert Craft's,
copyrighted in 1956. Acknowledging that the composer's "solution is
the best one" (not further explained), Calvocoressi's letter to Stravinsky
of 5 November 1913, thanking him for Entry 4, perhaps refers to the
matter of translation. At any rate, Calvocoressi acknowledged receipt of
the opera's "second act for translation" on 16 January 1914. He was to
publish an important interview with Stravinsky about the opera that
June, coinciding with its London production. Maurice Delage, a pupil

of Ravel, was an early Parisian friend and a frequent correspondent. He was photographed already in December 1910 at Stravinsky's apartment in Beaulieu-sur-Mer and is mentioned in Entry 6, written on an identical pre-stamped Swiss postcard. (See also Entry 3.)

Works Consulted

Calvocoressi, Michel-Dimitri. "M. Igor Stravinsky's Opera: 'The Nightingale'." *The Musical Times* 55 (1 June 1914): 372-4.

SAc. pls. on pp. 36-7.

SP&D. pl. on p. 73.

SP&RK. vol. 1. p. 518 (index: Delage); vol. 2. p. 156 (trans. Stanislav Shvabrin and Michael Green), p. 744 (index: Delage).

SSC. vol. 1. nn. 1-2 on p. 23; vol. 2. pp. 9, 100-2.

Walsh, Stephen. *Stravinsky, A Creative Spring: Russia and France, 1882-1934.* New York, NY: Alfred A. Knopf, 1999. p. 198.

5

(1914). Original, unsigned Russian picture postcard, 13.6 × 8.6 cm, taken c. 1898, depicting "Fedor Strawinsky / (1843-1902)" with a facsimile of his signature above and numbered "180" at lower left; on reverse (in Russian): "Music Store of Russian Music. Published Moscow. St. Petersburg 1914."

Acquisition: H. Colin Slim in New York on 22 April 1995 from Wurlitzer-Bruck.

Provenance: Same as Entry 2.

Commentary

The photograph itself in the postcard had already appeared in 1898 in the *Russian musical gazette* for March. Fyodor Ignatyevich Stravinsky, father of the composer, was a celebrated basso at the Maryinsky Theatre in St. Petersburg from 1876 until shortly before his death. Many photographs of him survive in and out of costume. Entry 5 is framed (left) with Entry 2.

Works Consulted

Craft, Robert. *Stravinsky: Glimpses of a Life.* London: Lime Tree, 1992; New York, NY: St. Martin's Press, 1993. pp. 282-3.

Spencer, Jennifer and Edward Garden. "Stravinsky, F.I." NG. vol. 18. pp. 239-40.

SC&I. pls. [2-5].

SE&D. pl. 1.

SM&C. 1960. pl. on p. 48; 1981. pl. 4.

SP&D. pp. 42-4.

SP&RK. vol. 1. pp. 410-13, no. 2.

SSC. vol. 1. pp. 435-6, app. K.

Taruskin, Richard. *Stravinsky and the Russian Traditions.* Berkeley and Los Angeles, CA: University of California Press, 1996. pp. 77-92, esp. fig. 2.1a on p. 79.

Walsh, Stephen. *Stravinsky, A Creative Spring: Russia and France, 1882-1934.* New York, NY: Alfred A. Knopf, 1999. pp. 4-5, 8-15, 48-50, 63-4, and pl. facing p. 172.

6

(1914). Autograph pre-stamped Swiss postcard, 9.0 × 14.0 cm, announcing the Schweizer. Landesausstellung, 15.Mai-15.Okt. 1914 BERN, postmarked Leysin 13.II.14.XI[a.m.], and written in French in blue ink on both sides, except for the place and date headed in red ink, 12 February 1914, to Edwin Evans (1874-1945):

Monsieur
Edwin EVANS
31, Coleherne road
Earls court
London S/W

[reverse] Leysin 12/II 1914

Cher ami, reçu votre lettre. Vous promet de faire mon possible auprès de Diaghilew. A ce moment ci je suis avec ma femme dans un sanatorium à Leysin (non loin de Montreux) à la hauteur de 1450 mètres, car apres l'accouchement à Lausanne (fillette-Milène) ma femme a eu une pleurisie avec une nouvelle poussée de son ancienne maladie (tuberculose).

Je viens d'écrire à mon Editeur que vous avez traduit mes poésies japonaises. Voulez vous lui ecrire de votre part qu en lui demandant quant il faut les envoyer. Il vous payerons comme d'habitude 25 francs [on address side] pour pièce ce qui fera 75 fr. le tout. C'est ce qu'il ont payé à Delage pour sa traduction française. Il fau que vous lui ecrivissiez à l'instant! On vous enverra la partition d'orch. de "Petrouchka" des qu'elle paraitera en 2ᵈᵉ tirage car le 1ᵉʳ est épuisé. Mon adresse est Strawinsky Tyrol (Grand Hotel) Leysin, Suisse.
    Bien affectieusement
    à vous I. Strawinsky

| Edwin Evans | Leysin |
| London | 12 February 1914 |

Dear friend, received your letter. Promise to do my best with Diaghilev. Right now I am with my wife in a sanatorium at Leysin (not far from Montreux) at an altitude of 1450 metres because after her delivery at Lausanne (baby girl: Milène) my wife had pleurisy with a renewed outbreak of her former disease (tuberculosis).

I have just written my publisher that you have translated my *Japanese Lyrics*. Would you please write him, too, asking him when they should be sent. He will pay you, as usual, 25 francs per poem which will make 75 francs in all. That's what he paid [Maurice] Delage for his French translation.

You should write him *immediately*! The orchestra score of *Petrushka* will be sent to you as soon as its second run is published because the first one is sold out. My address is Strawinsky Tyrol (Grand Hotel) Leysin, Switzerland.

    Very affectionately yours,
    I. Strawinsky

Acquisition: H. Colin Slim on 13 May 1995 from Gary E. Combs Inc. Autographs (3 Sheridan Square / New York) through Martin A. Silver Musical Literature (7221 Del Norte Drive / Goleta, CA.).
Provenance: Unknown.

Commentary

Stravinsky and his family had been in Switzerland since late September 1913, their home throughout the First World War and after it until June 1920. He had first met Edwin Evans in London early in February 1913. Unpublished in their correspondence (1913-37), Entry 6 is his response to Evans's letter of 5 February 1914 from London. Therein Evans tells the composer of his English translation of the *Three Japanese Lyrics* (1913) – already translated into French that year by Maurice Delage – and of Evans's interest in acting as a publicity agent for Diaghilev. For the translation Evans had apparently acted either on his own or on the initiative of Stravinsky because, on 28 February, Nicolas G. von Struve, head of the Russischer Musik Verlag in Berlin, wrote: "We received the letter from Evans in London, who writes that he has made a translation of your Japanese songs into English. We didn't order any translation from him!"

Reference to a forthcoming second edition of *Petrushka* is to the composer's work on a revised edition, in proofs by June 1914 but never published because of the First World War. Even during the war, however, there were plans to publish the revision. Reference to it appears again in a letter to Evans of 9 January 1918, partly edited by Craft.

Declaring his "Cher ami" a year later as "splendid (naive and not very intelligent)," Stravinsky is said to have attended a dinner in London on 21 January 1923 honouring Evans. For a six-roll edition for player piano of *The Firebird* in 1928-29, Evans translated program notes and synopses written by Stravinsky in 1927 which were printed directly on the rolls. Music critic for London newspapers and a frequent contributor to English musical journals, he wrote a booklet entitled, *The Fire-Bird and Petrushka,* published in 1933.

Catherine Stravinsky had suffered a renewed attack of tuberculosis following the birth on 15 January of her last child, Milène. This disease was eventually to kill her in 1939. As noted in the Introduction, some thirty-eight years later, in 1952, Milène was to journey to Vancouver with Stravinsky and her husband, André Marion, where she sketched her father conducting its Symphony Orchestra. (On Delage, see entries 3 and 4.)

Works Consulted

Colles, H.C., Frank Howes, and Rosemary Williamson. "Evans, Edwin." NG. vol. 6. p. 318.

"Dinner and Presentation to Edwin Evans." *The Musical Times* 64 (1 February 1923): 127.

Evans, Edwin. *Stravinsky. The Firebird and Petrushka.* Oxford and London: Oxford University Press, 1933.

Joseph, Charles M. "Diaghilev and Stravinsky." *The Ballets Russes and Its World.* ed. Lynn Garafola and Nancy Van Norman Baer. New Haven, CT, and London: Yale University Press, 1999. ill. p. 210.

Meyer, Felix, ed. *Settling New Scores. Music Manuscripts from the Paul Sacher Foundation.* Mainz: Schott, 1998. p. 72, no. 25.

Sotheby's. *Continental Printed Books, Manuscripts and Music.* London, 3-4 December 1992, lot 634.

SAc. pl. on p. 38.

SP&D. p. 527, n. 169 on p. 613.

SP&RK. vol. 2. pp. 105, 227 (trans. Stanislav Shvabrin and Michael Green), 254-5, 273, n. 6 on p. 276, p. 669, no. 120.

SSC. vol. 1. n. 23 on pp. 11-12, pp. 26-7, n. 30 on p. 66, pp. 75, 138, 391-2, app. C; vol. 2. pp. 116, 120, pl. [15] btn pp. 146-7.

Taruskin, Richard. *Stravinsky and the Russian Traditions.* Berkeley and Los Angeles, CA: University of California Press, 1996. n. 76 on p. 587, p. 589, Ex. 9.7a on p. 592.

Walsh, Stephen. *Stravinsky, A Creative Spring: Russia and France, 1882-1934.* New York, NY: Alfred A. Knopf, 1999. pp. 224, 283.

7   **(1914). Autograph pre-stamped Swiss postcard, 9.0 × 14.0 cm, in French in black ink on both sides, Salvan (Valois), Switzerland 27 VI 1914 [sic] (27 June 1914), but postmarked Salvan Valois 28 VII 14 1[a.m.] and thus written on 27 July 1914, to Alfredo Casella (1883-1947):**

Al Signor
Alfredo Casella
via Torino–Pont Canavese
per Cuorgnè
a Prascorsano
Italia.

[reverse]
Pension Bel-Air. Salvan (Valais)
Suisse 19 27/VI 14

Mon cher Alfredo,
Ne pensez pas que je vous oublie! Je suis comme toujours très
occupé. Je compose à ce moment ci des pièces pour Quattuor à
cordes, que le celèbre quattuor de Flonzalay va jouer cet hiver
à beaucoup d'endroits de l'Europe et Amerique. Quant à un
morceau de piano – je le ferai volontier en vous le dediant dès
que l'inspiration viendra. Pour le moment j'ai terminé 3 pièces
de caractère absolument different. D'ailleurs ce recueil portera
le nom de "Varieté" et sera le premier recueil de musique de
chambre. Je m'interesse à vos pièces de piano et je viens de
jouer votre morceau de piano et Flute. Cela est un heureux
travaile

[directly below: two bars of music on one three-stave system
marked "Fl." and "Piano" copied from the 5th and 4th bars,
and marked "etc," from the close of the *Sicilienne* of Casella's
Sicilienne et burlesque, op. 23 for flute and piano (Paris: Evette
et Schaeffer, 1914), but lacking the piano's sustained octave
low Cs]
[continuation on address side] et je vous en remercie pour le
plaisir que ça me fait. Egalement je vous remercie pour la
direction de L'oiseau de feu chez Mengelberg et l'étude
harmonique du "Sacre" et du "Rossignol"[.] Je suis fort
heureux que c'est vous qui le ferez! Ne preferiez vous pas peut
être de diriger Petrouchka? Quant à moi je dirige a Londres en
Avril chez Wood la 2ᵈᵉ moitié de son concert consacré à votre
aimable serviteur.
    Igor Strawinsky

[postscript upside down at top] Mille affections de nous deux à
vous deux. IStraw.

Alfredo Casella
Prascorsano

Salvan (Valois)
27 July [sic] 1914

My dear Alfredo:

Don't think that I'm forgetting you! I am, as always, very busy.
Right now, I am composing some pieces for string quartet which the
celebrated Flonzaley Quartet will play this winter in many places in
Europe and America. As for a piano piece, I shall gladly write one,
dedicating it to you, as soon as inspiration comes. Just now I have
finished three pieces of an entirely different kind. Moreover, this
group will be titled *Variety* and will be my first collection of chamber
music. I am interested in your piano pieces and I just played your
piece for piano and flute. It is a delightful work and I thank you for
the pleasure it gives me. I also thank you for conducting the *Firebird*
with Mengelberg's [orchestra] and for your harmonic study of *The
Rite of Spring* and of *The Nightingale*. I am mightily glad that it is you
who are doing these things! Do you not perhaps [also] want to
conduct *Petrushka*? As for me, I shall conduct in London in April [Sir
Henry] Wood's [orchestra], the second half of his concert devoted to
your obliging servant[,] Igor Strawinsky

p.s. A thousand affectionate greetings from us two to you two.

Acquisition: H. Colin Slim on 11 December 1997 from La Scala
Autographs.
Provenance: An unidentified dealer/collector in 1997 in England.

Commentary

The postcard is unpublished. Stravinsky was living with his family at the
pension Bel-Air in Salvan, Switzerland.

Although much later, Stravinsky failed to recall it, Alfredo Casella
first met Stravinsky on 12 November 1907 in St. Petersburg at an
orchestral rehearsal led by Alexander Siloti. Requesting Casella's recent
orchestration of Balakirev's *Islamey* for study, he returned it after two
hours, giving Casella his name. Meaning nothing to him, Casella forgot
the name until, according to Casella, Stravinsky reminded him four
years later, after the first performance of *Petrushka,* of their previous
meeting.

Entry 7 responds to Casella's letter from Prascorsano of 20 July 1914 (in the Paul Sacher Foundation at Basle). Clearly he had neglected writing for some time, for on 5 February Maurice Delage had urged him to write to Casella. Six days later Pierre Monteux wrote Stravinsky inviting him to play the important piano part in *Petrushka* at its concert premiere in Paris on 1 March. Owing to his wife's poor health, he declined. Casella reviewed Monteux's concert. Thus, Stravinsky's query "Ne preferiez vous pas peut être de diriger *Petrouchka?*" may refer to an ambition Casella already harboured, one fulfilled by conducting the Italian premiere at Rome in February the following year and then leading it at Paris that June. (See entries 8 and 9.)

The three compositions for strings by Stravinsky, finished 26 April, 2 July, and 25 July 1914, were his *Three Pieces for String Quartet,* prompted by a commission from the Flonzaley Quartet negotiated by Ernest Ansermet. (The first of these was originally a movement for piano four-hands.) On 26 July 1914, he described them as "three pieces from my new chamber-music album, which will consist of five pieces in all" (SSC 1, p. 407 n. 5). The Flonzaley Quartet played it the following year in Chicago on 8 November, the work apparently having received a private performance at Geneva earlier in the year. Although Casella reported that they were to be premiered in Paris on 19 May 1915, the first performance there was probably six days earlier.

The promised piano piece for Casella was the "Marche", one of three such four-handed works. Dated 19 December 1914, the "Marche" manuscript is headed "À Alfredo Casella!" and decorated with exploding cannons, referring to the First World War. Stravinsky did not immediately send the "Marche" to Casella who asked in postcards of 13 July and 3 September 1915 about "my piano piece." Although it had not arrived by 4 March 1917, Stravinsky dedicated it to him when it was published that year, seemingly acknowledged by Casella on 10 July.

What Stravinsky calls *Varieté* in Entry 7 is the above-mentioned *Three Pieces for String Quartet,* completed just two days earlier. The second piece of the three is an homage to the English clown and juggler, Little Tich (Harry Relph, 1868-1928), whom Stravinsky had seen in a London music hall in June 1914.

Stravinsky copied the musical excerpt by Casella on staves ruled by his special bronze stylus (rastrum). Inventing this device around 1911, he used it as early as his sketches that summer for *Le Sacre du Printemps*. (See also entries 48–60, 62, 71, 76, 106, and 115.)

Casella's letter of 20 July informs him that he will conduct *The Firebird Suite* at Amsterdam on 15 October 1914. He also tells Stravinsky that he has promised to write for the coming October issue of the *Monde Musical* an "étude très detaillé" about *Le Sacre* and *Le Rossignol*, assuring him that he will send his essay before publication. In the event, Casella's study did not appear in France, but in Italy. On 17 March 1915 he requested his Roman editor to send Stravinsky a copy of his article, "Igor Strawinsky e la sua arte," *La riforma musicale* 3 (7–14 March 1915). Although hardly an "étude harmonique," this essay, which also discusses *Petrushka,* duly arrived and is now in the Paul Sacher Foundation.

For his London concert in April 1915 with Sir Henry Wood and his Queen's Hall orchestra, Stravinsky wrote to his publisher, B.P. Jurgenson, on 24 July 1914, that he would be conducting excerpts from *The Firebird* and the *Scherzo Fantastique*. The concert never took place. His public debut as conductor of his own music had occurred at Montreux on 16 April 1914, his Paris debut in a similar capacity only on 29 December 1915. Apropos the Queen's Hall orchestra, the *Musical Times* noted in June 1915 that "the War also made it impossible to procure foreign novelties, even if it had been considered to introduce them here at such a moment."

Correspondence between him and Casella is larger than Craft's selection might initially suggest. In addition to entries 7-9, at least seven more communications were still in private hands in 1972 and one from 1913 was auctioned in 1990. Craft's opinion that "Stravinsky seems never to have had a good word for Casella" perhaps warrants modification, not only by these materials – above all the encomia in entries 7 and 8 – but also by an inscribed photograph: "A Alfredo Casella en souvenir d'une amitié de plus de vingt ans. Qu'elle dure au moins autant / Igor Strawinsky / Paris le 30 Janv. / 1934" [To Alfredo Casella in memory of a friendship of more than twenty years. May it last at least as long again. Paris 30 January 1934].

Works Consulted

Calabretto, Roberto, ed. *Alfredo Casella, Gli anni di Parigi. Dai documenti.* Florence: L.S. Olschki, 1997. p. 215, n. 27 on p. 350.

Casella, Alfredo. *Music in My Time*, trans. Spencer Norton. Norman, OK: University of Oklahoma Press, 1955. pp. 78, 99.

Colajanni, Anna Rita, F.R. Conti, M. de Santis, et al., ed. *Catalogo critico del fondo Alfredo Casella*, Florence: L.S. Olschki, 1992. vol. 1. p. 153, letter 805; vol. 2. p. 49, item 58.

Gordon, Tom. "Streichquartett-Komponist 'wider Willen' " in *Igor Strawinsky: Trois Pièces pour quatuor à cordes: Skizzen, Fassungen, Dokumente, Essays: Festgabe für Albi Rosenthal*. ed. Hermann Danuser, Felix Meyer, and Ulrich Mosch. Basle and Winterthur: Amadeus, 1994. pp. 34-8.

Meyer, Felix, ed. *Settling New Scores. Music Manuscripts from the Paul Sacher Foundation*. Mainz: Schott, 1998. p. 73, no. 28.

Musical Times 56 (1 June 1915): p. 340.

Nicolodi, Fiamma. "Casella e la musica di Stravinsky in Italia. Contributo a un'indagine sul neoclassicismo." *Chigiana* 29-30 (1972-73): 48-51 (trans. Leonard W. Johnson).

Sotheby's, *Fine Printed and Manuscript Music*. London: 21 November 1990, lot 295.

SConv. p. 38.

SP&D. pp. 58-9, 126-9, 176, n. 213 on p. 617.

SP&RK. vol. 2. pp. 441 and 748 (index: Casella).

SSC. vol. 1. pp. 130-1, n. 234 on p. 203, n. 5 on p. 407, p. 413; vol. 2. pl. on p. 21, pp. 125-34, 225.

Strawinsky. Sein Nachlass. Sein Bild [with] *Katalog der ausgestellten Bildnisse und Entwürfe für die Ausstattung seiner Bühnenwerke*. Basle: Kunstmuseum and Paul Sacher Stiftung, 1984. colour pl. on p. 62.

Tappolet, Claude, ed. *Correspondance Ernest Ansermet-Igor Strawinsky (1914-1967)*. Geneva: Georg, 1990-92. vol. 1. pp. 42, no. 38, 44, no. 40 (trans. H. Colin Slim).

Taruskin, Richard. *Stravinsky and the Russian Traditions*. Berkeley and Los Angeles, CA: University of California Press, 1996. n. b on p. 1446, pp. 1465-73.

—. "Stravinsky and the Subhuman: Notes on *Svadebka*" in *Defining Russia Musically*. Princeton, NJ: Princeton University Press, 1997. pp. 414-24.

Walsh, Stephen. *Stravinsky, A Creative Spring: Russia and France, 1882-1934*. New York, NY: Alfred A. Knopf, 1999. pp. 225, 232, 235-42, 250, n. 44 on p. 609.

Yastrebtsev, Vasiliy Vasilyevich. *Reminiscences [abridged] of Rimsky-Korsakov*. ed. and trans. Florence Jonas. New York, NY: Columbia University Press, 1985. p. 419.

8 (1915). **Autograph pre-stamped Italian postcard, 8.9 × 13.9 cm, with messages by Sergei Diaghilev, Alfredo Casella, Mimi [Marya Freund], and Stravinsky in French in various black inks on both sides, postmarked Rome 9-10/15.II/1915 [15 February 1915, 9-10 a.m.], countermarked Paris 17 February 1915, addressed by Casella, Sunday evening [14 February 1915], to his wife, Madame [Hélène] Casella in Paris:**

Mme Casella
12, Avenue de
la G^{de} Armée
Paris

Toutes mes felicitations de la grande victoire italo–russe[.]
S. Diaghilew.

[reverse]
Dimanche soir –
Le concert est admirablement passé. L'execution magnifique,
e Mimi★ merveilleuse. Nous dinons avec Igor et Diaghilew.
Baisers, A.

★merci – Mimi. Si contente d'avoir été la première à chanter
la Notte ici! –

Tout cela est parfaitement exacte et plus que cela.....
"Pétrouchka", particulièrement était admirablement bien
interpreté et la <u>Notta</u> de notre cher Alfred avait beaucoup
impressioné le publique par sa richesse sonore[.] Très
cordialement
    à vous Igor Strawinsky

Madame Casella   Rome
Paris   [14 February 1915]

All my congratulations on the great Italo-Russian victory.
S. Diaghilev.

Sunday evening. The concert went extremely well. The performance magnificent, and Mimi★ marvellous. We are dining with Igor
and Diaghilev. Kisses, A[lfredo].

★Thanks – Mimi. So pleased to have been the first to sing *La Notte*
here! [Marya Freund]

All this is completely accurate and even more than that ... *Petrushka,*
especially, was marvellously well interpreted and *La Notte* by our
dear Alfredo very much impressed the public by its rich sonorities.
Very cordially to you,
     Igor Strawinsky

Acquisition: H. Colin Slim on 11 December 1997 from La Scala
Autographs.
Provenance: Same as Entry 7.

Commentary
The postcard is unpublished. Leaving Geneva on 7 February 1915,
Stravinsky was in Rome from the 8th to the 17th, returning to
Switzerland the next day. The addressee was the first wife, Hélène (née
Kahn), pianist and singer whom Casella married in 1907 and separated
from in 1919, their union being annulled two years later.
     Correspondence between Stravinsky and Casella about obtaining
the score and parts for *Petrushka* for the Augusteo concert on 14
February is in a group of postcards from 26 December 1914 until 29
January 1915. Conducted by Casella, the program on 14 February was:
Suite française by Jean Roger-Ducasse (1873-1954); *Hymne à la justice* by
Albéric Magnard (1865-1914); *Petrushka*; Casella's *Notte di maggio*
(1913); and the second suite from *Daphnis et Chloë* by Maurice Ravel
(1875-1937). The glowing praise by Stravinsky of Casella's ability
contrasts sharply with the St. Petersburg newspaper review in *New*

Russian Word, 15 February 1915: "In spite of the undistinguished performance and the bad conducting by Casella, Stravinsky's music captivated the Roman audience, which gave the composer, present at the performance, a noisy ovation."

Just before the war, when he was in London for performances of *Le Rossignol,* Stravinsky had met the painter Filippo Tomasso Marinetti and the composer Luigi Russolo at a "Grand Futurist Concert of Noises" held in the Coliseum on 15 June. The day before the February 14 concert at Rome in 1915, the sculptor Umberto Boccioni (1882-1916) had been invited to a tea given by Diaghilev at the Grand Hotel to meet him: "He wants to meet me and do something with futurist ... color, dance, and costume" (Walsh, p. 249). At this tea he and Casella played four-hands the *Three Pieces* for string quartet. Following the performance of *Petrushka* on the 14th, Marinetti shouted from his loge: "Abasso Wagner, viva Stravinsky!" (SP&D, p. 152). On the return trip to Switzerland, he wrote his mother: "All of the Italian Futurists were there in person and greeted me noisily[;] Marinetti came especially from Milan for this" (SP&RK, vol. 2, p. 310).

The program of the 14 February concert reveals that "Mimi" is the singer, Marya Freund (1876-1966). Casella had known her since at least 1911, dedicated *Notte di Maggio* to her, and had premiered it with her at the Concerts Colonne in Paris on 29 March 1914. She and Casella had just given a concert in Turin on 21 December 1914 and had accepted another date together at Venice the following year. More-over, Stravinsky had accompanied her in some of his songs at Rome in the week preceding the Augusteo concert. (For more on her, see Entry 10.)

Works Consulted

Buckle, Richard. *Diaghilev.* New York, NY: Atheneum, 1979. p. 288, n. 17 on p. 563.

Casella, Alfredo. *Music in My Time,* trans. Spencer Norton. Norman, OK: University of Oklahoma Press, 1955. pp. 119-20, 123-4.

Colajanni, Anna Rita, et al., ed. *Catalogo critico del fondo Alfredo Casella,* Florence: L.S. Olschki, 1992. vol. 1. p. 194 letters 1138-39, p. 648 letters 4738-41; vol. 2. p. 218 P.13.

Garafola, Lynn. *Diaghilev's Ballets Russes.* New York, and Oxford: Oxford University Press, 1989. p. 77.

Nicolodi, Fiamma. "Casella e la musica di Stravinsky in Italia. Contributo a un'indagine sul neoclassicismo." *Chigiana* 29-30 (1972-73): 50-1 (trans. Leonard W. Johnson).

Regia Accademia di Santa Cecilia [Rome], Annuario dal 1° luglio 1914 al 30 giugno 1915. 330-2 (1915): 112.

SP&D. p. 152, n. 201 on p. 616.

SP&RK. vol. 2. n. 2 on p. 306, p. 310 (both trans. Stanislav Shvabrin and Michael Green).

SSC. vol. 2. n. 25 on pp. 17-18.

Walsh, Stephen. *Stravinsky, A Creative Spring: Russia and France, 1882-1934.* New York, NY: Alfred A. Knopf, 1999. pp. 248-9.

9

(1915). **Autograph Swiss picture postcard, 9.0 × 13.8 cm, in French in black ink, printed on front: "A. Lenzi édit. phot. Château d'Oex" and on reverse: "A. L. 148. Châteaux d'Oex – Vieux chalet" (also depicting at lower left the "Pension Richemont"), postmarked Clarens 20.III.15.XII [20 March 1915, 12 noon], to Alfredo Casella in Paris:**

Monsieur Alfredo Casella
12 Avenue de la Grande Armée
A-bas les Boches! Paris Vive la France!

Viex:
Suis ravi que vous jouer "Petrouchka"[;] dites mille choses à Massager de ma part et donnez moi de vos nouvelles ainsi que celles de "Petrouchka" apres son execution. Je suis encore à Clarens – je dis encore puisque je devais aller à Milan pour voir Diaghilew, Ricordi et encore des gents. J'attend toujours son telegramme pour y aller. Des qu'il y aura quelque-chose d'interressant je vous écrirai. Je vous embrasse
    votre viex Igor Strawinsky

[postscript upside down at top] Ou est Ravel? Si il est toujours à Paris – qu'il m'écrive un mot!

[second postscript top right of photo] Et ma lettre à vous et à l'orchestre de L'Augusteum etait-elle publié? – je n'en ai pas eu de novelles ...
[third postscript top left of picture] Mille chos à votre chère femme IStry
[fourth postscript below picture, upside down] Si je vais à Milan – j'y vais pour un, deux jours tout au plus et revien à Montreux avec Diaghilew.

Alfredo Casella   Clarens
Paris   20 March 1915
Down with Germans! Long Live France!

Old pal!
I'm delighted that you are to conduct *Petrushka*; say a thousand nice things to [André] Messager from me and give me your news as well as news about *Petrushka* after its performance. I'm still at Clarens – I say still because I'm supposed to go to Milan to see Diaghilev, [Tito] Ricordi, and other people. I'm still waiting for his telegram in order to go there. As soon as something interesting turns up, I'll write you. I embrace you.
      Your old pal Igor Strawinsky

p.s. Where is Ravel? If he is still in Paris, have him drop me a line.
p.p.s. And my letter to you and to the Augusteo orchestra, has it been published? I have had no news about it...
p.p.p.s. All the best to your dear wife, I Str[awinsk]y
p.p.p.p.s. If I go to Milan, I'll go there for one or two days at most and return to Montreux with Diaghilev.

Acquisition: H. Colin Slim on 11 December 1997 from La Scala Autographs.
Provenance: Same as Entry 7.

Commentary

The postcard is unpublished. Apparently the Stravinsky letter to Casella and the Augusteo orchestra mentioned in the postscript has not survived. Entry 9 is probably the communication hoped for by Casella who noted on 13 July 1915: "You have not written since March." Stravinsky and his family had moved at the beginning of January to the *pension* Hotel Victoria in Chateau d'Oex (east of Montreux), but returned to Clarens in March. Evident enough from Stravinsky's inscription to the left of the address, his dislike of Germans had already manifested itself in a letter of 20 September 1914 to Léon Bakst: "My hatred of Germans grows not by the day but by the hour," and soon resulted in his piano piece, *Souvenir d'une marche boche,* dated 1 September 1915.

A force in French musical life c. 1904-15 and general secretary 1911-14 of the Société Independante Musicale, Casella had already conducted *Petrushka* in Rome and was to lead it in Paris at the Odéon on 27 June 1915. At this time the composer-conductor André Messager (1853-1929) led the Société du Concerts du Conservatoire.

After many telegrams from Diaghilev, on 22, 28, 29 March and 1 April 1915, Stravinsky did travel briefly to Milan on 2 April, meeting there Sergei Prokofiev (1891-1953), Diaghilev, Casella, and the publisher, Tito Ricordi (1865-1933; retired in 1919). Asked by Stravinsky to introduce him to Ricordi, Casella did so, Stravinsky offering his *Three Easy Pieces* for piano duet (1914-15). Publisher and composer could not come to terms because of the high price Stravinsky wanted, despite a promised intervention by Diaghilev in March and additional queries from Casella in May.

Still other "gents" who awaited him at Milan in April included members of the "Movimento Futurista." Marinetti organized three evenings of performances honouring him and Diaghilev, where, among others there participated Francesco Pratella, Carlo Carrà, Boccioni, Léonide Massine, Prokofiev, Buzzi, both Russolo brothers, the director of La Scala, and Stravinsky himself; Francesco Cangiullo sketched the composer at least twice. As noted, he returned to Switzerland by himself. Diaghilev did not arrive in Montreux until 25 April.

Ravel had written from Paris on 2 January 1915, and Stravinsky was disappointed by the news that he was not coming there and doubting that he would be visiting him in Switzerland at the end of January. Although repeatedly trying to enlist during 1915, Ravel did not go to the front until the following January. (See also Entry 11.)

Works Consulted

Lesure, François. *Igor Stravinsky. La carrière européenne*. Paris: Musée d'Art Moderne, 1980. pp. 54-7.

Nicolodi, Fiamma. "Casella e la musica di Stravinsky in Italia. Contributo a un'indagine sul neoclassicismo." *Chigiana* 29-30 (1972-73): 54 (trans. Leonard W. Johnson).

Pratella, F. Balilla. *Autobiografia*. Milan: Pan Editrice, 1971. pp. 133-5.

SConv. p. 72.

SD. p. 41.

SD&D. p. 72.

SP&D. p. 151, n. 122 on p. 610, n. 250 on p. 621, n. 1 on p. 661.

SP&RK. vol. 2. p. 290 (trans. Stanislav Shvabrin and Michael Green), 755 (index: Messager).

SSC. vol. 2. pp. 20-1, 87, 126-7; vol. 3. p. 20.

Walsh, Stephen. *Stravinsky, A Creative Spring: Russia and France, 1882-1934*. New York, NY: Alfred A. Knopf, 1999. pp. 247-9, 252.

10

(1915). Autograph Swiss picture postcard, 9.0 × 13.5 cm, in French in black ink. [entire address side printed in red] CARTE POSTALE [at left] A. Zoller, Genève. No. 123. [and at right of a dividing red line] Adresse, and postmarked: Morges/25 VI 15.6 [25 June 1915, 6 a.m.]. Its reverse side depicts the "Villa Rogivue. MORGES." [avenue des Pâquis]. It is addressed in ink to Marya Freund (1876-1966):

Madame Maria Freund
2, Le Borromées
Lausanne
(Montriond)

Cher madame
L'unique raison de mon silence est que je suis completement absorbé par le travail. J'espère quand même vous voir avant votre depart. Ou allez vous?
　　Très respectieusement et cordialement à vous
　　Igor Strawinsky

Madame Marya Freund   Morges
Lausanne   25 June 1915

Dear Madame:
The sole reason for my silence is that I am completely absorbed by
work. Even so, I hope to see you before your departure. Where are
you going?
    Very respectfully and cordially yours,
    Igor Strawinsky

Acquisition: H. Colin Slim in New York on 17 June 1977 from
Wurlitzer-Bruck.
Provenance: Doda Conrad (1905-), son of Marya Freund.

Commentary

The postcard, unpublished, may be the earliest known communication
by Stravinsky from the Villa Rogivue in Morges, Switzerland, and
perhaps the earliest surviving one to Marya Freund. It and other notices
of her in this collection (entries 8 and 102), and Stravinsky's letters to
Vera Janacopulos (entries 23 and 26-7), effectively challenge Austin's
and Pasler's views of "Stravinsky's apparent lack of substantial
collaboration with singers."

    Photographs show Stravinsky and his family at the Villa Rogivue
(built 1880). For slightly more than two years, it was to be their first
stable home since leaving Russia. Evidence about precisely when the
family moved to the Rogivue is conflicting. Théodore "Fedik" (1907-
89) signed two watercolours of his father: "Morges 1915," recalling
their interiors as depicting this villa, and also stated that the family rented
the villa from the spring of 1915. In July 1915 and in April 1916
Stravinsky sent four postcards identical to Entry 10 from Morges to his
friend in Paris, Prince Vladimir Argoutinsky Dolgoroukov (1874-
1941). On the earliest of the four, 15 July 1915, and on the second one,
23 July, he circled an upper rear window on the right side of the villa
as "votre chambre." The Swiss writer Charles-Ferdinand Ramuz
(1878-1947) sent him a letter there dated 9 August 1915; and Fernand
Auberjonois, son of the painter René Auberjonois (1872-1957), also
located him there the same year.

Walsh hypothesizes that Stravinsky rented the Rogivue and, while renovating it, was still living at the Villa Les Sapins – for he believes that Stravinsky's letter to Alexander Siloti of 15 July was sent from Les Sapins, rather than from the Rogivue. The family certainly resided in the latter villa by the summer of 1915, although Walsh opts for "by September." Although at first glance Entry 10 – and the other four postcards – seems to depict him and his two sons, Théodore and Svyatoslav Soulima "Svetik" (1910-94), in the villa's garden with his first wife, Catherine, standing above on its balcony, closer inspection shows the figures to be too small for certain identification.

In 1928 Ramuz recalled the first Stravinsky residence in Morges as "the turreted villa with the slate roof ... in the outskirts" and that the composer had decorated his study with wallpaper "of an extraordinary blue, a washing-powder blue." Stravinsky and Ernst Ansermet were photographed in this study. He himself inscribed a copy of this photo-graph: "Moi avec Ansermet à Morges (Villa Rogivue) dans ma chambre bleu en 1915 ou en 1916" (Craft, Catalog). Craft identifies this as the Villa La Pervenche in Clarens, to which the family moved in December 1914, and again lived in during the following April-May. According to Ansermet, by July 1915, the Stravinskys had moved to the Villa Les Sapins in Morges. Two friends visiting him in Switzerland in 1915-16, C. Stanley Wise, and the Princesse de Polignac (1865-1945) – the latter with a charming account of a dinner given by the Stravinskys at the Villa Rogivue on 5 or 6 February 1916 – offer their impressions of him at this period.

Marya Freund, mezzo soprano, made her Berlin debut in 1903 and her Parisian one in 1910. A letter from Catherine Stravinsky to the composer's mother early in January 1915 from Clarens reveals that Stravinsky had known her previously in Paris. Freund was rehearsing with him in Clarens his *Two Songs* (1908), *Two Poems of Balmont* (1911), *Three Japanese Lyrics* and would soon rehearse *Pribaoutki* (1914). Catherine believed, however, that the *Japaense Lyrics* were "not in the least suited to her."

Obviously, Freund had recently chastised Stravinsky for not writing. But "mon silence" in Entry 10 could not have exceeded four months. On 13 (or 15) February 1915, he had accompanied her in Rome in the first two of his *Japanese Lyrics* – and probably the other works he had been rehearsing with her at Clarens (see Entry 8). In a postcard of 22 November that year, he complimented her on her singing: "votre admirable *voix slave!*" His "travail" in June mentioned in Entry 10 included work on the *Cat's Cradle Songs* (1915), *Les Noces* (1923), and possibly *Renard* (1916).

Having heard Schoenberg's *Pierrot Lunaire* at Berlin on 8 December 1912, Stravinsky was also to hear Freund sing its French premiere with the text translated into its original French at Paris, early in 1922. Six months later, on 15 August, he called her "la reine des cantatrices" and was again to praise her work in *Mavra* (1922) in Frankfurt in November 1925. She made her American debut in Chicago on 3 December 1923 and, on 25-26 of the ensuing January, sang Monteverdi and Mahler with the Boston Symphony under Pierre Monteux.

Stravinsky's question in Entry 10 about Freund's departure may refer to her forthcoming trip to Breslau c. October 1915 where she would take and leave behind two of his *Pribaoutki* manuscripts. (She later signed a copy of the 1917 first edition.) Just before and during the first years of the First World War, Alfredo Casella often accompanied her. He also reviewed her two concerts at Paris in May 1913 and 1914.

Ravel, another close friend, accompanied her in a recital of his own music at Vienna in October 1920 and, in a letter of 18 December 1925 to Alexandre Tansman (1897-1986), another future biographer of Stravinsky, he wrote: "Whether or not Marya Freund sings Schoenberg better than Debussy is a matter of personal taste." Freund was again to sing *Pierrot Lunaire* under Schoenberg in Paris on 8 and 15 December 1927. In addition to the premiere of Satie's *Socrate* in June 1920 and her French premieres in Paris during the 1920s of Schoenberg's *Pierrot Lunaire, Das Buch der hängende Gärten,* and his *Second String Quartet,* Freund sang works by Tansman, Szymanowski, and De Falla and, in May 1930, the European premiere of *Offrandes* by Varèse. She was frequently reviewed by the Parisian press, which, for example, announced in mid-October 1934 her series of ten lecture-recitals about singing Debussy.

A decade after Entry 10, Cole Porter (1891-1964) wrote from Venice to his then-lover, Boris Kochno (1904-90) that he had just heard Freund sing one evening in 1925: "une soirée charmante ce soir – une vieille chanteuse qui a choisi toutes les chansons les plus tristes du monde – Madame [Marya] Freund."

A lifelong friend of Stravinsky, Freund attended the premiere at Venice of *The Rake's Progress* on 11 September 1951. While in London on 11 December 1956, he noted in his "Medical Diaries" her address c/o her son, Doda Conrad. For a letter to Conrad in 1957 from him (masquerading as his son-in-law secretary, André Marion), see Entry 102.

Works Consulted

Auberjonois, Fernand. "The Swiss Years of Igor Stravinsky: 1914-1920." *ADAM International Review* 39 (1973-74): 76.

Austin, William. "Stravinsky's 'Fortunate Continuities' and 'Legitimate Accidents,' 1882-1982." *Stravinsky Retrospectives*. ed. Ethan Haimo and Paul Johnson. Lincoln, NB, and London: University of Nebraska Press, 1987. p. 13.

Boston Symphony Program Notes. 25-26 January 1924. pp. 877, 902.

Buckle, Richard. *Diaghilev*. New York, NY: Atheneum, 1979. p. 288.

Colajanni, Anna Rita, et al., ed. *Catalogo critico del fondo Alfredo Casella*. Florence: L.S. Olschki, 1992. vol. 2. pp. 43, 47, items S. 6 and 46.

Cox, Lisa. *Catalogue B/6 Winter Spring 1995*. Exeter, 1995. no. 477.

Craft, Robert. "Catalog of the Library of Robert Craft." Typescript: Library of Congress, Music Division. XII, Photographs: Stravinsky with others, p. 187, no. 3.

—. *Stravinsky: Glimpses of a Life*. London: Lime Tree, 1992; New York, NY: St. Martin's Press, 1993. pp. 340-1.

—. *Stravinsky: Chronicle of a Friendship*. 2nd ed. Nashville, TN, and London: Vanderbilt University Press, 1994. p. 62.

Goubault, Christian. *Igor Stravinsky*. Paris: H. Champion, 1991. p. 36.

La Revue Musicale 3-4 (1922-23); 7 (October 1926): 252; 11 (June 1930): 540.

Le Figaro. 14 October 1934, 6.

Lesure , François. *Igor Stravinsky. La carrière européenne*. Paris: Musée d'Art Moderne, 1980. pp. 45, nos. 132-3, 137 (1915); 111 (June 1915).

"Memoirs of the late Princesse Edmond de Polignac." *Horizon* 12 (1945): 134-5.

Milhaud, Darius. *An Autobiography. Notes without Music*. trans. Donald Evans. New York, NY: Alfred A. Knopf, 1953. pl. facing p. 148.

Morelli, Giovanni, ed. *Alfredo Casella negli anni di apprendistato a Parigi*. Florence: L.S. Olschki, 1994. pp. 9, 149, 159.

Morton, Lawrence. Papers. Box 9. Special Collections 1522. Charles E. Young Research Library. University of California at Los Angeles.

Nicolodi, Fiamma. "Falla e l'Italia." *Manuel de Falla tra la Spagna e l'Europa*. ed. Paolo Pinamonti. Florence: L.S. Olschki, 1989. pp. 240, 243.

Orenstein, Arbie, ed. *A Ravel Reader*. New York, NY: Columbia University Press, 1990. n. 2 on p. 198, n. 3 on p. 205, p. 266 letter 258.

Pasler, Jann. "Introduction: Issues in Stravinsky Research." *Confronting Stravinsky: Man, Musician, and Modernist*. ed. Jann Pasler. Berkeley and Los Angeles, CA, and London: University of California Press, 1986. n. 12 on p. xviii (Austin: 1982-84).

Ramuz, Charles-Ferdinand. *Souvenirs sur Igor Stravinsky*. Paris: Nouvelle Revue Française, 1929. pp. 36-7 (trans. Leonard W. Johnson).

Schaeffner, André. *Strawinsky*. Paris: Les Éditions Rieder, 1931. pl. xxxiii, no. 2.

Sotheby's. *Collection Boris Kochno*. Monaco, 11-12 October 1991, lot 384.

–. *Fine Music and Continental Manuscripts*. London, 15-16 May 1997, lot 306.

–. *Fine Printed and Manuscript Music*. London, 17 May 1990, lot 270.

SAc. p. 47, pls. on pp. 48-50.

SC&I. pls. [52], [58], and [60].

SE&D. 1962: p. 79; 1981: p. 68.

SP&D. pp. 136-8, 273: poster (*recte:* 1921), nn. 215 and 227 on pp. 617-18, n. 275 on p. 623.

SP&RK. vol. 2. pp. 302-3 (trans. Stanislav Shvabrin and Michael Green), 333-5.

SSC. vol. 1. p. 160, n. 181 on p. 186, pl. [8] btn pp. 202-3; vol. 3. p. 28.

SScrbk. p. 159 (medical diaries).

Stravinsky, Igor. Four unpublished postcards (1915-16) to Prince Argoutinsky Dolgoroukov, Theatre Collection, Harvard University, Cambridge. [See also Sotheby's 1997 sale, lot 306.]

Strawinsky. Sein Nachlass. Sein Bild [with] *Katalog der ausgestellten Bildnisse und Entwürfe für die Ausstattung seiner Bühnenwerke*. Basle: Kunstmuseum and Paul Sacher Stiftung, 1984. item 255.

Tappolet, Claude, ed. *Correspondance Ernest Ansermet-Igor Strawinsky (1914-1967)*. Geneva: Georg, 1990-92. vol. 1. p. 34, no. 31; vol. 2. p. 21, no. 192.

Taruskin, Richard. *Stravinsky and the Russian Traditions*. Berkeley and Los Angeles, CA: University of California Press, 1996. pp. 1138-40, table 2.

Walsh, Stephen. *Stravinsky, A Creative Spring: Russia and France, 1882-1934*. New York, NY: Alfred A. Knopf, 1999. p. 253, n. 1 on p. 650.

Wiéner, Jean. *Allegro appassionato*. Paris: P. Belfond, 1978. pp. 48, 50-1.

Wise, C. Stanley. "Impressions of Igor Strawinsky." *The Musical Quarterly* 2 (1916): 249-56.

11 (1916). Autograph letter, 27.0 × 21.0 cm, folded four times, in French in black ink, 2 May 1916, to Jacques Rouché (1862-1957):

Cher Monsieur Rouché,

J'espère que vous ne m'envoudrez pas si je vous dis que je refuse à tout le monde toute collaboration quelconque au livret, si beau soit-il. C'est trop long à éxpliquer dans une lettre; j'éspère le faire quand je vous verrai ce qui aura lieu probablement au courant de ce moi (vers le milieu)[.]

   Je vous envoie, cher Monsieur Rouché [crossed out in ink] tous mes souvenirs les meilleurs

   Votre dévoué

   Igor Strawinsky

Je vous prie de presenter mes hommages respectieux à Madame Rouché.

Morges

2 Mai

1916

[postscript top left] Avez vous reçu le materiel de mon "Scherzo fantastique"? La maison Foeutich Frères attend de nos nouvelles.

[second postscript top right] Je ne vous envoie pas pour poste le livret de Me. Colette car cela sera plus sur que je le prenne avec moi, quand j'irai à Paris[.]

Jacques Rouché   Morges

Paris   2 May 1916

Dear Mr. Rouché:

I hope you won't be annoyed with me if I tell you that I refuse any collaboration whatsoever with *anyone* in the libretto, as fine as it is. That's too long to explain in a letter; I hope to do this when I see you which will probably be during the course of this month (toward the middle).

I send you, dear Mr. Rouché, my best regards,
Your devoted
Igor Strawinsky

Please convey my respects to Mrs. Rouché.
p.s. Have you received the orchestra parts for my *Fantastic Scherzo*? The firm of Foetisch Brothers is waiting to hear from you.
p.p.s. I am not sending you Madame Colette's libretto by post because it will be safer if I bring it with me when I come to Paris[.]

Acquisition: H. Colin Slim on 10 June 1997 from La Scala Autographs, bidding for him at Pierre Berès and PIASA (Picard, Audap, Solanet et associés), *Collections musicales du Docteur Barbier et du Professeur de musicologie en Sorbonne Jean Mongrédien. Vente aux enchères* (Paris: Drouot-Richelieu, 30 April 1997), lot 317.
Provenance: Probably estate of Jacques Rouché; Henri Barbier (Swiss or French musicologist and collector of Handel and Lully from the 1930s).

Commentary

The letter is published in facsimile in *Collections musicales,* opposite lot 317. Its envelope is missing. He wrote it on paper watermarked: Original / Special Bank. / 1090, at Morges in the Villa Rogivue (pictured in Entry 10).

Professor Jean Mongrédien (letter of 22 July 1997) kindly advises Entry 11 was not his property and that Henri Barbier was Swiss, although J. and J. Lubrano identify him as French. A provenance from Barbier is established by comparing lots 101, 178-79, 181, and 195 of the above catalogue with lots 107, 159-61 and 189, respectively, in Lubrano's 1998 *Catalogue 54* (also illustrating Barbier's bookplate, not present in Entry 11).

Early in the summer of 1914 Jacques Rouché, director of the Paris Opéra (1914-45), was requested by Sidonie-Gabrielle Colette (1873-1954) to send Stravinsky the scenario of her ballet which she variously called *Le Ballet pour ma fille, Divertissement pour ma fille,* and *Divertissement pour ma petite-fille.* Following the birth of a daughter in July 1913, she wrote it for Rouché who had commissioned shortly before the First World War a "féerie-ballet." She then wrote Stravinsky asking him to compose music for it in which the Swiss painter and pianist, Paul Thévenaz (1891-1921), would dance the role of "Fire." (Whether this is connected with a report of 30 March 1914 in *Rech'* that Stravinsky, collaborating with Thévenaz in Switzerland, was then "writing music for rhythmical dances," remains unknown.) Colette also tells Stravinsky how much she would miss performances of *Le Rossignol* – presumably she had attended one or both at the Paris Opéra, 26 and 28 May 1914.

Not long after Stravinsky mailed Entry 11 and then returned Colette's libretto to Paris, Rouché sent her ballet in 1916 to Ravel at the front, where it was lost. A second copy reaching Ravel only after his discharge from the army in 1917, he set it between 1920 and 1925 as his opera *L'Enfant et les sortilèges*.

Rouché not only received the orchestra parts of the *Scherzo fantastique* (1908) mentioned on the left side of Entry 11 which were forwarded by Foetisch Frères (a Swiss publishing company in Lausanne), but they were still at the Paris Opéra in March 1918. Stravinsky had also sent Rouché the orchestra score, which, on 5 October 1916, he asked the Princesse de Polignac to bring with her when she visited him in Switzerland.

Stravinsky's reason for sending Rouché these materials and for requesting the return of the full score was his forthcoming trip to Paris in mid-November 1916 to approve the choreography by Leo Staats for *Les Abeilles,* a ballet set to the *Scherzo fantastique*. He was planning to conduct its gala premiere on 10 January at the Opéra after rehearsing it there in December. In the event, severe illness – an attack of intercostal neuralgia – in mid-December prevented him from doing both, as reported in his letter of 27 December 1916 to Alexander Sakharoff (see Entry 12). In May 1919 Beata Bolm (wife of the celebrated dancer) wrote to him from New York, mentioning *Les Abeilles* as one ballet among several that her husband, Adolph, was considering mounting.

By this period, Stravinsky was apparently not yet ready to suppress his original program for the *Scherzo fantastique* based on Maurice Maeterlinck's *La Vie des Abeilles* (1901), a program he had communicated to Rimsky-Korsakov and others in 1907-8. Maeterlinck withdrew his threat to sue following the ballet's premiere when Stravinsky wrote on

6 February 1917 that he had not intended any deception. A description translated from the composer's signed but undated program note in French, which excludes, however, Maeterlinck's name, appears in program notes used for performances during his first (1925) tour of the United States, for example, in program notes of the Chicago Symphony Orchestra. He certainly prevaricated in 1959, however, not only in responding "No" to Craft's question whether he had had Maeterlinck's work in mind for the 1908 *Scherzo* but also in averring that the 1916 "bee" choreography was not authorized by him.

Works Consulted

Chicago Symphony Program Notes. 20-21 February 1925. pp. 296-7.

Colette. *Lettres à Anne de Pène et Germaine Beaumont.* ed. Francine Dugast. Paris: Flammarion, 1995. n. 3 on p. 100, no. 69.

Darbellay, Etienne. "Foetisch, Charles." NG. vol. 6. p. 685.

Lubrano, J. and J. *Rare Printed Music & Musical Literature, Catalogue 54.* Great Barrington, MA, Spring 1998, lots 107, 159-61, 189.

Orenstein, Arbie. "*L'Enfant et les sortilèges*: correspondance inédite de Ravel et Colette." *Revue de Musicologie* 42 (1966): 215-16.

Orenstein, Arbie, ed. *A Ravel Reader.* New York, NY: Columbia University Press, 1990. n. 4 on p. 437.

SP&D. pp. 47-8, 120.

SPR&K. vol. 2. n. 13 on p. 303, p. 448 (both trans. Stanislav Shvabrin and Michael Green).

SSC. vol. 2. n. 35 on p. 28; vol. 3. n. 11 on p. 29, n. 19 on p. 34.

Taruskin, Richard. *Stravinsky and the Russian Traditions.* Berkeley and Los Angeles, CA: University of California Press, 1996. pp. 6-8, 303, 316-18.

Walsh, Stephen. *The Music of Stravinsky.* Oxford: Oxford University Press, 1988. pp. 17.

—. *Stravinsky, A Creative Spring: Russia and France, 1882-1934.* New York, NY: Alfred A. Knopf, 1999. pp. 106-8, 227, 271-3.

12

(1916). Autograph letter, 27.7 × 21.7 cm, folded twice, in Russian in pencil, 27 December 1916, to Alexander Semyonovich [Sakharoff, (1886-1963)]:

Morges 27 XII
1916

Mnogouvazhayemyi Aleksandr Semenovich!
Prostite, chto pishu karandashem[.] Ya sil'no bolen. Pis'mo
Vashe prishlo v moem otsutstvii (byl v Rime i Parizhe gde
prozhil bez malogo mesyats)[.] Vernuvshis' domoi ya sil'no
zanemog revmatizmom i nevralgiei na gripal'noi pochve.
Bolezn' kraine muchitel'naya i popravlenie sovershenno
razshatannogo zdorov'ya po uvereniyu vrachei potrebuet nedel'.
Uzhasnaya perspektiva! Poetomu otkladyvayu vse razgovory i
dela do polnogo popravleniya. Zhelayu Vam vsego luchshego k
novomu godu[.]
    Igor' Stravinskii

Alexander Sakharoff   Morges
Lausanne[?]   27 December 1916

Much respected Alexander Semyonovich!
Forgive me for writing in pencil. I am seriously ill. Your letter
arrived in my absence (I was in Rome and Paris, where I resided just
short of a month). Returning home, I came down with rheumatism
and neuralgia based on the flu. This illness is extremely tormenting
and the recovery of my entirely shattered health will, in the opinion
of the doctors, require *weeks*. Dreadful prospect! Because of this I am
postponing all conversations and business until I am fully recovered.
I wish you all the best for the New Year.
    Igor Stravinsky

Acquisition: H. Colin Slim on 23 February 1998 from Lion Heart
Autographs Inc. (470 Park Avenue South / Penthouse, New York
10016-6819), their no. 10397, inventory no. 635. Entry 12 was repaired
by removing previous mending tapes; numerous edge tears and tears
along fold lines and thinning at corners and a loss at the lower left
corner, and a tear through the signature were repaired with Japanese
paper and rice starch paste by Linda K. Ogden of Berkeley, CA, on 24
March 1998.

Provenance: Kenneth W. Rendell, Inc. *Autograph Letters Manuscripts* (Somerville, MA, May 1973). Previous dealers' erased pencil markings at upper left margin: "R.A[?] / idoka[Iolas??], / A2304X / I S. T" and along the upper margin in a hand from 1973 (or earlier): "STRAVIN-SKY, I. ALS 12-27-16;" on reverse side in pencil (by Lion Heart Autographs): "#10397" and at upper right corner: "St."

Commentary

The letter, unpublished, is on paper watermarked with three randomly placed five-pointed stars. Its missing envelope would have furnished the family name of its addressee. Without citing his patronymic, Rendell's 1973 advertisement identifies the addressee as "the noted dancer Sakharoff."

Alexander Sakharoff, dancer, choreographer, teacher, and costume designer, was the last of seven sons born to Simon Zuckermann on 25 May 1886 in Mariupol, Russia. He died at Siena on 26 September 1963. His father, a rich Jewish banker, placed his son in a good school in St. Petersburg. Already as a nine-year-old, the boy was fascinated with painting. After finishing high school, Alexander went at age seventeen to Paris, where he initially studied law at the university and also enrolled in painting courses with Bouguereau. By 1904 he found himself interested in the theatre and shortly thereafter began serious study in dance. Following his dance debut in Munich in 1910, he attracted great attention and soon met his professional partner and future wife, the dancer, Clotilde von Derp (1895-1974). At the beginning of the First World War, Sakharoff moved from Munich to Lausanne. Joined by Clotilde (probably late in 1916), they lived at Zurich from 1917 and were married there two years later.

Sakharoff thus presumably mailed his letter to Stravinsky from Lausanne and it arrived at Morges between 7 and 21 November, the composer having left Lausanne for Rome on the 7th. There, he discussed *Le Chant du Rossignol* with Diaghilev from 8 to 14 November, after which he returned to Morges on the 21st by way of Paris. While not indicating an extremely close relationship between the two men, Entry 12 with its statements about health is sufficiently personal as to suggest that Sakharoff was already more than a mere acquaintance. Still, at this period nothing is known of any projects between them.

A postcard from Stravinsky to Sakharoff of 3 October 1930, however, informs the dancer that he is pleased with Sakharoff's projected restaging for his wife Clotilde of the "Berceuse" from *The Firebird,* advising that she be guided by his new Columbia recording of that work (November 1928). The program for their joint dance recital in Paris at the Théatre des Champs-Elysées on 29 November and 2 December 1930 duly announced that the Berceuse, "créée par Clotilde, est d'une conception absolument nouvelle qui a obtenu la complète adhésion d'Igor Strawinsky." Given his aversion to excerpts from his music, his permission, let alone his approval, is tangible evidence of his confidence in the Sakharoffs.

A search for additional known acquaintances of Stravinsky named Alexander has yielded no one else with the patronymic of Semyonovich. If the addressee lived in Russia, he might have been the St. Petersburg lawyer, Alexander Semyonovich Stishinsky, mentioned with disdain by Rimsky-Korsakov in 1905 as a newly appointed conservative senator to the Duma, and again in 1906. There is no evidence, however, that Stravinsky knew either him or an Alexander Semyonovich Archangelsky (1854-1926), a literary historian (the latter name kindly furnished by Stephen Walsh). Both Alexander Semyonovich Rabinovich (1900-43), born in St. Petersburg and Oles (Alexander) Semyonovich Chishko (1895-1976) were too young to have been addressed in 1916 as "Much respected" and nothing documents Stravinsky's knowledge of either composer.

The illness cited in Entry 12 and mentioned also by Diaghilev on 17 December 1916 in a letter to Catherine Stravinsky was intercostal neuralgia, owing to abuses of tobacco and alcohol. It prevented him from conducting at Paris the following January (see Entry 11). I am obliged to Richard Taruskin, to Michael Green, and especially to a young scholar visiting from the Nizhny Novgorod Pedagogical University, Stanislav Shvabrin, for the transliteration and translation.

Works Consulted

Muzykal'naia Entsiklopediia. [Music Encyclopedia.] ed. Y.V. Keldysh. Moscow: Sovetskiy Kompozitor, 1973-82. vol. 4. p. 509; vol. 6. p. 250.

Rimsky-Korsakov, Nicolai. *Polone sobranie sochinenii.* [Collected Thoughts on Composition.] Moscow: Muzgiz/Muzika, 1982. vol. 8b. pp. 171-2, no. 456 (n. 4), 229-30 (index).

Sakharoff, Alexander and Clotilde. Papers. Box 7, folder 9 (souvenir programs). dbMS Thr 398. Theatre Collection. Harvard University.

Sequi, Sandro. "Sakharoff," *Enciclopedia dello Spettacolo*. Rome: Casa editrice Le Maschere, 1953-68. vol. 8. pp. 1409-10.

SP&D. p. 47.

SP&RK. vol. 1. n. on p. 425.

SSC. vol. 2. p. 33, n. 3 on p. 182.

Stuart, Philip. *Igor Stravinsky – The Composer in the Recording Studio. A Comprehensive Discography*. New York, NY, Westport, CT, London: Greenwood Press, 1991. p. 27, no. 7.

Veroli, Patrizia. "'La vita che abbiamo danzato' itinerario attraverso la vita e l'arte dei Sakharoff" in *I Sakharoff un mito della danza fra teatro e avanguardie artistiche*. ed. Veroli. Bologna: Edizioni Bora, 1991. pp. 15-41, 164-5, 174.

Vuillermoz, Émile. *Clotilde et Alexandre Sakharoff*. Lausanne: Éditions Centrales, 1933. pp. 15, 22, with many pls. of both dancers.

Yastrebstev, Vasily Vasilyevich. *Nikolai Andreyevich Rimskiy-Korsakov: vospominaniya 1886-1908*. [Reminiscences of Rimsky-Korsakov.] ed. Alexander V. Ossovsky. Leningrad: Muzgiz, 1959-60. vol. 2. p. 386.

13

(1917). Signed typed registered letter, 28.1 × 24.0 cm, folded four times, with autograph addressed envelope, 9.7 × 15.3 cm, postmarked 22 V.17-4 but lacking its stamps, in German in black ink, 19 May 1917, to unnamed executives of the Genossenschaft Deutscher Tonsetzer (Anstalt für musikalisches Recht [sic, *recte:* Aufführungsrechte]) (Association of German Composers; Institute for Musical [Performing] Rights), Berlin:

[envelope]
[sticker] R Morges / No. 946

[written by Stravinsky] Die Genossenschaft
Deutscher Tonsetzer
Wilhelmstrasse 57/58
Berlin W. 66
<u>Deutschland</u>

Absänder: [stamp] IGOR STRAWINSKY à MORGES

[printed on reverse of envelope] Militärischerseits unter /
Kriegsrecht geöffnet / Berlin O 17, den [written] 25 V
[printed] 1917 / [signed] [illegible] / [printed]
Überwachungsoffizier [the same stamped below; envelope
postmarked] BERLIN 25.5.17.

[typed letter]
MORGES (Schweiz) den 19. Mai 1917

Eingeschrieben
Genossenschaft Deutscher Tonsetzer
(Anstalt für musikalisches Recht)
Berlin .W.66

Sehr geehrte Herren,
Herr Ad.HENN, mein Vertreter, hat ["mit" corrected to] mir
Ihren gesch. Brief vom 10. d.M. mitgeteilt.
 Ich beeile mich Ihnen zur Kenntniss zu bringen dass ich mit
dem Inhalte des letzten Paragraphen obergenanntes Briefes
einverstanden bin; d.h. dass die beiden Verträge die ich mit
Ihrer Genossenschaft unterzeichnet hatte mit dem 31. Dezember
d.J. aufgehoben werden und ab dieses Datum kein Wert mehr
haben.
 Hochachtungsvollst
 [in black ink] Igor Strawinsky

Association of German Composers	Morges
Berlin	19 May 1917

Very honoured sirs:
Mr. Ad[dolfe] HENN, my representative, has shared with me your
handwritten letter of the 10th of this month.
 I hasten to bring to your attention that I am in accord with the
content of the final paragraph of the above-mentioned letter; that is,

that both agreements that I had signed with your Association will be cancelled on the 31st of December this year and from that date have no further validity.

Most respectfully,

Igor Strawinsky

Acquisition: H. Colin Slim on 30 June 1998 from La Scala Autographs. Entry 13 had been attached to a single sheet of watercolour paper by hinges of glassine tape; Linda K. Ogden removed these and repaired small edge tears in the letter with Japanese paper and rice starch paste on 8 September 1998.

Provenance: Unidentified dealer at an antiquarian show, spring 1998, Palm Beach, Florida.

Commentary

Unpublished, the letter is on paper watermarked EXPRESS Z.P.S. The reverse side of its accompanying envelope shows that it was opened by the military censor in Berlin before reaching its addressee. Entry 13 was written at the Villa Rogivue, the family not leaving it for the mountains that summer until 14 July.

The precise nature of a previous letter of 10 May sent by the Anstalt of the Genossenschaft – both organizations founded at Berlin in 1903 – to Adolphe Henn (1872-1954), bookseller and music publisher in Geneva from 1896 until his death, remains unknown. The Anstalt functioned to administer copyright in Germany and to collect royalties for musical works by members of the Genossenschaft. By 2 February 1913 Stravinsky had acknowledged: "I am a member" (SP&RK vol. 2, p. 17). As a Russian citizen, even though living in neutral Switzerland, he would have been regarded by Germany as an enemy. After the abdications by the czar and his son (15 and 16 May 1917), Russia's provisional government continued war against the central powers until the Bolsheviks concluded an armistice on 15 December, followed on 3 March 1918 by the Treaty of Brest-Litovsk.

Two weeks later Stravinsky was to sign a contract, on 1 June 1917, with Henn. The 10 May letter to Henn had perhaps originated from knowledge concerning Henn's forthcoming publications of five works at Geneva during July and August: *Pribaoutki* (1914), *Three Easy Pieces*

(1914–15), *Cat's Cradle Songs* (1915), *Renard* (1916), and *Five Easy Pieces* (1917). Because Koussevitsky's Russische Musikverlag had had to discontinue its operations in wartime Berlin – its final Stravinsky publication there was *Three Little Songs* (1913) in 1914 – and owing to the chaos in Russia during 1917, it seems possible that Entry 13 also relates to Henn's (short-lived) emergence as his publisher – all five works later being taken over by J. and W. Chester of London in the 1920s.

Works Consulted

Gaillard, P.-André. "Henn." MGG. vol. 6. col. 150-1.

McFarlane, Gavin. "Copyright Collecting Societies." NG. vol. 4. p. 755, item 6.

Schulze, Erich. "Gesellschaften für musikalische Urheberrechte." MGG. vol. 5. col. 2.

SP&RK. vol. 2. pp. 17 (trans. Stanislav Shvabrin and Michael Green), 417, 439, 447.

SSC. vol. 2. pp. 117, 143-4, n. 19 on p. 148, n. 16 on p. 218.

Walsh, Stephen. *The Music of Stravinsky*. Oxford: Oxford University Press, 1988. pp. 300-01.

–. *Stravinsky, A Creative Spring: Russia and France, 1882-1934*. New York, NY: Alfred A. Knopf, 1999. pp. 272, 280, 294, 299, 545.

14 (1918). Autograph letter, 27.2 × 21.3 cm, folded twice, in French in pencil, 19 December 1918, to Paul Laffitte:

Morges   Monsieur
19 Déc. 1918   Paul Laffitte
                                                     à <u>Paris</u>

Monsieur

Je vous retourne ci joint un exemplaire de notre contrat muni de ma signature, l'autre exemplaire reste donc chez moi. J'attire seulement votre attention sur le § III où vous avez oublié de mentionner la <u>Souède</u> où [crossed out] ~~est reserves également~~ les droits de reproductions, d'exécutions etc sont également reserves, comme dans la Norvège, le Danemark[,] l'Amer. du Sud. J'espère que cette omission ne créera aucun malentendu dans l'avenir. Par contre je suis plainement d'accord, quand au privilège de la 2ème édition que vous avez voulu vous reservé dans le présent contrat.

Je vous enverrai dans quelque jours la copie de la partition de piano du Rag-time.

En attendant le plaisir de vous lire je vous prie de trouver ici, Monsieur mes salutations les meilleurs

Igor Strawinsky

Paul Laffitte   Morges
Paris   19 December 1918

Sir:

Enclosed, I'm returning to you one copy of our contract signed by me, the other copy, of course, I'm keeping. I would draw your attention only to article III where you have forgotten to mention Sweden where rights of reproduction, of performances, etc., are likewise reserved, as in Norway, Denmark, South America. I hope that this omission will create no misunderstanding in the future. On the other hand, I fully agree with the licence for the second edition that you wanted to keep for yourself in the present contract.

I shall send you the copy of the piano score of *Ragtime* in a few days. Awaiting the pleasure of your reply, I remain, Sir, yours faithfully,

Igor Strawinsky

Acquisition: H. Colin Slim on 12 September 1996 from Les Autographes – Thierry Bodin, Paris, his *Catalogue 72* (July 1996), item 275. The letter is accompanied by a release, "Certificat pour un bien culturel," dated 27 August 1996, from the Ministère chargé de la culture.

Provenance: Unknown; below the signature in another hand in blue pencil is "Stravinsky," now mostly erased.

Commentary

The envelope of this letter and its enclosed contract are lacking. But the latter's terms can be deduced from a contract proposal Stravinsky had made to the poet Blaise Cendrars (1887-1961) on 11 November 1918 in which he also asked Cendrars to: "remind Picasso of his promise to design a cover ... for the *Ragtime*."

Stravinsky wrote Entry 14 with a hard pencil to make a good carbon copy, traces of which still appear on this letter's reverse side. It is also available in a different English translation by Craft (probably made from the copy in the Paul Sacher Foundation, Basle). At this period he was at his last Swiss residence before departing for France. He had moved his family from the Villa Rogivue early in October 1917 to the Maison Bornand in the Place St. Louis, Morges.

Laffitte, the addressee, was director-in-chief of the Éditions de la Sirène (12 rue La Boétie, Paris). With Cocteau, Cendrars was its co-founder and director. Negotiations by Cendrars with Stravinsky for the publication of the piano reduction of *Ragtime* had begun on 14 May 1918 and concluded on 22 December 1919 with his receipt of "two completely crumpled copies *Ragtime*" and a "frightful [spelling] error in dedication to Madame [Eugenia] Errazuriz [1860-1951]," his patroness in Paris from 1916 (SSC, vol. 2, pp. 184-9). (The autograph which he dated "Hiver 1918/Morges" and presented to her is now in the Pierpont Morgan Library, Lehman Deposit.) The delay resulted from the printing house used by La Sirène having gone out of business and from Picasso having designed a succession of covers, of which four preceded the final version. Stravinsky had first met the artist at Rome early in April 1917, at which time Picasso drew an initial portrait of the composer.

With its famous Picasso cover, *Ragtime* was finally published in 1919 by La Sirène. Released the following January in an edition of 1000 copies, exemplars are now rare, one being offered in 1996, and another in 1999. The Music Library at UBC acquired the first edition in 2000. A 1920 reprint of *Ragtime,* London: J. and W. Chester, is in the personal library of H. Colin Slim.

Works Consulted

Cox, Lisa. *Catalogue B/7 Keyboard Music Winter/Spring 1996*. Exeter, 1996, item 811.

—. *Cox's Gallimaufrey, 4 February 1999*. Exeter, 1999, item 148.

Geelhaar, Christian. "Strawinsky und Picasso – zwei ebenbürtige Genies" in *Strawinsky. Sein Nachlass. Sein Bild* [with] *Katalog der ausgestellten Bildnisse und Entwürfe für die Ausstattung seiner Bühnenwerke*. Basle: Kunstmuseum and Paul Sacher Stiftung, 1984. pp. 288-93.

SP&RK. vol. 2. pp. 439-40, item 7.

SSC. vol. 2. pp. 184-9.

Walsh, Stephen. *Stravinsky, A Creative Spring: Russia and France, 1882-1934*. New York, NY: Alfred A. Knopf, 1999. pp. 276, 283, 294-5, 546.

15

(1920). **Autograph picture postcard of CARANTEC (Finistère), Le Grand Hôtel du Kélenn et la Rue de l'Eglise, 9.0 × 13.8 cm, in French in black ink, postmarked Carantec 28 June, 27 June 1920, to Roland-Manuel (1891-1966):**

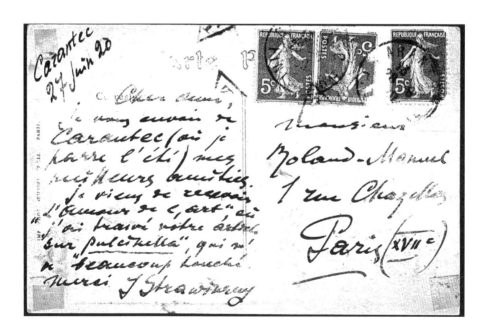

Monsieur
Roland–Manuel
1 rue Chazelles
Paris(XVIIᵉ)

Carantec
27 Juin 20

Cher ami,
Je vous envois de Carantec (où je passe l'été) mes meilleurs amities.
    Je viens de reçevoir "L'amour de l'art", où j'ai trouvé votre article sur "Pulcinella", qui m'a beaucoup touché.
    Merci
    I Strawinsky

Roland-Manuel   Carantec
Paris   27 June 1920

Dear friend:
I send you my best regards from Carantec (where I am spending the summer).
    I have just received *L'amour de l'art* in which I found your article about *Pulcinella* which touched me greatly.
    Thank you,
    I Strawinsky

Acquisition: H. Colin Slim in Los Angeles on 26 September 1999 from La Scala Autographs.
Provenance: Thierry Bodin, Paris, summer 1999 (perhaps from the 14 May 1986 auction at Paris by Paul Renaud of the Roland-Manuel archives, part 1).

Commentary
The postcard is unpublished. With family and in-laws, Stravinsky had left Morges on 8 June 1920, bypassed Paris, and arrived two days later at sea-side Carantec in Brittany, remaining there three months. House-hunting with his wife in Paris late that July, they ran into Gabrielle

Bonheur (Coco) Chanel (1883-1971), who invited them all to her house at Garches, to which they moved in mid-September (see Entry 16). The full extent of his Carantec correspondence in the summer of 1920 is not known. Another letter, this time in Russian, of 7 July to Jacques Handschin (1886-1955) in Basel, has only recently surfaced.

Ravel had introduced Stravinsky in 1911 to his (Ravel's) young student, the later composer and critic Roland-Manuel, a pseudonym of Roland Alexis Manuel Lévy. *Pulcinella* opened in Paris on 15 May 1920 and in London on 10 June. The critic's short essay, "*Pulcinella,* Ballet de Stravinsky-Pergolèse," marvels at the happy and fraternal collaboration with a composer who likewise possessed such a sense of concise musical expression devoid of parasitic ornamentation. In it, Roland-Manuel quotes Stravinsky as having confided: "Je suis le fiancé de la mélodie italienne."

Even after a less-than-enthusiastic review of *Mavra* two years later by Roland-Manuel – to which Stravinsky responded with uncharacteristic gentleness (even with "beaucoup de plaisir") – they remained friends. Commuting between Paris and Sancellemoz in the summer of 1939, he was to ghost-write with the composer six lectures (later entitled *La Poétique musicale*) which Stravinsky delivered at Harvard University as the incumbent of the Charles Eliot Norton Chair of Poetry, 1939-40. (See also entries 17, 64, 78, 86 and 94.)

Works Consulted

Cox, David. "Roland-Manuel." NG. vol. 16. p. 111.

Knjazeva, Janna. "Jacques Samuel Handschin – Igor' Stravinskij: Eine noch unbekannte Seite des Dialogs." *Die Musikforschung* 52 (1999): 207-11.

Lesure, François. *Igor Stravinsky. La carrière européenne.* Paris: Musée d'Art Moderne, 1980. p. 83, no. 267.

Renaud, Paul, and Thierry Bodin. *Archives Roland-Manuel [part 2].* Paris: 24 March 2000, lots 229-34. p. 69.

Roland-Manuel. "*Pulcinella,* Ballet de Stravinsky-Pergolèse." *L'Amour de l'Art* 1 (1920): 71.

Samuel, Claude. "Roland-Manuel." *Encylopédie de la Musique Fasquelle.* Paris: Fasquelle, 1958-61. vol. 3. p. 582.

SAc. pl. on p. 76.

Walsh, Stephen. *Stravinsky, A Creative Spring: Russia and France, 1882-1934.* New York, NY: Alfred A. Knopf, 1999. pp. 315-18, 351-2.

16 (1920). Autograph letter, 26.2 × 21.0 cm, folded twice, in French in black ink, 24 September 1920, to Robert Lyon (1884-1965):

Monsieur
Robert Lyon
à Paris

Cher Monsieur
Il y a deux fois que j'étais venu vous voir au magasin et chaque fois vos employers me disaient que vous étiez toujours souffrant. J'etais vraiment navré de l'apprendre. Comment allez vous maintenant et si vous pouvez m'écrire un mot de vos nouvelles vous me feriez grand plaisir. J'espère qu'il n'y a rien de grave.
  Croyez moi cher Monsieur votre bien devoué
  I Strawinsky

[stamped lower right] IGOR STRAWINSKY / VILLA BEL RESPIRO / Av. Alphonse de Neuville / GARCHES (Seine-à-Oise) / France
[dated below by him in pen] 24/IX 20

  Robert Lyon   Garches
  Paris   24 September 1920

  Dear Sir:
  I've been to see you twice at the shop and each time your employees told me that you are still unwell. I was really sorry to learn this. How are you now and if you could drop me a line with news about yourself, you would give me great pleasure. I hope it's nothing serious.
    Believe me, dear Sir, your very devoted
    I Strawinsky

Acquisition: H. Colin Slim on 8 November 1994 from Wurlitzer-Bruck.
Provenance: Unknown.

Commentary

The letter is unpublished, its envelope missing. The Garches address – "the very command center of Paris chic" in Taruskin's memorable phrase – is that of Gabrielle Bonheur (Coco) Chanel, briefly then Stravinsky's mistress. Her villa served as his family's temporary residence until he moved himself in April 1921 to Paris in a studio in the Maison Pleyel, then moved with his family that May to Anglet, near Biarritz.

Offering him a studio at the Maison Pleyel in February 1921, Robert Lyon – later director of Pleyel et Cie in Paris until c. 1930 and of the magazine, *Musique* (ed. Marc Pincherle) – was a friend and business manager of Stravinsky until at least 1932. He appears a final time in Vera Sudeykina's published diary on 21 February 1931. From early July 1910, Stravinsky had known the Lyon family, at whose home he first met Nadia Boulanger. (Further on the friendship and business association with Robert Lyon, see entries 21 and 23.)

Works Consulted

Rosenstiel, Léonie. *Nadia Boulanger. A Life in Music.* New York, NY: W.W. Norton, 1982. pp. 90-1.

SAc. pl. on p. 88 (Anglet).

SBu. p. 53: 21 February 1931.

SP&D. pp. 47, 210, 254, n. 173 on p. 614, n. 20 on p. 628.

SP&RK. vol. 2. n. 1 on p. 480, n. 1 on p. 497, p. 515, n. on p. 533.

SSC. vol. 1. pp. 188, 195, n. 288 on p. 221; vol. 2. n. 51 on p. 41, n. 23 on p. 250, pp. 268-9, 364, n. 1 on p. 475; vol. 3. n. 58 on p. 55, n. 70 on p. 82, p. 203.

ST&C. (both ed.) pl. facing p. 33.

Taruskin, Richard. *Stravinsky and the Russian Traditions.* Berkeley and Los Angeles, CA: University of California Press, 1996. pp. 1516-17.

Walsh, Stephen. *Stravinsky, A Creative Spring: Russia and France, 1882-1934.* New York, NY: Alfred A. Knopf, 1999. pp. 318-23, 385-6.

17 (1920). Autograph singly folded express letter, 16.0 x 11.5 cm, half the reverse side forming its envelope, in French in black ink on pinkish paper serrated on all sides, 19 November 1920, to Roland-Manuel. The lower half of the envelope is postmarked: Paris 44 20-11 20 R. de Grenelle; next to two stamps of 25 and 10 centimes (affixed to the top of the envelope) is printed: HOTEL CONTINENTAL / 3 RUE CASTIGLIONE / PARIS. Above the stamps Stravinsky wrote: <u>Pneumatique</u> and below them:

Monsieur
Roland-Manuel
42, rue de Bourgogne
<u>Paris</u>

[reverse of envelope]
Cher Monsieur,
Mon ami Serge de Diaghilew ne connaissant pas votre adresse m'a prié de vous demander si vous pouvez venir ce dimanche vers 12¾ à l'hotel Continental pour dejeuner avec nous. Vous seriez bien gentil de lui envoyer un mot de reponse au Continental qu'il habite.

   Dans l'espoire de vous voir après demain je vous serre bien cordialement la main
   Igor Strawinsky

19/XI/20

Roland-Manuel	Paris
Paris	19 November 1920

Dear Sir:
My friend, Sergei Diaghilev, not knowing your address, has requested me to ask if you could come this Sunday about 12:45 to

lunch with us at the Hotel Continental. Please be so kind as to send him a reply to the Continental where he is living.

Hoping to see you the day after tomorrow, I very cordially shake your hand,

Igor Strawinsky

Acquisition: H. Colin Slim on 5 August 1997 from La Scala Autographs. *Provenance:* Thierry Bodin, Les Autographes, (Paris, March 1996); Les Autographes, *Catalogue 76* (Paris, May 1997), item 277 (perhaps from the 14 May 1986 auction at Paris by Paul Renaud of the Roland-Manuel archives, part 1).

Commentary

The letter is unpublished. Diaghilev was perhaps interested in commissioning a work from Roland-Manuel for the Ballets Russes, although no such work is known (see also Entry 15).

Diaghilev first introduced Stravinsky in 1921 to Vera Sudeykina, who later became his second wife. Vera, who knew Diaghilev since at least 1913, realized better than anyone the extent of his influence on the composer. For example, in 1949, she cited "certain aesthetic attitudes as virtually parroted from him," stating that Stravinsky only paid attention to criticism when made by Diaghilev. Furthermore, in Moscow in 1962, Craft reported that she believed Stravinsky was affected by Diaghilev. Charles Joseph's study of their "tangled relationship" explores the composer's feelings about Diaghilev: "gratitude, indebted-ness, admiration, anger, guilt, hostility."

Works Consulted

Craft, Robert. *Stravinsky: Chronicle of a Friendship*. 2nd ed. Nashville, TN, and London: Vanderbilt University Press, 1994. pp. 28, 319.

Joseph, Charles M. "Diaghilev and Stravinsky." *The Ballets Russes and Its World*. ed. Lynn Garafola and Nancy Van Norman Baer. New Haven, CT, and London: Yale University Press, 1999. pp. 189-215.

Renaud, Paul, and Thierry Bodin. *Archives Roland-Manuel [part 2]*. Paris: 24 March 2000, 2.

18

(1921). Autograph fragment of a single-page two-sided love letter signed "I.," 13.4 × 20.9 cm, folded seven times, in Russian in black ink on both sides (some fading and also browning of paper), undated and without place or heading (but probably mailed shortly after mid-November 1921 from Biarritz to Boris Kochno in London for delivery there), to Vera Sudeykina:

[... ot-]pravila mne etikh pisem ne dozhidayas' moego otcheta o svidanii s S. Yu. ved' ya tak zhdal ot tebya imenno seichas zhe po priezde pisem i vse tekh zhe slov[,] kot.[orye] mne tak nuzhny, esli by ty tol'ko znala. Verochka[,] pishi mne chasto, k[a]k tol'ko zakhochetsya, a chto khochetsya teper' i byt' mozhet budet prodolzhat'sya khotet'sya <u>ya khochnu v etom byt' uverennym</u>, ibo vse chto sluchilos' mezhdu nami slishkom sil'no menia obozhglo i khranitsya u menya kak svia- [reverse] tynya ochen' gluboko, no ob etom govorit' ya ne khochu i ne lyublyu, tak uzh ya sozdan, mne kazhutsya vsegda moi slova men'she togo chto vo mne delayetsya i chto ya chuvstvuyu – muzyka anonimneye i ot togo mne stydno vyskazyvat'sya, a mozhet byt' muzyka i sovsem drugaya[.] <u>No ty</u> pishi[;] ya strastno zhdu ot tebya slov liubvi tvoei ko mne, kotoraya mne <u>bezumno</u> <u>nuzhna</u>[,] beskonechno nuzhna! Pishi ezhe[-]dnevno, esli mozhesh tol'ko[,] Verochka[,] moya dorogaya dorogaya lyubov'[.]
    I.

Vera Sudeykina   Biarritz
London   c. 15 November 1921

[...] you sent me these letters not waiting for my account of my meeting with S[ergey] Yu[ryevich Sudeykin]. You see, I was so much awaiting a letter from you and right away with words like "I need you so much, if you only knew." Verochka, write me often, as soon as you want, and since you want to now, perhaps you'll continue to want to write me. *I want to be certain of that,* since everything that has happened between us is too powerful; it has seared me, and is watched over by me like something sacred [reverse] deep inside me, but I don't want to talk about it, and I don't care to: that's just the way I am created. It always seems to me that my words are less than what is going on inside me and what I feel – music [is] more anonymous [impersonal(?)] and for this reason I feel less strongly ashamed to speak out [through it], but perhaps music is something completely different. *But write,* I passionately await from you words of your love for me, which is *insanely needed* by me, infinitely needed! Write every day, only if you can, Verochka, my dear dear love.

    I.

Acquisition: H. Colin Slim on 31 October 1997 from Lion Heart Autographs.

Provenance: Boris Petrovich Mikhailovich Kochno (1904-90); Sotheby's, *Collection Boris Kochno* (Monaco, 11-12 October 1991), lot 405, rightly conjectured that the letter may be incomplete; dealer's pencil mark on p. 1, top left: 22:95.

Commentary

The fragmentary letter is unpublished, its envelope missing. Dr. Slim is indebted to Simon Karlinsky, to Stanislav Shvabrin, and to Michael Green for the transliteration and translation. Readings by the latter two scholars differ in several respects from the brief excerpts in Sotheby's auction catalogue and from the translation provided by Lion Heart Autographs. In particular, the reading by Sotheby's of "anonimneye" as "instinktivenii," and subsequent translations of this word, are, therefore, incorrect.

Although its exact date is difficult to establish, Entry 18 may be among the earlier surviving love letters from Stravinsky to Vera Arturovna de Bosset-Luryi-Shilling-Sudeykina – and, ultimately, Stravinskaya – which the seventeen-year-old Boris Kochno passed to her late in 1921 and early the next year. Entry 18 was among half a dozen which the young poet-balletomane either never delivered, or did so and she then asked him to retain. Living with Diaghilev at the Savoy Hotel in London during most of the run of *The Sleeping Princess* (November 1921-February 1922), Kochno was acting as intermediary between the two lovers – separated by the English Channel – during

November and early December 1921. These undated letters – lots 400-05 in the above-cited 1991 Sotheby sale, which assigned them dates accepted by Craft in 1992, Walsh in 1999, and Varunts in 2000 – are perhaps all that have survived. Vera declared that, at the request of Stravinsky, she burned all his love letters in 1940 before emigrating to the United States. Craft reports that he burned Stravinsky letters to Vera after the composer's death, on his instructions.

With Sergei Yuryevich Sudeykin (1882-l946), her third husband, Vera had been introduced to Stravinsky by Diaghilev in Montmartre on 19 February 1921 during an evening at the Chauve-Souris, a theatre troupe relocated from Moscow. Stravinsky was soon involved in a brief affair in Paris with the troupe's young dancer, Yevgeniya (Zhenya) Nikitina, following one with Coco Chanel, and before that (1916) with Lydia Lopukhova, future wife of Maynard Keynes. (On Chanel, see Entry 16.)

Shortly thereafter, Vera and Stravinsky fell in love and, by March, had apparently rendezvoused behind the backs of their respective spouses. Before he left a month later for Spain with Diaghilev and Kochno on 16 March, Stravinsky had inscribed at Paris in one of her albums the opening of *The Firebird,* over which her husband later spitefully drew a bird having thistles for its tail. Although Stravinsky may have had a brief affair in London in June with another married woman, Juanita Gandarillas, by Bastille Day 1921, the affair between Stravinsky and Vera had been consummated, the pair thereafter celebrating 14 July as their "marriage."

About 26 February 1921, the Sudeykins, who had known Kochno in the Caucasas in 1917-18, had introduced that young man to Diaghilev. For a short while the impresario's lover and, by that spring, his secretary for life, Kochno was soon courting the bisexual Sudeykin, who had himself briefly been Diaghilev's lover in 1906.

A group of summer letters from Vera to Stravinsky, from late July to 19 September 1921, suggests that Kochno was already their confidant. While Stravinsky and Kochno were in London, 7-10 June 1921, for the premiere of *Symphonies of Winds Instruments* and for a concert performance of *Le Sacre,* and there again late that month for performances by the Ballets Russes, he had invited Kochno to write the libretto for *Mavra.* Back in Paris on 30 September, while Sudeykin was away in London, Stravinsky and Kochno inscribed the same page in one of Vera's albums.

Near the beginning of October, Diaghilev invited Vera to play the mimed role of the Queen in the Ballets Russes's revival in London of Tchaikovsky's *The Sleeping Beauty,* which Diaghilev renamed *The Sleeping Princess.* For this production, Stravinsky orchestrated two numbers and some transitions. By mid-October, Diaghilev had arrived in London with Kochno to supervise rehearsals, which included Vera who was there by 27 October.

In letters of October to Ansermet and Ramuz, Stravinsky noted that he would be going to London on 24 or 25 October, adding in Ansermet's that he would be staying "close to a week, at the Savoy," that is, in the same hotel as Vera, Diaghilev, Kochno, and Léon Bakst (the ballet's designer). From the Savoy he wrote Ramuz on 30 October stating that he would be leaving London "on my way home (in a week)," that is, 6 November, and that he would have only a little time in Paris because he was proceeding directly to Biarritz.

Because he wired Kochno from Biarritz on Tuesday 15 November, "Astonished a week without news," Stravinsky must have arrived there by the 8th. An undated Thursday letter to Vera (lot 401) states that he had received a letter from Kochno the previous day, that is, the 16th, so lot 401 may well date from the 17th. A letter which Ansermet addressed to him in Biarritz on 16 November assumes that he had already returned home and one of 19 November from Ramuz to him indeed suggests that he did not stay in Paris on his return to Biarritz. (A translation of a letter to Ansermet of 22 November placing the composer in Paris, is really dated 22 February of the following year.)

Opening in London at the Alhambra Theatre on 2 November, *The Sleeping Princess* closed there on 4 February 1922. At some point – presumably after he had left London for Biarritz early in November – Stravinsky wrote Kochno to hand some letters to Vera and to mail others: "give the enclosed yellow letter to Vera, post the other one with an English stamp and write the address so that the handwriting will not be recognized by someone" (Sotheby's *Kochno,* lot 399).

On what Stravinsky called "that Thursday which was so memorable for me" in an undated letter (lot 401), itself headed "Thursday" (perhaps of 17 November), Sudeykin had confronted him. (Craft and Varunts place the meeting in his Pleyel studio at Paris – and Varunts as *before* Stravinsky went to London – Walsh at Biarritz.) This must be "my meeting with S. Yu." referred to in Entry 18 and also "our meeting" mentioned in Entry 19 (formerly lot 403). In this "Thursday" letter (lot 401), he also reported to Vera that he and Sudeykin parted "in harmony and peace, and seemingly reconciled." Unless he stayed in Paris on his way home to Biarritz about 7 November or returned there almost immediately upon reaching Biarritz, the "Thursday which was so memorable" in lot 401 can only be Thursday 10 November.

An undated letter (probably of late November) by Sudeykin from Paris to Diaghilev mentions a breakfast between Stravinsky and Sudeykin at which Stravinsky experienced the full force of his jealous rage. (From this letter, Walsh concludes that Sudeykin visited him at Biarritz, and probably on Thursday 10 November.) Writing Ansermet from Biarritz on Friday 2 December, Stravinsky reported he had seen no one for three weeks. Three weeks earlier would be Friday 11 November, so 10 November for the "memorable" Thursday of lot 401 seems probable.

Presumably Stravinsky had written Vera immediately following his encounter with Sudeykin at Biarritz on the 10th. But Entry 18 responds to letters from Vera which she wrote *before* receiving any news from him of his "Thursday" encounter on the 10th in Biarritz with Sudeykin. Entry 18 thus dates shortly after 17 November. (For what it is worth, Stravinsky mailed Kochno a letter on 21 November, as can be deduced from the postmark of its envelope, lot 399, though whether it contained Entry 18 is not known: see also Entry 19.)

Entry 18 includes a reference to Stravinsky's expression of his feelings. Taruskin rightly observed: "Stravinsky's later – and oh so celebrated – squeamishness about the use of the word *express.*" He points to an early lack of squeamishness about *exprimer* evident in a Stravinsky article published 29 May 1913 which, despite his later protestations, he had certainly authorized. "Ce que j'ai voulu exprimer dans *Le Sacre du Printemps*" uses the identical French infinitive twice more on the same page.

Though contesting on 25 August a few lexical meanings in its Russian translation of 3 August, Stravinsky allowed an equivalent verb, *vyrazhat'*, to stand for *exprimer*, being assured by his Russian editor that its translator "has a mastery of French like a born Parisian" (SP&RK, vol. 2, p. 133). Dictionary meanings of *vyrazhat'* are "to express, show" and, when followed by *slovamii,* "to put into words." Less than a year later, under the influence of Jacques Rivière, Stravinsky adopted a quite different attitude about *exprimer.* Interviewed at Paris – presumably in French – in May 1914 by his friend Calvocoressi about his opera *The Nightingale,* he now averred: "I want neither to suggest situations or emotions, but simply to manifest, to express them" and "I always aim at straightforward expression in its simplest form."

The sentence seven years later in Entry 18, "music [is] more anonymous and for this reason I feel less strongly ashamed to speak out [through it]" with its verb, *vyskazyvat',* thus deserves some examination. This verb, "to express, tell, give," when used reflexively (*vyskazyvat'sya*), as here means "to speak up (or out), to express one's self, opinion, thoughts (about something); to declare one's self (for, or against, something)." In that most private of communications, a love letter – one which he certainly never expected to see printed – he frankly admits his aim, so strongly contrasting with all his other public statements except one – that of February 1934. In Entry 18, he not only uses a different Russian verb, one which is more intimate (*vyskazyvat',* "to speak out") but he also employs it reflexively, personally, (*vyskazyvat'sya*).

In light of Entry 18, Taruskin's observations require amplification, although the matter is too lengthy for discussion here. Such a study will want to consider additional uses by Stravinsky of such verbs, for instance, in 1924 to a Warsaw interviewer (French); 1929 to Walter Nouvel (Russian); 1934 to Walter Cameron and Maurice Perrin (both in French); 1939–40 in the *Poétique musicale*; 1945 to J. Nizon (French; see Entry 83); and 1962 to Craft (English).

Finally, the music to which Stravinsky refers in Entry 18 is surely *Mavra,* which he was then composing. In another love letter to Vera about two weeks later (lot 402), he calls *Mavra* "such music as would touch you" and in yet another (lot 404), "Oh, how I wish you could hear it now!" (See also entries 43, 46, and 54.)

Works Consulted

Bowlt, John E., ed. and trans. *The Salon Album of Vera Sudeikin-Stravinsky.* Princeton: Princeton University Press, 1995. nos. 48–9b and 123; item S5 on p. 98.

Calvocoressi, Michel-Dimitri. "M. Igor Stravinsky's Opera: 'The Nightingale'." *The Musical Times* 55 (1 June 1914): 374.

Craft, Robert. "Catalog of the Library of Robert Craft." Typescript: Library of Congress, Music Division. IX: Vera's archive, C, nos. 3-8 on p. 174.

—. *Stravinsky: Chronicle of a Friendship.* 2nd ed. Nashville, TN, and London: Vanderbilt University Press, 1994. pp. 228, 569.

—. *Stravinsky: Glimpses of a Life.* London: Lime Tree, 1992; New York, NY: St. Martin's Press, 1993. pp. x–xiii.

—. Review of Taruskin's *Stravinsky* in the *Times Literary Supplement.* 13 September, 1996. p. 5.

Kochno, Boris. *Diaghilev and the Ballets Russes.* trans. Adrienne Foulke. New York, NY, and Evanston, IL: Harper and Row, 1970. pp. 152-5.

Lesure, François, ed. *Le Sacre du Printemps. Dossier de Presse.* Geneva: Éditions Minkoff, 1980. p. 76.

Perrin, Maurice. "Strawinsky dans une classe de composition [1934-35]." *Feuilles musicales et revue suisse du disque* 3 (December 1951): 207-12.

Scherliess, Volker. "'Je déteste l'Ausdruck' – Über Strawinsky als Interpreten" in *Traditionen – Neuansätze Für Anna Amalie Abert (1906-1996).* ed. Klaus Hortschansky (Tutzing: Hans Schneider, 1997). pp. 475-92.

Sotheby's. *Ballet Material and Manuscripts from the Serge Lifar Collection.* London, 9 May 1984. lot 225, ill.

SAc. pl. on p. 89 (Biarritz).

SBu. pp. 13-16, esp. n. 2 on p. 13.

SChron. vol. 1. pp. 116-17; vol. 2. p. 160.

SE&D. (1962) pp. 114-15; (1981) p. 101.

SI&V. pl. 51 on p. 52.

SP&D. pp. 199, 240-1, 524-5, nn. 228 and 231 on p. 618, n. 10 on p. 627.

SP&RK. vol. 2. pp. 133, 489-515, nos. 1016-17 (trans. Stanislav Shvabrin and Michael Green).

SSC. vol. 1. n. 17 on p. 54, pp. 57, 152; vol. 3. pp. 63, 65.

Stravinsky, Igor. "I – AS I SEE MYSELF (In an interview with Norman Cameron)." *The Gramophone* 12, 135 (August 1934): 85-6.

—. "Quelques mots de mes dernières oeuvres." *Muzyka* 1, 1 (December 1924): 12-15.

Tappolet, Claude, ed. *Correspondance Ernest Ansermet-Igor Strawinsky (1914-1967).* Geneva: Georg, 1990-92. vol. 1: pp. 179-80, no. 158, p. 196, no. 173, pp. 198-99, no. 175.

Taruskin, Richard. *Stravinsky and the Russian Traditions.* Berkeley and Los Angeles, CA: University of California Press, 1996. pp. 990-95, figs. 13.6a-b on pp. 1000-01, pp. 1107-8, 1546.

–. "Stravinsky and the Subhuman: Notes on *Svadebka*" in *Defining Russia Musically*. Princeton, NJ: Princeton University Press, 1997. pp. 365-88.

Tuohy, William. "Vera Stravinsky's Rite of Spring: Work, Memories," *Los Angeles Times*. 16 March 1978, 28.

Walsh, Stephen. *Stravinsky, A Creative Spring: Russia and France, 1882-1934*. New York, NY: Alfred A. Knopf, 1999. pp. 265-6, 318-19, 324-8, 333, 344-5, 395, 459, 549, n. 6 on p. 630, n. 3 on p. 632.

White, Eric Walter. *Stravinsky: The Composer and His Works*. 2nd ed. Berkeley and Los Angeles, CA: University of California Press, 1979; repr. 1984. p. 585.

19

(1921). Autograph single-page two-sided love letter, signed "I," 27.0 × 21.0 cm, folded four times, in Russian in black ink on both sides, dated only "Subbota" (Saturday), without place (but probably mailed from Biarritz on 26 November 1921 to Boris Kochno in London for eventual delivery), to Vera Sudeykina:

Subbota

Verochka, Verochka moya[,] chital pis'mo tvoe, gde ty pishesh' o svoem vozvrashchenii (cherez 2 nedeli) k S. Yu. v Parizh[.] Chital i perechityval po mnogu raz ego i ne mog otorvat'sya ot nego! Akh Verochka – dumayu, chto eto neizbezhno, chto, verno tak i dolzhno byt', chto ty dolzhna vernut'sya k nemu. Odno ili drugoye, tret'ego ne mozhe byt', ibo ya soglasen s toboi chto svoego schast'ya nel'zya stroit' na chuzhom gore – eto nachalo antikhristianskoye. Dushevno zhe mne tvoi vozrat v Parizh bezumno tyagosten[.] Ya etogo ot tebya skryt' ne mogu. Tyagosten i za sebya i glavnym obrazom za tebya[,] moya Verochka. Dai Bog tebe sprav it'sya s tvoim chuvstvom ko mne a nichem ego ne obnaruzhit' S. Yu. Pisal li on tebe podrobno ob nashem svidanii? ili tol'- [page 2]-ko namekami kosnulsya ego, potomu chto ty pishesh' chto on skazal "my s Igorem rasstalis' v khoroshikh otnosheniyakh", a do etogo v etom pis'me pisal li on chto-nibud'? Ya tebe zavtra napishu ofitsiyal'nye pis'ma v Savoyu i kosnus' vskol'z' i mimokhodom S. Yu., ego nervoznogo nastroyeniya i posovetuyu tebe ego ne

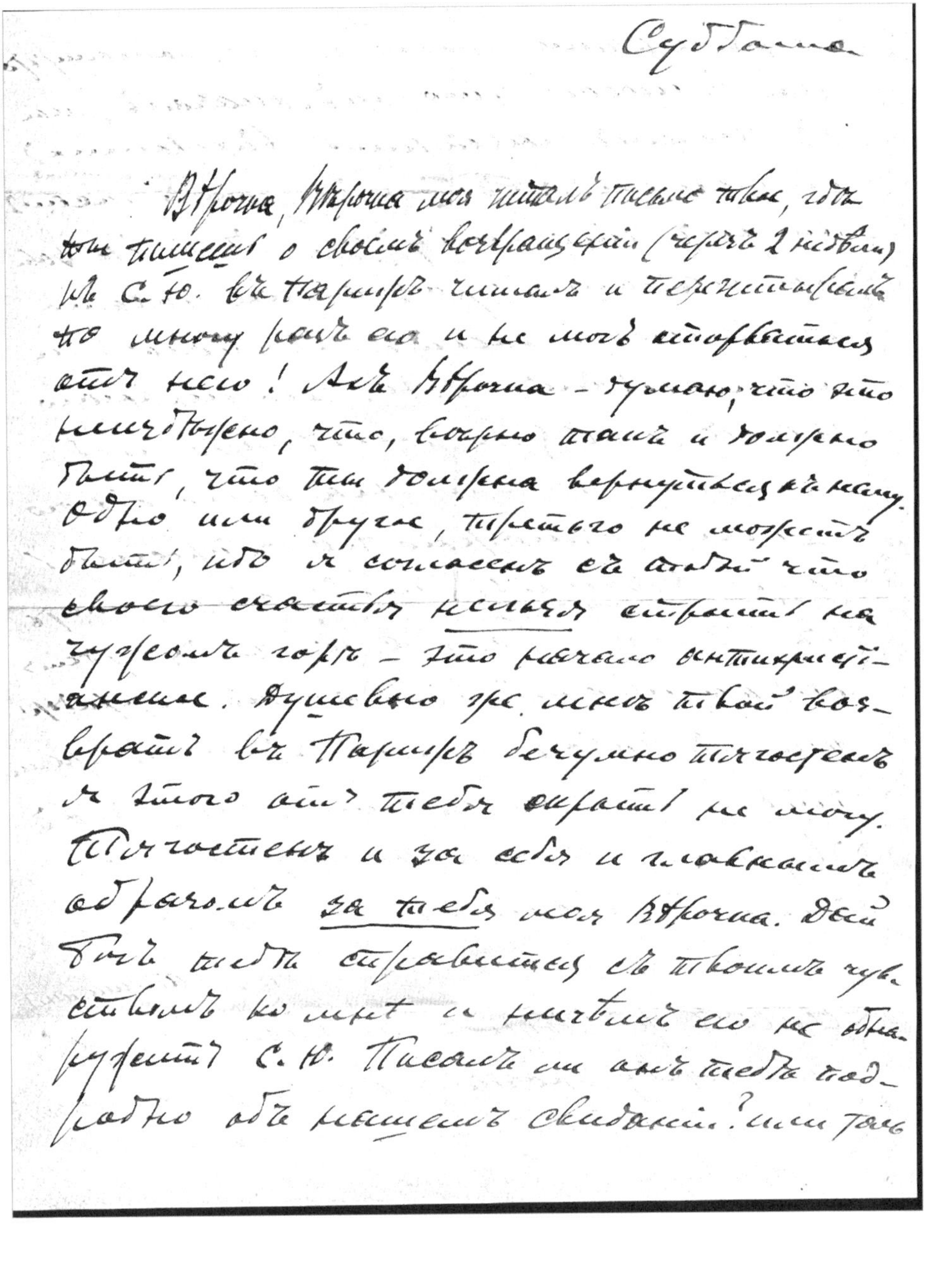

Суббота

Верочка, Верочка моя читалъ письмо твое, гдѣ ты пишешь о своемъ возвращеніи (черезъ 2 недѣли) къ С. Ю. въ Парижъ читалъ и перечитывалъ по многу разъ его и не могъ оторваться отъ него! Ахъ Верочка – думаю, что это неизбѣжно, что, вѣрно такъ и должно быть, что ты должна вернуться къ нему. Одно или другое, третьяго не можетъ быть, ибо я согласенъ съ тобой что своего счастья нельзя строить на чужомъ горѣ – это начало антихристіанское. Душевно же мнѣ твой возвратъ въ Парижъ безумно тяжелъ я этого отъ тебя скрыть не могу. Тяжелъ и за себя и главнымъ образомъ за тебя моя Верочка. Дай Богъ тебѣ справиться съ твоимъ чувствомъ ко мнѣ и ничѣмъ его не обнаруживать С. Ю. Писалъ ли онъ тебѣ подробно объ нашемъ свиданіи? или такъ

ostavlyat' nadolgo odnogo – esli vozmozhno ty poprosish'
dazhe Dyagileva tebya otpustit' v Parizh. Esli S. Yu. tebya
budet sprashivat' v kakom korridore ty v Savoe zhila, v tom
zhe li chto i ya[,] skazhi chto sovsem v drugom etazhe[,]
pol'zuyas' tem, chto ty seichas v tom etazhe gde Bakst i
Valechka. Napishi mne seichas zhe tozhe ofitsiyal'noye
pis'mo[.] Ya[,] mezhdu prochim[,] Ek. Gavr. rasskazal o stsene
revnosti S. Yu., no[,] razumeyetsya[,] etim i ogranichilsya. Ya
skazal ei[,] chto lyublyu tebya [left margin] k[a]k sestru.
Verochka[,] konchayu na segodnya, bezkonechno sil'nymi
ob"yatiami i uveryayu tebya[,] chto <u>ty tozhe ne podozrevaesh'</u>
k[a]k u menya rastet i krepnet samoe bol'shoe chuvstvo k tebe.
    I

| Vera Sudeykina | Biarritz |
| London | Saturday, 26[?] November 1921 |

Verochka, Verochka mine, I read [past tense] your letter where
you speak of your return (in two weeks) to S[ergey] Yu[ryevich
Sudeykin] in Paris. I read it and reread it many times and couldn't
tear myself away from it! Ah, Verochka, I think it unavoidable, and
that's exactly how it should be, that you must return to him. There's
either one solution or another, there can't be a third, for I agree with
you that it is *impossible* to build your happiness on another's misery –
that's an anti-Christian principle. Spiritually, for me, your return to
Paris is overwhelmingly burdensome. I can't hide this from you. It
burdens me and especially burdens *you*, my Verochka. May God give
you the ability to deal with your feeling for me and not let [it] be
revealed in any way to S. Yu. Did he write you in detail about our
meeting? or did [page 2] he simply touch on it because you write
that he said "Igor and I parted on good terms." But did he write
anything in that letter before that? Tomorrow I'll write you official
letters to the Savoy [Hotel, London] and I'll make passing mention
of S. Yu. and his rather nervous mood, and I'll advise you not to
leave him alone for long – if possible you should even ask Diaghilev
to let you go to Paris. If S. Yu. should be asking you what corridor
was yours at the Savoy, whether it was the same one that I stayed on,

tell him it was a completely different floor, taking advantage of the fact that you stayed on the same floor as [Léon] Bakst and Valechka [Walter Nouvel]. Write me an official letter right now as well. Among other things, I told Ek. Gavr. [Ekaterina Gavrilovna, Stravinsky's wife] about the jealous scene made by S. Yu., but naturally I stopped at that. I told her that I loved you [left margin] like a sister. Verochka[,] I'm stopping there for today, with infinitely strong embraces, and I assure you that *you also don't suspect* how the greatest feeling grows and strengthens within me toward you.

I

Acquisition: H. Colin Slim on 13 October 1998 from Lion Heart Autographs.

Provenance: Same as Entry 18; Sotheby's 1991 catalogue, lot 403, dating it "Biarritz, 19 November 1921." (Written the same day, a second love letter of three pages, sold at Sotheby's, lot 404, was available in 1998 from Lion Heart Autographs; it has since been sold.)

Commentary

The letter is unpublished, its envelope missing. Transliteration and translation were kindly provided by Stanislav Shavbrin and Michael Green. Their translation of Entry 19 differs in several details from the one provided me by Lion Heart Autographs and from the excerpts in Sotheby's catalogue.

Headed only "Saturday," Entry 19 is said to be of 19 November 1921. The parenthesis "(in two weeks)" is not likely, however, to refer to any return to Paris by Vera about 16 November after only two weeks of performing in London – a period dating from her first appearance on 2 November in London as the Queen in *The Sleeping Princess*. Instead, the parenthesis more likely refers to plans she had recently made to return to Paris in two weeks from the time she wrote to Stravinsky her now-destroyed letter, to which Entry 19 responds. Moreover, another letter (lot 404) Stravinsky wrote to her on the same Saturday as Entry 19 places her still in London.

During the run of the ballet, Vera became ill. On Saturday, 19 November (this date kindly confirmed by M. Elizabeth Bartlet at Paris in 1998), some two and a half weeks after its opening, her husband telegraphed Diaghilev in London about her health and the care being taken for her, asking whether he should come: "Priere de repondre immediatement comment va la sante de ma femme[.] J[']espere a tous les soins necessaires[.] Faut il venir[?] – Soudeikine." An undated letter from Stravinsky to Kochno in London, presumably also from about this time, expresses the same concerns: "Write to me what Vera's condition is like, how is her health and how does she feel about herself. Does she go out yet?" (lot 399).

Two undated letters from Sudeykin to Diaghilev (probably late November and early December) beg Diaghilev to return Vera to him. In the second of these he states that he had not expected the ballet to run for two months, that she had been away fifty days, and had given thirty performances. Obviously these letters postdate Sudeykin's telegram of 19 November to Diaghilev about her health. She had certainly arrived in London by 27 October for rehearsals and perhaps even earlier, with Diaghilev on 15 October. If the former, Sudeykin's second letter would have been written about 4 December.

An approximate date for her withdrawal from her role as Queen in the ballet is probably found in a note to Vera which Léon Bakst signed "London 27 Novembre 1921" wherein he declared himself a "loyal subject" of the "beautiful Queen of 'Sleeping Beauty'." This could mark either his own farewell upon leaving London or her coming departure from that city. Presumably Bakst gave her this note while she (and he) were still in London together. (He himself was in Paris by 12 December.)

By early to mid-December the cast of *The Sleeping Princess* had altered slightly, as a second edition of the program booklet reveals. A copy of the first edition, inscribed merely "December 1921" on the cover by its owner Edward Knoblock (1874-1945), has Vera playing the non-dancing role of the Queen and an English actor playing the King. On the second edition of the program its (unknown) owner inscribed the cover in ink "January 25 1922." Here Vera and the actor have been replaced by two dancers from the company.

Approximately when this revised program for the ballet was printed can be deduced from an advertisement newly added in it for a memorial exhibition of works by the artist, C. Lovat Fraser (1890–1921). The Fraser memorial was first announced in issues of the *London Times* on 19 and 28 November, stating that it would open privately on 2 December and publicly the following day; it was duly reviewed on 3

December. The advertisement in the second edition of *The Sleeping Princess* program, however, gives no opening date for the Fraser memorial exhibition, but states it would be "Open daily until Christmas." Since the opening date of the exhibition is not mentioned, the revised program was probably printed after 3 December. Just when Vera left the ballet company cannot, therefore, be precisely ascertained, but it was probably early that month, and, as suggested below, before the 13th.

Therefore, on the one hand, Entry 19, revealing knowledge of Vera's plan to return to Paris, can scarcely date from 19 November, the very Saturday that Sudeykin telegraphed Diaghilev. It was most likely written on the following Saturday, the 26th. Somewhat less than two weeks from 26 November would place her return to Paris around December 10, which is compatible with the date of 13 December entered in her album by Mikhail Struve in Paris (see below).

On the other hand, dating Entry 19 as the first Saturday of December seems too late. On that very Saturday, 3 December, Stravinsky telegraphed Kochno at the Savoy Hotel: "[Dite Vera que] poste livrera lettres seulement contre pièce [d'identité do]nc ne pourrais envoyer lettres qu'a son nom [stop agira]i pas autrement craignant la laisser sans mes [nouvelle]s Igor" [Tell Vera post office will only deliver letters if shown identity card so could only send letters in her name – (stop) will do this afraid to leave her without hearing from me] (incompletely reproduced in lot 399, provisional reconstruction and translation by Leonard W. Johnson, the former kindly confirmed by Stephen Walsh who had copied it out in 1994). This telegram of 3 December suggests that new love letters cannot be safely forwarded to her in Paris and also that Stravinsky was now concerned about how to communicate with her. Craft's report that "she returned in December" is perhaps confirmed by a poem, "To the Sudeykins," by Struve (1890–1948) entered in one of Vera's albums, which poem he signed "Paris, 13 December 1921." Moreover, she wrote a letter from Paris to Diaghilev on 28 December, in which she thanked him on that date: "very belatedly." (Although very late in life, she recalled requesting Diaghilev to release her from the ballet in mid-January 1922, in fact her diary for 1922 records her back in Paris by 3 January.)

Writing in Entry 19 that he will pretend ignorance in his "official letters" to her at the Savoy Hotel about her forthcoming return to Paris and that he will reflect anxieties (previously expressed to him in Biarritz, probably on 10 November) by her husband, Stravinsky obviously already knew of Vera's plan to return to Paris by the time he wrote Entry 19. He had also learned – presumably from her or from Kochno – of Sudeykin's telegram to Diaghilev of 19 November and perhaps even about one of her husband's undated letters. Clearly his ruse in Entry 19 was meant to hide from Sudeykin his secret communications with her by letters through Kochno.

Quarrelling with Sudeykin over an invitation from Stravinsky to attend the gala premiere of *Mavra* on 29 May 1922 in the ballroom of the Hotel Continental in Paris, Vera separated from her husband about 4 June. On 19 August, he emigrated permanently to the United States, where he died in 1946.

Léon Bakst (Lev Samoylovich Rosenberg, 1866-1924), the designer of the sets and costumes for *The Sleeping Princess,* was associated with Diaghilev's enterprises as early as 1898. He designed many Ballets Russes productions, 1909-17, and had an extensive correspondence with Stravinsky, for example, proposing in 1917 their collaboration in a production of Shakespeare's *Anthony and Cleopatra* (which never materialized with music by Stravinsky). His only other professional association was as an assistant designer for *The Firebird,* a costume design for Anna Pavlova surviving at the St. Petersburg Theatre Museum.

"Valechka," Walter Nouvel (Valter Fyodorovich Nuvel', 1871-1949), was a classmate of Diaghilev; in Taruskin's words, he was a "Sunday composer," a co-founder of the Evenings of Contemporary Music at St. Petersburg in 1901, and also a life-long friend of Stravinsky. In 1934-35, Nouvel collaborated with him in writing the *Chroniques de ma vie* (see entries 42-3, 46, 83, 103).

Stravinsky informed his wife, Catherine, about his liaison with Vera in the spring or summer of 1922. After Catherine's death in Paris in 1939, he emigrated to the US and Vera arrived the following year. They were married at Bedford, Massachusetts, on 9 March 1940.

Works Consulted

Baer, Nancy Van Norman, ed. *The Art of Enchantment. Diaghilev's Ballets Russes, 1909-1929.* San Francisco: Fine Arts Museums, 1988. pl. facing p. 91, p. 142 (*L'Oiseau de Feu*), pp. 157-58, nos. 123-36.

Bowlt, John E., ed. and trans. *The Salon Album of Vera Sudeikin-Stravinsky*. Princeton, NJ: Princeton University Press, 1995. pl. 163; p. 95, no. 163.

Buckle, Richard. *Diaghilev*. New York, NY: Atheneum, 1979. p. 394, n. 100 on p. 573.

Craft, Robert. *Stravinsky: Glimpses of a Life*. London: Lime Tree, 1992; New York, NY: St. Martin's Press, 1993. pp. xii-xv.

—. *Places. A Travel Companion for Music and Art Lovers*. New York, NY: Thames and Hudson, 2000. p. 171.

Garafola, Lynn. *Diaghilev's Ballets Russes*. New York, and Oxford: Oxford University Press, 1989. p. 386 (*Firebird*).

Knoblock, Edward. Papers. *The Sleeping Princess* [December 1921]. Theatre Collection. Harvard University.

Kochno, Boris. *Diaghilev and the Ballets Russes*. trans. Adrienne Foulke. New York, NY, and Evanston, IL: Harper and Row, 1970. pp. 168-75.

—. Fonds. Pièce 93. Bibliothèque de l'Opéra. Paris.

Kodicek, Ann, ed. *Diaghilev. Creator of the Ballets Russes. Art. Music. Dance*. London: Barbican Art Gallery/Lund Humphries, 1996. p. 161: *The Firebird*.

Lesure, François, et al., ed. *Diaghilev. Les Ballets Russes*. Paris: Bibliothèque Nationale, 1979. pp. 104-8.

London Theatres. A-ARG, folder. "Alhambra," *The Sleeping Princess* [January 1922]. Theatre Collection. Harvard University.

MacDonald, Nesta. *Diaghilev Observed by Critics in England and the United States 1911-1929*. New York, NY, and London: Dance Horizons, 1975. pp. 277-80.

Schouvaloff, Alexander. *The Art of Ballets Russes: The Serge Lifar Collection of Theater Designs, Costumes, and Paintings at the Wadsworth Atheneum, Hartford, Connecticut*. New Haven, CT, and London: Yale University Press, 1997. pp. 87-101.

SBu. pp. 13-16, esp. n. 1 on p. 14 (Sudeykin's request is misdated).

SI&V. pl. 54 on p. 55.

SP&D. pl. on p. 230.

SP&RK. vol. 1. n. 1 on p. 376, p. 512 (index: Bakst), p. 527 (Nouvel); vol. 2. pp. 513-14, nos. 1016-17 (trans. Stanislav Shvabrin and Michael Green), pp. 734-5 (index: Bakst), p. 758 (Nouvel).

SSC 2. pp. 92-7, app. K on pp. 487-502.

Taruskin, Richard. *Stravinsky and the Russian Traditions*. Berkeley and Los Angeles, CA: University of California Press, 1996. pp. 374-75, fig. 7.1 on p. 425, fig. 8.8b on p. 517, fig. 8.9 on p. 520, p. 1511.

Walsh, Stephen. *Stravinsky, A Creative Spring: Russia and France, 1882-1934*. New York, NY: Alfred A. Knopf, 1999. pp. 140, 334-6.

20
(c. 1921). Autograph calling card, 5.6 × 9.4 cm, in French, engraved *Igor Strawinsky* in italic and inscribed (though unsigned) by him in French in black ink to an unknown recipient, possibly in Paris:

avec mes meilleurs
compliments

[to unknown recipient]   [Paris, c. 1921]
with my best regards

Acquisition: by kind gift to H. Colin Slim, 9 April 1979, from Howard Mayer Brown (1930-93) and Roger W. Weiss (1932-91), both then professors at the University of Chicago.
Provenance: Probably Marya Freund; her son, Doda Conrad; Wurlitzer-Bruck (1979).

Commentary

An identically sized engraved calling card to "Mme Soudeikine" (Vera) dates from 1921 as does probably another to a "Dr. Talliro" [sic] in London and still another, sent to Rudolph Ganz in August 1922 inscribed "Villa Les Rochers/Biarritz." (The London doctor Talliro of Stravinsky is probably Diaghilev's "Dr. Talariko" there.)

Retaining the same spelling of his surname, Stravinsky later had this card reprinted on larger-sized papers, often using them for brief correspondence. One, 7.9 × 10.9 cm, of 8 December 1962, is to Ginny Carpenter Hill; another, the following day, concerns a Columbia contract he had signed and endorsed; another of 19 March 1965 is in the Chicago Symphony Archives; and still another one is inscribed to Warren Kirkendale on 19 September 1963. Kirkendale owns yet another, 6.3 × 8.3 cm, inscribed 13 December 1962; see also cards inscribed 16 November 1960 and 4 July 1963 to Mario Bois; and one to Deborah Ishlon of 9 March 1961.

An unemployed Russian taking the name Prince Serge de Temmenoff also had such a card printed in the 1920s, writing messages and forging the composer's signature. Entry 20 is, however, surely authentic – compare its "meilleurs" with the same word in his 1925 letter to Dr. Garbat, Entry 30. Since the provenance of Entry 20 is Doda Conrad, Stravinsky may well have sent the calling card to Conrad's mother, Marya Freund, whom he knew from at least 1915 and who was in Paris during the 1920s (see entries 8 and 10). A visiting card inscribed c. 1912 by him "Clarens Hôtel de Châtelard, Suisse" was offered by Lisa Cox in 1998 for £200. Entry 20 is framed with Entry 33.

Works Consulted

Bois, Mario. *Près de Strawinsky 1959-70*. Paris: Marval, 1996. pls. on pp. 11, 122.

Buckle, Richard. *Diaghilev*. New York, NY: Atheneum, 1979. pp. 398, 528.

Carpenter, John Alden. Papers. Box 1, folder S. The Newberry Library, Chicago.

Chicago Symphony Orchestra, Archives.

Cox, Lisa. *Gallimaufrey 3 August 1998*. Exeter, 1998, no. 177.

Erasmushaus. *Katalog 903. Autographen*. Basle, October 2000, item 194 on p. 81 with ill.

Ganz papers. Incoming Correspondence (excluding family) S-Z, folder 332. The Newberry Library, Chicago.

Kirkendale, Warren. Personal archive, Rome.

Schneider, Hans. *Katalog Nr. 156*. Tutzing, 1970. p. 47, no. 124.

Schulson, David, Autographs Limited. *The January Sale Catalog*. New York, January 2000, item 108 on p. 40.

Stargardt, J.A., *Katalog 672*. Berlin, 16-17 November 1999, lot 819, pl. on p. 321.

SP&D. n. 258 on p. 621.

SScrbk. pl. 294 on p. 149.

21

(1923). **Autograph sketches in pencil near the close of the second tableau for *Svadebka* (*Les Noces*), arranged for player piano on one side of the severed lower portion of a twice-folded page, now 17.9 x 27.0 cm with only fourteen printed staves, marked by Stravinsky in blue pencil: "Les Noces" and with additional autograph annotations in pencil: "page 67 A B C; x y z; 1 2 3 4 5 6; Chorus; les femmes hommes." Neither 1915-17 in pencil near the top of the left margin (partially erased but visible under ultraviolet light) nor 1800 within an ellipse at the upper right**

corner is autograph. The reverse side, with fourteen printed staves, has only non-autograph pencil annotations by various dealers.

Acquisition: H. Colin Slim on 11 October 1995 from Lisa Cox Antiquarian Music, Books, Autographs & Ephemera (20 Old Tiverton Road Exeter / Devon, England), *Catalogue 30. Autumn 1995,* item 181. *Provenance:* Possibly Dr. Ernst August Schröder of Essen who, in November 1988, had described his collections – containing player piano sketches for *Les Noces* (now at the Pierpont Morgan Library, Cary MS 567) – for the German auctioneer, Stargardt: "Autographen – das war etwas für mich. Von allen Gebieten, die die Stargardt-Kataloge anbieten, liegt mir das Gebiet 'Geschichte' am meisten, neben Literatur und Musik"; Kenneth W. Rendell, Inc. (Wellesley, MA, and New York) marked on reverse side: STRAVINSKY, I. AMusMS N3133 SBMX, followed by another hand: 11302 / Les Noces / 102; unidentified dealer in England (1995).

Commentary

The sketches are unpublished. Rex Lawson observes: "on the whole the similar sketches for other arrangements [of Stravinsky's works] are either not in public hands or simply do not exist" (Liner Notes, p. 10).

In 1921, Stravinsky signed a six-year contract with Pleyel at Paris for player piano (i.e., Pleyela, pianola) transcriptions of all his works, *Les Noces* being the thirteenth of these to appear. A notice published in the Pleyel house journal in October 1923 of his works for sale on these rolls does not yet include *Les Noces,* but it was advertised as available on four of them from 1 January 1924. It must, however, have been ready for sale the previous December when the back cover of a special Stravinsky issue of the *Revue musicale* advertised it that month.

Lawson correctly estimates the date of its commercial issue as "late 1923." Stravinsky must, however, have finished working on it with the head of the music rolls department at Pleyel, Jacques Larmanjat (1878-1952) and his assistants well before the premiere of the ballet at Paris on 13 June that year. Indeed, he played excerpts from *Les Noces,* apparently on the player piano, for the poet Vladimir Mayakovsky (1893-1930), who arrived in Paris on 18 November 1922 for a week's stay: "He played for us at Lyon's [Pleyel]. He played [from] *The Nightingale, The [Chinese] March, The Two Nightingales, The Nightingale and the Chinese Emperor,* and also his latest things: *Spanish Etude* for pianola [recorded September 1921], *Les Noces,* a ballet with chorus, which is to be performed in the spring by Diaghilev, and fragments from his opera, *Mavra.*" Mayakovsky observed the composer's vivid enthusiasm for the player piano – "writing for eight, for sixteen, for twenty-two hands!"

The Harvard Theatre Collection owns a souvenir program of the Ballets Russes at the "Gaité Lyrique 1923" (the theatre where the premiere of *Les Noces* took place), which includes an advertisement in the form of an inserted slip-sheet. Its contents are very close to that of the advertisement in the December 1923 issue of the *Revue musicale* cited above. The slip-sheet reads in part: "Sous Presse / pour paraître incessamment / en Exclusivité / Les Transcriptions, enregistrées et adaptées par Igor STRAWINSKY pour le PLEYELA 88 Notes, des OEuvres suivantes." Among the works listed is "Les Noces, (6 rouleaux)" (as opposed to the "4 rouleaux" advertised in the December *Revue musicale*).

Stravinsky would have given rough musical sketches, similar to those in Entry 21, to the technicians who then marked up master rolls and punched them out for his corrections and approval. The November 1923 issue of the *Revue Pleyel* contains an illuminating comparison by Larmanjat between the piano reduction of *Le Chant du Rossignol* and its player piano transcription from the orchestral score.

Player piano sketches of *Les Noces* antedate the work's private concert premiere – at the home of the Princesse de Polignac on 10 June and the choreographed public one three days later – for two other reasons. Serge Lifar (1905-86) reported that Stravinsky, who played the piano and supervised the rehearsals of *Les Noces* at Monte Carlo in the spring of 1923, "fit venir de Paris un orgue de Barbarie sur les bandes duquel était inscrite la musique du ballet. On assista alors à ce spectacle surprenant de l'accompagnatrice métamorphosée en mécanicien et tournant la manivelle!" [had brought out from Paris a barrel organ with the ballet's music on its rolls. Thus we saw the surprising spectacle of the (woman) accompanist transformed into a worker and turning the handle!] Lifar, auditioned in Paris by Diaghilev on 13 January 1923 and travelling to Monte Carlo the next day to join the corps-de-ballet, was among the twenty-one male dancers at its premiere. Stravinsky, who had installed his family in Biarritz, was in Paris most of January and February, in Biarritz most of March and briefly in Paris at its close, and was in Monte Carlo from early in April, returning to Paris by mid-May. Therefore, the incident reported by Lifar took place in April or May at Monte Carlo. Ninette de Valois observed that, for *Les Noces,* "we always had to rehearse with a pianola," but her first performance in this ballet was in the following year.

Second, at the invitation of Stravinsky on the day following the premiere of *Les Noces,* George Antheil (1900-59) and his future wife visited Pleyel's: "where he [Stravinsky] said, he would play the rolls of the pianola version of *Les Noces* for us ... and Stravinsky himself played *Les Noces,* this time on an electric pianola. I liked the second version even better than the one which we had heard last night; it was more precise, colder, harder." Craft has the date correctly as 1923 for the pianola transcription.

More than a year later in the September 1924 issue of the *Revue Pleyel* listing "Les Noces 4 rouleaux," Stravinsky self-endorsed the player piano rolls, "adaptés par l'auteur," for his works: "Igor Strawinsky, en particulier, s'est donné à cette tâche avec sa puissante maîtresse et une ardente conviction, réalisant même des arrangements spéciaux pour certaines de ses oeuvres pianistiques ou vocales. Il a trouvé, dit–il, dans le *Pleyela* des ressources et une précision que lui refuse l'orchestre." [Igor Stravinsky, in particular, devoted himself to this task (of transcription) with his powerful mastery and fervent conviction, even working out special arrangements for his piano and vocal works. He found, he said, in the Pleyela certain possibilities and a precision that he can't get from an orchestra.]

Because he was still a Russian citizen and the US did not recognize any copyrights by him, his friend Robert Lyon of Pleyel (see Entry 16) assisted him by signing each of these rolls: "Special Arrangement for Piano Player by Robert Lyon," thereby maintaining copyright. Several other contemporaries, including Vera Sudeykina and Jean Cocteau, observed him making the rolls and an August 1923 photograph shows him at work seated at the Pleyela.

Although at one time Entry 21 certainly belonged to some companion pages, it was not in 1988 among twenty-four pages of sketches for mechanical piano on six different kinds of paper (with thirty-two, twenty-eight, twenty-six, twenty, fourteen, and eight staves) plus two small slips with instructions. These pages are now held by the Pierpont Morgan Library, which bought them in March 1988 for DM32,000.

The dimensions of Entry 21 and the size of its staves, 21.5 × 0.5 cm, show that it came from twenty-eight–staved paper, 35.2 × 27.0 cm. The single extant full sheet of such sized paper in the Morgan Library is folded (in the same way that Entry 21 is) at stave 14 and down the middle. On one side only, this full sheet contains notations for "[p.]44 [at rehearsal] **46**, **49**, **55**." From the same sized paper, the Morgan Library's collection also includes one double half-sheet (of four pages), and one single half-sheet (two pages marked, on one side only, "page 100 [at rehearsal] **92**"), these also torn at stave 14.

The nature of the tear on Entry 21 suggests that it could well be the lower half of the Morgan Library's four-paged double half-sheet. This latter contains annotations on its four sides: "p. 99/p. 96;" "p. 95 [at rehearsal] **90**;" "p. 56;" and "4/4."

The majority of notations in Entry 21 relates to the second tableau, pp. 56-8 at rehearsals **62-3**, of the full score of the final instrumentation of *Les Noces,* finished in 1923 and published that year in London. Employing French (as do the Morgan's pages) rather than Russian, signalling the presence of a verbal text merely by "les femmes hommes," and locating these sketches at a "page 67," all suggest revising something already composed and perhaps even printed, rather than beginning composition.

Indeed, final versions of most of these "page 67" sketches do occur on a "p. 67 [at rehearsal] **63**" in a 140-page holograph manuscript, including autograph page and rehearsal numbers, dating from 1921-23. This manuscript comprises the instrumental accompaniment only – four pianos and percussion – and is on deposit in the British Library from the London publisher of *Les Noces,* J. and W. Chester. A similar holograph with the same instrumentation and pagination is in the Paul Sacher Foundation at Basle. For Entry 21, Stravinsky was working either from his manuscripts or from Chester's printed piano/vocal edition of 1922. In the latter, to which the technicians at Pleyel would have had access, the vocal music used from [rehearsal] **63** appears on p. 68, but the three musical figures marked "A B" and "C" do in fact precede on p. 67.

The music in Entry 21 on staves 3-5 directly below "A B" and "C" corresponds to eighth-note passages in pianos 1, 2, and 3 and the xylophone from rehearsal **62** through **64** in the printed score. "A B" and "C" could thus signify pianos 1, 2, and 3 (piano 4 playing the ostinato only). As musical materials, however, "B" and "C" each appear only once (between rehearsals **62** and **63**), whereas "A" appears four times, followed by three more statements during which its rising third interval expands to a rising fifth. (A similar use of majuscules appears in sketches for *The Rite of Spring*.)

The music copied below numbers "1 2 3 4 5 6" corresponds most closely to pianos 1 and 3 during the first two measures at rehearsal **63**, except for a missing initial eighth rest. The part marked "Chorus" is the initial four measures after rehearsal **63**, but written here entirely on just one staff (the 11th) in the treble clef and lacking text (Russian or French). It begins with tenors and basses and continues with sopranos and altos: "les femmes," but the sketch does not musically notate the ensuing answer by the tenors and basses: "hommes."

A wavy line through staves 1-7 separates their materials from related ideas not used in the final 1923 version set for four pianos and percussion. Here Stravinsky's observation to Ramuz on 18 August 1921 about preparing his works for player piano is relevant: "This mechanization interests me a great deal, and I have invented some splendid tricks." Directly below on staff 12 alternating "X" "Y" and "Z" notate similar chordal materials found in pianos 1, 2, and 3, this time with the requisite eighth rest. Obviously, he wanted to combine "X" and "Z" with the group of quintuplet triads notated on staves 13-14, which gradually become more thickly textured during their next three appearances. (For an autograph quotation from the fourth tableau of *Svadebka,* see Entry 55; for his citations about the ballet, see entries 23-4.)

Works Consulted

Antheil, George. *Bad Boy of Music.* Garden City, NY: Doubleday, Doran, 1945. p. 104.

"Avis Divers." *Revue Pleyel* 1 (15 October 1923): 20.

Craft, Robert. *Stravinsky: Glimpses of a Life.* London: Lime Tree, 1992; New York, NY: St. Martin's Press, 1993. p. 264.

Goubault, Christian. *Igor Stravinsky.* Paris: H. Champion, 1991. p. 187.

Hirsbrunner, Theo. "La musica di Stravinskij per 'Les Noces,'" *Oskar Schlemmer, Les Noces.* ed. Manuela Kahn-Rossi. Milan: Fabbri, 1988. p. 75.

Jans, Hans Jörg, and Lukas Handschin, ed. *Igor Strawinsky. Musikmanuskripte.* ("Inventare der Paul Sacher Stiftung," 5 [Winterthur: Amadeus, 1989].) 26: "Partitur (1923; 141 pp)."

Joseph, Charles M. "Diaghilev and Stravinsky." *The Ballets Russes and Its World.* ed. Lynn Garafola and Nancy Van Norman Baer. New Haven, CT, and London: Yale University Press, 1999. pp. 206-7, n. 16 on p. 374.

Larmanjat, Jacques. "Transcriptions des Oeuvres d'Orchestre pour le Pleyela." *Revue Pleyel* 2 (15 November 1923): 29-30.

Lawson, Rex. "Stravinsky and the Pianola" in *Confronting Stravinsky: Man, Musician, and Modernist.* ed. Jann Pasler. Berkeley and Los Angeles, CA, and London: University of California Press, 1986. p. 297, no. 5, p. 300, nos. 37-41.

–. "Stravinsky and the Pianola (part 2)." *The Pianola Journal* 2 (1989): 14.

–. Liner Notes (1993) to CD, *Igor Stravinsky, Pianola Works.* Music Master Classics, 1994. pp. 10-11.

"Les Rouleaux 'Pleyela' de transcription d'orchestre." *Revue Pleyel* 12 (15 September 1924): 28 (trans. Leonard W. Johnson).

Lesure, François. *Igor Stravinsky. La carrière européenne.* Paris: Musée d'Art Moderne, 1980. pp. 89-92, n. 4 on p. 105.

Lesure, François, and Nanie Bridgman, ed. *Collection Musicale André Meyer.* Abbeville: F. Paillart, 1960. pls. 250-1.

Lifar, Serge. *Ma Vie.* Paris: R. Juilliard, 1965. p. 51 (trans. Leonard W. Johnson).

Mayakovsky, Vladimir. "Parizhskiye Ocherki." *Polnoye Sobraniye Sochineniy.* Moscow: Gosudarstvennoye Izdatelstvo Khudozhestvennoy Literaturï, 1957. vol. 4. p. 229 (trans. Stanislav Shvabrin and Michael Green).

Schouvaloff, Alexander. *The Art of Ballets Russes: The Serge Lifar Collection of Theater Designs, Costumes, and Paintings at the Wadsworth Atheneum, Hartford, Connecticut.* New Haven, CT, and London: Yale University Press, 1997. pp. 208-11.

"Service du Pleyela." *Revue Pleyel* 6 [15 March 1924]: 29.

Stargardt, J.A. *Autographen aus allen Gebieten. Katalog 641.* Marburg, 9-10 March 1988, lot 1067. pp. 354-5.

−. *Beschriebenen Autographen aus allen Gebieten. Katalog 642.* Marburg, 30 November-1 December 1988. p. 6.

SBu. p. 18.

SI&V. pls. 56-60 on pp. 56-7.

SP&D. pp. 157-8, pl. on p. 242, pl. on p. 245 (lower).

SSC. vol. 1. n. 61 on p. 151, pp. 165-8; vol. 3. p. 61.

Stravinsky, Igor. *The Rite of Spring: Sketches 1911-1913. Facsimile Reproductions from the Autographs.* London: Boosey and Hawkes, 1969. p. 88.

Taruskin, Richard. *Stravinsky and the Russian Traditions.* Berkeley and Los Angeles, CA: University of California Press, 1996. fig. 18.3a on p. 1454.

−. "Stravinsky and the Subhuman: Notes on *Svadebka*" in *Defining Russia Musically.* Princeton, NJ: Princeton University Press, 1997. pp. 389-467.

Walsh, Stephen. *Stravinsky, A Creative Spring: Russia and France, 1882-1934.* New York, NY: Alfred A. Knopf, 1999. pp. 361-2.

22

(1923). Inscribed photograph, 13.9 × 9.5 cm, of Stravinsky standing outside a wooden structure, in French in black ink (lower left), 12 February 1923, to Georges Auric (1899-1983):

A Georges Auric
mes oreilles encore
pleines de sa très
bonne musique
des Facheux
I Strawinsky
Paris le 12 II 23

Georges Auric   Paris
Paris   12 February 1923

For Georges Auric, my ears still full of his very fine music for *Les Fâcheux*,

    I Strawinsky

Acquisition: H. Colin Slim in Los Angeles on 26 September 1999 from La Scala Autographs.
Provenance: Lisa Cox, *Catalogue 36* (Exeter, Summer [July] 1999), item 120.

Commentary

When and where the photograph was taken remain uncertain. A dealer's pencil remark on its reverse side: "Unofficial informal photo, signed and inscribed to Auric" is duplicated in Cox's catalogue. Above this is "AM 63," the number repeated in red pencil below. He inscribed a copy of the same image in 1923 to Boris Kochno and the following year one to Ansermet: "Genève/27/Nov./1924."

Auric wrote incidental music for the four performances of Molière's *Les Fâcheux* staged by the Comédie-Française at the Théâtre de l'Odéon in mid- and late April 1921, celebrating the 300th anniversary of the dramatist's birth. (Confusion about the year of these performances – even by Auric himself! – probably stems from the later run of Molière's play with incidental music by Beauchamp and Lully at the Comédie-Française from 1 October 1921 into 1922.)

Having heard one of these April 1921 play performances, Diaghilev was sufficiently impressed to commission the twenty-two-year-old Auric for music to a ballet by Boris Kochno after Molière, in which Jean Cocteau also had a hand. The latter entitled his undated drawing: "Georges Auric écrit les Fâcheux." Stravinsky, too, may have heard Auric's incidental music to Molière's play, or had early access to the piano score of Auric's ballet: "Avignon. Eté 1921 / Malines. Février 1923" (published at Paris late in 1923). Whatever the case, Auric played his score to Stravinsky the very day the latter inscribed Entry 22, as shown by Auric's letter to Paul Collaer: "Vu aussi Strawinsky, à qui je vais cet après-midi jouer *Les Fâcheux*" (reference kindly provided in July 2000 by Walsh). Perhaps then, the photograph was indeed taken in Paris.

Although the inscription in Entry 22 contradicts Walsh's earlier assertion that: "What Stravinsky thought of Auric's *Les Fâcheux* ... is not directly recorded," it confirms his intuition that Stravinsky would have liked it. In reviewing the 1924 Ballets Russes premieres of Auric's ballet score at Monte Carlo in January and at Paris in June, neither de Schloezer nor Prunières mention Auric's earlier incidental music to Molière's play.

Stravinsky may have met Auric as early as the fall of 1920, when he was invited to attend a series of concerts in Paris with Satie and Auric. Emerging with the latter from his Pleyel studio one evening in 1923, Stravinsky asked him to play one of the four piano parts at the forthcoming premiere of *Les Noces* on 13 June. Auric and Francis Poulenc – the latter ailing at the premiere and initially replaced by Édouard Flament – continued to be the pianists at later performances in 1924 (on the same program, 4 June, with the Parisian premiere of *Les Fâcheux*); in 1926 in Paris and at its London premiere; and in 1928 at Paris and London.

Works Consulted

Ansermet, Anne. *Ernest Ansermet, mon père*. Lausanne and Tours: Payot, 1983. pl. on p. 161.

Auric, Georges. *Quand j'étais là*. Paris: B. Grasset, 1979. pp. 52, 181-6.

Bordier-Nikitine, Michèle, ed. *Visages d'Igor Strawinsky*. Le Mans: Musée de Tessé, 26 February-25 April 1976. pl. 191 (Stravinsky and Auric at Biarritz in 1923).

Buckle, Richard. *Diaghilev*. New York, NY: Atheneum, 1979. pp. 428-9, 471, 501, 504.

Collaer, Paul. *Correspondance avec des amis musiciens*. ed. Robert Wangermée. Liège: P. Mardaga, 1996. p. 126, nos. 23-7.

Garafola, Lynn. *Diaghilev's Ballets Russes*. New York, and Oxford: Oxford University Press, 1989. p. 254.

Hitchcock, H. Wiley. "Molière." NG. vol. 12. p. 464.

Houle, George, ed. *Le Ballet des Fâcheux: [Pierre] Beauchamp's Music for Molière's Comedy*. Bloomington and Indianapolis: Indiana University Press, 1991.

Kochno, Boris. *Diaghilev and the Ballets Russes*. trans. Adrienne Foulke. New York, and Evanston, IL: Harper and Row, 1970. pls. on pp. 190, 194, pp. 210-13.

Le Figaro, 11 January 1921, p. 3; 3 April 1921, p. 3; 4 April, p. 5; 7, 14, 18, 24 April, each on p. 3; 30 September, p. 5.

Lesure, François. *Igor Stravinsky. La carrière européenne*. Paris: Musée d'Art Moderne, 1980. p. 89.

Lesure, François, and Nanie Bridgman, ed. *Collection Musicale André Meyer*. Abbeville: F. Paillart, 1960. pls. 49, 249 (1926 or 1928).

Lesure, François, et al., ed. *Diaghilev. Les Ballets Russes*. Paris: Bibliothèque Nationale, 1979. pp. 113-14, 122-4, 163-4.

Prunières, Henri. Review of *Les Fâcheux* (at Paris). *La Revue Musicale* 5, 9 (July 1924): 61-3.

Renaud, Paul, and Thierry Bodin. *Archives Roland-Manuel [part 2]*. Paris: 24 March 2000, lots 2 and 4. pp. 3-4.

Schloezer, Boris de. Review of *Les Fâcheux* (at Monte Carlo). *La Revue Musicale* 5, 4 (1 February 1924): 166-7.

Schouvaloff, Alexander. *The Art of Ballets Russes: The Serge Lifar Collection of Theater Designs, Costumes, and Paintings at the Wadsworth Atheneum, Hartford, Connecticut*. New Haven, CT, and London: Yale University Press, 1997. pp. 147-9.

SAc. pl. on p. 102 (Stravinsky and Auric at Biarritz in 1923).

SP&RK. vol. 2. pp. 476-7 (trans. Stanislav Shvabrin and Michael Green).

Steegmuller, Francis. *Cocteau: A Biography*. Boston, MA, and Toronto, ON: Little, Brown, 1976. p. 321.

Walsh, Stephen. *Stravinsky, A Creative Spring: Russia and France, 1882-1934*. New York, NY: Alfred A. Knopf, 1999. pp. 391-2.

23

(1923). **Autograph three-page letter, pp. 1-2 on one twice-folded sheet, 20.9 × 27.0 cm, on Pleyel (Paris) letterhead, with p. 3 on a severed twice-folded half-sheet, 20.9 × 13.4 cm, in French in black ink, 19 April 1923, to an unnamed Parisian woman, established as Madame Vera Janacopulos-Staal (1892-1955):**

Montecarlo 19 Avril 1923

Bien chère Madame,
Je vous remercie beaucoup de votre lettre et des intéressantes
nouvelles que vous m'annoncez.

Il m'est difficile de vous repondre en ce moment d'une
manière précise au sujet des mélodies à instrumenter pour notre
concert d'Anvers. Nous pourrons nous entendre à ce sujet à
Paris et je ferai ce travail pendant les vacances.

Quand à votre proposition pour le concert du 29 mai, vous
comprendrez que je dois réserver ma participation personnelle
aux concerts seulement pour les cas qui [page 2] peuvent
comporter des cachets assez élevés car ma situation financière
m'oblige à ménager cette source de gain! Mais votre lettre m'a
suggéré une idée que je me permets de vous exposer entr toute
franchise. Des tractations pour l'édition de plusieurs de mes
oeuvres manuscrites qui trainent en longueur me mettent juste
en ce moment dans une situation des plus difficiles. Je vous
avoue que je dois absolument trouver dans le délai de dix
jours une somme d'environ 4000 fr. S'il vous était possible de
trouver pour moi cette somme à titre de prêt, vous me rendriez
un grand service et je participerai avec plaisir à votre concert
comme vous le désirez, trop heureux de trouver là une occasion de vous témoigner ma reconnaissance dans la mesure de
mes possibilités actuelles.

Repondez moi je vous prie à l'hôtel des Princes –
Montecarlo où [page 3] je me trouve pour les répétitions des
"Noces" avec le "ballet russe."

En attendant votre reponse je vous prie de croire, chère
Madame à mes sentiments tout devoués
Igor Strawinsky

p.s. Mon ami Ansermet qui est ici à Montecarlo également me
dit qu'il compte fermement obtenir pour vous un engagement
en Suisse pour cet hiver ainsi que je lui en avais souvent parlé[.]

Vera Janacopulos-Staal   Monte Carlo
Paris   19 April 1923

Very dear Madame:
Thank you very much for your letter and for the interesting news
you tell me.

It is difficult for me to reply at this time in an exact way about
orchestrating the songs for our Antwerp concert. We can discuss this
in Paris and I could undertake this work during summer vacation.

As for your proposal about the May 29 concert, you understand
that I must reserve my personal participation in concerts only for
those occasions which can provide quite high fees, because my
financial situation obliges me to pursue this source of income! But
your letter has suggested an idea which I allow myself to share with
you in all frankness. Negotiations for the publication of several of my
works [still] in manuscript which have dragged on have put me just
now in a very difficult position. I confess that I absolutely must find
within ten days the sum of about 4,000 francs. If it were possible for
you to find this sum for me as a loan, you would render me a great
service and I would participate with pleasure in your concert as you
desire, too happy to find there the chance to demonstrate my
gratitude as far as my present circumstances allow.

Please reply to me at the Hotel Princes – Monte Carlo where I
am staying for rehearsals of *The Wedding* with the Ballets Russes.

Awaiting your reply, I am, dear Madame, yours very sincerely,
Igor Strawinsky

p.s. My friend, Ansermet, who is also here in Monte Carlo, tells me
that – just as I have often asked him – he firmly counts on obtaining
an engagement for you in Switzerland this winter.

Acquisition: H. Colin Slim on 11 December 1997 from La Scala
Autographs.
Provenance: An unidentified collector in England in 1997.

Commentary

The letter is unpublished, its envelope missing. Stravinsky was with
Ansermet for rehearsals by the Ballets Russes of *Les Noces* in Monte

Carlo, where, almost a year earlier, he had signed proofs on 11 May 1922 for the piano/vocal score. On the day he wrote Entry 23, *Les Noces* was rehearsed at Monte Carlo from 10 a.m. to 1 p.m.

Unnamed, the addressee of Entry 23 is identifiable from mention of her concert in Paris on 29 May 1923 and from another one forthcoming in Antwerp (7 January 1924) (see Entry 26). Because only one musical dictionary cites Janacopulos – and that very briefly – the following sketch of her career may be found useful not only in itself but for the light it sheds on her collaboration with many composers, including Stravinsky. It draws on her *Memórias* (requiring caution in respect to relevant dates in French) and on information in Boston Symphony program notes, and in US newspapers and in several music journals of the period. Dr. Slim thanks Seymour Menton for his translations from the Portuguese.

Born in Petropolis near Rio de Janeiro, Vera Janacopulos went as a child to France in 1896. She studied violin with George Enesco until 1908 when she began singing lessons with Reja Bauer, giving her first vocal recital at the Salle Gaveau in May 1915. She spent the First World War partly in Geneva and in Paris, where she studied with Jean de Reszke, continuing with Jean Périer, W. Thorner in New York, and lastly with Lilli Lehmann in Salzburg in 1923-24.

Making her US debut in Aeolian Hall, New York, on 14 December 1918 – where Prokofiev was to have accompanied her – Janacopulos gave a second New York concert on 29 December in the Hippodrome with the Russian Symphony Orchestra led by Modeste Altschuler. She remained in New York to give the premiere of *Three Poems* (1918) by Charles Griffes, with him at the piano on 22 March 1919, at which Prokofiev also accompanied her in three of his own songs and Maurice Dambois in several of his, to laudatory reviews. After two further concerts in New York on 12 April and 23 May, she sailed to Brazil and Argentina, performing in the latter country under Felix Weingartner.

Janacopulos returned to New York to sing on 1 November in Aeolian Hall. On the 13th she sang with the Boston Symphony under Pierre Monteux in Sanders Theatre at Harvard. Two days after a "Musical Morning" held at the Copley Plaza Hotel on 8 December by a local Boston voice teacher, she was in New York to give the US premiere of *Pribaoutki* (1914) in Aeolian Hall, her audience including

Prokofiev and Michel Fokine. The former wrote Stravinsky in Switzerland that she was "a very talented singer … approaching them lovingly and singing them excellently, except, perhaps, for Kornila ["Uncle Armand"], which is too low for her voice. It was a great success; all four pieces were encored." (Dating his letter as 10 December, Prokofiev understandably led Craft and Varunts to identify the date of her concert as the 9th.)

In the 1920s and early 1930s, Janacopulos ranked among the chief singers of new music in Paris. During May 1921, she gave four successive concerts at the Salle des Agriculteurs. At the last one – (20 May) which also included music by Villa-Lobos, Ravel, and Prokofiev – she sang *Pribaoutki* with instrumental accompaniment. At a fifth concert on 31 May with the Colonne orchestra conducted by Pierre Monteux, she performed Ravel's *Schéhérazade* (1903) to the great pleasure of the composer in the audience who inscribed her copy. By 1924 she had sung the Ravel also under Ernest Ansermet, Franz Ruhlmann, and Serge Koussevitsky.

For a "Friends of Music" concert in New York on 10 February 1924, Janacopulos sang *Schéhérazade* at Town Hall with Erwin Bodansky and Ernest Bloch's *Two Psalms* (1912-14) with the composer conducting the Metropolian Opera orchestra. Olin Downes wrote a glowing review of her 27 February recital in Aeolian Hall, which included *Pastorale* (1907) and "Tilim-bom" (1917) by Stravinsky, following which she journeyed to Boston. There she sang *Schéhérazade* again under Monteux on 29 February and 1 March with the Boston Symphony, its program notes reporting that she had sung in France, Belgium, Switzerland, Spain, and Portugal. Her repertoire of 500 songs in seventeen languages included concerts with Stravinsky, Prokofiev, de Falla, Milhaud, Poulenc, Enesco, and Griffes, with these composers playing piano or conducting.

In Paris, Janacopulos premiered works by Carlos Pedrell and her countryman, Heitor Villa-Lobos, the latter who dedicated to her *Historietas* (1921), and a *Suite para canto e violino* (1923) to her, her husband – A. Staal, and violinist Yvonne Astruc. With Artur Rubinstein, she gave two important concerts of Villa-Lobos's music in April and May 1924 and with Villa-Lobos conducting she sang the premiere there of his *Tres poemas indigenes* on 5 December 1927.

Rubinstein observed that, during the 1920s, he and Prokofiev were often in Paris together, and sometimes both of them with Janacopulos, "who sang Prokofiev's songs to his liking (she had a dreadful husband, however, a bearded Russian who drank vodka in great quantities)." Helping to translate Prokofiev's opera *The Love for Three Oranges* into French in 1919, she gave a recital with him in Paris on 28 October 1922.

Janacopulos sang with de Falla in Amsterdam on 26 April 1926 and the following year on 22-23 June performed with him in London. She was active with such other composers as Milhaud and Arthur Honegger in December 1927 and with Albert Roussel in 1932. By this latter date, she had sung in all the major cities of Europe, not only with the above-mentioned conductors, but also under Willem Mengleberg, Bruno Walter, Clemens Krauss, Walter Abendroth, Vladimir Golschmann, and Dimitri Mitropolous. In 1929 she undertook a tour of the Dutch East Indies, giving some thirty-two concerts in Java, Sumatra, and the Celebes.

Not only Prokofiev's favourable assessment of her in 1919, but her extraordinary beauty undoubtedly attracted the attention of Stravinsky. They may have first met in 1920 when he came from Switzerland to Paris for the premieres of *Le Chant du Rossignol* and *Pulcinella* at the Opéra on 2 February and 15 May, respectively, she having recently returned from Brazil. Perhaps he coached her for a concert she gave in the Salle des Agriculteurs on 2 June which included Russian music, by which time she could converse in that language "without an accent." She retained his inscription in Russian (probably on one of his compositions): "To Vera Georgievna / JANAKOPOULOS / with kind recollection / from / the author / Paris 23 V 20" – the day before Picasso's celebrated drawing of the composer seated (see entries 46 and 86). Curiously, by late 1923 he misspells her maiden name and again in 1924 (see entries 26-7).

Darius Milhaud, who inscribed a work to her in 1923, conducted a concert that she gave in Paris including compositions by Stravinsky, perhaps that year's concert of 29 May, to judge by the presence she reports of Serge Koussevitsky in the ensemble. There she sang *Pribaoutki,* the *Three Japanese Lyrics,* and the "Song of the Bear" (1916) from the *Three Tales for Children* (1916-17) with Koussevitsky playing its two-note ostinato accompaniment on his double bass.

Entry 23, with a request by Stravinsky for a short-term loan in exchange for his co-operation, exudes a palpable whiff of gentle extortion. His reference to forthcoming concerts with her: at Paris on 29 May (1923), at Antwerp (7 January 1924), and mention of his previous recommendations of her to Ansermet, obviously demonstrate an already considerable acquaintance. Indeed, two letters from him of 26 February and 4 May 1923, recommending her to concert agencies, are preserved at the Sacher Foundation in Basle.

Their continuing professional and social relationships to the mid-1930s (documented in entries 26-7) and in Vera Sudeykina's diary (from 1 January 1924) could well mean that Janacopulos found the requested sum for him. But the fact that, on 29 May 1923, he only attended and apparently did not accompany her concert in Paris at the Salle des Agriculteurs might also indicate that she did not come up with the loan. There, his friend de Falla accompanied her in several songs and she sang several works by Stravinsky, including his "Tilim-bom" from the *Three Tales for Children,* accompanied by a Pleyela player piano roll. This concert was noted as the "dernier concert donné par Vera Janacopulos avec le concours de MM. de Falla et Darius Milhaud. Oeuvres des ces auteurs, de Strawinsky et Poulenc." A year later on 22 May at a Sorbonne conference organized by Milhaud called "Les Ressources Nouvelles de la Musique (jazz-band et instruments mécaniques)," she preceded "Tilim-bom" with "Les canards, les cygnes et les oies" from the *Three Tales,* both of which were accompanied by the Pleyela. In Entry 23 the "mélodies à instrumenter," *Pastorale* and "Tilim-bom," were for her Antwerp concert with Stravinsky on 7 January 1924 (see Entry 26).

He had certainly already written Ansermet on her behalf for, on 17 September 1923, the Swiss conductor reported to him that she would sing "Parasha's aria" from *Mavra* and Ravel's *Schéhérazade* at Geneva on 10 November. With Ansermet she was also to perform "Tilim-bom" and de Falla's *El Retablo de Maese Pedro* in Paris on 11 January 1929 and songs by Handel, Purcell, and Lully as well as *El Retablo* in Geneva on 14 February 1931.

Works Consulted

Anderson, Donna K. *Charles T. Griffes*. Washington and London: Smithsonian Institution Press, 1993. p. 149 and n. 5.

Boston Symphony Program Notes (29 February–1 March 1924). pp. 1212-14.

"Ce soir." *Le Figaro*, 29 May 1923, p. 4.

Collaer, Paul. *Correspondance avec des amis musiciens*. ed. Robert Wangermée. Liège: P. Mardaga, 1996. p. 112: nos. 22-7, p. 147: nos. 23-5.

Craft, Robert. "Catalog of the Library of Robert Craft." Typescript: Library of Congress, Music Division. IV: Proofs, p. 9.

Downes, Olin. "Modern Songs Well Sung." *New York Times*. 28 February 1924. p. 22.

Fergison, Drue. "Bringing *Les Noces* to the Stage." *The Ballets Russes and Its World*. ed. Lynn Garafola and Nancy Van Norman Baer. New Haven, CT, and London: Yale University Press, 1999. p. 177.

França, Eurico Nogueira. *Memórias de Vera Janacópulos*. Rio de Janeiro: Ministério da Educaçao e Cultura, 1959.

" 'Geniuses are International' says Vera Janacopulos." *Musical Courier* 79, 2 (10 July 1919): 15 (also reporting that she learned Russian in 1917).

Janacopulos, Vera. Clipping file. Music Division. New York Public Library.

Mariz, Vasco. *Dicionario Biografico Musical*. rev. 3rd ed. Belo Horizonte: Villa Rica, 1991. pp. 126-7.

Orenstein, Arbie, ed. *A Ravel Reader*. New York, NY: Columbia University Press, 1990. no. 287.

Peppercorn, Lisa M. *The World of Villa-Lobos in Pictures and Documents*. Aldershot: Scolar Press, 1996. pp. 74-5, pl. 192 on p. 89.

Prokofiev, Sergei. *Prokofev o Prokofeve: stati i interviu*. [Prokofiev on Prokofiev: articles and interviews.] ed. V.P. Varunts. Moscow: Sovetskiy Kompozitor, 1991. pp. 36-7.

Robinson, Harlow. *Sergei Prokofiev*. New York, NY, and London: Robert Hale, 1987. pp. 175-6.

Rodriguez, Natalia, and Malcolm Herrick Brown. "Prokofiev's Correspondence with Stravinsky and Shostakovich." *Slavonic and Western Music: Essays for Gerald Abraham*. ed. M.H. Brown and Roland John Wiley. Ann Arbor, MI, and Oxford: University of Michigan Press, 1985. p. 275, no. 4 (trans).

Rubinstein, Artur. *My Many Years*. New York, NY: Alfred A. Knopf, 1980. p. 47.

Sopeña, Federico. *Vida y Obra de Manuel de Falla*. Madrid: Turner Libros, 1988. pp. 173, 177.

Stargardt, J.A. *Katalog 671*. Berlin, 30-31 March 1999, lot 896.

SP&RK. vol. 2. n. 1 on p. 184, p. 469.

SSC. vol. 2. n. 10 on p. 163.

Tappolet, Claude, ed. *Correspondance Ernest Ansermet-Igor Strawinsky (1914-1967)*. Geneva: Georg, 1990-92. vol. 2. p. 74, no. 229.

—. *Ernest Ansermet: Correspondances avec des compositeurs européens (1916-1966)*. Geneva: Georg, 1994. pl. 37 on p. 185, pl. 38 on p. 188.

"Three Composers at Janacopulos Recital." *Musical Courier* 78, 18 (1 May 1919): 39.

"Vera Jancopoulos Sings Songs of Stravinsky." *New York Times*. 11 December 1919. p. 11.

Walsh, Stephen. *Stravinsky, A Creative Spring: Russia and France, 1882-1934*. New York, NY: Alfred A. Knopf, 1999. n. 27 on p. 637.

Wiéner, Jean. *Allegro appassionato*. Paris: P. Belfond, 1978. pp. 81, 106.

24 (1923). Autograph two-page letter, 26.8 × 21.0 cm, folded twice, in Russian in black ink, 26 July 1923, to Vasiliy Fyodorovich [Kibalchich] (c. 1880-c. 1965):

Biarritz, 26 Juli
1923.

Dorogoi Vasilii Fedorovich,
Vsiyakiya dela i zanyatiya ne pozvolili mne svoyevremenno –
pis'menno* poblagodarit' Vas za Vashe dobroye, liubovnoye
otnosheniye k "Svadebke" i za eya userdnuyu[,] polnuyu
dostoinstv vyuchku. Delayu eto teper' i khochu dumat' chto Vy
poverite v moyu iskrennyuyu blagodarnost' Vam i v goriachem
moyem zhelanii snova uslyshat' s Vashem uchastiyem etu
doroguyu nam veshch'[.]

[hand-drawn rule across width]
*) "Chto napisano perom, togo ne vyrubish' toporom."

[page 2] Dast Bog na budushchii god chto[-]libo ustroitsya v
smysle eya kontsertnogo ispolneniya i ya tak budu schastliv
snova priniat'sya za rabotu s Vami, Ansermet i prochimi
nashimi userdnymi ispolnitelyami.

Klanyaites' Vashei miloi zhene, i sebe sokhranite moyu
iskrennyuyu k Vam druzhbu[.]

Vash
Igor' Stravinskii

igor STRAWINSKY
LES ROCHERS
[stamp] <u>BIARRITZ</u>

Vasiliy Kibalchich   Biarritz
[Geneva?]   26 July 1923

Dear Vasiliy Fyodorovich:
All kinds of affairs and business have not allowed me at the appropri-
ate time – *in letter format*★ to thank you for your kind and affectionate
attitude to *Svadebka* and for its full high-quality mastery. I am doing
this now and I want to think that you will believe in my sincere
gratitude to you and in my ardour of a desire to hear again with your
participation this thing which is dear to us.

★ "What is being written by a pen, you won't hack out with an
axe[.]" [a common Russian proverb, still in use]

[page 2] God willing, next year either [sic] it will be arranged in the
sense of its concert performance and I will be so happy again to get
down to work with you, Ansermet, and the rest of the devoted
performers.
    Pay my respects to your dear wife and for yourself be assured of
my sincere friendship for you.
    Your
    Igor Strawinsky

Acquisition: H. Colin Slim on 23 April 1998 from La Scala Autographs.
Provenance: George T. Cosmatos (1941-), Los Angeles (director of the
movie, *Rambo*); Sotheby's *The Collection of George Cosmatos including
autograph letters, manuscripts, music and film* (London, Aeolian Hall, 31
March 1998), lot 424.

Commentary

The letter is unpublished and its envelope is missing; a reduced facsimile of the second page of Entry 24 appears in Sotheby's catalogue, lot 424. Both pages are watermarked: PLANTAGENET / BRITISH MAKE / 8.P /. Dr Slim is obliged to Stanislav Shvabrin and Michael Green for the above transliteration and translation.

Kibalchich had prepared the chorus for the premiere of *Les Noces* by the Ballets Russes in Paris on 13 June 1923, his singers listed in the program as "Choeurs russes de Kibaltchitch" [sic]. Stravinsky may have considered him for this task as early as 1917. That year the poet Charles-Albert Cingria wrote the composer recalling their recent excursion to Rolle (near Morges), Stravinsky playing *Les Noces* and Kibalchich there: "with his brick-shaped head and admirable gold glasses. He was the chorus, not an individual, but a race: the whole of sacerdotal and administrative Russia" (Walsh, p. 279).

More than a year before the premiere, however, Ansermet aired some doubts about him to Stravinsky on 1 July 1922: "il parait que les choeurs de Kil[balchich] ont été très faibles aux concerts K[oussevitzky, in Paris]." Ansermet proposed not only that rehearsals for *Les Noces* should soon begin, but also that he take over a rehearsal now and then in Paris, for, as he wrote Stravinsky: "Vous savez que pour votre musique on ne peut pas improviser."

Just three days before writing Entry 24 to Kibalchich, Stravinsky had received a letter from Ansermet in Geneva wherein Ansermet hoped for a festival there in April 1924 which would include *Les Noces*. Therefore, it was probably this envisaged performance – "God willing, next year" – as least as much as the politeness of a formal note of thanks which prompted Entry 24. Three days after writing it, he wrote Ansermet of a possible performance of his music at Paris on 7 November 1923 which, ultimately, did not include *Les Noces*.

Although Kibalchich was later described as having been a disciple of Rimsky-Korsakov and director of the Archangelsky and of the Petrograd Conservatory choirs, Stravinsky apparently first met him in Château d'Oex in 1915. Possibly, however, this took place even earlier in Geneva, where, by 26 April 1914, Stravinsky had joined the "Society of Friends of Russian Music" founded by Kibalchich, "choirmaster of the Russian (Embassy) church in Geneva." While living in Chateau d'Oex and obviously in answer to his request, Stravinsky received from Ansermet on 1 February 1915 Kibalchich's address in Geneva. Kibalchich was organizing a concert of Russian music there for 15 May which Stravinsky apparently attended with Ansermet. Kibalchich later conducted the first performance of the *Four Russian Peasant Songs* (1914-17) at Geneva in 1917, the last song of which was dedicated to him. Photographed two years later with Stravinsky and two others in Switzerland, he (like Stravinsky) emigrated to France.

Kibalchich made his US debut conducting the Russian Symphonic Choir in New York in April 1924, taking it on annual tours thereafter. (He also made several recordings for the Victor label.) During these tours in the 1940s he would visit Stravinsky in Hollywood, one of these occasions being a luncheon with Stravinsky's University of St. Petersburg friend, Dr. Alexis Kall, on 15 July 1943. Although Stravinsky reported last having heard about Kibalchich in December 1950: "gravely ill in Philadelphia" – in fact, Kibalchich wrote him as late as 17 November 1964, as shown by a letter in the Paul Sacher Foundation.

Works Consulted

Fergison, Drue. "Bringing *Les Noces* to the Stage." *The Ballets Russes and Its World*. ed. Lynn Garafola and Nancy Van Norman Baer. New Haven, CT, and London: Yale University Press, 1999. pp. 168-9, n. 3 on p. 370.

Musical America 44 (26 June 1926): pl. on cover, p. 25.

"Russian Symphonic Choir." *New York Times*. 7 April 1924. p. 14.

SBu. p. 128 (15 July 1943).

SP&D. n. 43 on p. 604.

SP&RK. vol. 2. n. 12 on p. 303 (trans. Stanislav Shvabrin and Michael Green), pp. 305-6, pp. 693-4, no. 37.

SSC. vol. 1. pp. 169-70; vol. 3. n. 4 on p. 111, pl. [3, lower] btn pp. 242-3.

Tappolet, Claude, ed. *Correspondance Ernest Ansermet-Igor Stravinsky (1914-1967)*. Geneva: Georg, 1990-92. vol. 1. pp. 27-9, nos. 24-5, pp. 32-3, no. 29; vol. 2. pp. 1-2, no. 180, pl. 33 on p. 59, p. 60, no. 219.

Taruskin, Richard. *Stravinsky and the Russian Traditions*. Berkeley and Los Angeles, CA: University of California Press, 1996. pp. 1155-8, esp. fig. 15.4.

Walsh, Stephen. *Stravinsky, A Creative Spring: Russia and France, 1882-1934*. New York, NY: Alfred A. Knopf, 1999. pp. 279 (trans.), 545, n. 43 on p. 615.

25

(1923). **Signed typed coloured picture postcard, 8.6 × 13.8 cm, in French: [no.] 32 – BIARRITZ, Rocher dit "La Loge de Théâtre," postmarked BIARRITZ BSES PYRENEES/16 45/6 -8/23 [4:45 p.m. 6 August 1923], with address typed by Stravinsky, 6 August 1923, to Jean Cocteau (1889-1963):**

Monsieur
JEAN COCTEAU
Piquey
par ARES
Gironde

Cher Jean,
    Je pars ces jours à Weimar; on y joue l'Histoire du Soldat au théâtre.Les Reinhart qui s'en occupent me demandent de venir. Je n'ai jamais vu rien au monde de plus drôle que le portrait du monsieur auquel appartient l'énorme perroquet qui a mordu les dactylos anglaises. Je t'embrasse
    [in black ink] Igor Strawinsky

Jean Cocteau   Biarritz
Piquey   6 August 1923

Dear Jean:
    Within a day or two, I'm leaving for Weimar; they're staging *The Story of a Soldier* there. The Reinharts, who are arranging this, have asked me to come. Never in this world have I seen anything funnier than the portrait of the gentleman who owned the enormous parrot that bit the English typists. Love,
    Igor Strawinsky

Acquisition: H. Colin Slim in New York on 23 September 1994 from Wurlitzer-Bruck.
Provenance: Possibly collection Henri Lefèbvre; Sotheby Parke Bernet, *Catalogue of Music, Continental and Russian Autograph Letters, Literary*

Manuscripts and Historical Documents with Some Printed Music (London, 14-15 April 1982), lot 82, p. 38.

Commentary

Entry 25 is not included in the selected correspondence of Stravinsky and Cocteau (1913-62). It is the composer's reply to Cocteau's letter of 2 August 1923 which also contained the artist's portrait of "the gentleman who owns the very large parrot that bit the English typists." Cocteau's drawing has not been traced. (The auction catalogue translates "dactylos" as "secretaries," Craft as "typewriter.") Why Stravinsky qualified the typists as "English" remains unknown, unless it is a pun on the nearby town of Anglet. He may have recalled a letter to him of 9 October 1921 from Ramuz, who had punned on "Anglet" and "anglais."

That Stravinsky typed Entry 25 himself and other correspondence as well is clear. A letter to Ansermet of 29 July the same year from "Les Rochers" begins: "As you see, I type my letters on the machine, improving all the while"; in another to him from Nice of 2 October, 1924: "I type, hurting my fingers, on my 'Continsouza' machine, awaiting the opportunity to employ a secretary who can do this for me."

Stravinsky was in Biarritz at the Villa des Rochers to which he had moved his family from nearby Anglet in mid-October 1921. This postcard is the only surviving example of his correspondence in 1923 with Jean Cocteau, living that summer at Piquey with the young poet Raymond Radiguet (1903-23) and Georges Auric (perhaps the typists assaulted by the parrot). By August Stravinsky was spelling "perroquet" correctly, unlike a year earlier in his letter from Biarritz to the painter René Auberjonois wherein he twice omitted an "r."

The performance at Weimar of *L'Histoire du soldat* (1918) to which Stravinsky was bidden was to be conducted by Hermann Scherchen (1891-1966) on 19 August. Rehearsals began at the Bauhaus on the 16th, as documented in letters of 28 July and 10 August from his Swiss patron, Werner Reinhart (1884-1951), urging him to attend and enclosing a check enabling him to do so. For this particular occasion Vera Sudeykina met him in Paris on the 10th and accompanied him to Weimar, both of them returning to Paris on the 22nd. Four days earlier she took a photograph of him and Scherchen at Weimar. His detailed reaction to the Bauhaus production – one deemed by Craft as "celebrated" – is in his letter to Ansermet of 9 September. (For an autograph quotation from *L'histoire,* see Entry 52.)

Works Consulted

Lesure, François. *Igor Stravinsky. La carrière européenne.* Paris: Musée d'Art Moderne, 1980. pp. 52, no. 158, 83-4.

Steegmuller, Francis. *Cocteau: A Biography.* Boston, MA, and Toronto, ON: Little, Brown, 1976. n. on p. 310, p. 538 (Stravinsky III).

SAc. pl. 92 (Biarritz in 1923).

SBu. p. 18 (16-19 August 1923).

SP&RK. vol. 2. p. 750 (index: Cocteau).

SSC. vol. 1. pp. 92, 169, 181, item 5; vol. 2. p. 429; vol. 3. pp. 62, 148-9, pl. [4, lower] btn pp. 242-3, n. 1 on p. 461.

Tappolet, Claude, ed. *Correspondance Ernest Ansermet-Igor Stravinsky (1914-1967).* Geneva: Georg, 1990-92. vol. 2. pp. 60, no. 220 (trans. H. Colin Slim), 67-70, no. 225, 103-4, no. 253 (trans. H. Colin Slim).

Walsh, Stephen. *Stravinsky, A Creative Spring: Russia and France, 1882-1934.* New York, NY: Alfred A. Knopf, 1999. pp. 369-71.

26   (1923). Signed typed letter folded twice with autograph place of origin, date, and postscript, 26.8 × 20.6 cm, in French in black ink, 4 December 1923, to Vera Janacopulos-Staal:

[in black ink] Biarritz le 4 Dec 1923
Madame
Vera Janocopulos-Staal
<u>PARIS</u>.

Chère Madame,

Reçu votre réponse du 3 dec. et suis en même temps un peu inquiet au sujet du rouleau contenant le chant-piano de la Suite "Faune et Bergère" que je vous avais également envoyé (non recommandé) [typed over] S̶o̶ en même temps que ma lettre; j'espère quand-même qu'il vous est bien parvenu et vous prie de me le renvoyer par retour du courrier car c'est le seul exemplaire que je possède.

Quand au programme du concert d'Anvers en ce qui concerne votre partie voici les morceaux et leur ordre:

1º Prélude, chant du Pêcheur et air du Rossignol

2º Trois mélodies de la lyrique japonaise.

3º Pastorale et "Tilim-bom"

Il me semble que si nous ajouterions deux Pribaoutki et une Berceuse du Chat nous, risquerions de l'alourdir et d'autre part je m'arrête aux Japonaises vu [hole in paper] qu'elles forment unrecueuil. homogène.

Puisque vous insistez sur l'instrumentation du Tilim-bom et de la Pastorale je vous demanderai de m'envoyer également par ret. du ⊠ c[ourrie]r. cette dernière car je n'ai pas un seule exemplaire chez moi et il me serait impossible d'en procurer ailleurs.

Je vous prie de me donner vos adresses en Espagne et au Portugal pour que je puisse en cas de besoin vous atteindre.

En attendant de vos bonnes nouvelles, je vous prie, chère Madame de croire à mes sentiments bien dévoués.

[sideways, in black ink] Igor Strawinsky

[postscript left margin in black ink] Excusez je vous prie le trou et l'horrible fin de cette lettre – je suis très pressé d'envoyer cette lettre

| Vera Janacopulos-Staal | Biarritz |
| Paris | 4 December 1923 |

Dear Madame:

Received your reply of 3 December and am still a little worried about the roll containing the piano-song from the suite, *Faun and Shepherdess*, which I likewise sent you (unregistered) at the same time as my letter; I hope, however, that it has arrived safely and I ask you to send it to me by return mail because it's the only one I own.

As for the program for the Antwerp concert and your role in it, here are the pieces and their order:

1. "Prelude," "Song of the Fisherman," and the "Nightingale's aria."
2. Three songs of the *Japanese Lyrics*.
3. "Pastorale" and "Tilim-bom."

It seems to me that if we were to add two *Pribaoutki* and a "Cat's Cradle" song, we would risk overloading it and, on the other hand, I've decided on the *Japanese* [*Lyrics*], because they form an homogenous group.

Since you insist on an orchestration for "Tilim-bom" and for the *Pastorale*, I also ask you to send the latter by return mail because I have no copy here and I wouldn't be able to get it anywhere else.

Please give me your addresses in Spain and Portugal so I could reach you if need be.

Awaiting good news from you, I am, dear Madame, yours very sincerely,

Igor Strawinsky

p.s. Please excuse the hole and the dreadful close to this letter – I'm in a great hurry to send this letter.

Acquisition: H. Colin Slim on 11 December 1997 from La Scala Autographs.
Provenance: An unidentified collector in England in 1997.

Commentary

The letter is unpublished, its envelope missing. A copy of the letter is in the Paul Sacher Foundation, which holds much of their correspondence. Its full extent remains unknown, but he had mailed Janacopulos a postcard from the Maison Pleyel on 24 August 1923, noting that he was in Paris for a few days and wanted to see her one afternoon. Sending her the commercially unavailable piano roll of *Le Faune et la Bergère* (1906) was to stimulate her interest in performing the song cycle with him in Antwerp in January 1924 and in the US in 1925, as documented in Entry 27.

Janacopulos's first appearance in Vera Sudeykina's diary on 1 January 1924 as a daytime visitor was probably for rehearsals with him for their Antwerp concert six days later, a copy of its program held by the Sacher Foundation at Basle. Having been invited to Antwerp by the Société "Nouveaux Concerts" to conduct a program of his earlier works, Stravinsky led her performance there on 7 January. For this concert he had finished arranging late in December 1923 at Biarritz *Pastorale* (1907) for voice and woodwind quartet and "Tilim-bom" for voice and orchestra, the third item in Entry 26 (the "mélodies à instrumenter pour notre concert d'Anvers" mentioned in Entry 23). He reported to his editor on 19 January and to Ansermet on 24 March the great success of their Antwerp concert. She may be the unidentified woman seated next to him in a group photograph taken by Vera Sudeykina at Brussels on 14 January 1924 where the Société "Pro Arte" had organized a concert of his music.

Some notion of her voice, c. 1925, can be gained from Arthur Hoérée (1897-1986), critic and composer, who wrote in *Le Ménestrel*:

Mme. Vera Janacopulos, qui nous n'avions plus entendu depuis quelque temps à Paris, a été comblée des dieux. Elle possède un organe d'une qualité exceptionnelle et un art de s'en servir tout aussi exceptionnel. Il y a des timbres qui émouvent par leur seule présence. Celui de la cantatrice en est un exemple: plénitude dans la douceur, roundeur dans la force, parfum quasi unique, étrange et enivrant comme l'Orient, et qu'exhalent des subtiles modulations dont elle colore sa voix. Au surplus, le souci d'exprimer le sens poétique des textes qui, pour nombre d'interprètes, sont lettre morte.

[Madame Vera Janacopulos, whom we hadn't heard in Paris for some time, has been gifted by the gods. She possesses a voice of exceptional quality and uses it with an equally exceptional art. Certain vocal timbres move one simply by being there. This singer's is one of these: fullness in soft, roundness in loud, an almost unique perfume, strange and intoxicating like the Orient, emanating from certain subtle modulations with which she colours her voice. In addition, she takes care to express the poetic meaning of the text, which for many singers is a dead letter.]

Works Consulted

França, Eurico Nogueira. *Memórias de Vera Janacópulos*. Rio de Janeiro: Ministério da Educaçao e Cultura, 1959. p. 67 (trans. Leonard W. Johnson).

Macnutt, Richard, Ltd. *Catalogue 112*. Tunbridge Wells, 1983, item 173.

SP&D. pl. on p. 249, n. 219 on p. 618.

SSC. vol. 1. p. 178.

Walsh, Stephen. *Stravinsky, A Creative Spring: Russia and France, 1882-1934*. New York, NY: Alfred A. Knopf, 1999. pp. 382-3.

27 (1924). Signed typed letter, 27.0 × 21.0 cm, folded five times, in French in brown ink, 6 August 1924, to Vera Janacopulos-Staal:

Madame Vera Janocopulos
PARIS

Chère Madame,

Ne m'en voulez pas si même pendant les vacances on ne vous laisse pas tranquille – c'est que je viens vous demander de penser à ma Suite "Faun et Bergère" pour chant et orch. que je voudrais beaucoup entendre chanter par vous.

Vu que probablement l'occasion se présentera pour que nous la fassions ensemble en hiver prochain aux Etats-Unis✗ [crossed out in ink] vous feriez bien,je pense,de la travailler dès aprèsent.

Donnez moi de vos nouvelles,dites bien des choses à votre époux et croyez,chère Madame, à mon fidèle dévouement
Igor Strawinsky

[in brown ink] Igor Strawinsky

"Les Rochers"
BIARRITZ,
6/VIII/24

Vera Janacopulos-Staal   Biarritz
Paris   6 August 1924

Dear Madame:

   Don't be annoyed with me even if during [your] vacation I don't leave you in peace; it's just that I want to ask you to consider my suite, *Faun and Shepherdess* for soprano and orchestra, which I would very much like to hear sung by you.

   Given that probably we'll have the chance to do it together next winter in the United States, you would do well, I think, to begin work on it now.

   Send me your news, dear Madame, give my best wishes to your husband,

   Yours faithfully,

   Igor Strawinsky

Acquisition: by W. Gibson Mann for H. Colin Slim on 20 December 1996 in New York from the Cambridge-Essex Stamp Co. Inc. (393 5th Avenue). The letter was restored in March 1997 by Linda K. Ogden who removed two white cloth hinges at the top, repaired two small tears at the bottom with rice paper, and removed from the reverse side a non-autograph "Stravinsky" written in blue crayon.

Provenance: Unknown dealer; pencil markings on the upper left corner: "1c / Abb..nante / £60°°," perhaps from the estate of Madame Janacopulos-Staal; the letter was framed by Cambridge-Essex some time after 1978.

Commentary

The letter is unpublished, its envelope missing. A copy of the letter is in the Paul Sacher Foundation. The typewriter is the same one used for entries 25-6 and 38. By an English manufacturer, the paper is watermarked: Victory / Extra Strong. Cambridge-Essex had had Entry 27 framed with a rephotograph – slightly cropped at the bottom edge and cut at the upper right hand edge – of a photograph of Stravinsky taken at Carantec in August 1920 where he and his family lived briefly from June to September after arriving in France from Switzerland (see Entry 15); the Cambridge-Essex rephotograph was a slight enlargement of a plate reproduced in 1978.

Stravinsky had earlier tried to interest Janacopolous in learning his orchestral song-cycle, *Le Faune et la bergère,* for her 7 January 1924 performance in Antwerp, but she declined to do so, probably on grounds suggested by Walsh that she would seldom be required to sing it. Reference in Entry 27 to his wish that she perform it during his coming US tour in 1925 is confirmed by his Amsterdam agent, Salomon Bottenheim, manager of the Concertgebouw Orchestra (on whom see Entry 38). In a letter of 29 August 1924 to Arthur Judson, manager of the New York Philharmonic, Bottenheim advises that she is the composer's choice for his US tour. By 16 October 1924, it was clear that she would not be going there. Before his departure, however, she sang with him and also with Mengelberg in Amsterdam on 23 November. In the end, the soprano Greta Torpadie (1890-c. 1970) sang with Stravinsky in New York on 15 and 25 January 1925.

Upon Stravinsky's return to Europe that spring, Janacopulos gave on 19 April at the Augusteo in Rome the Italian premiere of his "Prelude," "Fisherman's Song," and the "Nightingale's Aria" from *Le Rossignol.* Five days later she sang at the Sala Accademica di Santa Cecilia with him conducting the *Three Japanese Lyrics* and *Pribaoutki.* Casella reported that "the public – and Igor Stravinsky – warmly applauded Mme Vera Janacopulos who sang *Pribaoutki* with great intelligence and a voice of rich possibilities, gaining the liveliest success – and one not easily achieved." Five days later at Turin, Casella conducted her in an all-Stravinsky program.

Janacopulos appears in a group photograph (second from right) with, among others, her husband Staal (unbearded) and Stravinsky, taken 2 March 1926 in Amsterdam, probably having sung at a chamber-music concert there with him on 27 February. Vera Sudeykina's engagement diary has her at the Staals (by herself?) in December 1926 and in January, 1927; in March, May, October-November of 1927, Stravinsky was with her. The many visits late in 1927 may well concern another concert, this time led by Milhaud in the Salle Gaveau on 16 December where she sang several works by him including the *Pribaoutki* and, to judge by the announcement of three clarinets in the instrumental ensemble, his *Cat's Cradle Songs,* although they were surely rather low for her. Citing Janacopulos in her London concerts of de Falla's music, 22-23 June 1927, he recalled her in 1935 as "l'excellente cantatrice."

Travelling annually to Brazil, 1933-38, Janacopulos resolved to retire before she was fifty (in 1942). The outbreak of the Second World War frustrating her plans for one final worldwide concert tour before retirement, she instead taught briefly in Paris; after returning to her native Brazil in 1940, she learned that Nazi soldiers had looted her Paris apartment. In Brazil she taught first at São Paulo for eight years and then at Rio de Janeiro until her death there in 1955.

Works Consulted

Colajanni, Anna Rita, et al., ed. *Catalogo critico del fondo Alfredo Casella.* Florence: L.S. Olschki, 1992. vol. 2. pp. 229, P. 91, P. 92.

França, Eurico Nogueira. *Memórias de Vera Janacópulos.* Rio de Janeiro: Ministério da Educaçao e Cultura, 1959. pp. 28, 34, 58.

Macnutt, Richard, Ltd. *Catalogue 112.* Tunbridge Wells, 1983, item 172: nos. 6, 10, 14, 18.

Nicolodi, Fiamma. "Casella e la musica di Stravinsky in Italia. Contributo a un'indagine sul neoclassicismo." *Chigiana* 29-30 (1972-73): n. 1 on pp. 41-2 (trans. Leonard W. Johnson).

Regia Accademia di Santa Cecilia, Annuario 1924-1925. 340-41 (1925): 210-12.

SBu. pp. 31 (2 March 1926), 36-8.

SChron. vol. 2. pp. 79, 99.

SI&V. pl. 80 on p. 67.

SP&D. pl. on p. 223, p. 253.

Walsh, Stephen. *Stravinsky, A Creative Spring: Russia and France, 1882-1934.* New York, NY: Alfred A. Knopf, 1999. pp. 382-3, 401-2, n. 18 on p. 643.

28 (1924). Autographed photograph, 11.5 × 16.9 cm, of Stravinsky seated with the Amar-Hindemith String Quartet (clockwise): Licco Amar, Rudolf Hindemith, Paul Hindemith (standing), and Walter Caspar taken by N.V. Fotocentrale (no. 5943 / Amsterdam) in the small concert hall of the Concertgebouw, 15 November 1924; below his own image inscribed sideways in black ink:

I Strawinsky

Acquisition: H. Colin Slim on 27 October 1997 from La Scala Autographs. Overlapping edges of a small tear below the image of Stravinsky were rejoined with starch paste, and remains of some tape and residues were removed from the reverse side by Linda K. Ogden in December 1997.

Provenance: Kenneth W. Rendell, Inc. (Wellesley, MA, and New York) (marked in pencil: "STRAVINSKY,I SPHOTO [sic] N 4785);" La Scala Autographs and sold to a private customer: apparently Benedikt and Salmon, Record Rarities-Autographs, who offered it in their *Autograph/Book Auction, Catalog no. 19* (San Diego, 27 August 1997), lot 209, p. 16 (illustrated btn pp. 11-12), and from whom La Scala Autographs then repurchased it in 1997.

Commentary

Arriving from Prague on 15 November 1924 in Amsterdam, Stravinsky and Vera attended the quartet's concert at which Stravinsky first met Hindemith. The same image (now in the Paul-Hindemith-Institut, Frankfurt am Main), inscribed by him: "moi avec / le Amar Kwartett [sic] / Amsterdam, Nov. 1924," is published with its quartet members identified in Rexroth's edition of Hindemith's letters.

The quartet was formed in 1921 by Amar (1891-1959) and Hindemith (1895-1963) with his brother Rudolf (1900-74) playing cello and Walter Caspar second violin. Rejoined in 1927 by Maurits Frank (1892-1959) as cellist, the quartet dissolved itself two years later because of Hindemith's burdensome professorial responsibilities in Berlin.

Stravinsky also annotated a similar but differently posed photograph: "moi avec le Amar-Koortett [sic] à Amsterdam, Nov. 1924," in which only he and Rudolf Hindemith (not Maurits Frank) face the camera directly. In both photographs Stravinsky holds gloves and homburg. The quartet played his *Concertino* twice.

During concerts in Holland, he played his *Piano Concerto* with the Concertgebouw Orchestra led by Willem Mengelberg and conducted the orchestra on 23 November during which Vera Janacopulos also sang. A photograph taken that day by Vera Sudeykina shows him wearing homburg and gloves.

For whom and precisely when he inscribed Entry 28 is unknown. On its reverse side is written in ink:

Amsterdam, Concertgebouw, kleine zaal, / Concertgebouw-kammermuziek (III) / Amar-quartett met Strawinsky / als bezoeker 15 November 1924 / Programma: / Quartet van Haydn (?) [sic] / Quartet [no. 11] op. 34 [1924] van Ernst Toch / Concertino [1920] van Strawinsky / (2-maal) / Stryktrio [op. 34; 1924] van Paul Hindemith / Quartet in Es [1813] gr.t. [Quartet] op. 125 No. 1 [Schubert].

A recent listing of this program by Michael Kube omits Toch's quartet and reports Haydn's as his B-flat major, Op. 33, no. 4.

Because inscription must have followed production of the photograph, and because the program and comments on it are written in Dutch, someone probably obtained the photograph during the eight days he spent in Amsterdam and requested him to inscribe it. It is unlikely that it was a quartet member who surely would have recalled which Haydn quartet was played. Below the program in a different hand in ink is: "4 en heer" (four and an important man) and in a still different hand: "Alt-violist: Paul Hindemith."

As the above program suggests, the quartet was known throughout Europe for its expertise in playing contemporary music. Stravinsky and Hindemith remained friends over many years, although in private correspondence with his wife Hindemith was occasionally critical (see the Preliminary Remarks to entries 48-60).

Works Consulted

Briner, Andres, Dieter Rexroth, and Giselher Schubert. *Paul Hindemith. Leben und Werk in Bild und Text*. Zurich: Atlantis, and Mainz: Schott, 1988. pp. 60-4.

Hindemith, Paul. *Briefe*. ed. Dieter Rexroth. Frankfurt am Main: Fischer Taschenbuch, 1982. pp. 100-01, pl. 6.

Kube, Michael. "Am Quartettpult. Paul Hindemith im Rebner- und Amar-Quartett." *Hindemith-Jahrbuch* 21 (1922): 202, no. 470.

SD. p. 102.

SD&D. pp. 50-1, pl. 1 facing p. 112.

SP&D. pp. 250-2.

Stravinsky, Igor, and Craft, Robert. "Some Composers." *Musical America* 82, 6 (June 1962): 8 and pl.

Strobel, Heinrich, ed. *Paul Hindemith. Zeugnis in Bildern*. Mainz: Schott, 1962. pp. 14, 22.

29 (1925). Autographed photograph, 23.6 × 34.6 cm, of Stravinsky at the piano in Aeolian Hall, New York, glued on original mat, 34.0 × 36.0 cm, 9 February 1925, signed by the photographer [Horace] Scandlin at right edge of the mat in pencil: "Scandlin" and inscribed below by Stravinsky in English in black ink, 9 February 1925:

To the Duo-Art Aeolian Organ
with best regards
Igor Strawinsky
New York, 9/II/25

Acquisition: H. Colin Slim in London, June 1981, from Burnett Simeone (at the same time as entries 30 and 81).
Provenance: Unknown.

Commentary

Evidently this particular image taken by Scandlin pleased him. A framed copy of it appears on his piano in a photograph taken in 1927 at his house in Nice and he inscribed another copy of it: "Pour Mr Cesare Barison Igor Strawinsky Nice le 28 I/28" (the latter offered for sale in 1997 by La Scala Autographs).

In 1925, he was in New York for his first American tour, 4 January to 13 March. The Duo-Art company, with which he had signed a seven-year contract the year before, took out a large and laudatory notice about him in the *New York Times* early in January. That month he recorded in New York for the Duo-Art pipe organ "Berceuse" and "Finale" from *The Firebird* and the "chorale" from *Symphonies of Wind Instruments,* their publication being announced the following April.

The hall in Scandlin's photograph is surely the one in New York (not London). Stravinsky had just conducted and played in Aeolian Hall (34 West Forty-Third Street), on 25 January, his *Ragtime, Renard,* and *Octet,* and accompanied the New York soprano, Greta Torpadie, in his *Pastorale,* and in excerpts from *Le Rossignol, Cat's Cradle Songs,* and his *Children's Stories.*

Identified as Aeolian Hall, the same building appears in another signed photograph of Stravinsky at the piano: "New York / Janvier 1925." This January photograph also appears in the April *Vanity Fair,* there identifying the photographer as Horace Scandlin. The hall was already famous for the premiere of George Gershwin's *Rhapsody in Blue* the year before Stravinsky arrived. He met Gershwin (1898-1937) at an evening party on 7 January 1925 hosted by mutual friends, Paul and Zozia Kochanski, again the following evening at a party given by Mary Hoyt ("Hoytie") Wiborg after his first Carnegie Hall concert, and once again the following morning in his hotel room.

Works Consulted

Hoover, Cynthia Adams. "Aeolian Co." NG. vol. 1. p. 115.

Jablonski, Edward. *Gershwin. A Biography.* New York, NY: Doubleday, 1987; repr. 1998. pp. 92-4, pl. 7 btn pp. 102-3.

Lawson, Rex. "Stravinsky and the Pianola." in *Confronting Stravinsky: Man, Musician, and Modernist.* ed. Jann Pasler. Berkeley and Los Angeles, CA, and London: University of California Press, 1986. p. 301, nos. 1-4, 11-12.

New York Times. 7 January 1925. p. 12.

Peyser, Joan. *The Memory of All That. The Life of George Gershwin.* New York, NY: Simon and Schuster, 1993. pp. 96-7 (the occasion cited for 7 January is incorrect).

SBu. pl. 21 on p. 28, pl. 33 on p. 39.

SD. p. 101.

SD&D. p. 49.

SP&D. pp. 165, 253, n. 274 on pp. 622-3.

SSC. vol. 2. p. 262.

Stravinsky, Igor, and Craft, Robert. "Some Composers." *Musical America* 82, 6 (June 1962): 6.

Stuart, Philip. *Igor Stravinsky – The Composer in the Recording Studio. A Comprehensive Discography.* New York, NY, Westport, CT, London: Greenwood Press, 1991. pp. 4-5, 26, nos. 2-5.

Thomson, Virgil. "How Modern Music Gets That Way. Some Notes on Stravinsky, Schoenberg, and Satie, as Representative Moderns." *Vanity Fair* 24, 2 (April 1925): pl. on p. 46.

"Torpadie, Greta." *Musical Americans. A Biographical Dictionary 1918-1926.* ed. Mary DuPree. Berkeley, CA: Fallen Leaf Press, 1997. p. 184.

Walsh, Stephen. *Stravinsky, A Creative Spring: Russia and France, 1882-1934.* New York, NY: Alfred A. Knopf, 1999. pp. 399-408.

30

(1925). Autograph twice-folded letter, 21.3 × 13.9 cm, in French in green ink on Hotel Sherman Chicago stationery, 25 February 1925, to Dr. A[braham Leon] Garbat (1885-1968):

D^{eur} A. Garbat
New York

Profondément touché de votre bonne lettre, je vous envoie,
mon cher Docteur mes souvenirs les meilleurs
    Votre bien reconnaissant
    Igor Strawinsky
    25/II/25

Dr. A. Garbat   Chicago
New York   25 February 1925

Deeply touched by your good letter, I send you, my dear Doctor,
my best regards,
    Yours very gratefully,
    Igor Strawinsky

Acquisition: H. Colin Slim on 17 June 1981 from Burnett Simeone,
Catalogue No. 3 (London, 1981), item 278.
Provenance: Unknown.

Commentary

The letter is unpublished, its envelope missing. Arriving in Chicago on
Tuesday morning 17 February 1925, Stravinsky conducted the
Chicago Symphony Orchestra there on 20 and 21 February, sharing the
podium with Frederick Stock. (Formerly at Randolph and Clark, the
Hotel Sherman no longer exists.)

Polish-born Dr. Abraham Leon Garbat was Stravinsky's New York
physician from 1925 until at least 1945. Entry 30 suggests that Garbat
offered some treatment while he was in New York. They were
probably introduced through mutual friends in New York, the violinist

Paul Kochanski (1887-1934) or perhaps George Gershwin (see entries 29 and 35).

Works Consulted

Schulson, David. *Autographs. [Catalog] 94.* New York, May 1998, item 40.

SBu. pp. 114 (20 May 1940), 132 (30 January 1945).

SSC. vol. 2. n. 2 on p. 293.

Walsh, Stephen. *Stravinsky, A Creative Spring: Russia and France, 1882-1934.* New York, NY: Alfred A. Knopf, 1999. p. 408.

31

(1925). Autograph twice-folded letter, 16.5 × 26.0 cm, in French in black ink on opposite sides and sectors of a doubled sheet of Langdon Hotel stationery, 13 March 1925, to Steinway and Sons. Above and to the right of the printed logo – L / THE LANGDON / 2 East 56th St. / New York – Stravinsky wrote:

13/III/25
Steinway Sohns
New York City

Chers Messieurs,
En quittant l'Amérique après deux mois de tournée artistique, je tiens à vous dire ma grande reconaisssance pour les extraordinaires instruments que vous avéz mis à ma disposition. [page 2] Je ne savrai vous dire combien j'en apprécie leurs qualités extraordinairs et je me joint sans reserve aux opinions des grand artistes d'aujourd'hui et d'autrefois qui tous également appréciaient hautement leurs valeur
    Croyez moi, Chers Messieurs votre bien devoué
    Igor Strawinsky

Steinway [&] Sons New York
New York 13 March 1925

Dear Sirs:
Upon leaving America after two months of concert touring, I must tell you of my great gratitude for the extraordinary instruments you have placed at my disposal. I hardly know how to tell you how much I appreciate their extraordinary qualities and I agree entirely with the opinions of great artists of the present and the past who all likewise highly esteem their worth.

Very sincerely yours,
Igor Strawinsky

Acquisition: H. Colin Slim on 5 August 1997 from La Scala Autographs. A small tear at the upper left corner from a staple was mended by Linda K. Ogden on 15 September 1997.

Provenance: Swann Galleries, Inc. (104 East 25th Street / New York), *Autographs ... featuring letters of endorsement from the Steinway Family Archives ... Public Auction Sale 1760* (New York, 3 June 1997), lot 226: bought by La Scala Autographs. (The Swann 1997 sale encompassed 23 lots sent 1856-1953 to the Steinways; another and similar letter of endorsement in 1925 by George Gershwin sold at Swann on 10 February 2000.)

Commentary

The letter is unpublished, its envelope missing. A week after arriving in New York, Stravinsky was joined by many other musicians in Old Steinway Hall for a reception given in his honour on 11 January 1925 by Frederic T. Steinway; this reception was one commemorated by Stravinsky's own inscribed copy of a photograph of the occasion. The Steinway Company put at his disposal some eighteen different pianos for his various concerts. He wrote Entry 31 for this firm the day before he sailed for France on the *S.S. Acquitania,* having appeared as pianist and/or conductor in New York, Boston, Chicago, Detroit, Cincinnati, Philadelphia, and Cleveland.

A decade later Steinway placed an advertisement in the program for concerts by the Los Angeles Philharmonic which he led there on 21-22

February. It reads: "Igor Stravinsky famous composer says 'Steinway and Sons' matchless instruments have inspired and aided me by their gorgeously rich and responsive qualities'."

Works Consulted

Philharmonic Orchestra of Los Angeles. Symphony Magazine. 21-22 February 1935. p. 238.

SBu. pl. 20 on p. 27.

SE&D. (1962): pl. 10 facing p. 73; (1981): pl. 9.

Swann Galleries Inc. *The Trumpet, an occasional newsletter* 14, 3 (Spring/ Summer 2000): 2.

Walsh, Stephen. *Stravinsky, A Creative Spring: Russia and France, 1882-1934.* New York, NY: Alfred A. Knopf, 1999. p. 401.

32 (1925). Autograph single-page two-sided letter, 17.8 × 22.7 cm, folded twice, in French in black ink, sent from Nice (or nearby), 21 August 1925, to unnamed friends presumably living on the French Riviera:

le vendredi
21/VIII/25

Mes Chers Amis,

Dites moi si votre choffeur connais quelqu'un comme mécanicien pour ma voiture – mon choffeur me quitte dans une huitaine et je reste sans pouvoir bouger ce qui est emmerdant.

Il me faut quelqu'un de toute confiance et qui pourrait se loger en face de chez moi en pension – le mien ne peut plus rester chez moi à cause qu'il loge trop loin de chez moi à Nice ce qui fait que pour [reverse] tous les repas il est obliger de rentrer chez lui. Je paye 800 net (je ne le nourris pas et je ne loge pas) – si je sort pour 1 journée entière ou plusieurs jours il reçoit en plus 25 fr par jour et il s'arrange pour la nourriture et le logement lui-même.

Nous avons tellement regretté l'autre jour de ne pas vous avoir trouvé. Il me semblait que le rendez-vous était fixé chez Picasso; c'est vous qui m'aviez donné son l'adresse.

Mille choses très sincères et très amicales de votre
Igor Strawinsky

Nice [?]
Friday 21 August 1925

My dear friends:
Let me know if your chauffeur knows someone who could drive my car – my chauffeur quits in a week and I'm stuck here, which is extremely annoying.

I need someone perfectly reliable who could board and room across the street from me – my man can no longer work for me because he lives too far away from me at Nice, which means that for every meal he has to go home. I pay 800 [francs] net (I don't feed or house him) – if I leave for an entire day or for several days he gets 25 francs extra per day, and he himself takes care of his food and lodging.

We were extremely sorry at not finding you the other day. I thought the meeting was set for Picasso's place; it's you who gave me his address.

A thousand very sincere and friendly regards from your
Igor Strawinsky

Acquisition: H. Colin Slim on 30 June 1998 from La Scala Autographs. Tears at the end of each crease were repaired with Japanese paper and rice starch paste by Linda K. Ogden on 8 September 1998.
Provenance: Florence Arnaud, Autographes-Dessins (10, rue de Saintonge / 75003 / Paris), accompanied by an export certificate, 1 May 1998, from the Ministère de la culture et de la communication.

Commentary
The letter, unpublished, lacks its envelope which surely contained the names and location of its addressees and the place from which Stravinsky mailed it. These addressees are not easily identified, owing to

the loss of Vera Sudeykina's diary for 1925 and of all correspondence between her and Stravinsky for that year.

Stravinsky had moved his family from Biarritz to Nice at the Villa des Roses, 167 boulevard Carnot, Montboron, in late September 1924. Financial successes of his 1925 winter concert tour in the US enabled him not only to purchase an automobile but also to employ a Parisian chauffeur then living in Nice, whom he had hired on 21 July and about whom he had boasted in a letter of 29 July written from that city.

Back home from the US at Nice with his family on 7 April, Stravinsky was to take frequent one-day automobile trips with summer guests along the Riviera during August as well as longer ones that month. Occasionally Vera drove, Stravinsky not receiving his driver's licence until 25 December.

Presumably it is the excursion mentioned in Entry 32 to which his niece Tanya refers in her letter of 22-23 August 1925: "Three days ago Uncle left for Marseilles, taking with him aunt Katya, Fedya, and Mika. From Marseille they went to Aix where they spent a second night, stopping briefly at Toulon on the way back. They returned yesterday evening." In late August he apparently remained home – composing, swimming, practising the piano, and dealing with a blackmail attempt by a former valet employed on his US tour. The day after writing Entry 32, he had dinner at home in Nice with Jean Cocteau who was living in nearby Villefranche-sur-Mer.

Evidently a previous mention to Stravinsky of Picasso's address by the recipients of Entry 32 cannot have been the artist's residence at Paris in the rue La Boëtie, one which Stravinsky well knew. The reference is instead to one among the changing summer addresses of Picasso: in 1925 it was Juan-les-Pins, where he and Olga also vacationed in 1920 and 1923-26. An undated photograph variously cited as 1925, 1926 and 1927 – but probably taken by Vera in the summer of 1925 – depicts Cocteau, Picasso, Stravinsky, and Olga at Juan-les-Pins. In this photograph the sweater, trousers, and shoes Stravinsky wears are identical to other photographs securely documented at Monte Carlo and Venice in August and September 1925, clothing not worn by him in pictures taken in the summers of 1926 and 1927.

Concerning the identity of the "chers amis" who had a chauffeur in Entry 32, two couples seem possible, both of whom then maintained villas on the Riviera. The American painter Gerald Murphy (1888-1964) and his wife Sara (1883-1975) arrived in Paris in September 1921. They were perhaps introduced to Stravinsky in Paris by Sara's sister, Mary Hoyt "Hoytie" Wiborg (1887-1964). She had feted him in New York in January 1925 and Vera later mentions visiting her three times with Stravinsky at London in June 1927 and again at Cincinnati in November 1940. And on 9 February 1946 they attended a dinner party in New York with Gerald Murphy. Early in the 1960s, Stravinsky reported: "The Murphys were among the first Americans I ever met" (perhaps forgetting C. Stanley Wise at Clarens in 1915: see Entry 10).

At any rate, both Murphys attended a rehearsal of *Renard* early in May 1922 (at which he berated the choreographer, Bronislava Nijinska). Soon the Murphys were close friends. A collation of excerpts published from Vera Sudeykina's diary for 23 February and 22 March 1923 with documents about the Murphys reveals attendance by both couples at plays, premieres, and parties. Murphy not only helped paint sets for *Les Noces,* but he and his wife attended all ten rehearsals before its premiere on 13 June. In Paris on Sunday 1 July (*not* 17 June), they gave a party – among their guests were Picasso and Cocteau – for Stravinsky on a converted barge in the Seine to celebrate *Les Noces.* Vera's diary records having supper on Murphy's boat that evening and he preserved his invitation to the party. Later that same summer the Murphys vacationed on the Riviera, renting a villa at Antibes where Picasso and Olga stayed with them.

By July 1925, the Murphys were living at Antibes in their own place they called "Villa America," remaining there most of that summer before returning to Paris late in September. Picasso rented a villa in 1925 at Juan-les-Pins, on the northern side of Antibes, a short drive from Nice where Stravinsky lived. Sara no longer driving, the Murphy's employed at their villa an automobile mechanic and chauffeur called Albert, to whom "votre choffeur" in Entry 32 may allude.

Another close Parisian friend of the composer from the mid-1920s was Count Guy de Matharel (d. 1944) and his wife Rosette. They owned the Villa Isthmia at Cap Brun in Toulon which he had already visited in May 1925. Stephen Walsh believes they too employed a chauffeur, although a decade later Vera described Rosette as "penniless" and Guy as earning nothing. It was probably one or the other of these couples who gave Stravinsky Picasso's summer address in 1925 at Juan-Les-Pins and who for some reason failed to show up.

Works Consulted

La Scala Autographs, *Spring 2000 Catalogue*. no. 98 (1925 Venice photograph).

Lesure, François. *Igor Stravinsky. La carrière européenne*. Paris: Musée d'Art Moderne, 1980. p. 76, no. 235.

Miller, Linda Patterson, ed. *Letters from the Lost Generation*. New Brunswick, NJ, and London: Rutgers University Press, 1991. pp. 13-14.

Rubin, William, ed. *Pablo Picasso: A Retrospective*. New York, NY: Museum of Modern Art, 1980. pp. 222, 225, 249-53.

Stravinskaya, Kseniya Yuryevna. *O I.F. Stravinskom i evo blizkikh*. [I.F. Stravinsky and his intimates.] Leningrad: Muzïka, 1978. p. 67.

SBu. pp. 18, 26 (1 March 1925), n. 1 on p. 31, n. 11 on p. 36, p. 38 (27 October 1927), p. 77 (October 1935), p. 117 (22 November 1940), p. 136 (9 February 1946).

SI&V. pl. 77 on p. 66, pl. 87 on p. 69.

SM&C. (1960): pl. facing p. 120 [as 1926]; (1981): pl. 19.

SP&D. pl. on p. 271 [as 1925], p. 454, n. 260 on p. 621.

SSC. vol. 2. pp. 480-1; vol. 3. p. 89.

Tompkins, Calvin. "Living Well is the Best Revenge." *The New Yorker* 38 (28 July 1962): 32.

Vaill, Amanda. *Everybody Was So Young: Gerald and Sara Murphy, A Lost Generation Love Story*. Boston and New York, NY: Houghton Mifflin, 1998. pp. 107, 110-13, 117-18, 160.

Walsh, Stephen. *Stravinsky, A Creative Spring: Russia and France, 1882-1934*. New York, NY: Alfred A. Knopf, 1999. pp. 411, 414, 418.

33

(c. 1925). Etching (said to be after Théodore Stravinsky) entitled at left "IGOR STRAVINSKY," 35.0 × 18.0 cm, marked "No. 40" at lower right corner in pencil by the engraver who signed in pencil "M. Amiguet" below at the lower right on the same sheet bearing the etching.

Acquisition: by kind gift to H. Colin Slim on 9 April 1979 from the late Professors Howard Mayer Brown and Roger W. Weiss of Chicago, who purchased it from Wurlitzer-Bruck in 1979.
Provenance: Unknown.

Commentary

Marcel Amiguet was a Swiss sculptor, active at Paris in the 1920s, who made a series of fourteen such etchings of composers, including Ravel and Schmitt. A reproduction of Entry 33 (said to be from the André Meyer collection) is called in Robert Siohan's 1959 book on Stravinsky a "dessin" by Théodore Stravinsky, although its later English edition has no such attribution.

Stravinsky's niece, Tanya, remarked in 1925 about Théodore's paintings of his parents and of Cocteau that year as having an "elongated" style. Théodore, however, often portrayed his father – in 1915, 1917, 1929, 1932, and in later years – and not always in this style. Whether or not the model for Entry 33 was drawn by Théodore, and for what it is worth, Stravinsky first appears wearing a tie with double stripes in photographs of 1924. Entry 33 is framed with Entry 20.

Works Consulted

Bischoff, Luc. "Le peintre Théodore Strawinsky." *Cahiers de Belgique* 3, 10 (December 1930): 339-43.

Hucher, Yves. *Florent Schmitt*. Paris: Plon, 1953. [270] Iconographie.

Lesure, François. *Igor Stravinsky. La carrière européenne*. Paris: Musée d'Art Moderne, 1980. pl. 10 on p. 12, and nos. 132-3, 142.

Musical America 41, 14 (24 January 1925): cover.

Schaeffner, André. *Strawinsky*. Paris: Les Éditions Rieder, 1931. pls. XLVIII, no. 2 and LVIII (misdated as 1929).

Siohan, Robert. *Stravinsky*. Paris: Éditions du Seuil, 1959. pl. on p. 168 (sub 1924), and [189]; ed. and trans. Eric Walter White. London: Calder and Boyars, 1965; repr. New York, NY: Grossman, 1970. pl. on p. 164 (sub 1924).

SP&RK. vol. 1. p. 415; vol. 2. p. 767 (index: F.I. Stravinsky).

Stravinskaya, Kseniya Yuryevna. *O I.F. Stravinskom i evo blizkikh.* [I.F. Stravinsky and his intimates.] Leningrad: Muzïka, 1978. pp. 54-6 (letter of 16-18 June 1925) and pls. on pp. 70, 72-3.

Strawinsky. Sein Nachlass. Sein Bild [with] *Katalog der ausgestellten Bildnisse und Entwürfe für die Ausstattung seiner Bühnenwerke*. Basle: Kunstmuseum and Paul Sacher Stiftung, 1984. pl. on p. [13]; *Katalog,* no. 155.

Walsh, Stephen. *Stravinsky, A Creative Spring: Russia and France, 1882-1934*. New York, NY: Alfred A. Knopf, 1999. pp. 412, 491-2.

34

(1926). Autograph picture postcard, 8.7 × 13.6 cm, reproducing a photograph, 13.6 × 8.7 cm, taken by Erik Satie of Claude Debussy and Stravinsky, autograph identification and date of 1912 in French in black ink, 1 May 1926, to Princesse Edmond de Polignac (1865-1943):

[crossed out in ink] Princesse
[crossed out in ink] Edm. de Polignac
[crossed out in ink] 43 avenue Henri Marten
[crossed out twice in ink] Palazzo Polignac
[crossed out twice in ink] Venezia
[crossed out twice in ink] Italia
[in a different hand] Paris
France

Nice, le
1 Mai
1926

Ma très chère, grand Amie, – heureux d'avoir votre gentil mot.
– Je vais très probablement pour tout le moi de mai à Milan
pour conduire à la Scala "Petrouchka" et "Le Rossignol,"
Toscanini tombé malade. J'espère vous voir à Paris fin mai-
commencement juin – De tout [upside down at top] coeur
votre
   I Strawinsky

[reverse]
[below photograph] Debussy et moi chez lui
(Av. du Bois) en 1912.

Princess Edmond de Polignac	Nice
Venice and Paris	1 May 1926

My very dear great friend:
Happy to have your kind note. I am very probably going for
the whole month of May to Milan to conduct *Petrushka* and *The*

Nightingale at La Scala, Toscanini having fallen ill. I hope to see you in Paris at the end of May, beginning of June.

Yours affectionately,

I. Strawinsky

[reverse] Debussy and I at his home (avenue du Bois) in 1912.

Acquisition: H. Colin Slim on 11 December 1997 from La Scala Autographs.
Provenance: Undisclosed collector/dealer, England. Below the stamps are dealer markings in pencil: "*1533* ... Z27" and some erased pencil markings: "Mettre dans ..."

Commentary

The postcard's text is unpublished. At some point, Stravinsky changed his mind about the destination of Entry 34: he cancelled with double lines only Palazzo Polignac, Venezia, and Italia and then squeezed in 43 Henry-Marten. Cancelling the entire address in blue ink, a later hand readdressed it to Paris / France. Her Paris address was apparently not 43, but 57, avenue Henri-Martin.

Princesse Edmond de Polignac (née Winnaretta Singer) was a major patroness of Stravinsky from 1912. She commissioned *Renard* (1916) and he dedicated his piano *Sonate* (1924) to her. She is pictured in 1925 with him in Venice and with him and Artur Rubinstein that year at her Palazzo Zaffo Contarini.

Toscanini's illness – referred to in Entry 34 – was feigned and diplomatic in order to avoid confronting Mussolini. Stravinsky conducted *Petrushka* in Milan on 9 and 12 May 1926. On the 14th he led his opera, *Le Rossignol,* there, as a La Scala poster announces.

Stravinsky variously recorded the date of the photograph of Debussy and himself as 1910, 1911, 1912, and 1913. At some time on the envelope containing the broken glass negative, he inscribed: "Negativ Debussy-Stravinsky 1910 Paris 80 Av. du Bois chez Debussy." On a slip of paper he also wrote: "Debussy-Stravinsky / 1910 / Paris 80 Av. du Bois / chez Debussy." Following the premiere of *The Firebird* (25 June 1910), Debussy invited him to dine and apparently he did so. Whether Satie was then also present is unknown. (Craft states that Satie was indeed there and photographed Stravinsky and Debussy together.) Stravinsky recalled in 1962, however, that shortly after the premiere of *Petrushka* (13 June 1911), he had lunch with Debussy at his home. After lunch they were joined by Satie whom Stravinsky photographed with Debussy; Satie then photographed him with Debussy. Moreover, in responding on 8 December 1962 to an enquiry from Ginny Carpenter Hill – daughter of Stravinsky's composer-friend, John Alden Carpenter (1876-1951) – he again recalled the date as 1911: "*Trouve* your letter with the photo (I with Debussy 1911)."

In 1959, though, Stravinsky hinted that the date of the photograph might be 1913: "I met [Satie] in 1913, I believe; at any rate, I photographed him with Debussy in that year." The first edition of Debussy's letters assigns the photograph to Satie in 1910, but its re-edited translation places it among letters of 1912 and between other plates of 1911 and 1913. Entry 34 was dated "1912" only some thirteen to sixteen years after the photograph was taken and this date, perhaps, deserves some authority. Walsh reproduces the image from the Sacher Foundation as "probably 1912."

Works Consulted

Brooks, Jeanice. "Nadia Boulanger and the Salon of the Princesse de Polignac." JAMS 46 (1993): 421-68.

Carpenter, John Alden. Papers. Box 1, folder S. The Newberry Library, Chicago.

Cossart, Michael de. *The Food of Love: Princesse Edmond de Polignac (1865-1943) and Her Salon*. London: Hamish Hamilton, 1978. pp. 147, 194, 206, and pl. 11a.

Craft, Robert. "Catalog of the Library of Robert Craft." Typescript: Library of Congress, Music Division. XII: Photographs, p. 213 (envelopes inscribed by Stravinsky containing negatives), no. 1.

–. Booklet accompanying *Stravinsky The Composer*, vol. IX, *The Firebird,* Music Masters CD 0612-67177-2. Oakhurst, NJ: 1997. p. 8.

Debussy, Claude. *Lettres 1884-1918*. ed. François Lesure. Paris: Hermann, 1980. pl. on p. 267, p. 291 (as 1910); *Debussy Letters*. ed. and trans. François Lesure and Roger Nichols. Cambridge: Harvard University Press, 1987. [257], pl. 32.

Lesure, François. *Igor Stravinsky. La carrière européenne*. Paris: Musée d'Art Moderne, 1980. p. 35, no. 100 (as 1910).

SBu. pl. 25 on p. 29, p. 31 (9 May 1926).

SConv. p. 75.

SE&D. (1962): pp. 149, 157-8; (1981): pp. 130-1, 138.

SI&V. pl. 24 on p. [37] (as 1910).

SP&D. pl. on p. 258, p. 262.

SP&RK. vol. 1. p. 518 (index: Debussy); vol. 2. p. 744 (index: Debussy); pp. 760 and 764 (index: Polignac, Satie).

Vlad, Roman. "L'architettura di un capolavoro: ancora sulla 'Sagra della primavera' III." *Nuova rivista musicale italiana* 33 (1999): 497 (as June 1911).

Walsh, Stephen. *Stravinsky, A Creative Spring: Russia and France, 1882-1934.* New York, NY: Alfred A. Knopf, 1999. pp. 429-30; lower pl. facing p. 364.

35

(1926). Autograph picture postcard, 8.9 × 13.5 cm, in French and Russian in black ink, 8 September 1926, postmarked: NICE PL. GR. ALPES [MARITIMES] 12.4[5] 9-[9] 26 NICE UN COIN DU PARADIS TERRESTIAL (i.e., 12:45 a.m., 9 September 1926, some of the date and place being obliterated). The face of the card probably depicts an Austrian hotel. Its other side is addressed to Paul Kochanski (1887-1934):

M^eur^ Paul Kochanski
Hôtel d'Angleterre
St Jean de Luz
(B^asses^ Pyr.)

[two printed lines crossed out in ink at upper left]
S ... / B[ad?] ... O[Schoenau?] ... N.[ieder] Oe.[sterreich]

Nice, le 8 Sept
1926

Dorogoi Pavlusha
Oba tvoi milye pis'ma i posylku-korrekturu poluchil. Spasibo. Ya, esli Bogu ugodno budet, priyedu v Parizh v to vremya kogda ty budesh tam – t.e. chisla 20^go^. Do skorogo, nadeyus', svidaniya. Tseluyu Vas oboikh.
 Tvoi I Stravinskii

Mr. Paul Kochanski   Nice
St-Jean-de-Luz   8 September 1926

Dear Pavlushka:
I received both of your nice letters and your package – galley proofs.
Thank you. I, if God wills it, will arrive in Paris when you are there
– i.e., on the 20th. So I hope soon to have a rendezvous. I kiss you
both.
    Thine, I Stravinsky

Acquisition: H. Colin Slim on 19 October 1995 from David Schulson
Autographs (11 East 68th Street / New York / 10021) through Martin
A. Silver.
Provenance: From a group of Kochanski items owned, c. 1988, by an
unidentified New York dealer (possibly Lion Heart Autographs, Inc.
[470 Park Avenue South / New York], which in October 1997 owned
a 1925 letter from Stravinsky to Kochanski and an undated one
mentioning the dedication of the *Pulcinella Suite* to him).

Commentary

The postcard's text is unpublished. Manufactured by "Kilophoto/
Wien," its face shows a large hotel in a hilly, park-like setting. To judge
from "N. Oe." (Nieder Oesterreich) on the card, from the manufacturer's mark, and from the hotel's architecture, the hotel is Austrian
and probably located in the environs of Vienna. Stravinsky's purchase of
this postcard may stem from the three-week concert tour he took in
March 1926, visiting Budapest, Vienna, and Zagreb. Two days before
mailing Entry 35, he finished sketching Act I of *Oedipus Rex* at Nice –
167, boulevard Carnot, where he had moved his family in September
1924 from Biarritz. I am indebted to Stanislav Shvabrin and Michael
Green for the transliteration and translation.

    Using the diminutive "Pavlushka" betokens affection. Paul
Kochanski, a Polish violinist and professor of violin at the Imperial
Conservatory in St. Petersburg, 1913-15, taught from 1921 at the
Juilliard School. He and his wife were introduced to Stravinsky in June
1914 by Artur Rubinstein in London. Kochanski was waiting on the
dock on 4 January 1925 when Stravinsky first arrived in New York.
Three days later he met George Gershwin in Kochanski's New York

apartment, a photograph surviving of Stravinsky and Kochanski from this period (see Entry 29). After he returned to Nice, he sent Kochanski and his wife a letter containing a New Year's greeting, which also thanked them for their help on his first visit to New York.

Shortly before sending Entry 35, he and Vera Sudeykina had dined three times in June and July with the Kochanski's in Paris. In fact, Stravinsky did not arrive there in September from Nice until the 21st, a day later than he had hoped for.

A five-movement suite from *Pulcinella,* completed on 24 August 1925, for violin and piano was intended for Kochanski. (Sketches of one movement read: "I Stravinsky à Paul Kohansky, London 1921.") An undated letter (c. 20 August 1925) in Russian from Stravinsky to Kochanski sets out the dedication to him in French and announces that the work will be completed tomorrow or the next day. The Library of Congress owns both the autograph with his instructions to insert the dedication to Kochanski, and a set of proofs from the first engraving, RMV 428. In response to a question on 16 May 1967 from an orchestra violinist of the Toronto Symphony, Stravinsky replied: "I played [it] with Kochanski only once, many times with [Samuel] Dushkin."

Although the *Pulcinella* suite is surely the subject of "the galley proofs" in Entry 35, it was premiered not by Kochanski but by Alma Moodie and Stravinsky at Winterthur on 12 November 1925. Kochanski wrote on 14 September 1925 to thank Stravinsky for the dedication of the *Pulcinella* suite to him, indicating that he liked the fingerings. Already by October, in writing to Werner Reinhart, Stravinsky had refused to extend exclusivity for Mlle Moodie beyond 1 June 1926, for the reason that Kohanski, who had learned the suite with Stravinsky, also wanted to perform it when he came back from the United States (SSC, vol. 3, p. 160). When published in 1926, the suite was dedicated to Kochanski, Stravinsky perhaps having interrupted his work on *Oedipus Rex* to read these proofs.

Late in 1926 he finished arranging for violin and piano the "Prelude" and the "Ronde des Princesses" from *The Firebird,* "dedié à Paul Kochanski," with editing by Kochanski. Since he did not begin them until after 1 November and sent them with the "Berceuse" to his publisher on 23 December, the "galley proofs" mentioned in Entry 35 cannot refer to these *Firebird* arrangements. All three were published in

1929 and dedicated to Kochanski. Stravinsky also dedicated to him in 1934 a new version of the 1925 *Pulcinella* suite. A photograph taken at Paris in the 1930s shows Kochanski holding his violin with Prokofiev seated at the piano.

Reference to "both of your nice letters" is to Russian letters in the Paul Sacher Foundation of 30 August and 3 September 1926 sent from St. Jean de Luz to Stravinsky at Nice. "I kiss you both" includes Kochanski's wife, Zosia. Just before Kochanski's death in the US and for many years thereafter, Zosia was close friends with Vera and Stravinsky.

Works Consulted

Cahoon, Herbert, ed. *The Mary Flagler Cary Music Collection. The Pierpont Morgan Library*. New York, NY: Pierpont Morgan Library, 1970. p. 48, no. 202.

Craft, Robert. "Catalog of the Library of Robert Craft." Typescript: Library of Congress, Music Division. IV: Proofs, no. 10.

Duke, Vernon. *Passport to Paris*. Boston, MA, and Toronto, ON: Little, Brown, 1955. pl. btn pp. 246-7.

Hanuszewska, Mieczyslawa. "Kochanski, Pawel." NG. vol. 10. p. 134.

Joseph, Charles M. *Stravinsky and the Piano*. Ann Arbor, MI: University of Michigan Research Press, 1983. pp. 196-7 and pl. 15.

—. "Stravinsky Manuscripts in the Library of Congress and The Pierpont Morgan Library." *Journal of Musicology* 1 (1982): 336, no. 34 and 337, no. 6.

Shepard, John. "The Stravinsky *Nachlass*: A Provisional Checklist of Music Manuscripts." *Music Library Association Notes* 40 (June 1984): 738.

Sotheby's, *Fine Printed and Manuscript Music* (17 May 1990), lot 294.

Stargardt, J.A. *Katalog 670*. Berlin, 7-8 July 1998, lot 997. p. 378 (DM 1200).

SBu. pp. 31, 51, 114, 118, 123, 132, 161.

SD. p. 101.

SD&D. p. 49.

SP&D. p. 122, n. 205 on p. 616.

SP&RK. vol. 1. pp. 494-5, no. 21 (1-2); vol. 2. n. 2 on p. 491, pp. 707-8, no. 55 (2, 4).

SSC. vol. 1. n. 180 on p. 185; vol. 2. nn. 2 and 5 on p. 293; vol. 3. p. 160.

Stravinsky, Igor, and Craft, Robert. "Some Composers." *Musical America* 82, 6 (June 1962): 6.

"Stravinsky Pays Tribute to Kochanski's Art with Promise of Violin Work." *Musical America* 41 (18 April 1925): 33.

"Stravinsky at 85." Canadian Broadcasting Corporation. Toronto, 16 May 1967. Telecast.

Walsh, Stephen. *Stravinsky, A Creative Spring: Russia and France, 1882-1934.* New York, NY: Alfred A. Knopf, 1999. pp. 399, 404.

White, Eric Walter. *Stravinsky: The Composer and His Works.* 2nd ed. Berkeley and Los Angeles, CA: University of California Press, 1979; repr. 1984. p. 609, App. C, no. 48a.

36

(1927). Autograph singly folded express letter on tan serrated paper, 11.2 × 14.2 cm, in Russian in black ink, half the reverse side forming its envelope with typed address in French, postmarked Nice 19.00 [p.m.] 24.1 1927, 24 January 1927, to Arthur Lvovitch Rabeneck (c. 1900-52):

[typed] Monsieur A-L. Rabeneck
S.A.des Gr.Ed.Musicales
22 Rue d'Anjou
PARIS,8°

[typed] I67,Brd.Carnot,Nice,
le 24 janv./27

Mnogouvazhayemyi Artur L'vovich,
Uyekhal-li v Germaniyu Gavri. Greg.? Dumayu chto da, t[a]k
zhe k[a]k dumayu, chto on zabyl prislat' mne tol'ko chto
vyshedshii Chant du Ross. v 2 ruki. Sdelaite eto pozhaluista za
nego i skazhite, kogda ia poluchu korrekturu moyego nov.
sochineniya. Bud'te dobry dostat' mne tetradku s V-Cell'nymi
su[i]tami Bakha po prilagayemoi zapisochke. Spasibo zaraneye.
  Iskrenne uvazhayushchii Vas I Stravinskii

Arthur Rabeneck
Paris

Nice
24 January 1927

Much respected Arthur Lvovitch:

Has Gavri[yil] Greg[orievich Païchadze] left for Germany? I think so, but I also think that he has forgotten to send me *Chant du Ross.* for [piano] two hands which has just appeared. Do this, please, in his place and tell me when I shall receive the proofs for my new work. Be good enough to obtain for me the cahier with the Bach V-Cell' [sic] suites, according to the little note attached here. Thanks in advance.

    Sincerely respecting you, I Strawinsky

Acquisition: H. Colin Slim on 3 April 1998 from La Scala Autographs. *Provenance:* Saggiori, Geneva, c. October 1997, lot 325.

Commentary

The letter is unpublished; there is no trace of the attached little note mentioned in the text. Dr. Slim is indebted to Stanislav Shvabrin and Michael Green for the transliteration and translation.

    Arthur Lviov Rabeneck was the assistant to Gavriyil Gregorievich Païchadze (1881-1976), director in Paris, 1926-46, of the Édition russe de musique founded by Serge and Nadia Koussevitsky in 1909. Païchadze was a major correspondent. At least two photographs show Païchadze with Stravinsky and Koussevitsky: one taken at Combloux in 1928 including Prokofiev, and another taken c. 1937 in France with family members of both Stravinsky and Koussevitsky. Writing to Stravinsky in 1952, Nicolas Nabokov characterized Rabeneck as "brilliant and wise."

    Entrusted to Jacques Larmanjat in 1924, the piano reduction of "Chant du Ross" – i.e., *Le Chant du Rossignol* – was indeed published by the Édition russe at the beginning of 1927 (see entries 51 and 62).

    The "new work" being engraved was probably Act I of *Oedipus Rex* for which he received proofs shortly before 10 February 1927. It might also have been his *Pater Noster* (not published until 1932) because, on 17 October 1926, he wrote Païchadze: "I am waiting to send my *Pater Noster* in order to make a piano reduction which it lacks" (SP&D, n. 18 on p. 628).

Although the "little note attached here" (probably an advertisement) does not survive, the edition of Bach's cello suites that he requested was probably the facsimile of the six suites by Diran Alexanian, published at Paris in 1927 by Francis Salabert. (This music is not, however, in the Paul Sacher Foundation.) In 1931, André Schaeffner, who probably had it confirmed from the composer himself, twice observed: "un passage de la variation d'Apollon, elle-même inspirée par les Suites pour violoncelle de J.-S. Bach" and "A l'époque d'*Apollon,* Strawinsky découvrit les suites pour violoncelle solo de Bach." If true, then Entry 36 reveals that he was already concerned with these suites some six months before he began composing *Apollo* in mid-July 1927.

Over the years, Stravinsky's opinions about Bach changed. Interviewed in London in 1913, he stated: "There is little that interests me in the music of the past. Bach is too remote" but, by 1924, "Bach ... has all my veneration." Citing Bach's cantatas in 1962, he praised "the wonderful jolts, the sudden modulations, the unexpected harmonic changes, the deceptive cadences."

As Cantoni observes, Bach's spirit is felt as early as the *Octet* of 1922-23 and increasingly so in fugal movements from the 1930s, such as those in the *Symphony of Psalms* and the *Concerto for Two Solo Pianos,* and in the concertante style of the *Dumbarton Oaks Concerto.* After arranging and orchestrating Bach's *Chorale-Variations on Von Himmel hoch* in 1956, he returned to the composer for a final time with his orchestration in April and May 1969 of four preludes and fugues from the *Well-Tempered Clavier.*

Works Consulted

Bach, Johann Sebastian. *Neue Ausgabe Sämtlicher Werke.* ed. Hans Eppstein, *Kritischer Bericht.* Cassel, Basle, London, New York, NY: Bärenreiter, 1990. 6, 2 [11].

Cantoni, Angelo. *La référence à Bach dans les oeuvres néo-classiques de Stravinsky.* Hildesheim, Zurich and New York, NY: G. Olms, 1998. p. 38 and passim.

Kirstein, Lincoln. "Pictures from an Album." *High Fidelity* 7 (June 1957): 39.

Schaeffner, André. *Strawinsky.* Paris: Les Éditions Rieder, 1931. p. 92, n. 1 on p. 115.

SE&D. (1962) pp. 90-1; (1981) p. 64.

SP&D. pp. 197, 488-90, n. 24 on p. 602, n. 18 on p. 628.

SSC. vol. 1. p. 102, n. 61 on p. 151; vol. 2. n. 53 on p. 42, pl. [2] btn pp. 338-9, p. 383; vol. 3. n. 7 on p. 328.

Stravinsky, Igor. "Chronological Progress in Musical Art." *The Étude* 44, 8 (August 1926): 559.

White, Eric Walter. "Stravinsky in Interview." *Tempo* 97 (1971): 7.

37   **(1927). Autograph picture postcard, 8.3 × 13.5 cm, in French and Russian in black ink with greetings also from Vera Sudeykina, of the Caserne Blandan (converted to a hospital at) Nancy, postmarked: NANCY-ENTREPOL MEURTHE ET MOSELLE/23/22 2/27 [11 p.m. 22 February, 1927] and countermarked: Paris IX/14ᵒᵒ/23. I/[1]927, addressed by Stravinsky to Serge de Diaghilev):**

Monsieur
Serge de Diaghilew
Le Grand Hôtel
<u>Paris</u>

Sovershayem divnoye puteshestvie, kakaya zhratva! Kakie vina!!
Tseluyu
    Igor' Stravinskii

i ya tozhe
Vera

Sergei Diaghilev
Paris

Nancy
22 February 1927

We are on [our] marvellous journey, what [good] grub! What wines!! I kiss you,
    Igor Stravinsky

and I also,
    Vera

Acquisition: from Richard MacNutt in May 1984, bidding for H. Colin Slim at Sotheby's London on *Ballet Material and Manuscripts from the Serge Lifar Collection* (London, 9 May 1984), lot 222.

Provenance: Sergei Diaghilev (1927-29); Serge Lifar (1905-86), the postcard bearing his collection stamp, "*Lifar*" (1929-84).

Commentary

The postcard, unpublished, is mentioned by Craft who notes that Vera and Stravinsky travelled by car from Paris and stayed overnight in Nancy on the way to Strasbourg. (Presumably Craft either had access to the Lifar Collection before its dispersal or he consulted Sotheby's auction catalogue.) I thank Michael Green and Stanislav Shvabrin for the transliteration and translation.

Gustatory and oenological raptures about Strasbourg are certainly understandable but what prompted the couple's bizarre choice of illustrated postcard for Diaghilev remains a mystery. Entry 37 precedes by more than a year the final rupture between the two men over the commissioning in January 1928 by Ida Rubinstein from Stravinsky of *Le baiser de la fée* (1928) and the unauthorized cut Diaghilev made in *Apollo* that autumn (see entries 45 and 58, respectively).

Works Consulted

Griffiths, Paul. "Dyagilev, Sergey Pavlovich." NG. vol. 5. pp. 792-3.

Schouvaloff, Alexander. *The Art of Ballets Russes: The Serge Lifar Collection of Theater Designs, Costumes, and Paintings at the Wadsworth Atheneum, Hartford, Connecticut.* New Haven, CT, and London: Yale University Press, 1997. pp. 18-23.

SBu. p. 36 (22 February 1927).

Walsh, Stephen. *Stravinsky, A Creative Spring: Russia and France, 1882-1934.* New York, NY: Alfred A. Knopf, 1999. pp. 469, 478.

38

(1930). **Signed typed letter, 27.4 × 21.5 cm, in French in pencil on his printed stationery: 167, Boulevard Carnot / NICE / Adresse Télégraphique: / STRAWIGOR–NICE, folded three times, 1 April 1930, to Sam [Salomon Adriaan Maria] Bottenheim (1880-1957):**

le I/4/30   Mr.Sam Bottenheim
                                             Amsterdam

Cher Monsieur Bottenheim,
Merci pour la réponse télégraphique malgré que cette dernière
ne me donne pas la satisfaction voulue.

   Il s'agit pour moi de savoir pas autant les dates des concerts
comme les dates entre lequelles se passeront les répétitions et
les concerts.Comme je vous avais écrit le I5 dernier j'ai un
concert à Bruxel-les I3/I4 déc. que j'éspère pouvoir transporter
au mois de novembre ce qui ne sera pas sans difficultés pour
moi et pour Ansermet qui m'accompagne mon Capriccio.Je vais
quand même tenter de le faire si vous me dites que l'époque
entre le I5 et 23 décembre pour une raison ou l'autre vous
semble trop courte pour plusieurs concerts.Vous m'aviez
demandé de commencer le I0 décembre dans votre lettre du I2
mars,ladessus je vous ai répondu que le I3/I4 j'étais
occupé.Entretemps Ansermet me faisait savoir que les dates du
I3/I4 déc. pouvaient peut-être être transportées au I5/I6 nov.
Avant de fixer cette alternative de Bruxelles vous comprenez
vousmême que j'attends vos dates limitant ma tournée en
Hollande.Tâchez de me fixer au moins cela en attendant
d'autres précisions – car ladessus vous ne m'avez encore rien
répondu: [in red type] Est ce que du I5 au 23 décembre cela
vous va? [in black type] Si c'est oui,je n'ai pas besoins de
deranger inutillement Bruxelles.

   J'attends votre réponse et vous envoie mes meilleures
salutations.
[in pencil] Igor Strawinsky

            Sam Bottenheim   Nice
            Amsterdam   1 April 1930

            Dear Mr. Bottenheim:
            Thanks for your telegram, even though it doesn't give me the
            answer I wanted.

I need to know not so much the concert dates as the dates between rehearsals and concerts. As I wrote you on the 15th of last month, I have a concert in Brussels 13-14 December which I hope to be able to move to November – which won't be without difficulties for me and for Ansermet who accompanies me in my *Capriccio*. I'm nevertheless going to try to do this if you tell me that the period between 15 and 23 December for one reason or another seems to you too short for several concerts. You had asked me to begin on 10 December in your letter of 12 March, to which I replied that I'm taken on the 13-14. Meanwhile, Ansermet let me know that the 13-14 December dates could perhaps be moved back to 15-16 November. Before settling on this Brussels alternative, you doubtless realize that I'm waiting for your dates determining my Holland tour. Try at least to settle that time, pending further details because you have not yet told me anything about that – [red type] does 15-23 December suit you? [black type] If so, I need not unnecessarily inconvenience Brussels.

I await your reply and send my best wishes.

Igor Strawinsky

Acquisition: H. Colin Slim in New York on 11 October 1997 from the Cambridge-Essex Stamp Company; sometime after 1948 this company had the letter framed with a rephotograph of Stravinsky, the original taken in 1947. Traces of red paint on the letter, cloth hinges at upper edge, and pressure-sensitive clear tape from lower edge were removed and tears along fold lines and lower edge were mended with Japanese paper and rice starch by Linda K. Ogden in December 1997. *Provenance:* Unknown.

Commentary

The letter is unpublished, its envelope missing. A copy is in the Paul Sacher Foundation. Entry 38 is perforated at its left edges by two circular holes for filing. Running down its right edge in an elaborately cursive script, the paper is watermarked: Iadon D.V. Ideal. Stravinsky typed Entry 38 on the same machine that he used for entries 25-7. He customarily typed Roman rather than Arabic letters for the numeral one and often failed to properly separate the final word of a sentence or phrase from the first word of the next sentence or phrase.

Cambridge-Essex's accompanying rephotograph depicted him at the corner of two walls cupping his left hand to his ear. Taken in New York by Irving Penn in 1947, this photograph was first published the following year in *Vogue*.

Salomon (Sam) Adriaan Maria Bottenheim, secretary to Willem Mengelberg (conductor of the Amsterdam Concertgebouw Orchestra), was the agent for a Stravinsky concert tour of Holland, 15-23 December 1930. By 5 March 1930, a festival of his music had been arranged for 13-14 December at Brussels. In addition to his letter to Bottenheim of 15 March mentioned in Entry 38, Stravinsky had also twice written from Nice to Ernest Ansermet on 24 and 27 March to enquire if the Brussels festival could be moved from December 13-14 back to November 15-16. On 3 April he wrote Ansermet in Brussels that, because his German agent had fixed concerts at Stuttgart for 16-17 November, it was impossible to change the Brussels dates back to November, shortly thereafter cabling the same information to Ansermet. A schedule of concerts which Stravinsky later drew up reveals that, in Brussels, he played the *Capriccio* (1929) with Ansermet who led the premiere there of the *Symphony of Psalms* (1930) and, in Amsterdam, he played the *Capriccio* with Mengelberg. Entry 38 is thus a good example of his frenetic concert schedule.

An earlier letter from Stravinsky to Bottenheim, 5 February 1926, was offered for sale in 1998 and another of 29 June 1925 was offered in 1999. His booking agent as early as the summer of 1924, the day Stravinsky led the Concertgebuow, the composer inscribed a photograph of himself playing the piano in his Pleyel studio: à Sam Bottenheim / souvenir amical / de Igor Strawinsky / Amsterdam/23/ XI/24.

Works Consulted

La Scala Autographs. *Winter 1998 [Catalogue]*. Pennington, 1997. item 84.

Pasler, Jann, ed. *Confronting Stravinsky: Man, Musician, and Modernist*. Berkeley and Los Angeles, CA, and London: University of California Press, 1986. frontispiece.

Stargardt, J.A. *Autographen aus allen Gebieten. Katalog 641*. Marburg, 9-10 March 1988, lot 1069. pl. on pp. 356-7.

SBu. p. 26 (23 November 1924).

SScrbk. pl. 223 on p. 110.

SSC. vol. 1. p. 208.

Tappolet, Claude, ed. *Correspondance Ernest Ansermet-Igor Strawinsky (1914-1967)*. Geneva: Georg, 1990-92. vol. 2. pp. 212-14, no. 332, pp. 217-23, nos. 336-7 and 340-1.

Walsh, Stephen. *Stravinsky, A Creative Spring: Russia and France, 1882-1934*. New York, NY: Alfred A. Knopf, 1999. n. 85 on p. 639.

39

(1935). **Pen and black ink drawing on a gray sheet, 38.5 × 24.0 cm (originally wider), lettered: IGOR STRAVINS[KY] and folded over at the extreme top right, signed below: ALINE/FRUHAUF (1907-78), undated, but executed in January or February 1935 for *Musical America*.**

Acquisition: H. Colin Slim in New York on 22 April 1995 from Wurlitzer-Bruck.

Provenance: Reverse side is stamped: Musical America / Made For Issue of 4/10/35; stolen from the artist shortly thereafter; a subsequent owner's initials, D B W, stamped on the two bottom corners, have not been identified. (The same initials appear in the bottom right-hand corner of Fruhauf's drawing of Arnold Schoenberg, offered by Lisa Cox in her autumn 2000 catalogue.)

Commentary

Aline Fruhauf related that she drew Stravinsky at a press conference in a New York hotel room in 1934; he did not arrive in that city, however, until the ensuing 3 January. She must have drawn Entry 39, therefore, during the period 3-12 January or 28 January to 9 February when he was there.

One of no less than seventy-five caricatures of musicians she executed for the *Musical Courier* and for *Musical America* published between November 1927 and August 1936, this drawing appeared in the latter journal on 10 April 1935. It was captioned: "Igor Stravinsky, Who Has Been Touring This / Country as Conductor and Performer of His / Own Compositions, Is Again in the Limelight, / Playing with Assisting Artists a Stravinsky / Program at the Library of Congress Festival / in Washington."

An (unfavourable) review by Alice Eversman of this program on 9 April – Stravinsky's second Washington concert – appeared two weeks later in *Musical America*. The program consisted of songs with Olga Averino; *Suite from L'histoire du Soldat, Divertimento* (a suite from *Le baiser de la fée,* 1934), and *Duo Concertant* (1932) with Samuel Dushkin; and *Concertino* (1920) by the Gordon String Quartet. Eversham's review began: "The largest crowd turned out for the evening program of Stravinsky's works. Expectancy charged the atmosphere, for the schedule promised to show the versatility of the composer through the years from 1913 to 1934." Only a few weeks later, on 1 May, Fruhauf's drawing, captioned "American caricature of Strawinsky," appeared in a Copenhagen newspaper, announcing his concert there. Like the reproduction in *Musical America,* the newspaper also suppressed the depiction of smoke issuing from Stravinsky's cigarette.

Printmaker and illustrator, Fruhauf was also a regular contributor to *Vogue, Vanity Fair, Theatre Arts Monthly, The Dance Observer,* and *Creative Art*. From Entry 39 she later made an undated watercolour on paper now in the National Portrait Gallery, Washington; in 1967, she made a second image of him, a woodcut. Her sharp eyes carefully observed the composer of 1935:

He was a small man with broad shoulders, a slim waist and a propulsive profile. At first his long, ovoid head suggested an Aztec carving; then it became a blanched almond ... At the first meeting, Stravinsky's hair was brownish and beautifully groomed, I was sure, with a pair of military brushes. He was well turned out in gray flannels, a chocolate-brown cardigan, a gray striped shirt with a white collar, and a brown foulard tie with copper dots. And his image was punctuated by a large onyx ring on his right hand, pointed black shoes, and a cigarette in a long black holder. I made a brush drawing [Entry 39] for *Musical America,* and when I went to the office to pick it up after it had been published, I found that one of my anonymous collectors had gotten there first. I made another drawing in watercolor [the one in the National Portrait Gallery] and exhibited it in a group show [New York, March 1938] at the ACA Gallery.

Works Consulted

Eversman, Alice. "Coolidge Festival Held at Library of Congress." *Musical America* 55 (25 April 1935): 18.

Fruhauf obituary. *New York Times*. 28 May 1978. p. 18.

"Strawinsky i Amerika." *Dagens Nyheder/Nationaltidende*. 1 May 1935, p. 11.

Vollmer, Erwin, ed. *Making Faces: Memoirs of a Caricaturist. Aline Fruhauf*. Cabin John, MD, and Washington, DC: Seven Locks Press, 1987. pp. 163, 227-9, 242.

"With Pen and Pencil." *Musical America* 55 (10 April 1935): 9.

40

(1935). Two unsigned photographs, taken 1 March 1935 in Hollywood: one, 16.5 × 11.4 cm, reproduced from the original negative, of Edward G. Robinson (1893-1973) and Stravinsky; the other, 16.5 × 10.1 cm, a rephotograph of Dr. Alexis Fyodorovich Kall [Kahl, Kal'] (1878-1948), Stravinsky, and Robinson.

Acquisition: H. Colin Slim, Winter 1995, courtesy of the Charles E. Young Research Library, University of California at Los Angeles, Special Collections, 601, Kall papers, Box 2: Kall photographs (negative) and Box 5: Stravinsky photographs (rephotograph).

Provenance: Papers of Alexis Fyodorovich Kall donated in 1950 by Jay Ledya and Sergey Bertensson to the University of California at Los Angeles.

Commentary

Both photographs were taken in front of the same house, probably Kall's residence at 143 South Gramercy, where Stravinsky was his guest during the second half of February. In a note of 15 May 1960 to Deborah Ishlon, his agent at Columbia Records, Stravinsky apparently refers to (Kall's) photograph of himself and Robinson. Although not reproduced until 1972, it was then captioned (correctly): "Hollywood, March 1935." A copy of the triple photograph is in the Paul Sacher Foundation. Reproduced in 1962 and 1981 and captioned (incorrectly) "Hollywood, May [sic] 1935," it all but truncates Kall's image – only a tiny part of his left shoulder is visible. On a concert tour of the United States, 10 January to 9 April 1935, with the violinist Samuel Dushkin

(1891-1976), Stravinsky lived at Kall's home on South Gramercy during his first visit to Los Angeles, 17 February to 1 March, mailing "Sweet Woof" (Kall's nickname) a thank you note on 2 March.

Stravinsky visited Robinson's home on 20 February at 910 North Rexford Drive, Beverly Hills, which Robinson called an "ersatz Tudor mansion." Robinson had the fortunate pastime of asking musicians to play his piano and then to inscribe their names on its soundboard. A photograph of this soundboard reveals, within the semicircle formed by Steinway & Sons / New York, the composer's inscription: "Igor Strawinsky / 20.II.35." As recorded in Kall's diary, six days later Robinson gave a reception for Stravinsky and saw him again on 1 March.

Because Kall owned the negative of the dual photograph in Entry 40, it probably came from his camera, someone else taking the other picture of all three men. Kall's former house at 143 South Gramercy has been remodelled, thus preventing secure identification, but the one in these pictures is obviously not Robinson's "Tudor mansion" on North Rexford (which he later remodelled).

Full histories of relationships between Stravinsky and Robinson and between Stravinsky and Kall remain to be written. Robinson recalled (although with some uncertainty and providing no date) that he first met Stravinsky at the home of the screenwriter Sonia Levien (1888-1960) and her husband, Carl Hovey (1875-c. 1950) in Los Angeles. Robinson could also have met him in New York with his friends the Gershwins on 7-8 January 1925, during the first trip Stravinsky made to the US.

Stravinsky sailed with the actor and his wife, Gladys, during his third transatlantic crossing, 18-23 December 1936, from France to New York aboard the *S.S. Normandie*. To honour Stravinsky, Robinson gave a dinner party in Hollywood c. 20 March 1937 which included Paulette Goddard, Charlie Chaplin, Douglas Fairbanks, Marlene Dietrich, Frank Capra, and George Gershwin at which Stravinsky and Dushkin performed, and he autographed a copy of his *Chroniques de ma vie* for Gershwin.

Less than a month after arriving in Los Angeles, Stravinsky and his new wife, Vera, attended the Robinsons' garden party on 19 June 1940. Robinson spoke on 16 May 1945 at an "American-Russian Friendship

Concert" conducted by Stravinsky and Otto Klemperer. The Stravinsky's continued to socialize with him during most of the 1940s. Much of the next decade, however, saw Robinson increasingly embroiled in political difficulties and his wife afflicted with mental illness.

The friendship between Stravinsky and Kall is particularly relevant here. (Their correspondence is not only at UCLA but also in the Sacher Foundation.) As the piano teacher of Dorothy Ellis McQuoid Hopper (1911-98), Kall forms the link between her and the composer, many of whose inscribed items to her are now in the present collection. Because information about Kall is not easy to find – Mrs. Hopper described him as exceedingly modest – a brief survey of his career follows.

In 1940, Kall recalled that he "first met Stravinsky in 1900, forty years ago" at St. Petersburg. A 1933 biography notes that Kall studied piano at the city's conservatory. In an appreciation about him prepared in 1939 by Mrs. Hopper (then Mrs. McQuoid), she noted that Kall had studied piano with "a famous pupil of Anton Rubinstein." This might have been Leokadiya Alexandrovna Kashperova (1872-1940) who was to teach Stravinsky from December of 1899. Kall certainly knew him no later than July 1901. Both men also studied with Rimsky-Korsakov and were remarked as there together on 9 November 1903, Kall also visiting Rimsky-Korsakov just before the latter's death in 1908.

Obtaining his Mus. Doc. at the University of Leipzig in 1902 with a dissertation, *Die Philosophie der Musik nach Aristoteles,* Kall taught from 1905 in the faculty of art at the University of St. Petersburg and then founded the Popular (Narodnaya) Conservatory there around 1908, which flourished until his final departure from Russia in 1917. Its 1910-11 poster announces, for example, that as *privatdocent* he will teach music theory and will also give twenty-four lectures on the history of music. Early in July 1913 he was living at 25, rue Madrid in Paris when the current stage-director for the Ballets Russes, Alexander Akimovich Sanin (1869-1956), wrote Stravinsky from London: "I'll be staying [in Paris] with my friend, Kall." Perhaps Kall had come to hear the *Rite of Spring*. Whether Kall then saw Stravinsky in Neuilly – where the composer was recovering from typhoid – before he and his family left for Ustilug on 11 July is unknown. "Prof. Kall from the musical section of the community People's University," along with Liberio Sacchetti (1852-1916), professor of music history at the Imperial Conservatory, and Walter Nouvel, was to welcome Debussy during his Russian visit late in November 1913. The following year in Petrograd Kall wrote scathingly about Prokofiev's music, for which the composer gently chastised him in January 1922. Drawn up not long after 1940, Kall's brief autobiographical sketch in his papers states that he knew both Tchaikovsky brothers, Rimsky-Korsakov, Lyadov, Glazunov, and Arensky. From the 1920s he corresponded with, among others, Rachmaninoff, Gretchaninoff, and Prokofiev.

After suffering a bayonet wound to his left hand, Kall had left Russia in the summer of 1917, ostensibly to study in China and Japan "avec le but scientifique" (as indicated on his passport of 25 August 1917). Late that autumn he arrived in Tokyo where for almost a year he gave concerts and taught music at Seisin Gaki In, the city's leading girl's school. Soon after sailing to San Francisco in 1918, he moved permanently to Los Angeles where, by 1919, he had opened a piano studio. Identified as the "Director of the Institute of Musical Art" in Los Angeles, he is pictured there with some of his piano students in 1926, highly respected as a piano teacher and musical savant until shortly before his death. Then president of the city's Russian Art Club, Kall played the *Tastiera per luce* [colour organ] at the Los Angeles premiere by the Philharmonic sponsored by the Club of Scriabin's *Prometheus* on 6 March 1926.

Described by Merle Armitage as "a huge, gentle Russian," Kall apparently renewed his old friendship early in 1935 when Stravinsky arrived in the US for his second tour. Kall's letter, dated 15 January 1934 (*recte:* 1935), included his photograph on a 15 May 1927 program by his piano students. One of them playing the Brahms *G-minor Rhapsody,* the then-unmarried Dorothy Ellis, was to be Stravinsky's future friend, Mrs. McQuoid. (Program and letter are in the Sacher Foundation.) Enclosing his own photograph, which does not survive in the Kall papers at UCLA, Stravinsky then wrote from Chicago on 19 January 1935 thanking Kall for his photograph and letter which had mentioned their former mutual friend, Andrey Rimsky-Korsakov (1878-1940), Kall's exact contemporary. At his request, Stravinsky sent a testimonial about Kall's teaching abilities from Paris, dated 17 March 1936, a copy of which is in the Sacher Foundation. Kall lectured about Stravinsky the following year in both San Francisco and Los Angeles.

In November 1939 at Cambridge, Kall recommended to Stravinsky his most famous piano student, Adele Marcus (1906-95), who had studied with him until 1922 when she left for Julliard. With the composer she played his *Concerto per due pianoforti soli* many times on the east coast during March 1940. (A recording of their performance on 8 March in Sanders Theatre, Harvard University, is extant.) She also performed the *Capriccio* in February 1941 under his direction with the Los Angeles Philharmonic in Los Angeles and in San Diego.

When Stravinsky first visited Los Angeles, in February 1935, Kall accompanied him to a meeting with members of the MGM music department, on the 25th. When he arrived in the city in March 1937 and in December 1939, he again stayed at 135 South Gramercy. Kall was secretary-factotum-translator on these occasions and again at Cambridge, October 1939 to May 1940, where he lived with Stravinsky *en pension* at the home of Edward Waldo Forbes (1873-1969), director of Harvard's Fogg Museum. Kall was a witness to the marriage of Stravinsky and Vera at Bedford on 9 March 1940, accompanying them on their move to Los Angeles by ship from Miami to Galveston the following May (as illustrated in Entry 69).

At Los Angeles in mid-December 1939, Kall had already introduced to Stravinsky another piano student (with him since 1923), Dorothy Louise Ellis McQuoid. With her first husband, Edwin Kerien McQuoid, who made at least three photographic portraits of Stravinsky, she was to prove helpful to him and to Vera when they arrived there on 20 May 1940 (see entries 67-8 and 70-5).

Although undergoing periodic strains owing to Kall's fits of drunkenness, these friendships endured until Kall's death in Los Angeles on 7 September 1948. In 1995 Mrs. Hopper recalled for Dr. Slim that the Stravinskys and the McQuoids attended Kall's funeral three days later, on 10 September 1948.

Works Consulted

Apollon 10 (1913) 82-3.

Armitage, Merle. "Stravinsky, musical milestone in our time." *Accent on Life*. Ames, IO: Iowa State University Press, 1965. p. 176.

Ellis [McQuoid], Dorothy. "Dr. Alexis Kall, a Gentleman and a Scholar." *The Baton of Phi Beta* (March 1939): 19-21.

Gretchaninoff, Alexander. *My Life*. trans. Nicolas Slonimsky. New York, NY: Coleman-Ross, 1952. p. 149.

Jablonski, Edward. *Gershwin. A Biography*. New York, NY: Doubleday, 1987; repr. 1998. pp. 92-4, 313.

Japan Advertiser [Tokyo]. 2 March 1918. p. 2.

Kahl [sic], Alexis. *Die Philosophie der Musik nach Aristoteles. Inaugural-Dissertation*. Leipzig: Breitkopf and Härtel, 1902. [ii]: "Vita."

Kall, Alexis. "Nationalism in Russian Music." *Art and Archaeology* 13 (1922): 82.

—. "Stravinsky in the Chair of Poetry." *The Musical Quarterly* 26 (1940): 283-96.

—. Papers. Boxes 1, 3, and 5, Special Collections 601. Charles E. Young Research Library, University of California at Los Angeles.

"Kall, Alexis." *Who's Who in California 1942-43*. ed. Russell Holmes Fletcher. Los Angeles: Who's Who Publications, 1941 [sic]. vol. 1. p. 469.

"Kall, Dr. Alexis." *Who's Who in Music and Dance in Southern California*. ed. Bruno David Ussher. Hollywood: William J. Perlman, 1933. p. 208, with photograph.

Morton, Lawrence. "Stravinsky in Los Angeles." *Festival of Music Made in Los Angeles*. ed. Orrin Howard. Los Angeles: Philharmonic Association, 1981. pp. 72-3.

Musical America 44 (4 September 1926): pl. on p. 19.

Philharmonic Orchestra of Los Angeles Programs. 1925-26 on pp. 138 and 302.

Prokofiev, Sergei. *Prokofev o Prokofeve: stati i interviu*. [Prokofiev on Prokofiev: articles and interviews.] ed. V.P. Varunts. Moscow: Sovetskiy Kompozitor, 1991. n. 1 on p. 77.

Robinson, Edward G., and Leonard Spigelgass. *All My Yesterdays: An Autobiography*. New York, NY: Hawthorn Books, 1973. pp. 147-8 and pl. btn pp. 152-3.

Robinson, Harlow, ed. *Selected Letters of Sergei Prokofiev*. Boston, MA: Northeastern University Press, 1998. p. 166 (31 December 1920).

Rosar, William H. "Stravinsky and MGM." *Film Music 1*. ed. Clifford McCarty. New York, and London: Garland, 1989. pl. on p. 110.

Rosenberg, Deena. *Fascinating Rhythm*. New York, NY: Dutton, 1991. p. 353.

Slim, H. Colin. "Unknown Words and Music by Stravinsky, 1939-44, for his longtime St. Petersburg and Los Angeles friend, Dr. Alexis Kall" in *Essays for Andrew Porter on his 75th Birthday*. ed. Claire Brook and David Rosen. Stuyvesant, NY: Pendragon, 2003. Forthcoming.

Stargardt, J.A. *Katalog 671*. Berlin, 30-31 March 1999, lot 963 (to D. Ishlon).

SBu. pp. 110-45, passim (1940-48).

SE&D. (1962) p. 83, pl. 13; (1981) p. 72, pl. 12.

SP&D. pp. 282, 336-7, 352, 354, 365-6, 556-7.

SP&RK. vol. 2. p. 103 (trans. Stanislav Shvabrin and Michael Green).

SSC. vol. 2. pp. 302, 307-10, n. 12 on p. 508.

ST&C. (1972) pl. facing p. 160.

Stuart, Philip. *Igor Stravinsky – The Composer in the Recording Studio. A Comprehensive Discography*. New York, NY, Westport, CT, London: Greenwood Press, 1991. p. 73 ("Sanders Theatre, Boston" [*recte:* Cambridge]).

Taruskin, Richard. *Stravinsky and the Russian Traditions*. Berkeley and Los Angeles, CA: University of California Press, 1996. pp. 96-9.

Walsh, Stephen. "Stravinsky and Los Angeles, First Encounter." *Performing Arts. Magazine, Los Angeles Philharmonic* 35 2 (2 February 2001) and 3 (March 2001): P. 10-12.

–. *Stravinsky, A Creative Spring: Russia and France, 1882-1934*. New York, NY: Alfred A. Knopf, 1999. pp. 52-3.

Yastrebstev, Vasily Vasilyevich. *Nikolai Andreyevich Rimskiy-Korsakov: vospominaniya 1886-1908*. [Reminiscences of Rimsky-Korsakov, 1886-1908.] ed. Alendrer V. Ossovsky. Leningrad: Muzgiz, 1959-60. vol. 2. p. 294 (trans. Stanislav Shvabrin and Michael Green).

Zarotschenzeff, M.T. "Fingalova Peshchera. K 70-letnemu yubileyu professora A.F. Kal'." *Novaya Zarya* ["Fingal's Cave. For the 70th Year Jubilee of Professor A.F. Kall," *Russian Daily*] [Los Angeles.] 28 January 1948, pp. 1-3 (trans. Stanislav Shvrabrin and Michael Green).

41

(1935). Autographed, printed eight-page program, 24.6 × 16.1 cm, signed in bluish-green ink on cover by Stravinsky and Samuel Dushkin and dated there "1935" in same ink, of a duo-concert, Sunday evening, 24 March 1935, in the National Theatre, Washington, DC.

[on front cover] Igor Strawinsky / Samuel Dushkin / 1935

Acquisition: H. Colin Slim in San Diego on 7 July 1998 from Benedikt and Salmon, Record Rarities–Autographs, San Diego; the back cover has in pencil: 175. Staples were removed and staple holes and small edge tears were repaired with Japanese paper and rice starch paste by Linda K.

Ogden on 8 September 1998. I have had affixed to the back of the frame a photocopy of p. 3 of the program.

Provenance: Unknown Washington, DC, concert patron, 1935.

Commentary

Handwritten below the printed/Washington/D.C./on the program, the 1935 date may or may not have been added by Stravinsky; in particular, its formation of the numeral 9 does not resemble those of other autograph dates by him in the present collection.

The condition of the program is poor. Its original owner stapled to it not only a photograph of Stravinsky by Hoyningen-Huené clipped from a November 1927 issue of *Vanity Fair* 29: 50, but also three favourable 1935 reviews from Washington newspapers, one each signed by Helen Buchalter and Ray C.B. Brown, plus stapling an earlier, more general, essay by Brown. In addition, two circular holes at its right edge were presumably for filing.

This concert, their first in Washington, was the fourteenth in a series of seventeen joint recitals which Stravinsky and Dushkin performed across the US from 10 January in New York until the last one in Washington at the Library of Congress on 9 April, cited in Entry 39. Like many other programs by them, this one for 24 March contained works specially arranged by Stravinsky for Dushkin. The program (p. 3) was: I. *Suite Italienne* (1932); II. *Divertimento* (1934); (Intermission) III. *Aria and Capriccio* from the *Violin Concerto* (1931); IV. *Airs du Rossignol, Marche Chinoise* (1932; from *Le Rossignol*), *Berceuse* (1931) and *Scherzo* (1932) (both from *The Firebird*), and *Danse Russe* (1932; from *Petrushka*).

Works Consulted

SSC. vol. 2. pp. 301-2.

42

(1936). Autograph letter, two sides of a card, 8.9 × 14.0 cm, in French in black ink, 28 January 1936, to E. Mounez:

M^r. E. Mounez
Dourdone (s. no.)

Monsieur,
Très touché de votre amicable lettre je vous envoie mes
remerciements les meilleurs.

Le livre en question (ouvrage que j'ai terminé l'année
dernière) s'appele "Chroniques de ma vie" etc 2 volumes. Il est
[reverse] paru dans l'édition <u>Denoël</u> et <u>Steele</u> et se trouve en
vente partout.

Je vous prie d'agréer, Monsieur, l'expression de mes sentiments très sincèrement sympathiques
Igor Strawinsky

Paris
le 28. I. 36.

E. Mounez   Paris
Dordogne (no number)   28 January 1936

Sir:
Very touched by your friendly letter, I send you my warmest thanks.

The book in question (a work that I finished last year) is entitled
Chroniques de ma vie etc., 2 volumes. It is published in the *Denoël and
Steele* edition and is for sale everywhere.

Very sincerely yours,
Igor Strawinsky

Acquisition: H. Colin Slim on 8 November 1994 from Wurlizter-
Bruck.
Provenance: Unknown.

Commentary

The letter is unpublished, its envelope missing. Its addressee remains
unidentified. Because Stravinsky apparently had his letter in hand, it

seems improbable that "E. Mounez" was Emmanuel Mounier (1905–50), a philosopher influenced by Jacques Maritain, the latter a friend of Stravinsky from 1926. (No correspondence under either Mounier or Mounez is in the Paul Sacher Foundation.)

Stravinsky wrote Entry 42 the day he returned to Paris at 25, rue Faubourg, St.-Honoré – where he had moved his family from Voreppe in October 1934 – from a two-day visit to his wife, Catherine. She was in the tuberculosis sanatorium at Sancellemoz, one which he himself had to enter in 1939, shortly after her death. (On the *Chroniques,* see entries 19, 43, 46, 83, and 103.)

Works Consulted

SBu. p. 77 (1936).
SSC. vol. 2. app. K on pp. 487–502; vol. 3. n. 95 on p. 102.

43

(1936). Inscribed first edition, 18.0 × 12.3 cm, IGOR STRAWINSKY / CHRONIQUES / DE MA VIE / *Avec six dessins hor texte* (Paris: Les Éditions Denoël et Steele, 1935), 2 vol. 187 pp. 6 pls., and 190 pp., respectively; vol. 1 (only) inscribed, in French, in brown ink, 5 February 1936, to David Ponsonby:

A Monsieur David Ponsonby
témoignage d'une sincère gratitude pour son très
précieux aide dans les nombreuses difficultés de la
traduction anglaise des ces "Chroniques"

l'auteur bien
reconnaissant
I Strawinsky

Paris
le 5.II.36

David Ponsonby   Paris
Paris   5 February 1936

For Mr. David Ponsonby, a token of sincere gratitude for his very
valuable assistance with the numerous difficulties in the English
translation of these *Chroniques,*
    the very grateful author,
    I. Strawinsky

Acquisition: Vol. 1, H. Colin Slim in Los Angeles on 11 February 2000
from La Scala Autographs; vol. 2, in Oakland, CA, on 17 August 1999
by purchase from J. Caleb Cushing, Oakland.
Provenance: Vol. 1 from Thierry Bodin, Paris, 1998, and subsequently
restored by La Scala Autographs; vol. 2 from Professor Charles Cushing
(1905-82), who bought his two volumes from a French bookseller in
November 1936; Piquette Cushing (1910-97), Berkeley, CA.

Commentary

The final *y* in the composer's surname forms the upper loop of the *P* in
Paris. The first volume, printed 14 March 1935, was issued early that
year which saw the second one printed on 12 December. The six
drawings, all reproduced in volume 1, are:

- Stravinsky seated, by Théodore Stravinsky, December 1932
  (frontispiece)
- Stravinsky portrait of C.F. Ramuz, 29 June 1917, Lausanne (pp. 64-5)
- Picasso and Stravinsky by Cocteau, Paris, mid-December 1920 (pp.
  80-1)
- Stravinsky by Picasso, 31 December 1920 (pp. 112-13)
- Picasso's cover for *Ragtime,* 1920 (pp. 128-9)
- Picasso's sketch for *Pulcinella,* early September 1919 (pp. 160-1)

In its complete form, the Cocteau drawing (frequently misdated as
1917) notes that, following the Parisian reprises of *Parade* (December

1920) and of *Le Sacre du Printemps* (15 December 1920), Picasso comforted Stravinsky, who "a but trop de vodka" [had drunk too much vodka].

Chroniques de ma vie was ghost-written by Walter Nouvel, a lifelong friend of Stravinsky and Diaghilev (see Entry 19). (Further, see entries 42, 46, 83, and 103.)

David Ponsonby, scion of a distinguished aristocratic British family, was a student of Nadia Boulanger in 1933. Described by Stravinsky as "a very serious person," he reviewed the anonymous English translation sent to Stravinsky in October and late December 1935 by the London publisher, Victor Gollancz. Ponsonby's suggestions for revising musical and aesthetic terms were accepted but not his proposal for a wholesale retranslation, owing to Gollancz's disagreement and his publication deadline of March 1936.

Works Consulted

Brooks, Jeanice. "Nadia Boulanger and the Salon of the Princesse de Polignac." JAMS 46 (1993): 430, n. 30.

Lesure, François, and Nanie Bridgman, ed. *Collection Musicale André Meyer.* Abbeville: F. Paillart, 1960. pl. 243.

Siohan, Robert. *Stravinsky.* Paris: Éditions du Seuil, 1959. ill. on p. 75; ed. and trans. Eric Walter White. London: Calder and Boyars, 1965; repr. New York, NY: Grossman, 1970. ill. on p. 73.

Steegmuller, Francis. *Cocteau: A Biography.* Boston, MA, and Toronto, ON: Little, Brown, 1976. n. on p. 189.

SAc. pl. on p. 129 (Nouvel with Stravinsky family in 1933).

SSC. vol. 2. pp. 496-8.

44 **(1936). Autographed photograph, 17.3 × 23.4 cm, in French in brown ink (partly faded), taken by L[azaro] Sudak of Buenos Aires who pencilled "Sudak" at lower left. Stravinsky inscribed it, 17 May 1936, to A[ída Victoria] Mastrazzi (c. 1913-):**

Pour cet excellent
artiste qu'est
M^{le} A. Mastrazzi
Souvenir bien
reconnaissant
de
IStrawinsky
Buenos Aires
le 17 V 36

Aída Mastrazzi	Buenos Aires
Buenos Aires	17 May 1936

For the excellent artiste [dancer], Miss A. Mastrazzi, a very grateful
memento from
    I. Strawinsky

Acquisition: H. Colin Slim on 4 December 1995 from Lisa Cox, bidding
for him at Christie's, *Valuable Printed Books and Manuscripts, Autograph
Letters and Music. Sale "Bookblock 5518"* (London, 29 November 1995),
lot 252, p. 187 (this photograph not illustrated).
Provenance: Unknown, but part of a large collection of musical
autographs.

Commentary
The photograph is unpublished. Although the orthography of the
dedicatee's surname is difficult, reading its first letter as "M" is confirmed by a comparison to the "M" of "*Mavra*" in Entry 54, inscribed
only a year later.
    Aída Mastrazzi danced in the corps de ballet at the Teatro Colón
from 1925 until reasons of health forced her retirement in 1938.
Afterward she taught at the Conservatorio Nacional de Música y Arte
Escenico, continuing in the present Escuela Nacional de Danzas until
her retirement on pension. In 1999 she was still living in Buenos Aires
(kind communication of 2 January 2001 from Michael Walensky).
    A photograph taken in 1926 of Mastrazzi in the ballet company
(2nd from left, first row) – she had joined it the year before – depicts a

young woman, probably not more than twelve or thirteen, approximately the age of her lifelong friend and the later prima ballerina, Maria Ruanova (1912-76), who had joined the company when she was twelve.

Two other photographs – one undated, the other of 1972 or 1973 – also include Mastrazzi. The undated photograph, wherein she appears to be in her early twenties, can be assigned to 1933 because of the simultaneous presence only then in Buenos Aires of the several international ballet stars depicted therein: Bronislava Nijinska, Ludmilla Schollar, her husband Anatole Wiltzak (Vilzak), and Anatole Obukhoff. Mastrazzi also participated in two ballets under Nijinska in a program at the Colón that year.

By 1936 Mastrazzi would have danced in Nijinska's staging at the Colón of *The Firebird* and *Petrushka* – which, during his South American tour, Stravinsky conducted on 7 and 10 May – and in both ballets plus *Le baiser de la fée* on 14 May. Not only Mastrazzi's skill in dancing and her training in piano, theory, and solfège, but also her beauty probably inspired his tribute in Entry 44. In 1985 she participated in celebrations memorializing Ruanova and was interviewed by Carlo Manzo for his book, perhaps as late as the following year.

In South America from April-June 1936 with his younger pianist son, Svetik Soulima, Stravinsky arrived in Buenos Aires on the *S.S. Cap Arcona* on 25 April. A photograph shows father and son leaning on each shoulder of their Argentinean hostess, Victoria Ocampo (1890-1979); another one shows all three on board ship to Rio de Janeiro; and still another of both men was taken shipboard during their return trip to Europe on 16 June. With rehearsals beginning on 27 April, he led concerts the next day at the Teatro Colón and on 2 and 9 May (apparently only attending on 11 May), as well as ballet performances on 7, 10, and 14 May and gave a recital with Soulima (see entries 61 and 82). (Further on Ocampo, see entries 45, 63-4, and 104.)

Sudak took Entry 44 just at this time, before or after a rehearsal. Posed in front of some kind of curtain with a towel around his neck, Stravinsky wears one sweater and a kind of jacket. Two copies of the same photograph, one signed but not dated, the other inscribed, signed, and dated "Buenos Aires May 36," were offered at auctions in 1991. A different photograph of him taken by Sudak, apparently at the same time, is in the Paul Sacher Foundation.

After rehearsing *Apollo* (concert performance) and *Perséphone* (with Ocampo as narrator) on 15-16 May, Stravinsky conducted these works at the Colón the very day he inscribed Entry 44. Another pose, probably also by Sudak, shows him in the same garb, but with eyeglasses on his forehead. Two photographs were taken in May at Buenos Aires, one during a rehearsal where he is similarly swathed, the other with Nijinska. (For an autograph manuscript signed by him in Buenos Aires the next day, see Entry 45.)

Entry 44 is by the theatre's official photographer. Its reverse side is stamped: FOTO / L. SUDAK / TEATRO COLON / Buenos Aires; written in ink above this stamp in an unknown hand is: "Igor Stravinsky 1936." (A photograph auctioned by Sotheby's of Claudia Muzio, for example, which she inscribed "Buenos Aires 1933," bears his label: L. SUDAK / FOTOGRAFO DEL / TEATRO COLON, as does one of Carlo Galeffi of 1933, offered by La Scala Autographs.) On the reverse side of Entry 44 and on its original mat (now discarded) appears "418" preceded on the mat by what seems to be "£" and, if so, possibly indicating a previous sale. Sudak also photographed a group of Mastrazzi's colleagues (though not including her) at the Colón in 1933. Both the dimensions of Entry 44 and the date "17 May 1926 [sic]" given in Christie's sale catalogue are incorrect.

Works Consulted

Caamaño, Roberto. *La historia del Teatro Colón 1908-1968*. Buenos Aires: Editorial Cinetea, 1969. vol. 2. pp. 233-4, 246; vol. 3. p. 301.

Giovannini, Marta, and Amelia Foglia de Ruiz. *Ballet Argentino en el Teatro Colón*. Buenos Aires: Ediciones Plus Ultra, 1973. pp. 33, 35, 81-2, 111-13, and pls. IV (undated), VII (1972; but dated 1973 by Manzo in his 1987 *Ruanova,* pl. 182 btn pp. 512-13).

La Scala Autographs, Inc. *[Catalog] Summer 1997*. Pennington, 1997, item 44.

Malinow, Ines. *Maria Ruanova*. Buenos Aires: Planeta, 1993. pl. on pp. 160-1 (persons unidentified).

Manso, Carlos. *La Argentina, fue Antonio Merce*. Buenos Aires: Ediciones Devenir, 1993. cover, p. 257.

–. *Maria Ruanova*. Buenos Aires: Ediciones tres tiempos, 1987. pp. 3, 57, and pl. 3 facing p. 142, pp. 836, 883, no. 3.

Meyer, Doris. *Victoria Ocampo. Against the Wind and the Tide*. New York, NY: G. Braziller, 1979. pl. [11] btn pp. 194-5.

Ocampo, Victoria. "*Perséphone* bajo la batuta de Strawinsky." *Testimonios*

Octava Serie (1968-1970). Buenos Aires: Sur, 1971. pp. 229-33.

—. "*Perséphone* con Strawinsky." *Testimonios. Décima Serie (1975-1977)*. Buenos Aires: Sur, 1977. pp. 242-51.

Schultz de Mantovani, Fryda. *Victoria Ocampo*. Buenos Aires: Ediciones Culturales Argentinas, 1963. pl. facing p. 65.

Sotheby's. *Music and Continental Manuscripts*. London, 16-17 May 1991, lot 474.

—. *Fine Printed and Manuscript Music including the Mannheim Collection*. London, 6 December 1991, lot 213.

—. *Fine Music and Continental Manuscripts*. London, 15-16 May 1997, lot 229.

SBu. pls. 77-8 on p. 80.

SD. pl. facing p. 80.

SP&D. pp. 328-30.

45 (1936). Autograph untitled working manuscript, on a single sheet (one half of a double sheet) folded twice on twenty-four–staved paper of varying heights, 26.6-26.4 cm, and widths, 34.55-34.65 cm, of the opening twenty-four bars of the Scherzo (movement III) from *Divertimento/Suite Symphonique "1934"* (Édition russe de musique, 1938) at rehearsals 83-86, copied on both sides in pencil and numbered "1" and "2." Heading p. 1 (lacking some woodwind triads) as: "Moderato ♩ = 88," and p. 2 as: "Un poco più mosso ♩ = 108," he inscribed the latter page, bottom right, in French in brown ink, 18 May 1936, to J[uan José] Castro (1895-1968):

A J. Castro, que j'aime, / son ami IStrawinsky B[uenos]Aires / 18.V.1936.

For my dear friend, J. Castro,
  I. Strawinsky
Buenos Aires
18 May 1936

Acquisition: H. Colin Slim on 16 November 1998 from La Scala Autographs. Small tears on all edges and a longer tear beginning at the lower edge along a previous fold line were mended with Japanese rice paper on 8 January 1999 by Linda K. Ogden.
Provenance: Unidentified Argentinean collector in Buenos Aires, 1998.

Commentary

These two pages in pencil are unpublished as such. Blind-stamped within an octagonal frame at the upper left corner of p. 1 is: LIMONAIRE / BAYONNE, the firm from which and the place where Stravinsky purchased the music paper. He had lived close to Bayonne, first at Anglet and then in Biarritz, from May 1921 through late September 1924, after which his family moved to Nice. To the right of the blind-stamp are traces of at least seven words once in ink but now erased, one of which is perhaps: "SC[HERZO]." Below p. "1" are traces of a word also erased. (These words may not be in his hand.) The music paper is distinctive with its two parallel lines below the twenty-fourth stave on both pages, suitable for adding words, or perhaps for a heading. This pair of lines and the larger band of blank paper below them rather than at the "top" suggest that Stravinsky turned the paper upside down when he notated it.

Entry 45 diverges in small but significant ways from all three publications of the *Divertimento* and also from its parent work, *Le baiser de la fée* (1928). The latter was a full-length ballet commissioned in January 1928 by Ida Rubinstein and composed that summer after music by Tchaikovsky.

Stephen Walsh kindly advises that on 3 March 1930 Stravinsky proposed to the Aeolian company in London that he make a piano-roll of fragments from *Le baiser de la fée,* a project that came to nothing. Later that month he proposed recording excerpts from the ballet and, in February 1931, he authorized Ansermet to conduct several extracts from it. Craft reports that two months later at Trieste Stravinsky himself conducted excerpts from *Le baiser* ("Prologue," "Village Festival," "At the Mill," and "Berceuse") on 24 April. Except for the "Berceuse" (and the perhaps-omitted Pas de deux), these excerpts might well prefigure the *Divertimento*. The Trieste performance could thus precede by several years what Walsh regards as the premiere of the *Divertimento* on

4 November 1934, when Stravinsky led "Fragments du ballet *Le baiser de la fée*" with the Orchestre Symphonique de Paris at the Salle Pleyel.

The day after finishing the sketch score at Nice of his ballet *Le baiser de la fée* (now in Basle, Paul Sacher Foundation), he made his score for solo piano (also in Basle), dating it 16 October 1928. Soon thereafter, a copy (probably by Soulima) for solo piano with its title page and first page in his hand and many other pages with his annotations (on ten-staved paper, 17.0 × 27.0 cm, also blind-stamped LIMONAIRE / BAYONNE), was prepared and then used for the engraving in 1928 (this manuscript now in the Pierpont Morgan Library).

At midnight, 30 October 1928, he finished his fair copy in pencil of the orchestral score of the complete ballet (now in the Library of Congress). Its twenty-four-staved paper is large double sheets, 26.8 × 70.0 cm, twice blind-stamped LIMONAIRE / BAYONNE. In poorer condition, Entry 45 uses but half of a double sheet of the same paper which has been slightly trimmed on all sides. Many years elapsed before an orchestral score of the entire ballet was published, but his solo piano arrangement of it was immediately printed, in 1928 by the Édition russe de musique (plate no. 455).

Goubault reports incorrectly that late in October 1932 Stravinsky performed with Samuel Dushkin at the Berlin Funkhaus (broadcasting studio) a work called *Divertimento,* a suite for violin and piano drawn from *Le baiser de la fée.* Walsh doubts that he and Dushkin worked together on it as early as the fall of 1933 at Fontainebleau. They first performed the violin and piano suite at Strassbourg on 12 December 1934. Printed that year as *Divertimento pour Orchestre … Transcription pour Violon et Piano* by the Édition russe de musique (plate nos. 592 and 595), it was reprinted in the 1950s by Boosey and Hawkes (plate no. 17269).

Drawing mostly on the same materials from the ballet as he had for the violin and piano suite, Stravinsky also created in 1934 his orchestral *Divertimento. Suite Symphonique.* The Édition russe de musique did not publish it until 1938 (plate no. 642).

After it was revised by Stravinsky in 1949, this orchestral *Divertimento* achieved a second publication by Boosey and Hawkes (plate no. 665) the following year. The full orchestral score of the entire ballet, *Le baiser de la fée,* had to wait, however, until 1952 when Boosey and Hawkes published it (plate no. 679), two years after its revision by Stravinsky.

Entry 45 is a unique and precious relic. No other autograph pages appear to survive for the orchestral version of the *Divertimento,* as opposed to the orchestral pages from *Le baiser.* The explanation is simple: he used the latter to make the former. For example, the pencil autograph of the complete ballet in the Library of Congress has his different and lighter pencil headings for the four sections he selected for the *Divertimento.* Cloth tabs attached to pages in the complete ballet bridge the cuts, and an inserted half double sheet which he headed: "Version de concert" was used to close the *Divertimento.*

In the western hemisphere, he led the first performances of the orchestral *Divertimento* with the Chicago Symphony on 14, 17, and 18 January 1935, followed by one at St. Louis on 10 February. For the premiere (at Milwaukee) the program called it "Divertimento," whereas the first Chicago performances called it both "Fragments" and "Divertimento." For all these performances he probably brought with him his set of orchestral parts which he had used at the Salle Pleyel the previous November. In a letter of 19 January from Chicago to Alexis Kall in Los Angeles he declined to perform it there on 21-22 February. As he explained, he and Dushkin would be playing the *Divertimento* in Los Angeles on 28 February and therefore he would not program its orchestral version with the Los Angeles Philharmonic. (He first conducted it there at the Shrine Auditorium during his next visit, in March 1937.)

Thus for purposes of comparison with Entry 45, some eleven sources are available in the US and Basle. For the *Divertimento* these include the autograph violin and piano arrangement made by Stravinsky and Dushkin upon forty-seven pages in the printed 1928 piano score of *Le baiser* as well as the three printed versions: for violin and piano in 1934; for orchestra in 1934 printed in 1938; and the 1950 revision of the latter.

For *Le baiser* there are: the sketches and sketchbook; the autograph 1928 arrangement for solo piano; the Library of Congress's orchestral autograph of 1928; the Morgan Library's 1928 partially autograph manuscript for solo piano and its printed edition of the same year; and lastly, the printed revision of the ballet in 1952.

The location of a twelfth source with the composer at Hollywood in 1949 (listed by White among the *Nachlass* but reported neither by Shepard in 1984 nor by Jans in 1989) remains unknown. It is (or was) a manuscript of the violin and piano arrangement of the *Divertimento*. Signing its cover and first page, he copied its fifty-two pages on unbound paper sheets, 14 × 10½ inches (c. 35.5 × 26.6 cm). According to Craft (as published by White), Stravinsky dated it "1928–32."

Among the first things one notices in Entry 45 is a complete lack of dynamic markings on p. 1. Neither page bears a key signature, the two sharps being added only after the final bar of p. 2. Also used in the Library of Congress autograph of the ballet (except for violins 1–2 and violas), this method obviates adding natural signs before F-sharps and C-sharps. The musical materials on p. 1 of Entry 45 do not appear in the violin and piano *Divertimento,* although they are in the orchestral *Divertimento* and, of course, in the orchestral *Le baiser,* as well as in its piano arrangement. Even though the parent autograph of the entire ballet at the Library of Congress has rehearsal numbers, neither the violin and piano *Divertimento* nor the two pages of Entry 45 have any.

Following the first three woodwind triads (mm. 2–4) and their rests (m. 5), p. 1 of Entry 45 lacks eleven subsequent following triads and their rests (mm. 6–16). Although the final triad is present (m. 17), breathing signs in woodwinds and strings follow it. These signs appear at this particular place in no other source.

On the other hand, breathing signs marked in the publications for earlier woodwind triads are lacking in Entry 45 as are a dynamic sign for the tremolo strings and their "con sordino," the latter present in the *Divertimento*. These woodwind breathing and dynamic signs and the indication, "con sordino," do not appear in the autograph orchestral score of *Le baiser.*

Lastly, the tie in the last bar for clarinet 2 present in the *Divertimento* is lacking in Entry 45 because its next bar (p. 2) is for clarinet 1 and is differently scored. (In *Le baiser,* the tie for its second clarinet is also lacking, though in this case, of course, the ballet continues differently from the *Divertimento*.) The first page of Entry 45 thus seems to have closer ties to the autograph of *Le baiser* than it does to the eventual orchestral *Divertimento.*

The second page also varies in several other respects from the violin and piano *Divertimento,* and from both publications of the orchestral *Divertimento*. This page differs in: key signature; tempo indication; omission of the initial low note of bassoon 1 and the octave displacement of clarinet 1; slurring of bassoon 1 and bass clarinet; and the final bar of violin 1. (A lack of key signature has already been mentioned.)

Found in no other source, the first two words of the tempo indication for p. 2, "Un poco più mosso ♩ = 108," suggest its origin. Because the "Scherzo" of the violin and piano 1934 arrangement of the *Divertimento* lacks the seventeen-bar introductory upper pedal point on A, it begins in 3/4 and is headed: "Allegretto grazioso ♩ = 126." At the same place, the autograph and the 1952 orchestral score of *Le baiser* and its 1928 printed and manuscript piano arrangements for piano, all at rehearsal **131**, as well as the 1950 orchestral *Divertimento* at rehearsal **85**, are marked just "Più mosso" with an "accelerando" during the concluding measures leading into the 2/4 "Allegretto grazioso." Thus the tempo indication on p. 2 of Entry 45 probably derives from the orchestral *Le baiser* and its piano arrangement, both finished late in 1928.

Omitting the opening low B in the bassoon part on p. 2 parallels a similar omission in the piano part of the 1934 violin and piano arrangement of the *Divertimento*. The low B appears in the sketchbook, in the orchestral autograph for *Le baiser* and in its 1952 edition, in its 1928 printed and manuscript arrangements for piano, and also in the printed 1938 and 1950 *Divertimento*. Despite the low B lacking in the bassoon part of Entry 45, its slurring and that for the bass clarinet notated directly above it are identical to slurrings for both instruments in the orchestral autograph of *Le baiser* and in the 1938 edition of the *Divertimento* prepared in 1934.

For the first measure of p. 2 in Entry 45, clarinet 1 in *la* sounds a D which then slurs downward to A. In the 1950 printed *Divertimento*, however, this sounding D is not only an octave lower, but it is assigned to clarinet 2 and ceases by the end of the first bar. Low D also sounds in the second clarinet in the orchestral autograph of *Le baiser* and in its 1952 edition and is at the same pitch in the 1928 piano arrangements. Using the upper sounding D in clarinet 1 in Entry 45 seems a less elegant solution to bridging the excision of rehearsal numbers **122–131** from the ballet than the solution he adopted in the orchestral *Divertimento,* where he allowed clarinet 2 to remain in its chalumeau register. This procedure again suggests that Entry 45 was an early experiment on the way to the final version of the orchestral suite.

Finally, a comparison of the printed copies owned by Stravinsky of the orchestral *Divertimento* and of *Le baiser,* copies which he notated for revisions, shows that he wanted the tied F-natural on the second beat of the final bar of violin 1 in Entry 45 to be altered to G-sharp. Despite his corrections, the F-natural reading, which also occurs in the autograph of *Le baiser* and in the 1934 (1938) *Divertimento,* continued to appear in the printed 1950 revision of the *Divertimento.* The desired G-sharp finally appeared only in the 1952 printed edition of *Le baiser.* F-natural in Entry 45 must also link it with the earliest stages of the music, that is, not long after the 1928 orchestral score for *Le baiser.* His several projected attempts in 1930-31 and his April 1931 performance at Trieste mentioned above suggest that as early as 1930 he was planning to draw a suite from *Le baiser.*

Therefore, the time of copying and the time of dedication to Castro for Entry 45 are probably separated by several years. Several scenarios seem possible. Obviously, the incomplete condition of the two pages (especially page 1) would have rendered them useless to copyist or printer of the 1934 orchestral *Divertimento* (not even published until 1938).

These two pages were copied on the same paper, bought years before at Bayonne, he had used in 1928 for the pencil orchestral *Le baiser* manuscript. He brought this (sole) orchestral score of the entire ballet with him in 1936 to Buenos Aires because he was to conduct it there. Perhaps Entry 45 was (accidentally?) packed along with the autograph score of the ballet, for it would seem odd that he would bring an empty half sheet of the latter's paper with him to Buenos Aires, copy out the two pages there (one of them incomplete), and dedicate them to Castro.

More probably, the sheet of Entry 45 with its differently scored clarinet parts was an abandoned attempt, c. 1930-34, to bridge the musical materials in *Le baiser* between its rehearsal numbers **122** and **131**. The question still remains that unless Entry 45 was merely packed away by accident with the full score of the ballet, why was Stravinsky carrying it around South America? Perhaps upon departing from France he had already intended to give it to someone on this tour.

One other possibility exists, of course. After returning to France and recalling their meeting at Buenos Aires, he found an abandoned page, inscribed it to Castro, and sent it there. This possibility, however, belies his usual method of dedicating materials on the spot.

In South America he would have had the music on these two pages very much on his mind. Only four days earlier he had led the complete

Le baiser de la fée with Bronislava Nijinska's choreography at the Teatro Colón in Buenos Aires. For this ballet performance he surely conducted from his sole autograph orchestral score. Shortly after the date of the Castro inscription, he was to conduct the *Divertimento* in Montevideo, on 23 May, for which he must also have utilized this same ballet score. As we have seen, apart from the autograph orchestral score of *Le baiser,* there is no evidence of any other orchestral score available for the *Divertimento* until it achieved print in 1938. For the Montevideo players, he probably brought the same set of parts he had just used in Buenos Aires.

Identifying the dedicatee "J. Castro" in Entry 45 poses only a few problems. The Castro family in Buenos Aires included several musicians whose first names began with J. They are Juan José (1864-1942), cellist and instrument maker, and his two sons: José Maria (1892-1964), also a cellist, composer and conductor; and Juan José II (1895-1968), violinist, pianist, composer, and conductor.

The elderly Juan José I seems least likely to have been the dedicatee. By 1936 he had long retired from playing cello in the Teatro Colón, devoting his last years to making instruments. Although both his sons were friends since 1925 of Victoria Ocampo who hosted Stravinsky and his son Soulima in 1936 at Buenos Aires, the more likely dedicatee is Juan José II. Ocampo seems to have been especially close to him. He often figures in her correspondence and, for Castro's seventieth birthday, she published a congratulatory essay and, in 1968, a moving obituary.

During the 1936 visit by Stravinsky to Buenos Aires, Juan José Castro conducted a broadcast concert on 11 May of four works by him. Moreover, in a photograph taken in the garden of Ocampo's home that May which shows Stravinsky in the act of photographing her, one sees behind him his son Soulima talking with Juan José.

In 1957 Castro wrote an essay celebrating the seventy-fifth birthday of Stravinsky. During concerts at Buenos Aires in August 1960, he inscribed a photograph of Juan José and himself: "To you, dear Castro / Yours / cordially as / ever / I Stravinsky / Buenos Aires / 1960." (For an autographed photograph signed by him in Buenos Aires on 17 May 1936, see Entry 44.)

Acquiring this page forges another link to his programming the *Divertimento* in Vancouver, Sunday afternoon 5 October 1952, the rehearsal for which Dr. Slim was privileged to attend that morning.

Works Consulted

Arizaga, Rodolfo. "Castro [family]." *Enciclopedia de la música argentina*. Buenos Aires: Fondo Nacional de las Artes, 1971. pp. 85-91.

—. *Juan José Castro*. Buenos Aires: Ediciones Culturales Argentinas, 1963. p. 29, pl. facing p. 80.

Caillois, Roger, and Victoria Ocampo. *Correspondance (1939-1978)*. ed. Odile Felgine, et al. Paris: Stock, 1997. p. 68, no. 3.

Chicago Symphony Program Notes. 14, 17-18 January 1935. pp. 215-17.

Craft, Robert. *Stravinsky: Chronicle of a Friendship*. 2nd ed. Nashville, TN, and London: Vanderbilt University Press, 1994. pp. 229-31 (26 August-3 September 1960).

Epstein, Ernesto. "Castro." MGG. vol. 15. cols. 1371-3.

Goubault, Christian. *Igor Stravinsky*. Paris: H. Champion, 1991. pp. 74, 234.

Jans, Hans Jörg, and Lukas Handschin, ed. *Igor Strawinsky. Musikmanuskripte*. ("Inventare der Paul Sacher Stiftung," 5 [Winterthur: Amadeus, 1989].) 26: "Partitur (1923; 141 pp)." pp. 14, 20.

Kall, Alexis F. Papers, Box 5 (Stravinsky: correspondence, 19 January 1935). Special Collections 601. Charles E. Young Research Library, University of California at Los Angeles.

Morton, L. "Stravinsky in Los Angeles." *Festival of Music Made in Los Angeles*. ed. Orrin Howard. Los Angeles: Philharmonic Association, 1981. p. 74.

Ocampo, Victoria. *Autobiografía IV Viraje*. Buenos Aires: Sur, 1982. pp. 31, 89-90, 108.

—. *Testimonios Séptima serie (1962-1967)*. Buenos Aires: Sur, 1967. pp. 194-5.

—. *Testimonios Octava serie (1968-1970)*. Buenos Aires: Sur, 1971. pp. 251-2.

—. *Testimonios Décima serie (1975-1977)*. Buenos Aires: Sur, 1977. p. 246.

Shepard, John. "The Stravinsky *Nachlass*: A Provisional Checklist of Music Manuscripts." *Music Library Association Notes* 40 (June 1984): 727.

Slim, H. Colin. "A Stravinsky holograph in 1936 for Juan José Castro in Buenos Aires: 'maître impeccable de la baguette'" in *Music Observed: Studies in Memory of William C. Holmes*. ed. Colleen Reardon and Susan Parisi. Warren, MI: Harmonie Park Press, 2003. Forthcoming.

SI&V. pl. 112 on p. [79] (caption).

SP&D. pp. 283-6, 329-30 (11, 14, and 23 May).

SSC. vol. 1. pp. 205-7; vol. 2. p. 294.

Taruskin, Richard. *Stravinsky and the Russian Traditions*. Berkeley and Los Angeles, CA: University of California Press, 1996. pp. 1610-18.

Vasquez, Maria Esther. *Victoria Ocampo*. Buenos Aires: Planeta, 1991. pl. [10, top] btn pp. 128-9, pp. 144-5.

Walsh, Stephen. *Stravinsky, A Creative Spring: Russia and France, 1882-1934.* New York, NY: Alfred A. Knopf, 1999. p. 548, n. 85 on p. 660.

White, Eric Walter. *Stravinsky: The Composer and His Works*. 2nd ed. Berkeley and Los Angeles, CA: University of California Press, 1979; repr. 1984. pp. 354, 610-11: nos. 52 and 60b-c.

46   (1936). Signed first US edition, 20.5 × 13.5 cm, STRAVINSKY: / AN AUTOBIOGRAPHY / (New York, Simon & Schuster, 1936), 288 pp. with 8 pls., inscribed in black ink across title page:

Igor Strawinsky

Acquisition: H. Colin Slim in Santa Barbara, CA, on 23 November 1995 through Martin A. Silver from Wahrenbrock Bookhouse (San Diego, CA).

Provenance: Auction sale (c. 1995) of a San Diego estate.

Commentary

This first edition in the US by an unknown translator of the two-volume *Chroniques de ma vie* (Paris, 1935) was published late in November 1936 (see entries 19, 42-3, 83, 103). Entry 46 increases the number of images found in volume one of the *Chroniques* in Entry 43. The new portrait of the composer (frontispiece) and the final new photograph of both his hands (p. 303) were taken on 12 November 1930 in Munich by Eric Schaal (later to photograph him rehearsing the New York Philharmonic in 1939). The other plates reproduce:

- Théodore Stravinsky's 1932 drawing of his father (p. 291)
- Picasso's portrait of 24 May 1920 (p. 293)
- the composer's 1917 sketch of Ramuz (p. 295)

- Cocteau's 1920 drawing of Picasso and Stravinsky and Picasso's 1919 sketch for *Pulcinella* (p. 297)
- Picasso's design for *Ragtime* and, additionally, his 1917 portrait of Stravinsky (p. 299)
- Picasso's December 1920 portrait (p. 301)

Although Entry 46 was surely not inscribed before 23 December 1936 when Stravinsky arrived in New York for his third US tour, his orthography suggests that he might have done so before 1945. From 1945 until 1952 he usually spelled his surname with a "v;" compare entries 80 (1943-44) and 81-2 (both 1944) clearly "w," with entries 83-6 (1945-48) apparently "v," and with entries 87-8 (both 1951) and entries 89, 91, and 93-4 (1952), all of these certainly "v."

On 26 December 1941 he observed that although "w" does not exist in the Russian language, his father had replaced the "v" with a "w" because of the German pronunciation of "v," which sounds like an "f." On 24 October 1942, he wrote that he spelled it with "w" because of German pronunciation. On 15 September 1952, however, he was persuaded to use "w" for a few years. The provenance of Entry 46 might suggest that he inscribed it on 18 February 1941 when he was in San Diego conducting the Los Angeles Philharmonic.

Craft has recounted the publishing history, from 9 December 1934 to 12 October 1937, of the *Autobiography* in the United States. It was later issued in an edition without plates in 1958 (New York, NY: M. and J. Steuer) and in paperback in 1962 (New York, NY: W.W. Norton) (see Entry 103). Joan Evans has discussed its history in Nazi Germany and later.

Works Consulted

Evans, Joan. "Some Remarks on the Publication and Reception of Stravinsky's *Erinnerungen*." *Mitteilungen der Paul Sacher Stiftung* 9 (March 1996): 17-23.

Lederman, Minna, ed. *Stravinsky in the Theatre*. New York, NY: Dance Index, 1949; repr. Da Capo Press, 1975. upper pl. on p. [175].

SBu. nn. 4 and 7 on p. 51.

SI&V. pl. 109 on p. [77].

SP&D. n. to colour pl. 1 facing p. 144.

SSC. vol. 2. pp. 494-9; vol. 3. p. 284.

47   (1937). Autograph singly folded letter, 16.8 × 13.3 cm, in French in black ink on a doubled sheet of WADE PARK MANOR / Cleveland / stationery, 1 March 1937, to Madame [Clara Gehring] Bickford (1903-85):

Chère Madame Bickford
Comment vous remercier du bon accueil que vous m'avez reservé à moi et ma musique
    J'en suis profondément touché et vous envoie toute ma gratitude
    Igor Strawinsky

le 1 mars / 37

Clara Bickford   Cleveland
Cleveland   1 March 1937

Dear Mrs. Bickford:
How to thank you for the kind reception that you accorded me and my music.
    I am deeply touched by this and send you all my gratitude.
    Igor Strawinsky

Acquisition: H. Colin Slim on 25 March 1997 from La Scala Autographs. The letter was backed with acid-free museum paper and inserted in a mylar envelope by Linda K. Ogden on 15 May 1997.
Provenance: Clara Gehring Bickford, Cleveland, OH (1937-85); Cleveland Institute of Music (1986-96); unidentified New York dealer (1996) with his printed label comprising a logo, followed by: Igor Stravinsky ALS/96B119 (net price only); La Scala Autographs, *Catalog Spring 1997* (Pennington, NJ), no. 123 (with a partial English translation).

Commentary
The letter is unpublished, its envelope missing. A small triangular tear, 1.3 × 0.1 cm, is at the upper right corner of the letter; discolouration on

three sides suggests previous matting and perhaps display. Residing at Wade Park Manor during his engagements in Cleveland, Stravinsky wrote Entry 47 two days after his final concert, 27 February 1937, with the Cleveland Orchestra.

Clara Bickford, née Gehring, civic patroness of the arts and amateur pianist, was elected Secretary of the Cleveland Institute of Music in October 1935 and organized its Women's Committee during her first year as President of the Board of Trustees of the Institute (1936-39). She remained a trustee until her death.

When Stravinsky visited in 1937, she was on the Board of Trustees of the Women's Committee of the Cleveland Orchestra, chaired its Music Memory and Appreciation subcommittee, and taught music appreciation courses for the orchestra, having in 1934-5 chaired the Speakers's Division subcommittee. In 1936 she was one of the founders of the Two Piano Club in Cleveland for women performers. She had studied piano at the Cleveland Institute where she also gave lessons and was a close friend of Beryl Rubinstein (1898-1952), who taught piano at the institute from 1921 and who was later its director (1932-52). She bequeathed to it not only Entry 47 but also thirteen autograph musical quotations by Stravinsky (entries 48-60).

She owned a vast collection of music manuscripts, autographs, letters, and photographs of composers only partly cited in *The Bickford Collection: An International Heritage of Music,* a memorial exhibition of some 104 selected items at the Cleveland Institute, in October 1986.

Her collection included materials by Bartok, Beethoven, Berg, Berlioz, Bernstein, Borodin, Brahms, Britten, Cherubini, Chopin, Debussy, Dvorak, Elgar, Stephen Foster, Franck, Gluck, Gounod, Grieg, Haydn, Humperdinck, Kern, Francis Scott Key, Liszt, Mahler, Mendelssohn, Meyerbeer, Milhaud, Mozart, Offenbach, Paganini, Poulenc, Prokofiev, Puccini, Rachmaninoff, Ravel, Respighi, Rimsky-Korsakov, Rossini, Schoenberg, Schubert, Robert and Clara Schumann, Shostakovich, Sibelius, Sousa, Johann and Richard Strauss, Stravinsky, Sullivan, Tchaikovsky, Vaughan Williams, Verdi, Wagner, Webern and many others. Late in September just before the exhibition, for example, *The Cleveland Plain Dealer* illustrated her Liszt signed photograph, two pages of one of her Schubert manuscripts, and Entry 52.

Some notion of her collection's present monetary value can be obtained from the following. At auction in March 1997 her 1803

Haydn manuscript sold at Berlin for DM 19 000 and her twenty-seven Clara Schumann letters for DM 38 000. The 1838 Robert Schumann letter was offered for $15 000, 1997-99, by Kenneth W. Rendell. Her Borodin letter of 1884 appeared at Sotheby's in May 1997, estimated at £3000-3500. Her 1873 Offenbach letter was offered by David Schulson in New York in 1997 for $500. Catalogues issued by La Scala Autographs in the spring seasons of 1997-98 included many items from her collection, for example: Bartok 1940 for $550; Bernstein 1954 for $1200; Cherubini 1837 for $1500; Humperdinck 1920 for $750; Kern 1944 for $600; Key 1840 for $950; Liszt 1850 for $3500; Poulenc 1942-43 for $750; Respighi 1932 for $500; Sibelius 1911 for $2000; Sousa 1920 for $1100; Richard Strauss 1898 for $800; Sullivan 1897 for $600; Von Buelow 1890 for $750; Vaughan Williams 1935 for $500. Her 1924 Webern appeared in Lisa Cox's winter 1998 and spring 2000 catalogues for £850 and £950, respectively.

According to her lawyer husband, George P. Bickford (1901-91), whom she married on 6 April 1933, she amassed her collection over some fifty years, beginning "with an almost impulsive purchase at an auction." In 1947, he wrote: "she is greatly interested in music, being an accomplished pianist, and music has played a large part in the lives of both of us. In addition, I have, with the assistance of Norm[an Alexander] Hall [bookseller from 1926 at Newton Center, MA], collected old books ... and musical autographs for my wife."

In 1925, (the unmarried) Clara Gehring probably did not meet Stravinsky when he conducted the Cleveland Orchestra on 12 and 14 February in Tchaikovsky's *Symphony no. 6* (a work he again performed with that orchestra during his 1937 tour), and his own *Fireworks, Le Chant du Rossignol,* and the 1919 *Firebird Suite* during his first visit to the US. (Given her future collecting habits, surely she would have requested his autograph that year and preserved it, as she did her 1937 items.) I thank Lenore Coral, Paul Cary, Carol S. Jacobs, Archivist of the Cleveland Orchestra, and especially my former student, Professor Katherine Powers, for kindly obtaining a printout of the exhibition catalogue and for checking Cleveland newspapers.

Works Consulted

"Bickford, Clara." *The* [Cleveland] *Plain Dealer.* 15 December 1985. p. 44A (obituary with photograph).

"Bickford, George P." *25th Annual Report, Harvard Class of 1922.* Cambridge: Harvard University Press, 1947. pp. 72-3.

Cleveland Orchestra. Twelfth Program; 12-14 February 1925. p. 405.

Finn, Robert. "A touch of musical greatness, CIM to show part of Clara Bickford collection." *The* [Cleveland] *Plain Dealer.* 20 September 1986. pp. 21-A, 24-A.

Kuehn, Alice. "Cleveland Orchestra Women." *The Cleveland Plain Dealer.* 18 April 1937. p. C-7 with photograph.

"Mrs. Crowell again Heads Music Board" [of the CIM]. *The Cleveland Plain Dealer.* 25 October 1935. p. 6.

Rendell, Kenneth W. *Catalogue 260.* Wellesley, MA, and New York, 1997. p. 34.

−. *Catalogue 267.* Wellesley, MA, and New York, 1998. p. 38.

−. *Catalogue 276.* Wellesley, MA, and New York, 1999. p. 38.

Rodda, Richard E., and David M. Thum. *The Bickford Collection: An International Heritage of Music.* Cleveland, OH: The Cleveland Institute of Music, 8-12 October 1986.

Schulson, David. *Autographs 94.* New York, 1997, item 69.

Sotheby's. *Fine Music and Continental Manuscripts.* London, 15-16 May 1997, lot 112.

Stargardt, J.A. *Katalog 666.* Berlin, 18-19 March 1997, lot 892 (ill. on p. 351), lot 1047 on p. 394-7.

SP&D. pp. 334-5.

SSC. vol. 2. p. 303.

Towns, Martha. "Clara Bickford's collection reflects her lifelong love of music." [unidentified Cleveland newspaper]. September 1986.

ENTRIES 48-60: PRELIMINARY REMARKS

These entries are thirteen undated autograph musical quotations with French titles (one also in Russian, and one in Latin) in black ink on variously sized slips of white paper, each signed by Stravinsky and mounted in 1937 (in the US or in France) for Clara Gehring Bickford of Cleveland. Five of the white paper slips (entries 52, 54-5, 57-8) are watermarked: B F K Rives (i.e., Blanchet Frères Kléber, Rives-sur-Fure [Isère]). Each slip is mounted on uniformly sized heavy dark green paper, 16.3 × 25.0 cm, from Annonay (Ardèche). Six of the latter (entries 48-50, 52-3, and 56) reveal various parts of an embossed manufacturer's mark: ANC[IEN]ᴺᴱˢ MANUF[ACTURE]ᴿᴱˢ CANSON & MONTGOLFIER ★ VIDALON-LES-ANNONAY ★.

Except for Entry 50 ("Le Sacre du Printemps"), each mount has on its lower right side dealer marks in pencil, running from 96B120 to 96B131; number 96B125 was also originally marked 96B124 (like its predecessor). On the reverse side of each mount (except for "Le Sacre") is 18667 in pencil, perhaps that of an inventory taker or of the dealer preceding La Scala Autographs Inc., but not in the hand either of Stravinsky nor of anyone at La Scala. As in Entry 47, the numbers are those of the unidentified New York dealer who purchased the Bickford collection. Mount 96B122 has 291 in pencil on its upper left corner, repeated from the same number in ink at the upper left of its musical quotation ("OEdipus Rex"), neither being in the hand of Stravinsky nor of persons working at La Scala.

Acquisition: entries 48-9 and 51-60, H. Colin Slim on 10 March 1997 from La Scala Autographs through Martin A. Silver; Entry 50 (the only one to lack its previous dealer's number) was acquired on 27 March 1997 from La Scala Autographs. Rather than risk attempting to remove them, the quotations were deemed stable enough by Linda K. Ogden in April 1997 to remain on their mounts. On 15 May 1997, she flattened several holes made by thumbtacks, backed each mount with acid-free museum paper and enclosed each in a mylar envelope. Because of their quantity, entries 48-60 are unframed.

Provenance: Clara Gehring Bickford, Cleveland (1937-85); Cleveland Institute of Music (1986 to fall 1996). *The Bickford Collection,* p. 8, "Panel 10 – Europe to America," noted: "**Igor Stravinsky** provided Clara Bickford with a remarkable set of thematic excerpts from thirteen of his most important works, each with his full signature, during his visit to Cleveland on his 1937 American tour" not mentioning the letter he wrote her (see Entry 47); unidentified New York dealer (late 1996); La Scala Autographs, *Catalog Winter 1997 [Part 1],* no. 123 with ill. "Le Rossignol" (see Entry 51).

Commentary

In Panel 10 of the 1986 Bickford memorial exhibition at the Cleveland Institute, her thirteen Stravinsky quotations, entries 48-60, were each mounted – equally spaced on each side and with a slightly narrower top margin than at the bottom – on a dark green sheet of paper. Many of these latter sheets have multiple holes from thumbtacks, some of which even pierce the mounted quotation. Probably his copying of the quotations followed the letter of appreciation that he wrote her on 1 March 1937 (see Entry 47), since it does not mention them and, in it, he wonders – even if perhaps rhetorically – how to thank her for her support. Mrs. Bickford may well have shown Stravinsky her collection of musical autographs or at least mentioned her hobby to him when he was in Cleveland.

Almost certainly he mounted the thirteen quotations himself. First, no other autographs belonging to Mrs. Bickford are mounted on this paper. Second, the mounts are all of the same heavy paper, French in origin. Although the thirteen excerpts provide an anthology of most of his important orchestral, choral, and chamber works from 1910 to 1931, curiously they do not include any music originally for piano, Mrs. Bickford's instrument.

The paper used for all but four of the quotations was made by the Société Blanchet Frères et Didier Kléber at Rives, a company established in 1820 and still flourishing. The paper for Entry 48 is unique; a still different paper was used for entries 49-51. That for the mounts was made by Canson and Montgolfier at their Vidalon mill situated on la Deume, a stream running through Annonay. Both Rives and Annonay are near Voreppe, where Stravinsky settled his family from August 1931 until near the close of 1934, though of course he could also have purchased such papers then or later in Paris or elsewhere.

Notwithstanding the Cleveland catalogue's indications, because the paper of each quotation and of its mount is French (and unlikely that Stravinsky would have travelled with the mount paper on his tour throughout the US), he probably copied the quotations in France after returning there in May and only then dispatched them to Mrs. Bickford (see the commentary to Entry 55). He would unlikely have presented her merely with a series of differently sized slips of white paper containing musical quotations. Craft has well noted his extreme fastidiousness.

La Scala Autographs purchased the letter and a dozen of these musical quotations from a dealer who took "Le Sacre" (Entry 50), for him/herself, the latter displaying no respect for an important historical collection. Fortunately, La Scala was able to obtain the *Rite* quotation in England for the present collection.

During his 1937 tour of Eastern Canada and the US (3 January–28 April), Stravinsky conducted many of the works he autographed for Mrs. Bickford: *Firebird, Petrushka, Pulcinella, Apollo, Symphony of Psalms,* and the *Violin Concerto*. With the Russian-born American violinist, Samuel Dushkin, he also played arrangements of several of them. Having toured on 18-20 February with the Cleveland Orchestra to Allentown, Pennsylvania, and Princeton, New Jersey, Stravinsky conducted on the 24th in Cleveland itself, at Severance Hall, and his *Fireworks, Violin Concerto* (with Dushkin), and *Petrushka* there on the 25th and 27th. Hearing Stravinsky conduct *Apollo* and his new *Jeu de Cartes* (1936) two months later at the Metropolitan Opera, Paul Hindemith wrote his wife: "the good Igor is a truly mediocre conductor and cunningly avoids any step in the direction of free and spontaneous music making."

Stravinsky drew the staves of these excerpts with his own patented invention, a special bronze stylus with a wheel, which he had used since the time of composing *Petrushka*. Called by Ramuz in 1928, "un certain instrument à roulettes qui servait à tracer les portées et dont Stravinsky lui-même était l'inventeur," this device is also cited by Dushkin in 1949 and by Vera Stravinsky in 1962. Several photographs by Arnold Newman taken 1966-67 show him using it. (For additional examples, see entries 7, 62, 71, 76, 106, and 115.)

Because the order in which he copied entries 48-60 is unknown, the entries appear below in their chronological order of completion. Each entry is followed by the mark assigned it by the dealer.

Works Consulted

Canson and Montgolfier. *Papeteries de Vidalon-les-Annonay (Ardèche)*. Vienne: Savigne, 1872.

Craft, Robert. *The Moment of Existence: Music, Literature, and the Arts 1990-1995*. Nashville, TN, and London: Vanderbilt University Press, 1996. p. 268.

Ganne, Bernard. *Gens du cuir. Gens du papier*. Paris: CNRS, 1983. passim.

Newman, Arnold, and Robert Craft. *Bravo Stravinsky*. Cleveland, OH, and New York, NY: World, 1967. pp. 13-17, 29.

Poncet, Marie-Thérèse. *Rives-sur-Fure*. Paris: Guenegaud, 1976. passim, esp. pp. 49, 54, 59.

Skelton, Geoffrey, ed. and trans. *Selected Letters of Paul Hindemith*. New Haven, CT, and London: Yale University Press, 1955. p. 105.

SP&D. p. 334.

SSC. vol. 1. n. 3 on p. 399; vol. 2. pp. 302-3.

"Stravinsky Leads Cleveland Forces." *Musical America* 57 (10 March 1937): pl. on p. 18.

48

(1937). Autograph musical quotation, one side of a sheet, 7.2 × 13.0 cm, in black ink on a single stave, of two bars headed: "L'Oiseau de Feu" and signed below: Igor Strawinsky. Dealer's pencil mark on original mount: 96B124.

Commentary

The excerpt, "Berceuse" from *The Firebird* (1910; publ. Jurgenson, 1912), is scored for bassoon 1; see the 1912 ed., p. 163, at rehearsal **183** and the 1919 *Suite*, p. [166], at rehearsal **1**. (For a different excerpt from the ballet, see Entry 115.)

49

(1937). Autograph musical quotation, one side of a sheet, 7.3 × 15.8 cm, in black ink on three staves, of two bars headed: PETROUCHKA, inscribed: Fag. C-fag. CB.pizz. at the beginning of the staves and signed at the right below the first stave: Igor Strawinsky. Dealer's pencil mark on original mount: 96B120.

Commentary

The excerpt, "The Magic Trick" from *Petrushka* (1911; publ. Édition russe de musique, 1912), is scored for double basses, bassoons 1-2 and contrabassoon; see the 1912 ed., p. 41, at rehearsal **30**. The contrabassoon part here agrees not with it, however, but with the revised 1948 edition, p. 35, m. 1, thereby corroborating Craft's observations about the revision process. (For a comment by Stravinsky in December 1939 to Dorothy Ellis McQuoid in Los Angeles about errors in the 1933 Kalmus reprint of the 1912 score, see Entry 68).

Claude Debussy particularly admired the passage quoted in Entry 49. On 13 April 1912, he wrote Stravinsky: "I do not know many things as good as the passage you call the Conjuring Trick. There is in it a kind of sonorous magic, a sort of mysterious transformation of mechanical souls, which become human by a spell of which, until now, you seem to be the sole inventor. Finally, there are orchestral certainties that I have found only in *Parsifal*." (For a different quotation from the same ballet, see Entry 119.)

Works Consulted

SSC. vol. 1. pp. 391-2.

Walsh, Stephen. *Stravinsky, A Creative Spring: Russia and France, 1882-1934.* New York, NY: Alfred A. Knopf, 1999. p. 164 (trans. S. Walsh).

50 (1937). Autograph musical quotation, one side of a sheet, 8.9 × 15.1 cm, in black ink on one stave, of three bars headed: Le Sacre du Printemps and signed below: Igor Strawinsky. There is no dealer's mark on the front of the mount, but on the reverse side appears: CBD [=?Clara Bickford] in pencil within a circle, written over something no longer legible.

Commentary

The excerpt, from the "Introduction" to part 1 of *The Rite of Spring* (1913; publ. Édition russe de musique, 1921), is scored for oboe 1; see the 1913 ed. (piano, 4 hands) and 1921 ed., p. 7, at rehearsal **9**. Stravinsky has made an erasure, perhaps of some other clef, from the beginning of the stave.

Works Consulted

Meyer, Felix, ed. *Settling New Scores. Music Manuscripts from the Paul Sacher Foundation.* Mainz: Schott, 1998. pp. 76-8, no. 22.

51
(1937). Autograph musical quotation, one side of a sheet, 7.0 × 14.8 cm, in black ink on a single stave, of four bars headed: "Le Rossignol" and signed below: Igor Strawinsky. Dealer's pencil mark on original mount: 96B126.

Commentary
The excerpt, "Andantino" from *The Song of the Nightingale* (1917; publ. Édition russe de musique, 1921), is scored for flute 1; see the 1921 ed., p. 15, at rehearsal **15**. This passage, not appearing in the opera, *Le Rossignol* (1908-14), was newly composed during the spring of 1917 at Morges for *Le Chant du Rossignol*. (For a different quotation from *Le Chant*, copied two years later, see Entry 62.)

Works Consulted
Taruskin, Richard. *Stravinsky and the Russian Traditions.* Berkeley and Los Angeles, CA: University of California Press, 1996. p. 1090, esp. n. 121.

52
(1937). Autograph musical quotation, one side of a sheet, 8.2 × 13.5 cm, in black ink on two staves, of five bars headed: Histoire du Soldat and signed below: Igor Strawinsky. Dealer's pencil mark on original mount: 96B129.

Commentary
The excerpt, the "Soldier's March" from *The Soldier's Tale* (1918; publ. Chester, 1924), is scored for cornet and trombone, then joined by clarinet, bassoon, violin, double bass and percussion (see the 1924 complete edition); the 1922 *Suite*; and the 1920 *Suite* for violin, clarinet, and piano, all at p. 1, mm. 1-5. Stravinsky erased a bar line from each stave in the fourth bar and incorrectly copied the final lower note in the double bass in bar five as low C instead of D. Entry 52 is reproduced in *The Cleveland Plain Dealer*, Saturday, 20 September 1986, p. 24-A.

Works Consulted
Meyer, Felix, ed. *Settling New Scores. Music Manuscripts from the Paul Sacher Foundation.* Mainz: Schott, 1998. pp. 279-81, nos. 143-5.

53

(1937). Autograph musical quotation, one side of a sheet, 8.3 × 13.5 cm, in black ink on a single stave, of two bars headed: Pulcinella (Finale), in the left margin: Tr.ba and signed below: Igor Strawinsky. Dealer's pencil mark on original mount: 96B127.

Commentary

The excerpt, "Finale" from *Pulcinella* (1920; publ. Édition russe de musique, 1924), is scored for trumpet 1; see the 1924 and 1966 editions, p. 151 at rehearsal **192** and the 1924 *Suite* (rev. 1949), p. 66, at rehearsal **107**.

54

(1937). Autograph musical quotation, one side of a sheet, 6.5 × 14.2 cm, in black ink on one stave, of three bars headed: M<u>avra</u>, with Russian text below: Drug moi milyi, kras-no solnysh-ko mo-e (Dear darling mine, my bright sun) and signed below: Igor Strawinsky. Dealer's pencil mark on original mount: MAVRA/96B130.

Commentary

The excerpt, "Parasha's aria" (or "Chanson Russe") from *Mavra* (1922; publ. Édition russe de musique, 1925), from which Stravinsky omitted the 3/4 and 5/8 time signatures, is for soprano. The 1947 revision of the 1925 full score published in 1969, p. 12, and the revised edition of the 1925 piano/vocal edition, p. 7, both at rehearsal **1–2**, have a different (singing) translation. The aria may have been much on his mind: in collaboration with Dushkin in April 1937 at New York, he arranged it for violin and piano.

Works Consulted

SSC. vol. 2. n. 9 on p. 294.

Walsh, Stephen. *Stravinsky, A Creative Spring: Russia and France, 1882-1934.* New York, NY: Alfred A. Knopf, 1999. pp. 120-1, ex. 28.

55 (1937). Autograph musical quotation, one side of a sheet, 8.0 × 13.5 cm, in black ink, on two staves of three bars headed in Russian and French: Svadebka [/] <u>Les Noces</u> in the left margin: Sopr.[/] { , and below the upper stave Russian text: I ia byla na sinem na mo-re na more [And I have been on the blue sea, on the sea], and signed below: Igor Strawinsky. Dealer's pencil mark on original mount: 96B128.

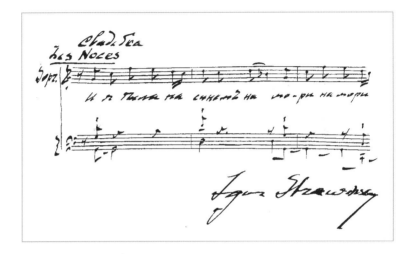

Commentary

The excerpt, "The Wedding Feast," from tableau 4 of *The Wedding* (1923; publ. Chester, 1923), is scored for solo soprano and piano 2; see the 1922 vocal score and the 1923 ed., p. 99, both at rehearsal **106**. Taruskin's discussions of the sources of music and text are indispensable. The choice of text in this quotation for Mrs. Bickford might well testify to the composer's various sea trips to and from the US in 1924-5 (December-January and March), 1934-5 (December-January and April), to and from South America in 1936 (April-June), and even specifically to his most recent one to and from the US in 1936-7 (December–April). If the text of Entry 55 does in fact pertain to his return to France, then the quotations would certainly have been inscribed there and not in the US. (For autograph sketches for player piano from a different part of *The Wedding*, see Entry 21.)

Works Consulted

Taruskin, Richard. *Stravinsky and the Russian Traditions*. Berkeley and Los Angeles, CA: University of California Press, 1996. table 4, facing p. 1422 and ff.

–. "Stravinsky and the Subhuman: Notes on *Svadebka*," in Richard Taruskin, *Defining Russia Musically*. Princeton, NJ: Princeton University Press, 1997. pp. 390-467.

56

(1937). Autograph musical quotation, one side of a sheet, 6.2 × 13.5 cm, in black ink on a single stave, of four bars headed: Octuor (TEMA) and signed below: Igor Strawinsky. Dealer's pencil mark on original mount: 96B121.

Commentary

The excerpt, "Andantino" from the *Octet* (1923; publ. Édition russe de musique, 1924), second movement, is scored for flute (octave higher) and clarinet (octave lower); see the 1924 edition, p. 15, and the revised 1952 edition, p. 12, both at rehearsal **24**.

57

(1937). Autograph musical quotation, one side of a sheet, 9.9 × 12.8 cm, in black ink on three staves, of five bars headed: OEdipus Rex, at left margin of top stave: OEd with Latin text below top stave: Lux fa-cta est. and signed below: Igor Strawinsky. The number 291 in ink at the upper left corner is not in the composer's hand. Dealer's pencil mark on original mount: 96B122.

Commentary

The excerpt, from *Oedipus Rex* (1927; publ. vocal score only: Édition russe de musique, 1927; full score: Boosey and Hawkes, 1949), act II, is scored for tenor and cellos, then followed by harp, two clarinets, and double basses; see the 1927 edition (rev. 1949), p. 115, at rehearsal **169**. Stravinsky has made an erasure preceding the second stave.

58

(1937). Autograph musical quotation, one side of a sheet, 8.1 × 12.7 cm, in black ink on a single stave, of five bars headed: Apollon-Musagète and signed below: Igor Strawinsky. Dealer's pencil mark on original mount: 96B123.

Commentary

The excerpt, the opening of the "Variation Terpsichore" from *Apollo* (1928; publ. Édition russe de musique, 1928), scene 2, composed 16-19 November 1927, is scored for first and second violins and violas; see the 1928 edition, p. 36, and the 1947 revised edition, p. 22, both at rehearsal **52**. Diaghilev had infuriated him by deleting Terpsichore's variation from later performances of the ballet during 1928 and 1929.

Perhaps he inscribed Mrs. Bickford's musical quotation not only for this reason, but also to salute her. In 1935 he had written: "Enfin, Terpsichore, réunissant en elle les rhythmes de la poésie et l'éloquence du geste, révèle au monde la danse et trouve ainsi parmi ces muses la place d'honneur à côté du Musagète." [Finally, Terpsichore, uniting in herself the rhythms of poetry and the eloquence of motion, reveals dance to the world and thus finds among these muses the place of honour beside the Musagete.]

Works Consulted

Joseph, Charles M. "Diaghilev and Stravinsky." *The Ballets Russes and Its World*. ed. Lynn Garafola and Nancy Van Norman Baer. New Haven, CT, and London: Yale University Press, 1999. p. 197.

SChron. vol. 2. pp. 101-2 (trans. Leonard W. Johnson).

Walsh, Stephen. *Stravinsky, A Creative Spring: Russia and France, 1882-1934*. New York, NY: Alfred A. Knopf, 1999. pp. 469, 478, 482.

59

(1937). Autograph musical quotation, one side of a sheet, 9.4 × 13.4 cm, in black ink on three staves, of four bars headed: Symph. de Psaumes, at left margin of upper pair of staves: Disc. [/] Alti and: Ten. [/] Bas. with Latin text between them: Al-le-lu-ia. Lauda-te, Laudate and signed below: Igor Strawinsky. Dealer's pencil mark on original mount: 96B125.

Commentary

The excerpt, from the opening of the third movement of *Symphony of Psalms* (1930; publ. Édition russe de musique, 1931), is scored for Discanti, Alti, Tenori, Bassi, cellos, double basses, harp, two pianos, and timpani; see the 1930 vocal score, and the 1931 edition (rev. 1948), p. 27, both at rehearsal **1**.

60

(1937). Autograph musical quotation, one side of a sheet, 9.9 × 19.0 cm, in black ink on two staves, of three bars headed: 1ᵉʳ Mᵉⁿᵗ du Concerto pour Violon [/] et orchestre, at left margin of upper stave: V.no and at the left margin of the lower one: { and signed below: Igor Strawinsky. Dealer's pencil mark on original mount: 96B131.

Commentary

The excerpt, from the first movement of the *Concerto in D for violin and orchestra* (1931; publ. Schott, 1931), is scored for solo violin, three bassoons and cellos; see the 1931 ed., p. 6, at rehearsal **10**. Stravinsky erased an incorrect E-sharp below the lower stave at the third eighth note of the first full bar.

Works Consulted

Meyer, Felix, ed. *Settling New Scores. Music Manuscripts from the Paul Sacher Foundation*. Mainz: Schott, 1998. pp. 73-4, no. 29.

61

(1938). Signed embossed concert program, 25.2 × 20.0 cm, Brussels, 19 May 1938, the program itself on inside page, Stravinsky's signature in black ink, right, on cover below coat of arms, Soulima signing below his printed name:

FONDATION MUSICALE REINE ELISABETH
[coat of arms] L'UNION FAIT LA FORCE
[signed] I Strawinsky
Concert Symphonique
SOUS LA DIRECTION DE MONSIEUR
IGOR STRAWINSKY
AVEC LE CONCOURS DE MONSIEUR
SULIMA STRAWINSKY
PIANISTE
[signed] S. Strawinsky
[fleuret]
Grande Salle du Palais des Beaux-Arts
19 Mai 1938

Acquisition: H. Colin Slim on 28 March 2000 from Joyce B. Muns, Fine Arts Book Dealer (1162 Shattuck Ave / Berkeley, CA / 94707).
Provenance: Probably at auction in Germany; the cover's upper edge bears an almost completely erased pencil inscription: "Aufführung / Stravinskys."

Commentary

In rather poor condition, the concert program has not been published. For whom it was inscribed is unknown. When signing its cover, Stravinsky (though not Soulima) obviously experienced considerable difficulty with the pen.

Vera's diary notes that he would be travelling from Paris to Brussels on 16 May. The inside page of Entry 61 prints the program: *Symphony no. 3 in D major* by Tchaikovsky, his own *Capriccio* with Soulima as soloist, and the 1919 *Firebird Suite.* (Stravinsky had himself played the *Capriccio* at Brussels in the same Grande Salle under Ansermet, on 13 December 1930.) Soulima first performed it under his father's baton at Barcelona on 16 November 1933. (See also Entry 82.)

Devotion to Tchaikovsky manifested itself during the 1920s and 1930s not only in *The Sleeping Princess, Le baiser de la fée* but also by Stravinsky conducting that composer's symphonies (see entries 47, 65, and 71). His own first symphony (1905-07) reveals in its slow movement and at the close of its finale profound debts to Tchaikovsky's fifth and sixth symphonies.

Works Consulted

SAc. pp. 132, pl. on p. 151 (1936 photograph of father and son).

SBu. p. 92 (15 May 1938).

SP&RK. vol. 1. pp. 416-17.

Taruskin, Richard. *Stravinsky and the Russian Traditions.* Berkeley and Los Angeles, CA: University of California Press, 1996. pp. 206-21.

Walsh, Stephen. *Stravinsky, A Creative Spring: Russia and France, 1882-1934.* New York, NY: Alfred A. Knopf, 1999. pp. 104, 492, 497, 529-31.

62   (1939). Autograph untitled musical quotation, one side of a card, 9.0 × 14.0 cm, in black ink on two staves, of two bars of *Le Chant du Rossignol* in a piano reduction especially made by the composer and inscribed January 1939 at Paris for [Dean Carl Trock]:

Igor Strawinsky / Janv. 1939 Paris

Acquisition: in May 1981 from Richard MacNutt, bidding for H. Colin Slim at Christie's London, *Valuable autograph letters, historical documents and music manuscripts* (29 April 1981), lot 246.

Provenance: Dean Carl Trock, Copenhagen (1939-81).

Commentary

Stravinsky scored the excerpt for bassoon 1, trombone 3, tuba, tamtam, cellos and double basses. Distribution of parts and rests in Entry 62 shows that he used neither his own piano reduction (publ. 1927) of his symphonic poem, *Le Chant du Rossignol* (1917; publ. 1921), at rehearsal **73**, nor the score of his opera, *Le Rossignol* (publ. Édition russe de musique, 1914 and 1923), at rehearsal **103**, for the above reduction. The tail of *y* in his signature also serves as the serif of *P* in Paris. Similar playfulness occurs in entries 43, 72, and 107.

In response to Dr. Slim's letter of enquiry about its provenance, its previous owner, Dean Carl Trock in Copenhagen, kindly wrote on 21 August 1981: "The history of the autograph is not very exciting, only this: When I was young, I collected autographs and I simply wrote [in 1938] to Igor Stravinsky and he sent me the notes and his autograph." Undoubtedly Trock's nationality played a role in Stravinsky selecting a composition based on a tale by Hans Christian Andersen. His choice of music for Entry 62, "Death in the Emperor's Bedchamber," however, surely reflects his mood so shortly after the death, 30 November 1938, of his elder daughter, Lyudmila. Craft discusses the publishing history of both opera and symphonic poem. (For a different excerpt from the symphonic poem, see Entry 51.)

Works Consulted

SSC. vol. 2. pp. 197-218.

63

(1939). Autograph picture postcard, 13.2 × 8.7 cm, in French in black ink, the reverse side with a photograph of Stravinsky probably taken by Gar Vic in 1936 at Buenos Aires, 21 May 1939, to Vittorio Gui (1885-1975):

A Vittorio Gui
Londres

Merci, cher ami, de votre si gentil mot. Dans 2 heures je dirige Perséphone avec votre admirable orchestre. Cela était une joie pour moi de travailler avec eux. Je regrette votre absence et vous, envois mes fidèles amitiés
   Votre
   Igor Strawinsky

Florence
le 21.V.39

Vittorio Gui   Florence
London   21 May 1939

Thanks, dear friend, for such a kind note. In two hours I shall conduct *Perséphone* with your fine orchestra. It was a joy for me to work with them. I'm sorry you're not here and send kindest regards.

    Your Igor Strawinsky

Acquisition: H. Colin Slim on 3 April 1998 from La Scala Autographs. *Provenance:* Parisian dealer.

Commentary

The postcard bears no stamps; the envelope in which it must have been mailed is lacking. The message side of Entry 63 bears a tiny printer's (or photographer's) logo: a building with two chimneys, flanked by towers. The same logo appears on a picture postcard Stravinsky was later to inscribe with music for Dorothy Ellis McQuoid in Los Angeles on 17 December 1939, although her photograph of him (wearing the same suit and tie) is full face, a cropped version of which he inscribed to Fernand Auberjonois in New York in August 1951. A copy of this latter photograph at the Paul Sacher Foundation is attributed there to Gar Vic, Buenos Aires, 1936. This date seems correct, another photograph from the same series appearing on a cover of *Musical America,* which contains a review of the world premiere in April 1937 of *Jeu de cartes.*

    In 1928, Vittorio Gui had founded the Orchestra Stabile Fiorentina from which, at his initiative, the Maggio Musicale festival in Florence developed in 1933. In 1939 he returned to Covent Garden where he conducted *Il trovatore, La traviata, Tosca,* and *Otello.* Gui made an Italian translation of *Perséphone* by André Gide for his own use in 1950, but Stravinsky proposed, reasonably enough, that Gui's percentage be deducted from Gide's royalties rather than from his own.

    Following his wife's death on 2 March 1939, Stravinsky and his younger daughter, Milène, had to enter the tuberculosis sanatorium at Sancellemoz (see Entry 64). Late in April he wrote his old friend Alexis Kall in Los Angeles that Sancellemoz's doctors had advised that his health was sufficiently improved that he could conduct concerts at Milan and Florence and safely travel to the US in late September to take up the Norton professorship for 1939-40 at Harvard. In this April letter, he also invited Kall to be his secretary-translator there.

On 18 May, Gui wrote Stravinsky from London greatly regretting not hearing *Perséphone* and hoping to see him when the composer would return to Paris (letter in the Paul Sacher Foundation). In Italy from 7 to 21 May 1939, Stravinsky led the Italian premiere of *Perséphone* on the 16th at the Maggio Musicale, again performing the work there on the 21st. Its first performance in Italy had been postponed from 29 May 1935 at Rome because Ida Rubinstein had cancelled her engagement there with him, and it was postponed once again from 29 November 1938 at Rome when the narrator, Victoria Ocampo, had fallen ill. Ocampo narrated at the performance he mentions in Entry 63 (on her, see entries 44-5, 64, and 104).

An admirer of Benito Mussolini since the mid-1920s, Stravinsky was received by the dictator in Rome at the Palazzo Venezia in 1930, in 1935, and again in 1936, when he presented an inscribed copy of volume two of his *Chroniques de ma vie* to the dictator. Near its close, he had written of fascist Italy's "remarquable effort régénérateur" over the past ten years. He had planned still another concert in Italy in 1939, at Venice on 4 September for the Biennale. The outbreak of the Second World War the previous day forced its cancellation, even though Italy remained neutral until the following June.

Works Consulted

Caillois, Roger, and Victoria Ocampo. *Correspondance (1939-1978)*. ed. Odile Felgine, et al. Paris: Stock, 1997. pp. 44-7.

Christie's. *Valuable Printed Books, Manuscripts and Music*. London, 25 June 1997, lot 89.

Craft, Robert. *Stravinsky: Glimpses of a Life*. London: Lime Tree, 1992; New York, NY: St. Martin's Press, 1993. n. 41 on p. 191.

"Vittorio Gui." *Opera* 26 (1975): 1128 (obituary).

Kall, Alexis F. Papers, Box 1. Special Collections 601. Charles E. Young Research Library, University of California at Los Angeles.

Musical America 57 (10 May 1937): cover.

Ocampo, Victoria. *Autobiografía IV Viraje*. Buenos Aires: Sur, 1982. p. 104.

—. "*Perséphone* bajo la batuta de Strawinsky." *Testimonios Octava Serie (1968-1970)*. Buenos Aires: Sur, 1971. p. 233.

SChron. vol. 2. p. 180.

SP&D. pp. 551–2.

SSC. vol. 3. n. 12 on p. 333.

Taruskin, Richard. "Stravinsky and the Subhuman: Notes on *Svadebka*" in *Defining Russia Musically*. Princeton, NJ: Princeton University Press, 1997. pp. 450-4.

64 (1939). Signed typed letter folded three times, 24.9 × 20.9 cm, in French, with typed envelope 8.1 × 14.1 cm, postmarked Sancellemoz Haute-Savoie 24-6 39, 24 June 1939, to Roland-Manuel:

[envelope] Monsieur Roland Manuel

42 rue de Bourgogne

PARIS VII

[letter]

Mr.Roland Manuel

42 rue de Bourgogne(et c'est ainsi que je vous câblé et non 44)

Paris

Merci de votre lettre,mon cher Roland.

Je retrouve la lettre de Victoria Ocampo du 3I mai où elle me parle de Mr. Marx. Lorsque je l'ai vu,il y a deux semaines à Paris,elle ne m'en a pas parlé et moi je n'ai pas pensé de la questionner la-dessus étant encore trop sous le coup de mon recent deuil. Voici ce qu'elle m'écrivait: "Ce mot pour vous dire que j'ai eu Marx à déjeuner aujourd'hui et que je lui ai parlé de votre affaire [one letter crossed out in ink].C'est arrangé. Il faut seulement que vous lui disiez quand vous partez et lui donniez vous même les détails." Que veut dire la phrase "C'est arrangé"? Qu'est ce qui est arrangé? Sachant que Victoria va voir Mr Marx à Paris je l'avais demandé à Florence de lui parler(à Mr Marx)de mon prochain voyage en Amérique et de voir avec lui si cela était possible [underlined in red] de me le faciliter(dans le sens d'une mission officielle:visas diplomatiques,recommandations aux frontières;bref,ce que l'on fait pour p.ex.Nadia Boulanger,Alfred Cortot etc.). Est-ce le passage gratuit aller-retour en Amérique qu'elle entend dans la phrase "c'est arrangé"? C'est ce que je vous demanderai d'éclaircir dans votre conversation avec le nommé Mr.Marx. Vous avez deviné,cela m'ennui de lui écrire et vous êtes vraiment gentil de me proposer votre médiation, je l'accepte avec reconnaissance. Je le connais Mr.Marx,c'est un mélange de Jean Zay et de Larmanjat,il est plustôt gentil,très impressionné de sa situation(héritage du front populaire,je crois,de Blum en tout cas),ce n'est pas une excellence. S'il faut que je lui écrive une lettre vous serez un amour de m'envoyer un échantillon. Quel est son prénom? Je suis un peu pressé de mettre tout cela au clair puisque je dois répondre à la Transatlantique que dont vous me faite connaître la lettre du I4 cr.

Pour ce que vous m'écrivez au sujet de la dactylographie en cinq exemplaires et la traduction anglaise des résumés – d'accord pour la somme d'environ 500 fr.

Attends avec impatience la 6-ème leçon. Quand l'aurai-je? Bientôt?

Et le bachot de Claud? Aucune trace dans votre lettre? Pourquoi?

Je m'em..... ici sans vous et ne prends plus d'Arquebuse à la tisane [one letter crossed out in ink] de mente-tilleul.

Je vous ambrasse bien affectueusement. Mes respectueuses amitiés à votre femme,je vous prie.

Sancellemoz
le 24 juin /39   [in black ink] votre Strawinsky

Roland-Manuel   Sancellemoz
Paris   24 June 1939

Thanks for your letter, my dear Roland.

I have before me the letter from Victoria Ocampo of 31 May which speaks of Mr. [Jean] Marx. When I saw her two weeks ago in Paris, she did not mention him to me, and I did not think to ask her, being still too much affected by my recent sorrow. This is what she wrote me: "This note to tell you that I had Marx to lunch today and that I spoke to him about your business. It's all set. You need only tell him when you will leave and give him the details yourself." What does the expression "It's all set" mean? What has been arranged? Knowing that Victoria was going to see Mr. Marx in Paris, I asked her in Florence [c. 21 May] to speak to him (to Mr. Marx) about my next trip to America and to see if it was possible for him *to help me with it* (in the sense of an official mission: diplomatic visas, introductions at frontiers; in sum, what was done, for example, for Nadia Boulanger, Alfred Cortot, etc.). Is free round trip to America what she means by her expression "It's all set"? This is what I want you to clarify in your conversation with the above-named Mr. Marx. You have guessed that it bothers me to write him and you are really kind to offer your intervention. I accept it gratefully. I know Mr. Marx, he is a combination of Jean Zay and [Jacques] Larmanjat, he is quite nice, very taken with his position (a legacy from the Popular Front, I think, and in any case, from Blum); he's not exactly pre-eminent. If I do have to write him a letter, you would be a love to send me a sample. What is his first name? I'm rather in a hurry to settle all this because I must respond to the [Cie] Transatlantique, whose letter of the fourteenth of this month you bring to my attention.

From what you write me about the typescript in five copies and the English translation of the summaries, I agree to the sum of about 500 francs.

I impatiently await the sixth lecture. When shall I have it? Soon? And Claude's graduation? No mention in your letter? Why?

I'm bored here without you and no longer take Arquebuse with linden-mint tea.

Yours very affectionately. My kindest regards to your wife, please,

Your Strawinsky

Acquisition: H. Colin Slim on 23 April 1998 from La Scala Autographs. *Provenance:* Private New York collector (perhaps from the 14 May 1986 auction at Paris by Paul Renaud of the Roland-Manuel archives, part 1).

Commentary

Entry 64 bears the watermark B F K Rives, a paper manufactured by the same company as used in several musical quotations Stravinsky made for Mrs. Bickford in 1937. (See Preliminary Remarks to entries 48-60.)

Brief excerpts from the letter have been published in translation and a chronology established for the collaboration – much of it at the tuberculosis sanatorium at Sancellemoz – between Stravinsky and Roland-Manuel in writing the six Harvard lectures for the Charles Eliot Norton Professorship at Harvard University, 1939-40 (see entries 78, 86, 94). Nineteen photographs of Stravinsky taken in 1938-39 by Roland-Manuel at this sanatorium were auctioned in March 2000. (On Roland-Manuel, see entries 15 and 17; on Victoria Ocampo, entries 44-5, 63, and 104.) "Le coup de mon recent deuil" refers to the death of Stravinsky's mother on 7 June 1939, his wife having died on 2 March.

Jean Marx (1884-c. 1965) was plenipotentiary to the French Minister of Foreign Affairs to whom Stravinsky had already written in May 1939. Jean Zay (1904-44) was Minister of Education in the Popular Front government (1936-37) of Léon Blum (1872-1950). A mixture of Socialists and supported by the Communists, the Popular Front was anathema to Stravinsky, whose politics at this period were right wing (see Entry 63). For example, six months before the electoral victory of the Popular Front, Catherine Stravinsky mentioned that the Stravinskys supported the candidacy of Pierre Laval (1883-1945) (SBu, p. 77).

Stravinsky was on the wrong side of history. Mussolini, whom he admired, was shot in April 1945; his candidate, Laval, became a puppet of the Nazi government and virtual dictator in Vichy from 1942 and was executed as a traitor in October 1945. But Zay, captured and executed by the Vichy government in June 1944, was a hero of the French Resistance.

Although at the time of Entry 64, Jacques Larmanjat (1878-1952) was director (1935-45) of the Rennes Conservatory, he had earlier served the French government during the period 1928-30 and also worked at the Salle Gaveau from 1930 to 1934. Stravinsky had known him from 1922, when Larmanjat was making player-piano rolls for Pleyel (1918-28) (see Entry 21). A letter of 29 September 1924 from Stravinsky to Larmanjat (with La Scala Autographs in February 2000) has been partially translated. It reveals Larmanjat making piano reductions for Stravinsky.

References to "résumés" and the "6-ème leçon" are to Roland-Manuel's work on the six lectures Stravinsky was to deliver in 1939–40 at Harvard, printed by Harvard University Press in 1942 as *Poétique musicale* (see Entry 78). "Le bachot de Claud [sic]" presumably refers to the graduation of Roland-Manuel's son, Claude (born 1922).

Works Consulted

Ferchault, Guy. "Larmanjat." MGG. 8: col. 220-1.

Lesure, François. *Igor Stravinsky. La carrière européenne.* Paris: Musée d'Art Moderne, 1980. pp. 102-4, nos. 343-9.

Renaud, Paul, and Thierry Bodin. *Archives Roland-Manuel [part 2].* Paris: 24 March 2000, p. 2, lot 234 on p. 69 (two pls. of Stravinsky at Sancellemoz).

SBu. p. 77 (first Entry sub 1936).

SP&D. pp. 242 (caption), 555, n. 12 on p. 662.

SSC. vol. 1. n. 61 on p. 151; vol. 2. pp. 503-15.

Walsh, Stephen. *Stravinsky, A Creative Spring: Russia and France, 1882-1934.* New York, NY: Alfred A. Knopf, 1999. pp. 520-22.

65 (1939). Signed typed letter, 27.9 × 21.5 cm, folded three times, in French with autograph corrections and annotations in black ink, 17 November 1939, to Pierre Monteux (1875-1964):

Monsieur Pierre Monteux,
Empire Hotel
San Francisco.

Mon cher Monteux,
    Comme Mr. Drake ne se dérange [crossed out in ink] pas même [written] pas [typed] pour m'avertir des jours des répétitions à San Francisco puis-je vous prier d'avoir l'amabilite de dire à votre secrétaire qu'il m'envoie les dates exactes de mes répétitions (indicant les jours et les heures) car je dois le savoir pour fixer la date de mon départ d'ici.

    Puis-je aussi vous demander de reserver deux chambres a
votre hôtel pour moi et le Dr. Kall?
    Très heureux de vous revoir je vous envoie mes fidèles
pensées ainsi que mes amitiées respectueuses à Mme Monteux.

[written] votre Igor Strawinsky
qui vous envoie cette [crossed out in ink] ~~lettre~~ copie par avion
pour avoir plus vite la réponse

[typed] Gerry's Landing,   November I7, I939
c/o Mr. edward W. Forbes
Cambridge, Mass.

[written, right] P.S. Avez-vous reçu le matériel de "Jeu de
Cartes"? Je le dirige ici le 1 et 2 décembre et si l'<u>Associated
Music Publ.</u> (réprésentant de la B. Schott édition) ne possède
pas un second exemplaire il serait indispensable que je prenne
ce materiel avec moi. Faites moi savoir ce que je dois faire, je
vous prie.

[written, left] La Symph N2 de Tchaïkovsky, je la prends avec
moi

Pierre Monteux   Cambridge, MA
San Francisco   17 November 1939

My dear Monteux:
Since Mr. [Richard] Drake does not even trouble himself to inform
me about days for the rehearsals in San Francisco, may I ask you
kindly to request your secretary to send me the exact dates for my
rehearsals (indicating days and times) because I must know this in
order to settle my departure date from here.
    Could I also ask you to reserve two rooms at your hotel for me
and for Dr. [Alexis] Kall?
    Very happy to see you again,
    Yours faithfully, with kindest regards to Madame Monteux,
    Igor Strawinsky

who sends you this copy by airmail so as to have your reply more quickly.

p.s. Have you received the orchestra parts for *The Card Game*? I'm directing it here on 1 and 2 December and if Associated Music Publishers (representing B. Schott) do not have a second copy, it will be absolutely necessary for me to bring these parts with me. Let me know what I should do, please.

p.p.s. I am bringing the Tchaikovsky *Second Symphony* with me.

Acquisition: H. Colin Slim on 3 December 1998 from La Scala Autographs.

Provenance: An undisclosed dealer in the US, 1998.

Commentary

The letter is unpublished and its envelope is lacking; corrections and accents by Stravinsky are in ink. On a different typewriter from the one used in Entry 64, Entry 65 was perhaps typed by Alexis Kall, who, as Vera Sudeykina noted in September 1939, was "practicing his typing to be worthy of being a secretary to Stravinsky." A much-corrected pencil draft of Entry 65 by Stravinsky in French of 17 November survives in Kall's papers at the University of California, Los Angeles. Then living with him at the Forbes' family house in Cambridge, Kall acted as his translator during sessions with composition students at Harvard, 1939–40 (see Entry 40).

Although sent by airmail, Entry 65 did not elicit an immediate response from Pierre Monteux who was on a brief vacation in California. Replying a week later from his apartment in San Francisco, he wrote that orchestra rehearsals would be on 10 and 12–14 December and that he would reserve two rooms at the Empire Hotel.

References to sets of orchestral parts owned by Stravinsky in Paris for the works he was to program in San Francisco first appear in a letter he wrote to Kall from Sancellemoz on 21 August 1939. He asks Kall to ascertain from Monteux if the program remains the same as earlier planned, that is, Tchaikovsky's *Second Symphony*, *Jeu de Cartes*, and *Petrushka*, adding: "J'ai besoin de le savoir *surtout pour la Sym. de Tchaïkovsky* étant donné que c'est moi qui apporte le matériel."

Apparently, however, he did not carry these parts with him when he sailed to the US on 25 September. On 19 October, in response to his letter of inquiry, Vera Sudeykina wrote from Paris that "the orchestra parts for *Jeu de cartes* and the two Tchaikovsky symphonies [presumably nos. 2 and 3] should be here with me." By 13 November the parts for *Jeu de cartes* had been found, but not those for the symphonies. On 25 and 30 November, however, only a single Tchaikovsky symphony is mentioned; Stravinsky led the second symphony in New York in January 1940 and both of them during February 1940 at Chicago. Because some of the music did not arrive until 20 December, by plane with Charles Munch, and the remainder by ship with Vera herself, on 12 January – too late for the San Francisco concerts – it seems improbable that his reference in the postscript of Entry 65 to the Tchaikovsky second symphony can be to these parts in Paris. In his reply, Monteux informed Stravinsky that the San Francisco Orchestra owned only the Tchaikovsky symphony. Whether Stravinsky had to bring the set for *Jeu de Cartes* he had used for his performances with the Boston Symphony at the beginning of December remains unknown (see Entry 66). The San Francisco concerts were on 15 and 16 December.

Some of the correspondence, 1912-57, between Stravinsky and Monteux reveals ambiguity and even plain jealousy about Monteux's conducting of his music. Despite all Monteux's support and his efforts on behalf of Stravinsky, he was among those slandered in 1919 in a vicious anti-Semitic letter to Misia Sert. Taruskin and Walsh document additional examples of his anti-Semitism from 1912, 1919, and 1928. The degree of Stravinsky's compartmentalization is revealed in his writing to Kall on 27 December 1937, wherein he describes Monteux as "a fine and conscientious musician" and in his *Greeting Prelude* composed for Monteux's eightieth birthday in 1955. Another example is his charming inscription of 23 March 1937 on his postcard photograph to Monteux's daughter, Nancy, offered for sale in 1999 by La Scala Autographs.

Walsh's criticism of Taruskin's "transparent determination to see anti-Semitism wherever there might be a *prima facie* expectation" is perhaps supported by a letter from Stravinsky to Kall of 31 December 1938 announcing the death of his daughter, Lyudmila, the previous month. It exhibits a tender concern for his Jewish son-in-law, the poet Yury Vladimirovich Mandelstamm (1908-43), subsequently murdered by the Nazis. Stravinsky wrote: "She left us her little two-year-old darling and her unfortunate, very needy husband, of whom I cannot but take care." And in respect to Mandelstamm's marriage to Lyudmila in October 1935, Denise Strawinsky, who had married Théodore in June 1936, reported in 1998 that "pour Igor et Catherine, l'antisémitisme n'a jamais eu de place" (SAc, p. 162).

On 16 December 1939, the day of his final concert in San Francisco, Stravinsky inscribed for Kall what has been well deemed a "minor jewel." Although published almost forty years ago, it has not yet drawn the attention of scholars. It is a mostly syllabic setting in C major (marked by Stravinsky "Andante") of: "DO NOT / THROW / PAPER TOWELS / IN TOILETS", which notice he probably detached from the washroom of the Empire Hotel in San Francisco. Arriving in Los Angeles on 17 December where he was to be a guest at Kall's home, the two men were met at the train by Kall's piano student, Dorothy Ellis McQuoid (see entries 67-8, and 70-5).

Richard Drake of Copley Management, New York, was Stravinsky's US agent following Richard Copley's death in February 1939, the latter having represented him since January 1935. Various letters in Kall's papers at UCLA show that, during the summer and early fall of 1939, Drake had tried, without success, to arrange concerts for Stravinsky with the Los Angeles Philharmonic in December 1939 and also to have him conduct performances with Theodore Koslov's ballet company there as he had done on his 1937 visit.

Works Consulted

Kall, Alexis F. Papers, Boxes 1 (Russian Correspondence) and 5 (manuscripts; Stravinsky: letters). (trans. Stanislav Shvrabrin and Michael Green). Special Collections 601. Charles E. Young Research Library, University of California at Los Angeles.

La Scala Autographs. *1999 Holiday Catalogue*. Pennington, NJ, November 1999. p. 20, item 113, ill.

"Minor Jewel." *UCLA Librarian* (10 February 1961): 47.

Sotheby's. *Collection Boris Kochno*, Monaco, 11-12 October 1991, lot 398.

SAc. pp. 142, pl. on p. 160 (Mandelstamm, Lyudmila, and baby), 162.

SBu. pp. 94, 97-100, 102-3, 105-6, 109 (letters 1, 6-8, 10-11, 13, 15, 17-19, 21).

SI&V. pl. 156 on p. 95.

SP&D. pp. 277-81, 336-7, pl. on p. 338, p. 353.

SP&RK. vol. 1. p. 525 (index: Monteux); vol. 2. p. 756 (index: Monteux).

SSC. vol. 2. p. 71 (24 November 1939), pl. 10 (top) btn pp. 338-9.

ST&C. p. 47, pl. facing p. 48.

ST&E. p. 39.

Taruskin, Richard. "Stravinsky and the Subhuman: Notes on *Svadebka*" in
Defining Russia Musically. Princeton, NJ: Princeton University Press, 1997.
p. 457.

W.F. "Harvard Students Taught Music by Russian Composer." The *Christian
Science Monitor*. 22 November 1939. p. 12.

Walsh, Stephen. Review of Taruskin's *Stravinsky and the Russian Traditions* in
Music and Letters 78 (1997): 452.

–. *Stravinsky, A Creative Spring: Russia and France, 1882-1934*. New York, NY:
Alfred A. Knopf, 1999. pp. 192, 300, 518-20, n. 31 on p. 573.

66 (1939). Autograph untitled musical quotation, on uppermost stave of at least six-staved printed music paper, 14.1 × 24.1 cm, cut down and folded once vertically, in black ink, of three measures from *Jeu de cartes* (1936), signed at lower right, probably inscribed c. 28-30 November 1939 for Dr. Moses Joel Eisenberg (1895-1969):

IStravinsky / Boston Nov 39

Acquisition: H. Colin Slim on 3 April 2000 from J. and J. Lubrano,
Music Antiquarians (8 George Street / Great Barrington, MA).

Provenance: Cleveland dealer, March 2000; musical autograph
collection (1939-69) of Dr. Moses Joel Eisenberg of Roxbury and
Chestnut Hill, MA.

Commentary

The music paper of Entry 66 was probably once a double sheet, as
revealed by its irregular left edge. Though now obscured by two thin
pieces of rice paper attached to its reverse side in order to stabilize the
vertical fold, staves are printed on both sides, originally at least six of
them, the uppermost line of stave six still being visible. An illegible
watermark, whether that of the music paper or of the strengthening
sheets, is faintly visible on the left side of the sheet.

Curiously, the musical quotation, from the "First Deal" of his three-movement ballet score, *Jeu de cartes* (Mainz: Schott, 1937) appears nowhere precisely as copied in Entry 66. Marked "Moderato assai," Flute 1 plays it twice between rehearsals **12** and **13**, though an octave higher and not preceded by the first note A-natural, but by a rapid scale upward including an A-flat. The flute's "Tranquillo" restatement at rehearsal **34** is likewise preceded by a run, this time, however, including an A-natural, but its initial F is a dotted half-note. The only statement at the pitch of Entry 66 is by clarinet 1 at rehearsal **36**, omitting, however, the A and beginning with the F (but transposed up a whole step, of course, for the B-flat instrument).

During his third visit to the US, Stravinsky led the first two performances of this ballet, commissioned by Lincoln Kirstein and choreographed by George Balanchine for the American Ballet, on April 27-28 1937, in New York (see Entry 103). Unauthorized cuts, which Ernest Ansermet insisted on making in *Jeu de cartes* for performances he conducted that October, precipitated a major rupture in their long friendship, not fully healed until 1966.

When Stravinsky returned to the US in 1939, he scheduled orchestral performances of it by the Boston Symphony on 1-2 December, two weeks later in San Francisco and, during January and February 1940, in New York, Pittsburgh, and Chicago. Lecturing at Harvard and meeting with its students, Stravinsky was living in the fall of 1939 with the Forbes family at Gerry's Landing in Cambridge. On 20 November, he dined in Boston with Serge Koussevitsky and began rehearsals there with the Boston Symphony on November 28. *Jeu de cartes* evoked interest among the city's musical public owing to newspaper publicity about its forthcoming Boston premiere. Probably he inscribed Entry 66 either for Dr. Eisenberg (a research dentist), attending one of these Boston rehearsals, or for someone else from whom Eisenberg later acquired it. (In Boston during March and May 1940, however, a Dr. Fink was the composer's dentist.)

Works Consulted

"Eisenberg, Moses Joel." *American Biographical Archive,* series II, no. 167 [np], entries 369-71.

Meyer, Alfred H. "Re-Enter Mr. Stravinsky." *The Christian Science Monitor.* 29 November 1939. p. 16.

SBu. p. 103 (21 November 1939), pp. 112-14.
SP&D. pp. 246-9, 331-3, 353-4.
SSC. vol. 1. pp. 225-33.

67

(1939). Original uninscribed photograph, 26.0 × 26.0 cm, of Stravinsky and Cary Ellis McQuoid (1934-97), taken 18 December 1939 and made from the square negative, 6.0 × 6.0 cm, owned by Dorothy Louise Ellis McQuoid Hopper until her death. Shortly after taking the photograph, she wrote on the envelope containing the negative: "Stravinsky / Dec. 18 '39." In 1995 below Entry 67 she kindly signed her name for Dr. Slim to a typed statement regarding the circumstances of her photograph.

Acquisition: H. Colin Slim from her negative on 31 October 1994 at The Darkroom (Laguna Beach, CA), courtesy Dorothy Ellis McQuoid Hopper, San Clemente, CA.
Provenance: Dorothy Ellis McQuoid, Los Angeles (1939-98).

Commentary

The photograph, unpublished in its complete form, was taken in Los Angeles during the composer's third trip to the city. Mrs. Hopper remembered in 1994 that she took Entry 67 about 11 a.m. near the house (now remodelled) at 143 South Gramercy, Los Angeles, of her piano teacher, Dr. Alexis F. Kall, with whom the composer was then living.

Kall had introduced her to Stravinsky the previous day, 17 December 1939, when she had met their train from San Francisco at Union Station in Los Angeles. She then drove them in her car to Kall's house where there was afterward a party, mostly, she recalled, of Russian-speaking guests (see entries 40 and 68). On this occasion, he presented her with a picture postcard of himself on the back of which he wrote a little four-bar tune in C major setting the words: "Dorothy, o [sic] Dorothy you are nice" and signed it: "IStrawinsky / Los Angeles / Dec 17th 39." At her death, this card passed to her surviving elder son, Ronald Richard McQuoid (1933-) and her married daughter, Alexis Larson (1942-).

She also recalled for Dr. Slim that her first husband, Edwin Kerien McQuoid, a professional photographer, assisted her with preparations for the camera, a Speed Graphic, and that he made suggestions about posing Stravinsky on 18 December, whom she remembered as a reluctant subject. An identical photograph, although cropped at the right and left sides to exclude her younger son, was said in 1985 – incorrectly – to have been taken by Edward G. Robinson on 23 December 1939.

Stravinsky wore the same wide pin-striped double breasted suit in nine different photographs taken by Edward Weston (1886-1958) at Los Angeles in February 1935 and in two photographs with Edward G. Robinson taken at Hollywood that March. (The latter appear in Entry 40.) He also wore the same suit in a photograph taken on board ship with Nadia Boulanger early in May 1937, again in the above-mentioned autograph musical postcard of his portrait he presented to Dorothy Ellis McQuoid on 17 December 1939 (its photograph taken at Buenos Aires in 1936), and in a photograph with Dr. Kall taken on 5 May 1940 by Elliot Forbes (1917-) at his father's home, Gerry's Landing, Cambridge.

The automobile parked at the right in Entry 67 is an inexpensive four-passenger 1940 Plymouth coupe, owned neither by the McQuoids nor by Kall, who did not drive. The vehicle, purchased late in 1939, was kindly identified in 1996 by Ronald W. Wakefield and Richard Romm.

Works Consulted

Armitage, Merle, ed. *Igor Strawinsky*. New York, NY: G. Schirmer, 1936. pl. facing p. vi.

Hinch, Robin. "Music was theme of Dorothy Hopper's life; Obituary." *The Orange County Register,* 28 February 1998. Metro section, p. 7.

Spycket, Jérôme. *Nadia Boulanger*. trans. M.M. Shriver. Stuyvesant, NY: Pendragon Press, 1992. pl. on p. 87.

SBu. pls. 72-6 on pp. 73-4, pl. 87 on p. 108, n. 2 on p. 109.

Strawinsky. Sein Nachlass. Sein Bild [with] *Katalog der ausgestellten Bildnisse und Entwürfe für die Ausstattung seiner Bühnenwerke*. Basle: Kunstmuseum and Paul Sacher Stiftung, 1984. 4 pls. on pp. 128-[9].

The New Yorker 16 (9 March 1940): automobile advertisement in colour, facing p. 35, lower right.

68

(1939). Autograph inscription on first page, 22.6 × 16.6 cm, in English in black ink, Christmas 1939, of a miniature score, IGOR / STRAVINSKY / PETROUSHKA / A Burlesque in four scenes (New York, Kalmus, 1933), no. 79, 156 pp., bearing on its outer cover the stamp of its first owner: "Dorothy Ellis / 10323 Ilona Ave., L.A." On the first page of music, upper right, he wrote:

To Dorothy Ellis
very very sincerely,
IStrawinsky
Los Angeles
Christmas
1939

Acquisition: H. Colin Slim in San Clemente on 29 July 1996 by purchase from Dorothy Ellis McQuoid Hopper. The score was restored in October 1996 by Linda K. Ogden.
Provenance: Dorothy Ellis McQuoid, Los Angeles (1939-96).

Commentary
By Christmas of 1939 Mrs. McQuoid had known Stravinsky for just over a week (see Entry 67). She recalled for Dr. Slim in 1994 that Stravinsky had inscribed her copy of this score at a Christmas party with mostly Russian-speaking guests at the house of her piano teacher, Alexis Kall, whom he was then visiting. This was the only time she ever sought his autograph. By Christmas he would not have known her very well and he surely inscribed her maiden name as it appeared stamped in her copy of the score rather than her married name, which he may not have recalled or even heard.

Because she and her first husband (whom she had married in 1931) did not live at Ilona Avenue in Los Angeles until 1938, and she did not meet Stravinsky until 17 December 1939, her copy of *Petrushka* cannot relate to when he conducted it in Los Angeles either first at the Philharmonic Auditorium, 21-22 February 1935, or again at the Shrine Auditorium two years later on 12-13 March. In 1937 it was choreographed and danced by Theodore Koslov (1881-1956), and then staged at the Bowl by Kozlov (without Stravinsky) on 2 September, following negotiations late in 1936 through Kall. Although he conducted *Petrushka* in San Francisco in mid-December 1939, he gave no concerts at Los Angeles during this visit. She believed that she probably purchased her copy of *Petrushka* in order that she could have him autograph it.

Mrs. Hopper recalled in 1994 that Stravinsky told her at the time he inscribed Entry 68 that her 1933 score – a pirated copy of the 1912 Berlin score of the Russischer Musik Verlag – was faulty. Complaining about misprints as early as 27 March 1912, he entered extensive pencil and red ink corrections in his own 1912 full score. Since he had left it in Europe, however, it was unavailable during the war. Charles Hamm's corrected 1912 score, published in 1967, incorporates notes made by Claudio Spies utilizing corrections Spies probably had from Stravinsky. (For autograph quotations from the "The Magic Trick" and the "Russian Dance" in *Petrushka,* see entries 49 and 119, respectively.)

Works Consulted

SP&D. p. 85 (27 March), pl. on p. 337.
SSC. vol. 1. App. C, pp. 391-7, esp. n. 3 on p. 392.
Stravinsky, Igor. *Petrushka: An Authoritative Score of the [1912] Original Version.* ed. Charles Hamm. New York, NY: W.W. Norton, 1967. p. [22].

69

(1940). Unsigned photograph, 16.8 × 10.7 cm, of Vera and Stravinsky during boat drill aboard the *S.S. Seminole* at Miami, taken by Alexis Kall, 18 May 1940, reproduced from the original negative in the Kall papers, UCLA.

Acquisition: H. Colin Slim on 9 November 1995 from the Charles E. Young Research Library, University of California at Los Angeles, courtesy Special Collections, 601, Alexis Kall papers, Box 2, Kall photographs, unidentified: negative.
Provenance: Alexis Kall, Los Angeles, CA (1940-48).

Commentary

The same photograph was reproduced, slightly cropped on all sides, by Vera Stravinsky and Craft in 1978. Because the negative is among Alexis Kall's papers, he probably took the picture (on him, see Entry 40). Their sea voyage – New York to Galveston, Texas, 15-21 May 1940 – and subsequent train trip to their eventual destination of Los Angeles included not only Kall but also his housemate, Gregory Golubeff (1891-1958). Owing to Kall's disorganized ways and his frequent bouts of inebriation, Golubeff was soon to succeed him as secretary to Stravinsky.

Works Consulted

"Golubeff, Gregory W." *Who's Who in California*. 1941. vol 1. p. 346.
SBu. n. 14 on p. 114.
SP&D. pl. on p. 366.

70　(1940). Autograph picture postcard, 8.7 × 13.7 cm, made by Gevaez, in English in black ink by Vera and Stravinsky, depicting two **CANTADORAS DEL BAJIO. MEXICO** (marked:) **1127/ OSUNA**, posed in front of La Virgen de San Juan de Los Lagos, Guadalajara. Postmarked on reverse, Mexico C[ity] (date not legible), the undated card, probably mailed c. 2 August 1940, is addressed by Vera in ink to E[dwin] and [Dorothy Ellis] McQuoid:

Mr an Mrs
E. McQuoid
10323 Ilona av.
<u>Los Angeles</u>
California
U.S.A.

[Vera] Dear friends – greetings loves and kisses from Vera Straw[insk]y

[Stravinsky] Dear friends we come back, we hope, in one week
with good news (we hope) Very very sincerely IStrawinsky

Acquisition: by gift to H. Colin Slim on 13 June 1994 from the
Department of Music, University of California, Irvine, on the occasion
of my retirement from the University.
Provenance: Mr. and Mrs. Edwin McQuoid, Los Angeles; kind donation
by Dorothy Ellis McQuoid Hopper (1940-94), widow of Edwin
McQuoid and Jerry Hopper, to the Department of Music.

Commentary

The postcard is unpublished. A complete reproduction of the statue of
the Virgin, including a small cross at the top of her halo – and, in front
of her, a different woman – is illustrated, but unfortunately not
identified, in *Nuestra México* for July 1932. The Bajio (heartland) is a
geographical area north of Mexico City, roughly the state of
Guanajuato and parts of the states of Queretaro and Michoacan.

In June 1994 Mrs. Hopper dated the envelope in which she
presented Entry 70 to the Music Department at the University of
California at Irvine as "circa 1941," believing that the postcard
stemmed from the second trip Stravinsky and Vera made to Mexico,
10-26 July 1941. It seems illogical, however, for them to have sent
Entry 70 to her and her husband in 1941. Having been coached in the
Capriccio by Stravinsky in Los Angeles in the summer and early fall of
1940, she was herself also in Mexico City that same July 1941, hoping
to perform the *Capriccio* with him in case he found the scheduled
Mexican soloist, Salvador Ochoa, unsuitable. Moreover, the date that
the Stravinskys would return to the US from Mexico was certain in
1941.

But the exact date of their return from the 1940 trip to Mexico (18
July-8 August) – during which he and Vera obtained permanent
resident visas to the US – was quite uncertain. Hence his closing
parenthesis in Entry 70: "we come back, we hope, in one week with
good news (we hope)." The good news was perhaps the arrival of their
US visas. On their way to Mexico City in 1940, they detrained on 21

July for one and a half hours and visited Guadalajara, its Cathedral, and other sights by taxi. Probably they purchased Entry 70 in that city, mailing it later from Mexico City. Stravinsky led concerts in Mexico City on 26 and 28 July and on 2 and 4 August.

Not long before the 1940 Mexico trip, Stravinsky took a photograph early in June of Dorothy and Edwin McQuoid with Vera Stravinsky at the Hollywood Farmers Market, reproduced (slightly cropped) in the edition of Vera's diary. Mrs. Hopper owned an uncropped copy of this photograph (now with her children). Vera mentions "Dorothy" [McQuoid] more times in her 1940 diary than the two published entries for 26 May and 9 June might suggest (additionally on: 28 and 30 May; 1, 2, 8, 14, 17 June; 28 August; 4 and 24 September; 23 October; and 2 November). And, on 8 July 1941, just before she and the composer went for a second time to Mexico, appears: "McQuoids and Bolms."

From Mexico City he and Vera sent another postcard, no. A202 (of ruins at Oaxaca) made by the same firm as Entry 70, with identical stamp and postmark, to Alexis Kall at 143 S. Gramercy, Los Angeles with a message from Stravinsky: "See you soon." Unfortunately the date of its postmark is also illegible. Because Kall changed residence in 1942, the Oaxaca card must be from either 1940 or 1941.

On 2 August 1940, Stravinsky and Vera also sent Manuel de Falla a postcard from Mexico City. If they likewise mailed Entry 70 from Mexico City on or about the same date, its statement about returning "we hope, in one week" would be accurate because they arrived in Los Angeles on 9 August 1940. Mrs. Hopper recalled taking their picture as they stepped off the train assisted by their friend, Adolf Bolm (1884–1951), a photograph that duly appeared in her local newspaper, the Hollywood *Citizen-News,* a clipping from which she preserved.

Between 1939 and 1941, he inscribed seven additional items to Dorothy Ellis McQuoid, and Vera herself wrote her a note late in 1942. Although Dorothy's name rarely appears in her daily diaries after the autumn of 1940, Vera kept track of her several changes of address throughout the 1940s (see Introduction and entries 68 and 71-5). Dr. Slim is grateful to Esperanza Martinez and Sally Avila for discovering the location of the image of the Virgin in Entry 70.

Works Consulted

Agea, Francisco. "Igor Stravinsky. Su Vista a México." *Boletín de la Orquesta Sinfonica de México* 1, 4 (June 1940): 63-5, 82, programs VI and VII on p. 68; 1, 5 (November 1940): pl. on p. [78]; 2, 1 (June 1941): 48 (program VI).

Kall, Alexis F. Papers, Box 5 (postcards). Special Collections 601. Charles E. Young Research Library, University of California at Los Angeles.

Nuestra México 1, 5 (July 1932): 52; (fac. ed.; Mexico City, 1981): p. [368].

SBu. pl. 90 on p. 113, pp. 114-16, 122-3.

SI&V. pl. 161 on p. [97].

SSC. vol. 2. p. 175.

71 (1940). Autograph letter folded three times, 24.7 × 19.3 cm, in English in brown ink with two untitled musical quotations (originally 27.9 × 21.4 cm on HARVARD UNIVERSITY / DEPARTMENT OF MUSIC / CAMBRIDGE, MASSACHUSETTS stationery; a surviving reverse print shows that Stravinsky lined out the university's heading and its location), 28 August 1940, to [Edwin and Dorothy Ellis McQuoid]:

Beverly Hills
August 28th
/ 40

My dear friends:

Your beautiful monometrical night-letter poetry (I was deeply touched) may become polymetrical one by putting [crossed out in ink] a music on its words; for instance:

[music stave in treble clef, 4 bars of first C-major theme from finale of Tchaikovsky *Symphony no. 2,* to which Stravinsky set below the stave]

Bravo Bravo Bravo Bra-vo Bra-vo

As answer to your so kind message I [crossed out in ink] can only only can say:

[two music staves in treble clef with five sharps, 8 bars of the second theme (antecedent phrase) from same finale, which he transposed from C major to B major and to which he set below the staves]

I thank you, fifty times thank you, fifty times thank you, thank you, I thank you, I thank you!

I Strawinsky

Acquisition: H. Colin Slim in San Clemente, CA, on 13 October 1996 by purchase from Dorothy Ellis McQuoid Hopper. The letter was restored in December 1996 by Linda K. Ogden who removed an acidic backing board and a discoloured coating of alcohol-soluble material. *Provenance:* Edwin and Dorothy Ellis McQuoid, Los Angeles (1940-96); (Mrs. [McQuoid] Hopper had entries 71-2 framed together.)

Commentary
The letter is unpublished, its envelope missing. On the back of the frame of Entry 71 Dr. Slim had had affixed a photographic reproduction of its complete original state, made from a reverse print of the original, kindly furnished by Mrs. Hopper in 1994. Its original state provides a good example of Stravinsky's habit of purloining stationery (another example being found in Entry 74). Entry 71 was probably mailed from the house (124 South Swall Drive / Beverly Hills) that he and Vera rented on 6 June 1940 to the McQuoid's house (10323 Ilona Avenue / Westwood).

Mrs. Hopper told Dr. Slim in 1994 that Stravinsky sent Entry 71 – or rather, its original state – in response to a night-letter from the McQuoids that he received after his conducting debut at the Hollywood Bowl, Tuesday evening 27 August 1940. After attending this concert, they sent a night-letter which contained the word "Bravo" repeated fifty times. Indeed, Vera's diary, now in the Paul Sacher Foundation, notes on 28 August: "telegram / 50 times Bravo / from Dorothy McQuoid." The term "monometric" first appears in his sketches for an unfinished work, *Cinq pièces monométriques*, begun in 1919.

The first half of his concert opened with the traditional arrangement of the *Star-Spangled Banner*. It continued with Tchaikovsky's *Nutcracker Suite* and his *Symphony no. 2 in C minor* (the "Little Russian").

Choosing to inscribe for the McQuoids themes from the finale of the Tchaikovsky symphony reflected Stravinsky's fondness for this work. In the US, he first performed it at mid-December concerts with the San Francisco Symphony in 1939 and then early in January 1940 with the New York Philharmonic and the Chicago Symphony on 22–23 February, the New York performance being preserved on a CD recording. Just a month before the Hollywood Bowl performance, he had conducted it in Mexico City, on 26 July. By these 1940 performances, he was commemorating the hundredth anniversary of Tchaikovsky's birth (see also entries 47, 61, and 65). Stravinsky celebrated Tchaikovsky's one hundred tenth anniversary by conducting it at Aspen Colorado with the Denver Philharmonic on 2 August 1950. He led it once again two years later in what Craft described as "a delectable performance" at the Hollywood Bowl on 12 August, just two months before Dr. Slim heard him rehearse it in Vancouver. (Although not released on LP until 1977, either his 1950 Aspen or his 1952 Hollywood Bowl performance was recorded. Uncertainty stems from the Italian record company identifying it as a: "Los Angeles 1950 [sic] registrazione del vivo." This confusion is compounded by the record jacket's relocation of Aspen to California and its commentary about one of his performances: an "evento pressoché unico verificatosi ad Aspen in California [sic] nell'estate del 1950.")

After intermission at the Bowl, Stravinsky's 1940 concert concluded with *The Firebird Suite* (1919), newly choreographed by Adolf Bolm, a close friend during the ensuing Hollywood years. Bolm had danced in *The Firebird* in 1912 at Covent Garden, in *Petrushka* at the Metropolitan Opera in 1916, 1919, and 1925 (the latter production also staged by him), and took the title role in the premiere of *Apollo* at Washington, DC, in 1928. (In the late 1940s the McQuoids sent their young daughter, Alexis, to him for ballet lessons.) Sets and costumes for the 1940 *Firebird* were by Nicolai Vladimirovich Remisoff (1887-1979) – the designer for *Apollo* in 1928 and for *L'Histoire du Soldat* at Chicago in 1931, and an art director for four Hollywood films in 1940. Intermission commentary was by Deems Taylor (1885-1966).

Commenting in the program booklet about *The Firebird*'s music and choreography, Bruno David Ussher and Dorathi Bock Pierre included details about Bolm with a photograph of him, Stravinsky, and Nana Gollner, the prima ballerina. Four photographs of the participants and of the production survive in the archives of the Los Angeles Philharmonic and in two of the city's newspapers, the *Los Angeles Times* and *Los Angeles Examiner*. Three useful descriptive reviews are by Jones, Ussher, and Richard Drake Saunders. (For autograph quotations from *The Firebird*, see entries 48 and 115.)

In September 1994, Mrs. Hopper's second son, Cary Ellis McQuoid – pictured in Entry 67 with Stravinsky and who predeceased his mother – reminded her of a Hollywood Bowl concert conducted by the composer. Both she and her first son, Ronald Richard McQuoid, remembered her wearing her cone-shaped "Firebird" red iridescent hat, close-fitting about the face with feathers of red, green, blue, and yellow, as well as those of black, predominating. On a shopping trip with Vera Stravinsky and suggesting that Vera buy it – who, perhaps wisely, declined – Mrs. McQuoid paid the then-fantastic sum of $90 for it. She kept the hat for many years afterward. (In 1995 she made Dr. Slim a drawing of it.) During the concert's intermission, Stravinsky hung up his sweat-soaked dress shirt to dry over a light bulb. Leaving the room and having accidentally forgotten to turn off the switch, he burnt a hole in it. Mrs. McQuoid mended it on the spot from the flap of his shirttail. She believed that this incident took place at the Hollywood Bowl concert on 27 August 1940 detailed above.

Unfortunately, Mrs. Hopper's now faded original Stravinsky letter was trimmed by its first framer to the present dimensions of Entry 71. With both its edges and the Harvard Music Department heading trimmed off, the original state of the letter thus survives only in her several reverse prints, these made, fortunately, before its first framing.

Works Consulted

Bellingari, Luigi. Jacket notes for Tchaikovsky, "Sinfonia n.2 in do minore, op. 17." *Grande concerti live*. Cetra Records, 1977. LO 505.

Canfield, David. *Canfield Guide to Classical Recordings*. 3rd ed. Bloomington, IN: Ars Antiqua, 1991. vol. 2. no. 49257.

Carbonneau, Suzanne. "Adolph Bolm in America." *The Ballets Russes and Its World*. ed. Lynn Garafola and Nancy Van Norman Baer. New Haven, CT, and London: Yale University Press, 1999. pp. 219-44.

Hollywood Bowl Program Notes. 27 August 1940. pp. 11, 13-17, 20-2, 42-4.

Jones, Isabel Morse. "Season at Hollywood Bowl Goes Into Its Final Week." *Los Angeles Times*. 25 August 1940. pt. 3, p. 5.

—. "Stravinsky, Ballet Share Bowl Honors." *Los Angeles Times*. 28 August 1940. p. 10.

Los Angeles Philharmonic Orchestra. Archives. Photographs nos. 36225, 36232, 1547: no. 47.

Merrill-Mirsky, Carol, ed. *Exiles in Paradise*. [Exhibition catalogue]. Los Angeles: Hollywood Bowl Museum, 1991. p. 59.

Morton, Lawrence. "Stravinsky in Los Angeles." *Festival of Music Made in Los Angeles*. ed. Orrin Howard. Los Angeles: Philharmonic Association, 1981. pp. 74, 76 (confusing Tchaikovsky's first and second symphonies).

New York Philharmonic. *The Historic Broadcasts 1923 to 1987*. New York, 1997. CD 3.

Saunders, Richard Drake. *Musical Courier* 122 (15 September 1940): 34.

Schubert, Hannelore. "Die Bühnenbilder der Uraufführungen." *Musik der Zeit* n.s. 1 (1958): 49.

Sotheby's. *Collection Boris Kochno*, Monaco, 11-12 October 1991, lot 398.

SBu. n. 2 on p. 115, p. 116 (17, 24, and 26 August 1940).

SI&V. pl. 162 on p. [97].

SScrbk. pl. 19.

SSC. vol. 2. p. 252 (no performances took place on 29 and 30 August).

Stuart, Philip. *Igor Stravinsky – The Composer in the Recording Studio. A Comprehensive Discography*. New York, NY, Westport, CT, London: Greenwood Press, 1991. pp. 69, 77.

Taruskin, Richard. *Stravinsky and the Russian Traditions*. Berkeley and Los Angeles, CA: University of California Press, 1996. pp. 1600-01.

Ussher, Bruno David. "Stravinsky, Bolm Ballet in successful bowl program." *The News, Los Angeles*. 28 August 1940. pp. 11 and 13.

72   (1940). **Autographed photograph (cropped), 20.3 × 15.4 cm, taken by George Hoyningen-Huené at Paris, 16 November 1934, printed on white background, 24.9 × 20.1 cm, with embossed stamp at lower right of Harcourt-Harris / New York, inscribed in summer/ fall 1940 at the upper right in English in black ink across the photograph into the background for Dorothy [Ellis McQuoid]. An elongated tail of the final *y* of Strawinsky encloses the date:**

Dorothy Dorothy ... _ _
for you
IStrawinsky
1940

Acquisition: H. Colin Slim in San Clemente, CA, on 13 October 1996 by purchase from Dorothy Ellis McQuoid Hopper. The photograph was restored in December 1996 by Linda K. Ogden, who removed its acidic backing board.

Provenance: Dorothy Ellis McQuoid, Los Angeles (1940-96). (Mrs. Hopper had it framed with Entry 71.)

Commentary

When he inscribed Entry 72, Stravinsky told Mrs. McQuoid – correctly – that it was taken by George Hoyningen-Huené (1900-68). Entry 72, however, is a rephotograph. A clue as to which season he inscribed it for her might lie in his inscription: "Pour Madame / Marcus / Koshland / Son admiratur / Igor Strawinsky / 1940" on a different photograph from the same series by Hoyningen-Huené where his final *y* similarly encloses the year. (Stravinsky dined with Mrs. Koshland on 8 September 1940 in San Francisco and was her house guest the next several days).

Cropping on all sides of Entry 72 was presumably done in New York by its US printer, Harcourt-Harris. The original photograph by Hoyningen-Huené was taken 16 November 1934. With the same long background shadow at the right, the original photograph also includes Stravinsky's glasses, nose, and moustache all in shadow. He inscribed a photo of an identical (complete) photograph to Madame Roland-Manuel in Paris in March 1936, a postcard of it to John Alden Carpenter (1876-1951) the same month in Paris, and again there in October the same (complete) photograph in Russian to his brother Yury (1878-1941). The original photograph has been incorrectly dated as 1927 by William Ewing, confusing it with another photograph of the composer that year in *Vanity Fair.*

Works Consulted

Carpenter, John Alden. Papers. Box 1, folder S. The Newberry Library, Chicago.

Ewing, William A. *The Photographic Art of Hoyningen-Huené*. London: Thames and Hudson, 1986. pl. 96, p. 242.

Hoyningen-Huené, George. 13.053. Theatre Collection. Harvard University.

Koshland, Mrs. Inscribed photograph. Vertical file. Music Library, University of California at Berkeley.

Renaud, Paul, and Thierry Bodin. *Archives Roland-Manuel [part 2]*. Paris: 24 March 2000, lot 232, pl. on p. 68.

Stravinskaya, Kseniya Yuryevna. *O I.F. Stravinskom i evo blizkikh*. [I.F. Stravinsky and his intimates.] Leningrad: Muzïka, 1978. pl. on p. 30.

SBu. n. 14 on p. 36, p. 116 (8-9 September 1940).

Strawinsky. Sein Nachlass. Sein Bild [with] *Katalog der ausgestellten Bildnisse und Entwürfe für die Ausstattung seiner Bühnenwerke*. Basle: Kunstmuseum and Paul Sacher Stiftung, 1984. pp. 126-[7], lower image.

Vanity Fair 29 (November 1927): pl. on p. 50.

73

(1940). Photograph, uninscribed and undated [28-29 October 1940], 12.7 × 18.0 cm (including borders), stamped lower right margin: Edwin McQuoid, the reverse side stamped: PHOTO BY / EDWIN McQUOID / 10323 Ilona Ave., L. A.

Acquisition: H. Colin Slim in San Clemente, CA, on 18 February 1997 by purchase from Dorothy Ellis McQuoid Hopper. It was restored in March 1997 by Linda K. Ogden, who dry-cleaned its reverse side and slightly reduced some cockling at the top and bottom where the photographic paper had expanded.

Provenance: Edwin and Dorothy Ellis McQuoid, Los Angeles (1940-97).

Commentary

The photograph is unpublished. Edwin McQuoid probably took this photograph not long after Entry 72, which Stravinsky had inscribed for McQuoid's wife in 1940. Obviously, Hoyningen-Huené's portrait influenced McQuoid stylistically. The date of 1940 Mrs. Hopper gave Dr. Slim in 1994 seems correct. Arriving in Los Angeles on 23 May

1940 and departing on 2 November, Stravinsky and Vera did not return there until 9 February 1941. Craft similarly dates two photographs by "Edwin McQuoid-Los Angeles" as 1940. Three of McQuoid's photographs of Stravinsky are in the Paul Sacher Foundation, including one identical to Entry 73, and the one next described.

Although it does not bear McQuoid's stamp, a different photograph of Stravinsky – now owned by Elliot Forbes of Cambridge, inherited from his parents – was also taken by McQuoid, as Mrs. Hopper instantly confirmed in 1996, when Dr. Slim showed her a copy of it kindly supplied by Professor Forbes. Stravinsky probably inscribed it for the elder Forbes when he and Vera were their guests, 12-19 January 1941, at Gerry's Landing in Cambridge. It reads: "Pour mes chers / amis Peg et / Edward/Forbes / avec toute / ma fidèle / affection /IStrawinsky / 1941." Here the composer is without jacket, but he wears the same sweater with the same shirt tabs visible, the shadow background appearing as in Entry 73.

According to Mrs. Hopper, still another, and different photograph of Stravinsky taken by McQuoid, appeared unacknowledged in the Los Angeles Philharmonic Program for concerts he led in February 1941 (copy courtesy of her of the program in the orchestra's *Symphony Magazine*). In all three photographs he wears the same black horn rim glasses and, in Entry 73, he wears the same jacket as in the Philharmonic photograph.

Mrs. Hopper remembered that these three photographs – and some others as well, unfortunately never located by her – were taken at one session in their home at 10323 Ilona Avenue because, as she explained, he posed as a favour for her husband and would not willingly have posed again. Nor would McQuoid likely have been able to schedule a series of photographs of him in 1941 during the busy and exhausting period of his rehearsals with the Los Angeles Philharmonic and with Adele Marcus, 10-12 February. And even had McQuoid done so, the picture would unlikely have been taken and then printed in the short time between his arrival in Los Angeles on 9 February and its appearance in the program for the 13th. A pair of unpublished entries in Vera's diary for 1940 settles the matter: 28 October "McQuoid photos" and 29 October "McQuoid."

Indicators of Edwin McQuoid's talent are reproductions of his prints in the *Los Angeles Times* in December 1940, one of them awarded the "best picture of the year" and another in the *New York Times* that December: "Grand prize winner in *Scientific American*'s annual contest."

Works Consulted

Brown, Robert W. "A Big Year for Camera." *New York Times*. 29 December 1940.

Craft, Robert. "Catalog of the Library of Robert Craft." Typescript: Library of Congress, Music Division. XII: photographs, nos. 53-4 on p. 208.

Philharmonic Orchestra of Los Angeles. Symphony Magazine. 13-14 February 1941. pl. on p. [142].

"Prize 'Stills' by Film Men." *The Los Angeles Times*. 15 December 1940. Rotogravure section, p. 12 (film star, Marsha Hunt).

74 **(1941). Autograph undated singly folded note, 20.7 × 14.0 cm, in English and French in black ink and red crayon on stationery with silver-striped borders; printed header reads: BARBIZON·PLAZA· HOTEL / 101 WEST 58th STREET ... CENTRAL PARK SOUTH ... NEW YORK; printed footer reads: cable address / "barbplaza" .... telephone CIrcle 7-7000; from Stravinsky and Vera, c. 1 January 1941, to unnamed addressees, established as Edwin and Dorothy McQuoid:**

A HAPPY
NEW YEAR [underlined above and below in red]
Igor and Vera [only her name in her hand]
Strawinsky
mercy pour la
belle photo et
le si joli dessin

Edwin and Dorothy McQuoid   New York
Los Angeles   c. 1 January 1941

A HAPPY NEW YEAR
Igor and Vera Strawinsky
Thanks for the beautiful photograph and the very pretty drawing[.]

Acquisition: H. Colin Slim in San Clemente, CA, on 29 July 1996 by
purchase from Dorothy Ellis McQuoid Hopper.
Provenance: Edwin and Dorothy McQuoid, Los Angeles (1941-96).

Commentary

The note is unpublished, its envelope missing. The addressees were Mr.
and Mrs. Edwin McQuoid, as in Entry 70.

In 1998 Mrs. Hopper no longer remembered what photo and
drawing she and her first husband had sent almost sixty years previously
to the Stravinskys. During 1940, the latter resided at the Barbizon Plaza
for several periods (31 March-7 April, 8-15 May, 26 November-14
December and 22-31 December; and then again in 1941: 1-3 January
and 19 January-6 February) before returning to Los Angeles.
Uninscribed sheets of the same note paper as Entry 74 – also purloined
by Alexis Kall during his stay with them at the Barbizon Plaza Hotel in
the spring of 1940 – are in Kall's papers at the University of California
at Los Angeles.

Entry 74 surely salutes the New Year beginning 1 January 1941.
For example, Stravinsky wrote Nadia Boulanger on 4 December 1940,
using the same hotel stationery. He also wrote two notes on this hotel's
stationery to Edward Forbes in Cambridge, dating them 4 December
1940 and 10 January 1941.

Mrs. Hopper believed that "mercy" in Entry 74 was some joke
between Stravinsky and herself since Edwin McQuoid did not speak
French. (Banter about "Merthi" passed between Vera and Robert Craft
in 1948.)

Although Mrs. Hopper did not concur, it seems possible that the
"belle photo" mentioned in Entry 74 was one of several photographs of
Stravinsky taken late in October 1940 by her first husband in Los

Angeles. Perhaps it was even the McQuoid photograph that Stravinsky shortly thereafter inscribed to Edward Forbes and his wife in 1941, now owned by their son and his wife, Professor and Mrs. Elliot Forbes, Cambridge, a copy of which is in the Paul Sacher Foundation (see Entry 73).

Works Consulted

Forbes, Edward Waldo. Personal papers. "Stravinsky." Harvard University Archives.

Kall, Alexis F. Papers. Box 4: Postcards. Special Collections 601. Charles E. Young Research Library. University of California at Los Angeles.

SBu. pp. 117-19, 145 (22 August 1948).

SI&V. pl. 163 and caption on p. 98.

SSC. vol. 1. n. 4 on p. 238.

75   (1941). Autograph inscription in English in black ink on title page of first edition, 31.2 × 23.1 cm, [twenty stars circumscribing title] THE / STAR-SPANGLED / BANNER / Words by FRANCIS SCOTT Key Music by JOHN STAFFORD SMITH / Harmonized and Set for Chorus by / IGOR STRAWINSKY / [star] / Price 30¢ / [star] / (New York: Mercury Music Corporation, [1941]), piano vocal score, 6 pp., December 1941, for Dorothy [Ellis] McQuoid:

To Dorothy McQuoid
with all my best
wishes
IStrawinsky
1941

Acquisition: H. Colin Slim in San Clemente, CA, on 29 July 1996 by purchase from Dorothy Ellis McQuoid Hopper. The piano vocal score, with its frayed title page and detached pages, was restored in October 1996 by Linda K. Ogden.

Provenance: Dorothy Ellis McQuoid, Los Angeles (1941–96).

Commentary

Mrs. Hopper was present when Stravinsky led the national anthem (not in his own arrangement) for the first time at the Hollywood Bowl on 27 August 1940 (see Entry 71). She could not recall for Dr. Slim whether she had discussed Entry 75 with Stravinsky or even whether she attended its premiere in Los Angeles at the Embassy Auditorium, Tuesday, 14 October 1941. The re-harmonized national anthem was the final work on a program by the WPA Symphony Orchestra, joined by the Los Angeles Oratorio Society and the Los Angeles WPA Negro Chorus conducted by James Sample, and was followed by "Remarks" by Stravinsky.

The Library of Congress preserves, however, her night-letter to him from Burbank, California, of 14 October 1941:

> Dearest Igor[:] For some unexplained reason we confused the date of your concert thinking it this Saturday[.] Ed is judging pictorial solon [sic][.] I am alone with boys, no way to reach concert[.] Cannot tell you what an intense disappointment it is[.] Many bravos and many kisses[.] Our deepest love[.] / Dorothy McQuoid / 8:37[pm].

Stravinsky inscribed another copy of the same 1941 piano/vocal edition: "To Eliott [sic] Forbes, to him and to his beautiful wife IStr/ 1942." I owe my knowledge of this copy to the kindness of Professor Forbes. Stravinsky also inscribed a copy to Dagmar Godowsky (1897–1975).

Stravinsky's arrangement for full symphony orchestra and chorus was published by Mercury Music Corporation in 1941. On its final page is printed: "Finished July 4 1941," the same date on which he says he composed his version of the anthem. Along with the manuscript presentation copy of his orchestration to President Franklin D. Roosevelt in August, he wrote a preface. (Both are in the Library of Congress.) Mercury's date of publication can be deduced from *Time*, 22 December 1941, which announced: "a new version of *The Star-Spangled Banner* published last week here ... should be welcomed by conductors." Mercury printed with it a facsimile of his preface:

Searching about for a vehicle trough which I might best express my gratitude at the prospect of becoming an American Citizen, I chose to harmonize and orchestrate as a national choral the beautiful sacred anthem the Star Spangled Banner.

It is a desire to do my bit in these grievous times toward fostering and preserving the spirit of patriotism in this country that inspires me to tender this my humble work to the American People.

Igor Strawinsky

October 1941.

Uniquely for him, Stravinsky had Mercury print at the bottom of the first page: "The Right to Public Performance for Profit is Extended by the Publisher to All with No Restriction Whatsoever No Fees need Be Paid and No Special Permission is Necessary."

Stravinsky also composed two other arrangements of the anthem, differently harmonized, for *a cappella* male chorus. One of these, set *a4*, he dated "Sept 41." The other, *a4-a6*, he dated only "1941." Recorded by Craft in 1993, the latter remains unpublished, although a facsimile is available. A mixture of dislike for existing arrangements of the national anthem, expediency, and patriotism seems to have prompted these versions. Stravinsky remained fascinated by the anthem's melody at least through Christmas 1941 (see Entry 76).

Several persons took or have been assigned the credit for suggesting the idea to him. He stated that Ernest Andersson (c. 1890-1943) – his composition student from late February 1941 – suggested he undertake the arrangement, but this belies the October 1940 sketch for it cited below.

In an interview in San Francisco two days before he conducted it himself with the San Francisco Symphony, on 9 January 1942, Stravinsky said: "I like the melody. Just right for a hymn, a national anthem. But – it is so poorly organized." Stating here that he had arranged it shortly before 4 July 1941, he explained that he had wanted to make it more suitable for schools, for large choruses, so he " wrote" his own orchestration.

Aaron Sapiro (1884-1959), the composer's lawyer, is also said to have made the suggestion. Sapiro was not Stravinsky's lawyer, however, until 1942.

Years later, in 1957, the son-in-law of Ernest Andersson, James Sample (1910-), who had led its premiere, not only wrote enthusiastically about it to Richard Hill (then head of the Music Division at the Library of Congress), but also took credit for it: "I had the privelege [sic] of premiering the Stravinsky version in late 1941, and off the record, of influencing him to attempt the job."

A sketch by Stravinsky for his arrangement is said to date from October 1940. This would be just two months after he had conducted the national anthem at the Hollywood Bowl for the first time.

After dating the manuscripts of his orchestral-choral score and his piano-choral arrangement 4 July 1941, he then had his composition student, Andersson, send the arrangement to be copyrighted on 28 July. On 14 August, Stravinsky dispatched it to Leonard Feist (1911-96), president of Mercury Music Corporation, informing him that it would be premiered in Los Angeles on 9 September. (Having already met with "editeur Feist" in New York on 31 December 1940, Stravinsky had signed a contract by early 1941 with Mercury: "for the publication of all of Stravinsky's light non-symphonic compositions for a period of years.") He again sent it to Feist on 9 October. Only a first rehearsal – one just for chorus – took place on 8 September 1941, however. There was one for orchestra on 13 October, the day before its premiere.

The program also included the *Nocturno and Scherzo* by Andersson, Sample's father-in-law. Both were perhaps works done under the tutelage of Stravinsky, as the program announces that, whereas the *Nocturno* had been played several times previously, the "*Scherzo* is a recent composition." Possibly both movements belonged to the symphony by Andersson, now lost, which Stravinsky was then rewriting for his student.

A letter of 30 September 1941 from Stravinsky to Sample authorized him to make a non-profit recording of the anthem. Sample again conducted it on 18 October.

Its world premiere seems to have been generally well reviewed by Los Angeles critics such as Jones, Saunders, and Ussher. Isabel Morse Jones reported: "the audience received it solemnly. They did not sing, although it was repeated three times" and also opined that, in Stravinsky's version, "the anthem was made easier to sing." Early the next year, San Francisco welcomed it and it continued to be played at WPA concerts in Los Angeles until the orchestra disbanded in April

1942. Problems occurred only at later performances – such as those at St. Louis, 19-20 December 1941, and above all in Boston, 14-15 January 1944 – where further performances were forbidden by the police on grounds of "tampering with national property."

Twenty-five years later, almost to the day that he had completed his arrangement of the national anthem, Stravinsky conducted it at a concert on 5 July 1966 for the opening of the season at the Hollywood Bowl, where he was photographed.

Works Consulted

Christie's. *Illuminated Manuscripts, Illustrated Books, Autograph Letters and Music.* London, 29 June 1994, lot 124.

Craft, Robert. *Stravinsky: Chronicle of a Friendship.* 2nd ed. Nashville, TN, and London: Vanderbilt University Press, 1994. p. 473 (16 December 1967).

Frankenstein, Albert. *San Francisco Chronicle.* 7 and 10 January 1942. pp. 11 and 19, respectively.

Jones, Isabel Morse. *The Los Angeles Times.* 15 October 1941. pt. 2, p. 10.

–. *Musical America* 61 (25 October 1941): 18.

Joseph, Charles M. "Stravinsky Manuscripts in the Library of Congress and the Pierpont Morgan Library." *Journal of Musicology* 1 (1982): 336, no. 38.

McPhillips, William. "Stravinsky in Spotlight. Bowl Opens 45th Season of Symphonies under the Stars." *The Los Angeles Times.* 6 July 1966. pt. 1, p. 3.

Meyer, Felix, ed. *Settling New Scores. Music Manuscripts from the Paul Sacher Foundation.* Mainz: Schott, 1998. p. 159, no. 84 with two pls. (1942 for publication and "John" Sample are incorrect.)

Morton, Lawrence. Papers. Box 85 (letter: 11 November 1957 to Richard Hill). Special Collections 1522. Charles E. Young Research Library. University of California at Los Angeles.

Roelofsma, H. Toni. *Pacific Coast Musician* 31 (17 January 1942): 4.

"Sample, James W." *Who's Who in California.* 1941. vol. 1. p. 799.

"Sample, James." *Music and Dance in California and the West*, ed. Richard Drake Saunders. Hollywood: Drake-William, 1948. p. 248.

Saunders, Richard Drake. *Musical Courier* 123 (1 February 1941): 133; (1 November 1941): 28; 124 (15 November 1941).

Shepard, John. "The Stravinsky *Nachlass*: A Provisional Checklist of Music Manuscripts." *Music Library Association Notes* 40 (June 1984): 730, 750 (C74).

Smith, Moses. "Stravinsky Meets the Boston Censor." *Modern Music* 21 (1944): 171-73.

SBu. facing title page, p. 123, n. 8 on p. 124, n. 6 on p. 125, p. 222.

SM&C. (1960) pp. 93-4; (1981) pp. 99-100.

SP&D. pp. 368, 556, n. 55 on p. 648.

SScrbk, pls. 16-17 and 19 at pp. 12-13.

Tussler, Adelaide. *Monday Evening Concerts. Lawrence Morton Interviewed.* University of California Los Angeles, 1973. p. 405.

Ussher, Bruno David. "Sounding Board." *Daily News. Los Angeles.* 16 October 1941. p. 26.

White, Eric Walter. *Stravinsky: The Composer and His Works.* 2nd ed. Berkeley and Los Angeles, CA: University of California Press, 1979; repr. 1984. p. 614, App. C, no. 73b.

Wolffers, Jules. "Boston." *Musical Courier* 130 (5 February 1944): 8.

76 (1941). Autograph annotated printed Christmas card, 19.0 × 29.0 cm (opened), in French in black ink, with musical quotation of initial two phrases of *The Star-Spangled Banner*, Christmas 1941, to unidentified correspondent:

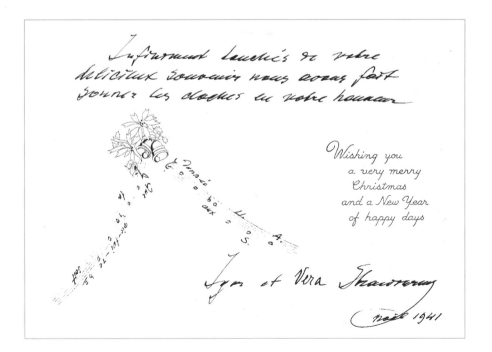

Infinement touchées de votre delicieux souvenir nous avons fait
sonner les cloches en votre honneur
[below, two of Stravinsky's rastrum-drawn staves with music of
the anthem and rhyming text emerging from two (printed)
bells]
Que la vic-toi-re soit
donnée aux U.S.A.
[beside staves, at right, printed] Wishing you
a very merry
Christmas
and a New Year
of happy days
[below, signed across opening]
        Igor et Vera [only her name in her hand] Strawinsky
                noël 1941

                        Hollywood
                  Christmas 1941

Extremely touched by your charming memento, we are making the
bells ring in your honour:
    May victory be given to the U.S.A.
    Igor and Vera Strawinsky

Acquisition: H. Colin Slim on 15 July 2000 in Santa Monica, CA, from
La Scala Autographs.
Provenance: R. and R. Enterprises (3 Chestnut Drive / Bedford, NH),
Autograph Auction Catalog 238 (21 June 2000), lot 1559 (no. 2381537).

Commentary

Its music unidentified in *Catalog 238,* the card is illustrated therein
(reduced); its envelope is missing. Presumably Entry 76 dates between
the declaration of war on Japan by the US on 8 December and
Christmas Day of 1941.

    The language chosen and the quotation from the isorhythmic
national anthem disguised in even whole notes and set to a rhyming
couplet might suggest the recipient was both French-speaking and a

musician. Such a person was the composer Richard Hammond (1896–1980), a friend since 1922, visited in New York by Stravinsky and Vera on 23 December 1940, who entertained him at their "first American party" in Hollywood on 1 November 1941 and who again dined with him there five days later. The possibility that Entry 76 was sent to him is increased by the same *Catalogue 238* including another Stravinsky Christmas greeting, lot 1560 (no. 238153), that one inscribed to "Dick Hammond" in 1945. In any event, Entry 76 reveals the continuing impact upon Stravinsky of the anthem of his newly adopted country.

Works Consulted

SBu. pp. 118 (23 December 1940), 124 (1 and 6 November 1941).
SSC. vol. 1. n. 78 on p. 155.

77   (1942). Signed single-folded typed letter, 20.8 × 15.2 cm, headed with blue printed address, in English, and typed envelope, 10.9 × 15.8 cm (without stamps), with same blue printed address on rear flap, 19 March 1942, to Julian Brodetsky (1894-1962):

[printed in blue ink, between margin-to-margin rules]
1260 NORTH WETHERLY DRIVE … HOLLYWOOD, CALIFORNIA
[typed]   March 19,1942

Mr.Julian Brodetsky
444.N.Alfred str.
Hollywood,Cal.

Dear Mr.Brodetsky,
    As I just read about the draft,I remembered our recent conversation at the Tansmans and your [one letter crossed out in ink] ~~w~~worrying about the future of your splendid organisation which depends so much on young musicians.

I sincerely hope that actual circumstances will not interfere with your activity,which personaly I consider as most gratifying and culturaly most important for the progress of the musical art.

I would be glad to know how the thigs turn and I wish most sincerely,you could quietly continue your so useful and high artistic effort,particularly precious in these actual dark moments.

Yours cordially

[blue ink] Igor Strawinsky

Acquisition: H. Colin Slim in Berkeley, CA, on 30 March 2000 from Joyce B. Muns.

Provenance: A California dealer, c. 1993; J.B. Muns, *Musical Autographs List 97* (Berkeley, 1997), "Julian Brodetsky Collection," no. 42.

Commentary

The several misspellings and typing errors, incorrect idioms, mistranslations from the French ("actual" for "actuel"), frequent lack of vertical alignment, and crowding in the typing all point to the composer himself at the typewriter, struggling with English. The absence of stamps suggests the letter may have been hand-delivered, perhaps passed on by the Alexandre Tansmans. To my knowledge, Brodetsky's name does not appear in the Stravinsky literature to date.

Vera's diary reports the same day: "Tansman for lunch. Igor irritable all day because of business letters," one of which that day in English to Associated Music Publishers is partly edited. No trace of irritation appears in Entry 77. In fact, Stravinsky wrote Brodetsky again, late in 1942, this time in Russian (see Entry 79).

Brodetsky was born near Warsaw, then a Russian possession. After graduating from the Petrograd Conservatory in 1916, and already concertmaster in Moscow's Bolshoi Theatre Orchestra during the beginning of the revolution, he left Russia for Latvia and from there to Cologne, joining the Brühler Schlossquartet. Emigrating to New York via England around 1923, Brodetsky joined the first violins of the San Francisco Symphony Orchestra, outside fifth desk, on 23 October

1925, remaining in that position throughout the 1926-27 season. Promoted to outside third desk in 1927-28, he became Assistant Concertmaster (outside second desk) in 1928-29, playing his last concerts in April 1929. During this final season he also placed advertisements in the orchestra's programs for "Violin Instruction."

Relocating to Southern California, Brodetsky joined the Los Angeles Philharmonic in October 1929, remaining in the inside third desk of its first violins under Artur Rodzinski until the autumn of 1932. Highly regarded in 1939-40 as one of the Philharmonic-endorsed "Prominent Teachers of Los Angeles," in the late 1930s he formed a group of thirty-two young players – comprising eight string quartets – which he named the Brodetsky Chamber Music Ensemble and which rehearsed *daily*. It is this group in Entry 77 that Stravinsky calls "your splendid organization." A newspaper review of 30 January 1942 reports him in the audience at the Wilshire-Ebell Theatre on 25 January where the Ensemble performed works by Tansman, Ernst Toch, Dimitri Shostakovitch, and Ralph Vaughan-Williams.

Tansman (1897-1986) – although first appearing in Vera's published diary only on 19 March 1942 (also the date of Entry 77) – knew Stravinsky well in Hollywood from the end of 1941 until April 1946, when he returned to France. Stravinsky not only gave him a manuscript of the *Four Norwegian Moods* (1942) but also inscribed on 31 March 1946 the manuscript of Tansman's sixth string quartet – dedicated to Brodetsky – at its first performance: "Heartiest thanks for this music and its wonderful performance by J. Brodetsky." Two years later Tansman was to publish in French his own book about Stravinsky.

By the date of Entry 77, of course, the US military draft, initiated two years previously, was in full force. Late in 1945, on 7-8 December, Brodetsky was one of the speakers at a Conference on American-Russian Cultural Exchange, held at UCLA. His Ensemble survived the war years and continued to play as late as 1953. According to Brodetsky's memoirist – who studied violin with him from 1955 – Stravinsky, Tansman, Mario Castelnuovo-Tedesco, Toch, and others often attended its two- and three-hour rehearsals. Between 1938 and 1949 all of them – including Reinhold Gliere (1875-1956) in 1945 from the Soviet Union – wrote Brodetsky to express their admiration for his superb training of young musicians.

Works Consulted

Brodetsky, Julian. "The New Chamber Music." *Music and Dance in California.* ed. José Rodriguez. Hollywood: William J. Perlman, 1940. pp. 60-4, 323 ("Brodetsky, Julian," with photograph).

"Brodetsky, Julian." *Music and Dance in California and the West.* ed. Richard Drake Saunders. Hollywood: Drake-William, 1948. p. 178.

Morton, Lawrence. Papers. Box 5, folder 9. Special Collections 1522. Charles E. Young Research Library. University of California at Los Angeles.

Muns, J.B. *Musical Autographs List 97.* Berkeley, 1997, nos. 33-46.

–. *Musical Autographs Lists 00-5 and 6.* Berkeley, 2000, nos. 61, 256.

Philharmonic Orchestra of Los Angeles Programs, 1929-32, and *Symphony Magazine*, 1939-40, p. 16.

Quinn, Alfred Price. "Brodetsky Ensemble Scores." *B'nai B'rith Messenger*, 30 January 1942.

San Francisco Symphony Orchestra [Programs]. 15-18 (1925-29).

SBu. p. 125 (19 March 1942).

SSC. vol. 3. pp. 279-81 (19 March), 521.

Tansman, Alexandre. *Igor Stravinsky. The Man and His Music.* trans. Therese and Charles Bleefield. New York, NY: Putnam, 1949. pp. 239-41.

Wibberley, Leonard. *Ah Julian! A Memoir of Julian Brodetsky.* New York, NY: Ives Washburn, 1963.

78

(1942). First edition, 22.7 × 15.0 cm (with original wrappers), POÉTIQUE MUSICALE / *SOUS FORME DE SIX LEÇONS* **/ PAR IGOR STRAWINSKY / Veritas (Cambridge: Harvard University Press, 1942), 95 pp. with 1 pl., uninscribed.**

Acquisition: H. Colin Slim in Oakland, CA, on 17 August 1999 by purchase from J. Caleb Cushing, Oakland.

Provenance: Charles Cushing, Berkeley (1942-82), who dated his copy (price: $2.00), "August 1942"; Piquette Cushing, Berkeley (1982-97).

Commentary

This first French edition of the six Charles Eliot Norton lectures by Stravinsky at Harvard in 1939-40 has for its frontispiece a photograph of the composer, a postcard copy of which he had inscribed to Dorothy

Ellis McQuoid in December 1939 (see Introduction and Entry 67). An identical photograph in the Paul Sacher Foundation is identified there as probably by Gar Vic, Buenos Aires, 1936.

The Norton lectures, ghost-written by Roland-Manuel, were apparently slated to be published in the fall of 1940. There was even a plan to publish an English translation that fall by Alexis Kall (see Entry 86). Funding problems delayed this, as revealed by correspondence of 27 March that year between Professor Edward W. Forbes, chairman of the Norton Committee and Jerome D. Greene, Harvard's Treasurer, and of 10 October between Forbes and Stravinsky. The October letter states that a Mr. Malone "doubts, owing to various difficulties and delays, if it will be possible actually to publish the book this autumn." (For the 1947 English translation and a French edition published in 1952 at Paris, see entries 86 and 94. Further, see entries 15, 17, and 64.)

Works Consulted

Forbes, Edward Waldo. Personal papers. "Stravinsky." Harvard University Archives.

79   (1942) Autograph letter, 20.8 × 15.2 cm, folded once, in Russian in black ink, and autograph envelope, 10.9 × 15.8 cm, with two one-cent stamps, postmarked Los Angeles 26 October 1942 3:30 p.m. (both letter and envelope on same stationery as Entry 77), 24 October 1942, to Julian Brodetsky:

[envelope:] Mr Julian Brodetsky [y altered from i]
444 No. Alfred Street
Hollywood,
Cal.

[printed in blue ink, between margin-to-margin rules]
1260 NORTH WETHERLY DRIVE ... HOLLYWOOD,
CALIFORNIA

24 Okt. 1942

Iskrenne blagodaren Vam, dobreishii Brodetski, za lyubeznyi present. Vash photostat moyego Apollona vyshel och.[en'] udachno.

S serdechnym privetom Vam oboim
Vash
IStravinskii

Julian Brodetsky	Hollywood
Los Angeles	24 October 1942

Sincerely grateful to you, kindest Brodetsky, for the kind present. Your photostat of my Apollon [Musagète] came out v[ery] successfully.

> With heartfelt greetings to you both,
> Yours,
> IStravinsky

Acquisition: H. Colin Slim in Santa Monica, CA, on 15 July 2000 from J.B. Muns.
Provenance: Same as Entry 77, her *List 97,* no. 43.

Commentary

The translation given in *List 97,* no. 43, is inaccurate. "Greetings to you both" includes Brodetsky's young wife, Anna May Nolan, whom he had married on 12 December 1937. A talented violinist, she later turned to biology.

Presumably, Stravinsky had requested or allowed Brodetsky to have a photostat made of a printed score of *Apollo,* since the manuscript itself was far away, in the Library of Congress. Dorothy Ellis McQuoid Hopper recalled for Dr. Slim in 1994 a similar incident in 1940 when her first husband, Edwin, had several copies duplicated at Paramount Studios for Stravinsky of her copy of the two-piano reduction of the *Capriccio* because the composer had only an orchestral score (see entries 67 and 70). Brodetsky could have delivered the photostat by mail, or perhaps in person at a party given by their mutual friends the Tansmans, attended by Stravinsky and Vera on 21 October 1942.

Whether Brodetsky's thirty-two student string ensemble (to which he would needs have added some double bass players) ever performed *Apollo,* or whether this photostat was related to corrections Stravinsky was making to *Apollo* on 22 March 1943 preparatory to conducting it in New York a month later, remain unknown.

Works Consulted

"Brodetsky, Julian." *Who's Who in California.* (1941): vol. 1, p. 117.
SBu. pp. 127-8 (22 March 1943).
Wibberley, Leonard. *Ah Julian! A Memoir of Julian Brodetsky.* New York, NY: Ives Washburn, 1963. p. 138.

80

(1943-4). Autograph fourteen-page calligraphic transparencies of *Scherzo à la Russe* arranged for two pianos by Stravinsky and signed: "June [19]44." pp. 1-2, 6, and 8-14: 30.2 × 24.2 cm; pp. 3-4: trimmed to 29.7 × 24.2 cm; p. 5: reassembled to 30.2 × 24.2 cm; p. 7: reassembled to 30.5 × 24.2 cm. Writing in black ink and with some traces of pencil on ten- and twelve-stave transparency paper for purposes of reproduction, Stravinsky added page numbers 2-14 at the top centre. Traces exist of previous autograph page numbers (now erased) "2, 3, 4, 5, 6, 7" on the upper corners of pp. 2-7, only. He inscribed the title "Scherzo a la Russe" in a kind of art-deco style on p. [1], signing at the right "Igor Strawinsky / 1943" and he printed in a slightly more formal hand on its lower left side "Copyright by Igor Strawinsky 1944." Cut and reassembled by him, pp. 5 and 7 of "Trio 1" suffered damage from his use of transparent tape. On p. 4, lower right, and mostly erased between the staves of piano 2 is: "IStr." and below it on the lower staff is: "21:4-43" or "2/:4-43" (perhaps signifying 1943 as the year of copying pp. 1-7). On p. 9, upper left margin to the left of Piano I, appears in pencil (visible only under ultra violet light): "6 25" (?=June 25). On p. 14, lower right, is "I Str. / June 44 / Hollywood."

Acquisition: on 4 August 1995 from J. and J. Lubrano, bidding for H. Colin Slim at Christie's, *Important Autograph Letters. Manuscripts and*

Music from the Richard Monckton Milnes Collection and other properties
(London: 29 June 1995), lot 476 (ill. of first page of manuscript at 127).
In February 1996, Linda K. Ogden removed yellowing transparent
tape, replaced it with rice paper, and encased each page, backed with a
sheet of acid-free museum paper, in a mylar envelope.
Provenance: John Wilson, Oxford (now Cheltenham), purchased by him
at Sotheby's, *Music and Continental Manuscripts* (London: 16-17 May
1991), lot 475, (ill. of first page of manuscript on p. 290).

Commentary
Stravinsky took his title from Tchaikovsky's piano piece, op. 1, no. 1
from 1867, a work which he incorrectly stated in 1956 that he had used
for *Le baiser de la fée* in 1928.

A detailed study of Entry 80 is in Dr. Slim's "Stravinsky's *Scherzo à
la Russe* and its Two-Piano Origins." The following excerpts from it
plus some supplementary remarks here may be found useful.

Copied on one side only of transparency paper and dated at its close
"June 44," Entry 80 is contemporaneous with and may well precede the
arrangement he began early in May that year on a $1000 commission
from the Blue Network of the American Broadcasting Company for
Paul Whiteman's jazz band, completing it by mid-June (see below,
Entry 81 [Exhibit A, p. 1, item 3]).

Three sets of ozalid reproductions of pages 1-6 together with three
separate ozalids of page 7 – all donated by Craft to the Library of
Congress – reveal an earlier and probably the earliest state of the
transparencies of Entry 80. These ozalid copies differ in four respects
from Entry 80:

1   page numbers 2-7 appear in their upper corners but not in the
    upper center of each page (as in Entry 80)
2   the octave F-sharps of piano I on page 4 are at the far right side of
    the first measure of Trio 1 and have "sub. p" marked between them
3   no small notes appear in Trio 1
4   page 7 is copied on twelve-stave paper

A different ozalid copy of just pages 1-7, held by the Paul Sacher
Foundation, follows the first of those just mentioned at the Library of

Congress, but immediately precedes Entry 80. Although it has the same page numbers at its upper corners, and page 7 is still on twelve staves, there are many indications for the May 1944 jazz-band scoring. On the Sacher ozalid Stravinsky notated very roughly in pencil and with hand-drawn staves the small notes of Trio 1, the very notes and staves he then so carefully copied in ink onto pages 4-7 of Entry 80.

Stravinsky copied all his music on the side of the transparency printed with blue staff lines except for page 1 and the upper half of the reassembled page 5, which two pages he copied on the reverse side inscribed with black staff lines. Pages 1-6 and pages 8-9 are on ten-stave transparencies. Staves on these pages are uniformly spaced at 1.95 cm, even on the reassembled page 5. As mentioned above, page 7 was originally copied on twelve-stave transparency paper. For some reason – perhaps because of copying errors and/or jazz-band indications – he reassembled page 7, using six fragments taken from twelve-stave transparency paper to form the sole eleven-stave page in the manuscript. The spaces between staves on page 7 are only 1.5 cm. Its paper thus emanated from the same stock of twelve-stave transparencies on which he copied the remainder of his music on pages 10-14. No manufacturer's mark appears on any of them.

Except for the first page, owing to the space the title occupies, and even on his reassembled pages, Stravinsky left on pages 2-9 staves 5 and 6 blank between each of his two systems of two-piano notation. There are two exceptions to this procedure. When he began copying the transition to the central E-flat section of Trio 2 and was copying that section itself within this Trio (pp. 10-11), he employed three systems per page on his twelve-stave paper and hence had no room to separate his systems. For the remainder of Entry 80 (pp. 12-14), he not only separated his two systems as before with a pair of empty staves, but the twelve-stave paper also allowed him a blank stave at the top and bottom of each page. Perhaps he ran out of ten-stave paper at the close of page 9, as a result of having reassembled page 5; and perhaps even page 7 was at one time copied on ten-staves. These variations in paper stock suggest that not all pages of Entry 80 were copied at the same time.

Copying pages 10-11 so densely without leaving staves between the systems is, however, probably for a practical reason. Although space between the systems could easily have been found by redistributing the three systems on each of these two pages as two systems each on three pages, such a distribution would have necessitated an extra page-turn for the pianists.

Entry 80 contains many deviations from the printed two-piano edition. The first edition was published early in October 1945 by Associated Music Publishers of New York (plate no. A.C. 19455, copyright 1945, 17 pp.). A copy of AMP's fall *Supplement* to their checklist that year in the New York Public Library (Music Division) is stamped: "Oct 16 1945." The two-piano *Scherzo* was reprinted about a decade later, by Schott in London (ED 10646: S. and Co. 6184, 17 pp.).

Differences appear at the very beginning – Entry 80 is marked "allegro e forte," whereas the printed versions are marked "Con moto" – and at the opening of Trio 1. In the Trio the publication inserts an extra measure at rehearsal **9**. Rehearsal numbers are in the printed editions only. Stravinsky's erasures in Entry 80 for piano I in the first measure of Trio 1, which show its F-sharps originally copied farther to the right (as mentioned above), may or may not mean that the extra measure (assigned to piano II in the publication) was once present, or even that he meant to insert it and forgot to do so. In the same trio at rehearsal **14**, beat 2 (extra staff), only Entry 80 and the printed two-piano edition of 1945 have the same reading. This 1945 printed edition for two pianos also contains many more dynamic indications, marks of articulation, and different slurring than does Entry 80.

The explanation for discrepancies between Entry 80 and its publication lies in a proof copy – yet another two-piano ozalid – held by the Library of Congress. Its first page is notated in red ink: "AM/7/31/45 (with I.S.'s answers to questions)." "AM" is Arthur Mendel (1905-79), editor for AMP from 1941 to 1947.

Annotated by Stravinsky and others, this proof consists of ozalid copies made from pages 3-14 of the present state of Entry 80. These ozalids are preceded by two music manuscript pages in pencil, not in the hand of Stravinsky. In addition, at the beginning of Trio 1 in the proof copy a small paste-down of three measures copied in pencil by the same hand substitutes for the final two measures there on page 4 of Entry 80. A note above asks: "I.S. – correct – avec une mesure ajoutée selon la partition?" followed by "Yes" in the composer's hand.

Because most changes made at the end of July 1945 to the LC proof copy also appeared in the 1945 orchestral score but not in the score for jazz band copied the previous year, Stravinsky (or, with his approval, Mendel at AMP) made these additions and alterations from the orchestral arrangement, "la partition," which Stravinsky had finished on 31 May 1945 and mailed to AMP sometime in June.

In Entry 80 at the close of the Scherzo proper on p. 4 below piano II, Stravinsky inscribed "fine" and following its double bar line – perhaps stimulated by his "fine" – he wrote "IStr." and below this "2/: 4 43" (now erased), as if he had finished copying. The two F-sharp dotted half notes already mentioned which open Trio 1 (in the right hand of piano I and one in its left hand) were, moreover, originally inscribed closer to the right side of the page. At the close of Trio 1 (p. 7) he wrote: "Sherzo [sic] da capo al fine" but at the close of Trio 2 (p. 14) only: "Scherzo da capo."

On page 5 (within Trio 1), which Stravinsky cut in half and joined with transparent tape, he continued carefully adding the same small staves he had already drawn on page 4 at the beginning of Trio 1, a procedure continued on page 6. On these extra staves he meticulously notated in small notes sixteenth-note passages he assigned to the violins, violas and muted trumpet in the 1944 jazz-band version (and to three solo violins, solo viola, and muted trumpet in the 1945 orchestral version). On reassembled page 7, however, between fragments one and three he inscribed the small notes on a regular-sized printed staff.

As stated above, such notations added in small notes to Entry 80 are not on its first ozalid at the Library of Congress, but appear roughly inscribed in pencil on a second ozalid at the Paul Sacher Foundation. In Entry 80 these small notes differ from the published versions at rehearsal **14**, beat 2. They also offer some additional material: at beat 4 preceding rehearsal **16**; and at beats 1-2 of rehearsal **16** (the extra music on beats 1-2 appears also in the printed 1945 and 1955 two-piano versions). The proof copy of 31 July 1945 in the Library of Congress excises them.

These additions to Entry 80 on Stravinsky's extra staves in Trio 1 are not to be confused with his several autograph corrections by erasure which appear at many places (pp. 1, 3, 4, 5, 8-11, and 13). Finally, the last note, D, in the left hand of piano I, page 9, m. 6, is correct, as shown by bassoon II and French horn IV in the orchestra score (2 mm. before rehearsal **20**), whereas both printed two-piano editions have an incorrect F. Here the proof copy of 31 July 1945 is correct, but the error is that of the printer, which escaped the proofreader.

Two performances are documented of Stravinsky playing the *Scherzo* arranged for two pianos: at its premiere with Nadia Boulanger at Mills College, Oakland, on Wednesday evening, 25 October 1944; and four months later with Vincent Persichetti (1915-87) at the Philadelphia Arts Alliance, 21 February 1945. For these performances, he probably used his personally edited – and somewhat simplified – ozalid copy (also held by the Library of Congress) made from Entry 80, which reveals that he played piano II.

On Sunday morning, 5 October 1952, I had the good fortune to hear him rehearse the symphonic version of the *Scherzo à la Russe* with the Vancouver Symphony Orchestra (see entries 91-2).

Works Consulted

Bernard, Matvey Ivanovich. ed. *Piesni Russkago Naroda*. Moscow: Jurgenson, c. 1886. no. 51 on p. 55.

Clough, Francis F., and C. J. Cuming. *The World's Encyclopaedia of Recorded Music*. London: Sidgwick and Jackson, 1966; repr. Westport, CT: Greenwood Press, 1970. p. 600.

Collaer, Paul. *Correspondance avec des amis musiciens*. ed. Robert Wangermée. Liège: P. Mardaga, 1996. pp. 375-6, no. 44-4.

Craft, Robert. "Catalog of the Library of Robert Craft." Typescript: Library of Congress, Music Division. IV: Proofs, no. 18 on p. 85; V: Facsimiles (ozalid copies and photostats), no. 36 on p. 85.

–. *Stravinsky: Chronicle of a Friendship*. 2nd ed. Nashville, TN, and London: Vanderbilt University Press, 1994. pp. 93 (19 January 1953), 445-6 (29 December 1966).

–. *Stravinsky: Glimpses of a Life*. London: Lime Tree, 1992; New York, NY: St. Martin's Press, 1993. pp. 300, 321.

–. Review of Taruskin's *Stravinsky* in the *Times Literary Supplement,* 13 September 1996. p. 5.

Crawford, Dorothy Lamb. *Evenings On and Off the Roof: Pioneering Concerts in Los Angeles, 1939-1971*. Berkeley and Los Angeles, CA, and London: University of California Press, 1995. p. 163.

Dahl, Ingolf. "Stravinsky on Film Music." *Musical Digest* (September 1946); repr. *Cinema. The Magazine for Discriminating Movie-Goers* 1, 1 (June 1947): 7-8, 21.

de Lerma, Dominique-René. *Igor Fyodorovich Stravinsky: A Practical Guide to Publications of his Music*. Kent, OH: Kent State University Press, 1974. p. 83 (S14).

DeLong, Thomas. *POPS: Paul Whiteman, King of Jazz*. Piscataway, NJ: New Century, 1983. pp. 268-9.

Downes, Olin. *New York Times*. 4 December 1946. p. 44.

Flamm, Christoph. Prefaces (1996) to his editions of Stravinsky, *Scherzo à la Russe*, for Jazz ensemble and Symphonic Version. London and Mainz: Eulenberg, 1999.

Frankenstein, Alfred. "Stravinsky Recital at Mills College." *San Francisco Chronicle*. 27 October 1944. p. 3H, col. 1.

Gessler, Clifford. "Stravinsky and Boulanger Are Heard at Mills." *Oakland Tribune*. 29 October 1944. p. 2-C.

Gold, Arthur, and Robert Fizdale. *Misia: The Life of Misia Sert*. New York, NY: Alfred A. Knopf, 1980. pp. 306-7.

Goldberg, Albert. *The Los Angeles Times*. 6 March 1956. pt. 2, p. 9.

Hellman, Lillian. *The North Star: A Motion Picture about Some Russian People*. New York, NY: Viking Press, November 1943. p. 29.

Jablonski, Edward. *Gershwin: A Biography*. New York, NY: Doubleday, 1987; repr. 1998. p. 336 ("1942" is incorrect).

Jans, Hans Jörg, and Lukas Handschin, ed. *Igor Strawinsky. Musikmanuskripte*. ("Inventare der Paul Sacher Stiftung," 5 [Winterthur: Amadeus, 1989].) 26: "Partitur (1923; 141 pp)." p. 34.

Joseph, Charles M. *Stravinsky and the Piano*. Ann Arbor, MI: University of Michigan Research Press, 1983. pp. 216-27.

Kober, Arthur. Collection. Box 1, folders 19-20; Box 2, folder 23, State Historical Society of Wisconsin, Madison, WI.

L., H.W. *Musical Courier* 134 (15 December 1946): 19.

L'Art ancien S.A. *Kostbare Autographen der neureren Musik und Literatur. Versteigerung*. Zurich, 17 November 1948. lots 19-22, pp. 35-41.

Lederman, Minna, ed. *Stravinsky in the Theatre*. New York, NY: Dance Index, 1949; repr. Da Capo Press, 1975. pl. on p. 132.

"Master Mechanic," *Time* 52 (26 July 1948): 46.

Mills College Weekly 28, 6 (23 October 1944): 1; 28, 7 (28 October 1944): 5.

Morton, Arthur, and Herbert Morton. *Monday Evening Concerts 1954-1971: The Lawrence Morton Years*. Los Angeles, CA: A. and H. Morton, 1993. p. 52.

Oakland Tribune. 22 October 1944. p. C2.

Oliver, Michael. *Igor Stravinsky*. London: Phaidon, 1995. pl. on p. 142 (incorrectly captioned).

Persichetti, Vincent. "Philadelphia's Lively Mid-Season." *Modern Music* 22, 3 (March–April 1945): 185.

Riordan, Mary Marguerite. *Lillian Hellman, A Bibliography: 1926-1978.* Metuchen, NJ, and London: Scarecrow Press, 1980. item B7 on p. 8.

Rollyson, Carl. *Lillian Hellman: Her Legend and Her Legacy.* New York, NY: St. Martin's Press, 1988. pp. 197-8.

Rothschild, Sigmund. "A Catalogue of Manuscripts and Documents: The Original Works of Igor Stravinsky [Inventory]." Music Division Special Collections, New York Public Library. vol. 2: 155.

Saturday Review of Literature 52 (26 July 1969): 52.

Schallert, Edwin. "News Clips from Studio Town." *The Los Angeles Times.* 1 December 1942. p. 26.

Scharlau, Ulf, ed. *Igor Strawinsky: Phonographie.* Frankfurt am Main: Deutsches Rundfunkarchiv, 1972. p. 127, no. 70.

Shepard, John. "The Stravinsky *Nachlass*: A Provisional Checklist of Music Manuscripts." *Music Library Association Notes* 40 (June 1984): 724, 742.

Slim, H. Colin. "Stravinsky's *Scherzo à la Russe* and its Two-Piano Origins" in *Essays on Music and Culture in Honor of Herbert Kellman.* ed. Barbara Haagh. Paris-Tours: Minerve, 2001. pp. 518-37.

Spycket, Jérôme. *Nadia Boulanger.* trans. M.M. Shriver. Stuyvesant, NY: Pendragon Press, 1992. pl. on p. 115 (top).

SBu. n. 6 on p. 116, pp. 127 (19 October 1943), 131, n. 6 on p. 132, p. 233 (5 January 1970).

SD. pp. 52-3.

SD&D. pp. 85-6.

SM&C. (1960) p. 102; (1981) p. 108.

SP&D. pp. 357, 373-4, 556, n. 21 on p. 644, n. 30 on p. 645, n. 58 on p. 648.

SSC. vol. 1. n. 72 on p. 359; vol. 2. n. 29 on p. 256; vol. 3. pp. 256, 259, 282-3, 293-9, 302, 305, 333, n. 27 on p. 364, p. 411.

Stuart, Philip. *Igor Stravinsky – The Composer in the Recording Studio. A Comprehensive Discography.* New York, NY, Westport, CT, London: Greenwood Press, 1991. pp. 11-12, no. 47x on p. 33, no. 50 on p. 34, no. 134 on p. 47, no. L11 on p. 71, p. 75.

Supplement to checklist A[ssociated]M[usic]P[ublishers] Fall 1945. New York, NY: AMP, 1945. pp. 2 (advertisement) and 5.

Taruskin, Richard. *Stravinsky and the Russian Traditions.* Berkeley and Los Angeles, CA: University of California Press, 1996. n. C.1 on pp. 1142-3, n. 19 on p. 1611, ex. E.5 on p. 1625, ex. E.6 on pp. 1627-9, pp. 1632-1647, and esp. ex. E.9a on p. 1634.

Thomas, Michael Tilson. *Viva Voce: Conversations with Edward Seckerson.* London and Boston, MA: Faber and Faber, 1994. p. 83.

Walsh, Stephen. *The Music of Stravinsky.* Oxford: Oxford University Press, 1988. p. 304, no. 89.

White, Eric Walter. *Stravinsky: The Composer and His Works*. 2nd ed. Berkeley and Los Angeles, CA: University of California Press, 1979; repr. 1984. pp. 131, 615, App. C, no. 79a, 629.

81 (1944). Signed carbon copies of 10 pages, 27.8 × 21.4 cm, in English in black ink, of typescripts of three legal contracts:

1. a two-sheet EXHIBIT A, pp. 1-2, dated 13 and 15 July 1944, of an unsigned confirmation of "mutual understanding" addressed to Stravinsky c/o Gretl Urban, c/o Associated Music Publishers Inc., New York. This agreement is between Stravinsky and THE BLUE NETWORK, N.Y. for: "an original orchestral composition for an orchestra of approximately thirty-five pieces of our selection ... for broadcasting over our facilities in a series of programs designed to present original compositions of outstanding composers ... you agree to accept the sum of $500 ... In addition, we agree to advance $500 to you at the time of the first radio performance." The agreement concerns the first orchestration of *Scherzo à la Russe* (1943-44), already commissioned in April 1944 by Paul Whiteman for his band, finished early the ensuing June, but apparently not printed until 1999. [Agreements nos. 2 and 3, below, concern the *Scherzo* and the *Sonata for Two Pianos* (1943-44).]

2. A seven-sheet agreement, pp. 1-7, dated 11 September 1944, between Stravinsky in Los Angeles and Associated Music Publishers Inc. and Chappell and Co. Inc. in New York. It is signed on p. 6, below right:

Igor Strawinsky

3. A single sheet of a clarification among all parties of 17 October 1944 with the engraved heading of Arthur E. Garmaize / Attorney at Law / One Cedar Street / New York, 5, signed below left:

Approved / Igor Strawinsky

Acquisition: H. Colin Slim in London on 17 June 1981 from Burnett Simeone.
Provenance: Unknown.

Commentary

The legal contracts are unpublished. Most pages of Entry 81 are watermarked MACADAM BOND / RAG CONTENT. Only Garmaize's clarification (no. 3) and page 6 of the agreement (no. 2) bearing the full signatures of Stravinsky are framed. The remaining sheets are in a folder.

Lack of a name in Exhibit A (no. 1) for the *Scherzo,* already commissioned by 11 April 1944, bothered Stravinsky who complained about it in his letter the following 15 July to Gretl Urban (his representative with AMP in New York, 1943-47). The Paul Sacher Foundation holds an undated typed list, "Radio Hall of Fame Orchestra Instrumentation." It has some notations in his hand with a total by him of "33 players," rather than the approximate number mentioned in Exhibit A. Previous telegrams and letters between him and Hugo Winter of AMP, 11-13 April 1944, are reproduced in the prefaces to the 1999 editions of the jazz band and symphony orchestra arrangements.

Nadia Boulanger and the Canadian pianist, Richard Johnston (1917-), offered a private premiere of the *Sonata for Two Pianos* (mentioned in agreements 2 and 3) for the Dominican Sisters of Edgewood College, Madison, Wisconsin, on 2 August 1944. Boulanger and Robert Stone Tangeman (1910-64) gave the public premiere at Indiana University six days later. Boulanger had written to Stravinsky in July 1944 requesting permission to give performances of the *Sonata.* Already on 19 October 1942, however, he had played some portion of his "4-hand sonata [sic]" with Marcelle de Manziarly at Santa Barbara. Published in 1945, the forty-one pages of transparencies of the *Sonata,* auctioned in 1991, are now in the Pierpont Morgan Library, Lehman Deposit.

Among the witnesses in no. 2 of Entry 81 was Aaron Sapiro (1884–1959), Stravinsky's Los Angeles attorney, 1942-59 (see pp. 3, 5: "A. Sapiro for I.S." and p. 6). A graduate of Hastings Law School at Berkeley, Sapiro was instrumental in 1948-49 in obtaining both the full score of *Orpheus* for about $3000 and the short score of it for the library of the Department of Music at the University of California at Berkeley. Sapiro apparently had a not inconsiderable influence on the composer at this period.

An almost geometric fiscal increase in commissions received by Stravinsky from the period of the *Scherzo* for $1000 can be deduced from the following examples: in 1944, *Scènes de ballet* for $5000; in 1946, *Orpheus* for $5000; in 1951, *The Rake's Progress* for $20 000; in 1953, *Agon* for $10 000; in 1957, *Threni* for $11 000; in 1958, *Movements* for $15 000. And twenty years after the $1000 *Scherzo* commission, Stravinsky telegraphed Boulanger on 17 November 1964 that he would charge: "no less than $25 000 commission for a short piece."

Works Consulted

Boulanger. Collection. Bibliothèque Nationale, Paris. Uncatalogued.

Flamm, Christoph. Prefaces (1996) to his editions of Stravinsky, *Scherzo à la Russe*, for Jazz ensemble and Symphonic Version. London and Mainz: Eulenberg, 1999. pp. vi-vii.

Roberts, John. "The Berkeley Music Library at Fifty." *Bene Legere. Newsletter of the Library Association* 51 (Fall 1998): pl. on p. 1 (*Orpheus*).

Sotheby's. *Music and Continental Manuscripts* (1991), lot 473, p. 298 (facsimile of title page of *Sonata*).

Spycket, Jérôme. *Nadia Boulanger*. trans. M.M. Shriver. Stuyvesant, NY: Pendragon Press, 1992. p. 135.

SBu. n. 6 on p. 125, p. 127.

SP&D. pp. 443, 452, 557, n. 49 on p. 648.

SSC. vol. 1. pp. 261, 265, 285, 305-6, n. 30 on p. 340, 359-60, 362, 366; vol. 2. pp. 253-6; vol. 3. pp. 293, 296-7, 299-300, n. 12 on p. 300, pp. 325, 338.

Tangeman, Robert. "Stravinsky's Two-Piano Works." *Modern Music* 22, 2 (January-February 1945): 93.

"Tangeman, Robert," *Harvard Class of 1932: Twenty-fifth Anniversary Report*. Cambridge: Harvard University Press, 1957. pp. 1104-5.

82 (1944). Signed typed single-sided unfolded letter, 13.9 × 21.5 cm, in French in black ink, 28 October 1944, to [Dr. Walter Adolphe] de Bourg (1888-1979):

le 28 octobre 1944

Cher Monsieur de Bourg,

Encore ce petit score et ce bref message a mon fils. Peut-etre aurai-je la chance que cela vous parvienne avant votre depart.

Excusez moi genereusement de vous avoir exploite ainsi et croyez, cher Monsieur de Bourg, a mon fidele et reconnaissant devouement.

Ma femme se joint a moi pour vous souhaiter a vous et a Mademoiselle votre fille nos meilleurs voeux de bon voyage.

[in black ink] Igor Strawinsky

Walter Adolphe de Bourg   Hollywood
Los Angeles[?] Washington, DC[?]   28 October 1944

Dear Mr. de Bourg:

In addition, this miniature score and this brief message for my son. Perhaps I shall be lucky enough for it to arrive before your departure.

Kindly forgive me for having thus exploited you, and please accept, dear Mr. de Bourg, my sincere gratitude.

My wife joins me in sending you and your daughter our best wishes for a good trip.

Igor Strawinsky

Acquisition: H. Colin Slim from Lion Heart Autographs, item 2299, on 1 July 1998 (also listed in their November 1998 catalogue: 5, no. 28). *Provenance:* Undisclosed, bought in 1993 by Lion Heart Autographs.

Commentary

The letter, on paper watermarked CHALLENGE / BOND, is unpublished and lacks its envelope as well its accompanying message for the (unnamed) son of Stravinsky and the "petit score" (a miniature score?) for said son. Absence of any fold plus the still clear impression made by a paper clip at the middle of the right side of Entry 82 suggest that it, the message, and the score were sent to Dr. de Bourg in an envelope considerably larger than this letter. Excellent typing in Entry 82 probably indicates not Stravinsky himself but his secretary until 1947, Beata Bolm (c. 1895-1967), who executed this letter.

Mention of the "petit score" and a short message destined for a son suggest the musician Soulima in Paris, rather than the artist Théodore in Geneva. Soulima continued to perform in Paris during the German occupation, being viewed by some as a collaborator, an accusation which was to cause his father acute embarrassment and grief in 1945 and which is said to have prevented Soulima from visiting him in the US until three years after the close of the Second World War.

Dr. Walter Adolphe de Bourg (also called von Burg) began his diplomatic service in Paris, going on to posts in Bucharest, London, and Munich. Transferred from Munich in May 1938 to Vienna as Swiss Consul General, he was recalled to Berne early in 1941 after a brief term in Bratislava. A member of the Swiss Legation in Washington during the Second World War, he had already met with Stravinsky in Los Angeles, on 26 April 1944.

Whether de Bourg was departing from Los Angeles with his daughter or from Washington late that October is unclear from Entry 82. By 1950, he was in Dublin, his last post after Washington until he retired three years later. Whether or not he was leaving the US in 1944, de Bourg would have encountered little difficulty in having score and message delivered to its destinee through Swiss diplomatic channels.

Works Consulted

Craft, Robert. *Stravinsky: Glimpses of a Life*. London: Lime Tree, 1992; New York, NY: St. Martin's Press, 1993. p. 142.

"de Bourg," *Who's Who in Switzerland including the Principality of Liechtenstein 1950/1951*. ed. H. and E. Girsberger. Zurich: Central European Times, 1952. p. 104.

—. *Who's Who in Switzerland including the Principality of Liechtenstein 1955*, ed. James Schwarzenbach and Stephen Taylor. Zurich: Central European Times, 1955. pp. 92-3.

—. *Who's Who in Switzerland including the Principality of Liechtenstein 1978/79.* [editor unnamed.] Geneva: Central European Times, 1978. p. 95.

Documents Diplomatiques Suisses 1848-1945. var. ed. Bern and Zurich: Benteli, 1979-97. vol. 12 (1937-38), pp. 754, 821; vol. 13 (1939-40), p. 556; vol. 14 (1941-43), n. 4 on p. 82, p. 434.

Les Archives Diplomatiques et Consulaires 3 (1938): 39, 240, 323.

SBu. n. 1 on p. 131.

SSC. vol. 1. n. 26 on p. 87, n. 34 on p. 341.

83   (1945). Signed typed singly folded letter, 11.7 × 18.3 cm, in French in black ink, with typed air mail envelope, 9.3 × 16.5 cm, 15 December 1945, addressed to J. Nizon:

Mr. J. Nizon
4 Rue de la Bretonnerie
Orlean, Loiret
France
[typed in red ink] EUROPE

[return address]
IGOR STRAVINSKY
1260 N.Wetherly Dr.
Hollywood 46, Calif., U.S.A.

[letter on Stravinsky's printed stationery]
1260 North Wetherly Drive . Hollywood 46, Calif. .
CRestview 1-4858

[typed]

le l5 DEC. 1945

Cher Monsieur Nizon,

    Juste ce mot en reponse a votre lettre du l0 decembre.

Quand je dis, "la musique est par son essence impuissante a
exprimer quoique ce soit", j'entends par la qu'elle n'est pas un
langage pareil a celui qui opere avec des mots, etant depourvue,
elle, des qualites immanentes a ce dernier, proprietes par
lesquelles un evenement, un sentiment, une attitude, un etat
psichologique, un phenomene de la natue peut etre transmis
(exprime, expose) et recu (compris). En somme, la musique
n'exprime pas autre chose qu'elle meme. C'est elle qui est a la
fois le sujet et l'objet de l'expression, son but et son moyen.

Esperant que ces quelques lignes pourront vous guider dans
vos recherches, je vous prie de croire, cher Monsieur Nizon, a
mes sentiments les meilleurs.

[in black ink] Igor Stravinsky

J. Nizon   Hollywood
Orleans   15 December 1945

Dear Mr. Nizon:

Just this note replying to your letter of 10 December.

When I say: "music is, by its nature, incapable of expressing anything
at all," I mean that it is not a language related to the one which uses
words, music being deprived of those immanent qualities of the
latter, characteristics by which an event, a feeling, an attitude, a
psychological state, a natural phenomenon, can be transmitted
(expressed, shown) and received (understood). To sum up, music
expresses nothing other than itself. It is itself both the subject and the
object of expression, its end and its means.

I hope, dear Mr. Nizon, that these few lines can assist you in
your research.

Kind regards,
Igor Stravinsky

Acquisition: H. Colin Slim on 20 January 1995 from Wurlitzer-Bruck.
Provenance: Unknown.

Commentary

Unpublished, the letter was typed on the same machine as Entry 85, probably by his secretary, Beata Bolm, and mailed one week later after she finished it. The envelope bears one postmark of Los Angeles 22 December 6:30 p.m. and three others marked 7 p.m.

Although its addressee, J. Nizon, has not been identified, Entry 83 suggests an interest by Nizon in the aesthetics of art. For example, just over a year later from Orléans, Nizon requested a sketch from Raoul Dufy (1878-1953), whom Stravinsky was later to memorialize in his *Double Canon* (1959) for string quartet.

The quotation in Entry 83 to which Stravinsky responds is from volume one of his *Chroniques de ma vie* (p. 116) written in collaboration with his old friend, Walter Nouvel: "Je considère la musique, par son essence, impuissante à *exprimer* quoi que ce soit: un sentiment, une attitude, un état psychologique, un phénomème de la nature, etc." Entry 83 thus contains an explication of what Craft justly observed as a statement that clung to Stravinsky all his remaining years. Stravinsky had also discussed this concept in February 1939 with Roland-Manuel, preserved in the latter's notes (see entries 15, 17, and 64). (Further on the *Chroniques,* see entries 19, 42-3, 46, 103.) In 1962 he made a further explication to Craft: "music expresses itself," these three words thus paraphrasing his sentence to Nizon: "la musique n'exprime pas autre chose qu'elle meme." (For a different view by him in 1921, see Entry 18.)

Works Consulted

Lesure, François. *Igor Stravinsky. La carrière européenne*. Paris: Musée d'Art Moderne, 1980. p. 102, no. 344.

Kenneth W. Rendell. *Catalogue 277,* Wellesley, MA, and New York, 1999. p. 13 (Dufy).

SE&D. (1962) p. 115; (1981) p. 103.

SSC. vol. 2. p. 491.

84 (1946). Autographed sepia photograph taken in 1944, probably by Paola Foa, 17.5 × 12.5 cm (including inscribed lower margin), in English in black ink, May 1946, to Harry Freistadt (1908-64):

To Harry Freistad as promised
sincerely
IStravinsky
Hollywood, Cal.
May 1946

Acquisition: H. Colin Slim on 27 April 1996 through Martin A. Silver from David Schulson.

Provenance: Unknown; probably from the addressee's widow or daughter in New York.

Commentary

Harry Freistadt played trumpet in New York for the Columbia Broadcasting System Symphony Orchestra. Stravinsky made recordings with this orchestra on 5 February 1945, returning a year later to rehearse it on 28 January for a broadcast on the 30th. On 11 February he rehearsed at the CBS Playhouse for a recording session the next day, cancelled, however, because of a strike by the Musicians' Union. His inscription on Entry 84 probably refers to his orchestral work with Freistadt early in 1946.

This sepia image is a detail from and is probably a rephotograph of a picture taken in 1944. It crops some of Stravinsky's right shoulder and all of his right hand, which rests on the arm of a chair or sofa in a photograph said to be of 1944 and taken in Hollywood. The photograph is owned by Boosey and Hawkes with whom he dealt from late 1945 and, from 1947, as his exclusive publisher. A copy in the Paul Sacher Foundation of this latter photograph, ascribed to Paola Foa, is said there probably to date from 1945. An even smaller detail of the photograph appears in 1951 on the cover of Columbia LP ML4398, a re-issue of 78 rpm recordings made in New York and Hollywood six years previously. Presumably the complete photograph was not among those taken in 1944 by Karl Bauer of Associated Music Publishers, New York – "I must confess that I do not like them: they do not resemble me" (SSC, vol. 3, p. 294). Perhaps, however, it was among "some much better ones" Stravinsky sent to AMP on 4 June 1944.

The photograph in Entry 84 may have been among the "packet of my photographs, to distribute to those people who constantly request autographed photographs" mentioned on 16 September 1944. Whether in 1946 Stravinsky also charged Freistadt for the photograph that he had inscribed for him is not known. Complaining a decade later about autograph seekers and the demand for photographs, he said that he ignored such requests unless the photo, envelope and stamps were enclosed "because they cost money."

Works Consulted

Craft, Robert. *Stravinsky: Chronicle of a Friendship*. 2nd ed. Nashville, TN, and London: Vanderbilt University Press, 1994. p. 161.

"Freistadt, Harry." *New York Times*. 17 December 1964. p. 41 (obituary).

Routh, Francis. *Stravinsky*. London: Dent, 1975. pl. [2] btn pp. 86-7.

SBu. pp. 132, 136 (28 January 1946).

SSC. vol. 2. n. 6 on p. 457; vol. 3. pp. 294-5, 298-9.

Stuart, Philip. *Igor Stravinsky – The Composer in the Recording Studio. A Comprehensive Discography*. New York, NY, Westport, CT, London: Greenwood Press, 1991. p. 59.

Tempo 8 (summer 1948): pl. on p. 12 (lower).

85

(1947). Signed typed letter, 27.1 × 18.0 cm, folded three times, in English in black ink, on Stravinsky's printed stationery of 1260 N. WETHERLY DRIVE / HOLLYWOOD 46, CALIFORNIA, 21 December 1947, to Nathan van Patten (1887-1956):

[typed] December 2l
1 9 4 7

Professor Nathan van Patten
STANFORD UNIVERSITY
Stanford, Calif.

Dear Professor van Patten:
This is my answer to your very interesting letter of early December, wherein you ask that I made available to your University an original manuscript of my music.

I shall be glad to be represented in this collection and in its catalogue of such a famous University. For this reason I select one of my late compositions, writen during my residence here in the United States, DANSES CONCERTANTES. This has been performed many times in this country and in Europe and is considered typical of this last period of my work.

I am happy to give this manuscript to Stanford University; and in return, I ask you to do something for unfortunate people, who are practically unknown to me but whose necessities distress me greatly.

Please send the persons on de enclosed list such packages foodstoffs or plain wearing apparel, as you may consider adequate, from time to time. This will gratify me deeply.

I shall forward the manuscript soon, after I withdraw it from the safety vault, to join your illustrious scores.

With my personal compliments, I am

Sincerely yours

[in black ink] Igor Stravinsky

Acquisition: H. Colin Slim in New York on 23 September 1994 from Wurlitzer-Bruck.

Provenance: Undisclosed; probably estate of Nathan van Patten.

Commentary

The letter is unpublished, its envelope and its "enclosed list" are missing. A copy of the letter is in the Paul Sacher Foundation. Entry 85 is typed on the same machine as entries 82-3.

Van Patten had made his request for a music manuscript on 8 December 1947. His papers at Stanford University also reveal that Van Patten (who perhaps kept Entry 85 for himself) typed a copy of it for the university's files, generally retaining the same line division but correcting the several errors in it. These slips may be those of Beata Bolm, then the usual typist for Stravinsky, or they may indicate that he typed Entry 85 himself.

On the following 16 January, Van Patten acknowledged the safe arrival the previous Monday of the manuscript of *Danses concertantes* (1942). Van Patten's food order of 17 March to Hammacher-Schlemmer and Co., New York, copies the missing Stravinsky "enclosed list" in Entry 85 of fifteen persons: ten dwelling in France, four in Germany, and one in Austria. This list (at Stanford) also includes his note of 29 May enquiring whether Van Patten had "received any confirmation of food packages from the persons the names and destinations I submitted to you at the time I have handed my DANSE CONCERTANTE [sic] manuscript."

The first person on the list, Mrs. Olga Ilinisha Sallard (c. 1890-1961), was a long-time and close friend of Vera Stravinsky. The matter of confirmation was settled in subsequent correspondence between van Patten and Aaron Sapiro, lawyer of Stravinsky. Entry 85 documents the composer's private generosity, he being better known for parsimony. Both aspects and the names of several other beneficiaries were cited by Craft in 1978. But even earlier, in 1956, he wrote sympathetically of the composer's generosity.

Professor of Bibliography at Stanford, van Patten was author of a *Catalogue of The Memorial Library of Music.* It contains a facsimile of the first page of *Danses concertantes,* and cites Stravinsky's inscribed title page: "I give this manuscript to Stanford University, Igor Stravinsky. Hollywood, Jan. 9th, '48."

Works Consulted

Craft, Robert. *Stravinsky: Chronicle of a Friendship.* 2nd ed. Nashville, TN, and London: Vanderbilt University Press, 1994. p. 156.

Patten, Nathan van. *Catalogue of The Memorial Library of Music: Stanford University.* Stanford, CA [Los Angeles]: Anderson and Ritchie, Ward Ritchie Press, 1950. pp. 255-8, no. 1028.

–. Papers. Box 4, folder 6. Special Collections, M639. Stanford University Libraries.

SBu. n. 10 on p. 18.

SP&D. p. 349, n. 10 on p. 642.

"van Patten, Nathan." *Who's Who in California* (1941): vol. 1. p. 934.

86

(1948). **Autographed first edition (with original wrappers), 18.7 × 13.5 cm, / by / IGOR STRAVINSKY / *Poetics of Music* / IN THE FORM OF SIX LESSONS / TRANSLATED BY ARTHUR KNODEL AND INGOLF DAHL / HARVARD UNIVERSITY PRESS . CAMBRIDGE . 1947. 142 pp., in English in dark blue ink below a**

reproduction of the 24 May 1920 drawing by Picasso of
Stravinsky which precedes the title page, in 1948, to Merle
Armitage (1893-1975):

Am very happy
you like it
dear friend
Merle Armitage
cordially
1948 IStravinsky

Acquisition: H. Colin Slim in Goleta, CA, on 5 March 1997 through
Martin A. Silver from Kenneth Karmiole Books Inc. (Santa Monica).
Provenance: Undisclosed; but probably from the sale in 1969 at
Dawson's Bookshop in Los Angeles of books belonging to Merle
Armitage.

Commentary

Among many other occupations, Armitage was a concert impresario
who, with Charles L. Wagner, sponsored Stravinsky and Samuel
Dushkin in recital on 28 February 1935 in Los Angeles. Stravinsky had
autographed a photograph of himself rehearsing the Los Angeles
Philharmonic: "To Merle Armitage / my wonderful ar- / tist manager
/ in gratitude / IStrawinsky / le 9 II 35."

Between 1929 and 1969 Armitage produced more than 150 books,
including the first one about the composer published in North America,
in 1936. Upon arrival on Stravinsky's second trip to New York early in
January 1937, he called Armitage: "un bon ami, très sympathique."
Apparently in response to unfavourable criticism about the design of the
1936 book, he wrote Armitage: "Ce que le public te reproche,
développe-le, c'est toi." Armitage may not have realized that Stravinsky
was quoting from lines addressed to himself before the First World War
by Jean Cocteau in *Le Potomak,* except that Cocteau wrote "cultive-le:"
for "développe-le." (Stravinsky would not normally have employed
the familiar "tu" form with Armitage, reserving it for only a few and
long-time close friends, chief of whom in the US was Alexis Kall.) A

revised edition of this 1936 book by Edwin Corle appeared in 1949, after the composer had settled in Hollywood. He wrote Armitage that the 1936 volume was a near "perfect marriage of content and design." Although Stravinsky had many complaints about the 1949 book, Armitage included in it a reproduction of a signed photograph: "To Merle Armitage / cordially as ever."

Harvard University Press did not issue its English translation of the *Poétique musicale* until November 1947, even though a letter of 27 March 1940 from Harvard Professor Edward Waldo Forbes to Jerome Greene reveals that: "most of the work of translating on Strawinsky's lectures has been at no expense to us." Kall's article about the Harvard lectures published that July noted "they have been translated by the writer [Kall] from French into English and will be published by the Harvard Press early in the autumn." Stravinsky gave his last lecture on 10 April and on 2 May Forbes's secretary requested Greene's approval for a voucher: "Dr. [Alexis] Kall has translated Mr. Strawinsky's book and resumés into English. Further work is being done by Mr. Forbes and Mr. [Irving] Fine [1914-62]." On 27 October 1943 Stravinsky thanked Forbes for sending him this Kall-Forbes-Fine translation, which he used for lectures, "Composing – Performing – Listening," he was to give in 1944-45 at Chicago, Madison, Oakland, and Philadelphia. His letter to Forbes noted: "Dr. Kall qui a sa traduction anglaise et aussi la version corrigée de Mr. I. Fine." (Both versions are preserved in Kall's papers at UCLA.) In the event, Harvard Press's final translation, too, was delayed, until 1947, with the publication of Entry 86.

Precisely when in 1948 he sent Entry 86 to Armitage is unknown. By 15 December of that year, however, he wrote Craft in New York: "Try, if possible to bring up the matter [of the forthcoming 1949 Armitage-Corle revision] with this, although nice, but rather unreliable man." Armitage records a visit by Stravinsky and Vera to an exhibition of his books held at UCLA in the spring of 1956. (For the original French edition published by Harvard in 1942, see Entry 78; for an inscribed copy of the 1952 French edition, see Entry 94.)

Works Consulted

Armitage, Merle. "Stravinsky, musical milestone in our time." *Accent on Life.* Ames, IO: Iowa State University Press, 1965. pp. 171-83, and pl. [13] btn pp. 208-9.

Armitage, Merle, ed. *Igor Strawinsky*. New York, NY: G. Schirmer, 1936; Edwin Corle, ed. rev. ed. New York, NY: Progress-Bulletin, 1949. pl. [7] (lower) btn pp. 104-5.

Baltensperger, André. "Strawinsky's 'Chicago Lecture' (1944)." *Mitteilungen der Paul Sacher Stiftung* 5 (January 1992): 19-23.

Cocteau, Jean. *Le Potomak 1913-1914 précédé d'un Prospectus 1916*. 2nd ed. Paris: Gallimard, 1924. p. 53.

Eaton, Quaintance. "Stravinsky: Apostle of Today." *Musical America* 57 (10 January 1937): 11.

Forbes, Edward Waldo. Personal papers. "Stravinsky." Harvard University Archives.

Kall, Alexis F. Papers, Box 5: "Stravinsky Lectures." Special Collections 601. Charles E. Young Research Library, University of California at Los Angeles.

—. "Stravinsky in the Chair of Poetry." *The Musical Quarterly* 26 (1940): 296.

Marks, Robert. *Merle Armitage. Bibliography*. New York, NY: E. Weyhe, 1956. p. 3, and foreword.

Meyer, Felix, ed. *Settling New Scores. Music Manuscripts from the Paul Sacher Foundation*. Mainz: Schott, 1998. pp. 134-5, no. 67.

Philharmonic Orchestra of Los Angeles. Symphony Magazine. 21-22 February 1935. p. 20 (advertisement for Stravinsky-Dushkin concert).

Purcell, Robert M. *Merle Armitage Was Here! A Retrospective of a 20th Century Renaissance Man*. Morengo Valley, CA: Sagebrush Press, 1981. item 40 on p. 48, pp. 56-7.

Ritchie, Ward. *Merle Armitage: His Loves and his Many Lives*. Laguna Beach, CA: Laguna Verde Imprenta, 1982. p. 31.

Shippey, Lee. "The Lee Side o' L.A." *The Los Angeles Times*. 28 February 1935. p. 4.

Steegmuller, Francis. *Cocteau: A Biography*. Boston, MA, and Toronto, ON: Little, Brown, 1976. p. 93.

SSC. vol. 1. p. 353, n. 65 on p. 353; vol. 2. n. 34 on p. 376, app. L, pp. 503-17.

87   **(1951). Autographed photograph, 19.6 × 17.0 cm, taken by Erio Piccagliani at Venice in 1951, probably in the Teatro La Fenice on 6 September, rehearsing Act III of *The Rake's Progress,* and inscribed in English in dark green ink at Venice, probably September 1951, to T[rudy] Goth (1914-74):**

To T Goth / sincerely IStravinsky / Venice 1951

Acquisition: H. Colin Slim on 15 May 1997 from La Scala Autographs.
Provenance: Unidentified New York dealer in October 1996.

Commentary

The photograph is unpublished. On its reverse side is a stamp in blue
ink: No. 6267 / ERIO PICCAGLIANI / Fotografo / TEATRO ALLA
SCALA / MILANO – Tel.89.77.78 (the number 6267 being repeated
in pencil on the upper right corner). At the top also in pencil but in a
different hand is: "Stravinsky, Igor / Russian Comp / Inscribed to
Trudy Goth (Eng) / 1951 / Conducting"; at the bottom in still another
hand are some indecipherable remarks in pencil, possibly instructions
for framing plus a diagram of a moulding, the photograph evidently
having previously been mounted. A different photograph of Stravinsky
taken by Piccagliani at the dress rehearsal in the Teatro La Fenice
appeared in *Musical America* early in the following year.

The music for "Violino II" at the bottom left corner of Entry 87
bears headings of: "Ballad Tune," "Stretto-Finale," and "Ballad Tune
(reprise)." They are from the close of scene 1, Act III of *The Rake's
Progress* (1951), at rehearsals **134–58** in the orchestral score, pages 315-
30. He led orchestra rehearsals for his opera at La Scala on 27-28, and
30 August, and on 1 and 3 September, 1951. Rehearsals at La Fenice
took place on 6-9 September. He wears, however, a different shirt and
trousers at his 30 August and 1 September La Scala rehearsals.

Because Stravinsky wrote "Venice" on Entry 87, Piccagliani
probably took it there at the Teatro La Fenice where he rehearsed Act
III on 6 September. Indeed, the conductor's stand depicted in Entry 87
seems identical to the one he used in La Fenice at the premiere.
Piccagliani is credited with another photograph of him and the
principals bowing after the premiere, which quickly appeared in
October's *Musical America*. Craft observed that Stravinsky did not
conduct a complete rehearsal in Venice until the day before the
premiere.

Trudy Goth, dancer and producer, founded the Choreographer's
Workshop in New York in 1946, later often writing for *Opera News,
Dance Magazine, Variety, Aufbau,* and other journals. A couple of years

after Stravinsky inscribed Entry 87 for her, she became the personal representative for Dimitri Mitropoulous (1896-1960), from about 1953 until the conductor's death. Born of Hungarian parents in Berlin, she had emigrated to the US in 1940, maintaining a home in New York as well as with her parents in Florence; she is buried on the island of Elba.

In 1951, from June through September, Goth participated in the management of the Florence and Venice Festivals, returning to New York at the beginning of November. Stravinsky probably inscribed Entry 87 for her in Venice early that September while she was working for the Festival, rather than in New York late in the fall when he was there, 22 November-29 December. She is incorrectly identified as a photog-rapher on the back of the accompanying cardboard frame.

Works Consulted

Craft, Robert. *Stravinsky: Chronicle of a Friendship*. 2nd ed. Nashville, TN, and London: Vanderbilt University Press, 1994. pp. 61, 69.

"Goth, Trudy." *Dance News* 59, 10 (June 1974): 6 (obituary).

"Goth, Trudy." *New York Times*. 14 May 1974. p. 40 (obituary).

Jenkins, Newell. "Stravinsky's The Rake's Progress." *Musical America* 71 (October, 1951): pl. on p. 3.

Skulsky, Abraham. "Igor Stravinsky. Sound is the defining element." *Musical America* 72 (February 1952): pl. on p. 27 (photo by Piccagliani).

SBu. pl. 111 on p. [152].

SP&D. pl. on p. 415 (upper).

"The Rake's Progress at Venice." *Tempo* 21 (Autumn 1951): pl. on p. 29 (right).

Trotter, William R. *Priest of Music: The Life of Dimitri Mitropoulos*. Portland, OR: Amadeus Press, 1995. pp. 11, 344-5.

"Trudy Goth Resumes Work." *Dance News* 19, 5 (November 1951): 3.

88

(1951). Autographed photograph, 23.0 × 17.2 cm, inscribed in German in blue ink, c. 18-21 October 1951, at Munich for Werner Hessenland (1909-79) with an autographed concert program, 21.0 × 14.8 cm, 8 October 1951, in German in green ink at Cologne and affixed at an angle on the lower right quarter of the photograph. These are mounted on cardboard, 39.8 × 29.8 cm:

[upper right corner of the photograph in blue ink, written with fountain pen]
An Werner Hessenland
in bester Erinnerung
an "Oedipus Rex"
und seinem Andenken

IStravinsky

München
1951

[across the upper half of printed program in foreground, in green ink, written with a ballpoint pen]
Tausend Dank
IStravinsky

Werner Hessenland   Munich
Munich   October 1951

For Werner Hessenland with happiest memories about *Oedipus Rex*
and his participation
    I. Stravinsky

A thousand thanks
    I. Stravinsky

Acquisition: H. Colin Slim on 15 July 1997 from David Schulson.
Provenance: Hartung and Hartung, *Auktion 85: Wertvolle Bücher Dabei Sammlung Adolf Funke, Aachen Manuskripte – Autographen* (Munich, 15 May 1997), no. 399, lot 2655 (with photograph); pencilled in the upper left corner of mat: "2655" in a circle; pencilled on the reverse side: "85/ 125/1."

Commentary

Both photograph and program are unpublished. The performance of *Oedipus Rex* on 8 October 1951 with Stravinsky conducting the

Cologne Radio Chorus and Symphony Orchestra, in which the forty-two-year-old film actor Werner Hessenland narrated, was taped by Columbia Records. Residing in Troisdorf, near Cologne, Hessenland's widow early in 1998 kindly recalled having seen Entry 88 to Dr. Ullrich Bethe.

The first post-war concert led by Stravinsky in Germany was one of three greatly acclaimed successes, the other two being concerts in Baden-Baden and in Munich. With a different cast of performers (except for Creon) and a different narrator, he again led *Oedipus Rex* at Munich on 21 October. In accordance with the composer's wishes, Hessenland's narration on the tape of 8 October was replaced with Jean Cocteau's (recorded Paris, 20 May 1952) when Columbia issued its recording in April 1953. A recorded copy of the 1951 performance with Hessenland survives, however, in the Cologne radio archives.

The final word in the inscription to Hessenland is difficult to decipher. The auction catalogue states it is "Announcer" (which quite obviously it is not). Dr. Bethe reads it as "Ausdauer." Dr. Monika Holl suggests "Ansager," "Interesse," and "Andenken"; I believe her last reading is correct.

As for the program, one cannot be certain whether he inscribed it on 8 October at Cologne or whether he did so two weeks later at Munich, when he inscribed the photograph for Hessenland. The considerable differences in the pen employed and in the ink colorations between the photograph (inscribed in blue ink with a fountain pen) and the program (written in green with a ballpoint) suggest he did so on different occasions. The impersonal nature of the inscription on the program also hints that it was not for Hessenland but perhaps for a member of the chorus or orchestra. Whether Stravinsky or Hessenland affixed program to photograph remains unknown; perhaps a dealer did so before Entry 88 came to auction. (For an autograph quotation from *Oedipus Rex,* see Entry 57.)

Works Consulted

Craft, Robert. *Stravinsky: Chronicle of a Friendship.* 2nd ed. Nashville, TN, and London: Vanderbilt University Press, 1994. pp. 66-7, 82 (20 May 1952).

Krafsur, Richard P., ed. *The American Film Institute, Catalog of Motion Pictures, Feature Films 1961-1970.* New York, and London: R.R. Bowker, 1976. vol. 2. p. 289 (index).

Ragan, David, ed. *Who's Who in Hollywood*. New York, NY: Facts on File, 1992. vol. 1. p. 742.

Scharlau, Ulf, ed. *Igor Strawinsky: Phonographie*. Frankfurt am Main: Deutsches Rundfunkarchiv, 1972. p. 87, no. 47.

"Strawinsky dirigierte in Deutschland" *Melos* 18 (1951): 324–5, 359.

Stuart, Philip. *Igor Stravinsky – The Composer in the Recording Studio. A Comprehensive Discography*. New York, NY, Westport, CT, London: Greenwood Press, 1991. p. 36, no. 65.

89   (1952). Autographed page, 34.5 × 21.5 cm, LOS ANGELES CHAMBER SYMPHONY ORCHESTRA / JANUARY 15th, 1952 / PROGRAM NOTES / (later folded), in English in black ink, the text by Stravinsky for the concert conducted by him on 15 January 1952, Royce Hall, University of California, Los Angeles:

Igor Stravinsky
Los Angeles
January 1952

Acquisition: H. Colin Slim in New York on 23 September 1994 from Wurlitzer-Bruck.
Provenance: An unidentified man of Viennese origin in New York.

Commentary

Entry 89 is only one of several identically autographed extant copies of which the Paul Sacher Foundation owns three. Evidently Stravinsky anticipated having to distribute autographs after his concert! As such, Entry 89 has not been published.

At this concert, Stravinsky conducted the *Octet, The Soldier's Tale, Concerto in E flat (Dumbarton Oaks)*, and *Danses Concertantes*. His notes in Entry 89 for the *Octet* differ from those he wrote for *Dialogues and a Diary*, used in *Igor Stravinsky Conducts 1961* (Columbia MS 6272) but closely resemble those in *Stravinsky conducts music for chamber and jazz ensembles* issued in August 1971 (Columbia M 30579). His notes here for *The Soldier's Tale* do not appear elsewhere, to my knowledge. Those for the *Concerto in E flat (Dumbarton Oaks)* differ from the ones in *Themes and Episodes* and in *Themes and Conclusions* as do his notes for the *Danses Concertantes*.

Preceded by two rehearsals on 12 January and one on the 13th, the concert took place an hour late because of a violent rainstorm and was followed by a party for Stravinsky at Alma Mahler-Werfel's, also attended by Vera, Craft, and Aldous Huxley. Two works performed on the 15 January concert, *Octet* and *The Soldier's Tale*, were privately recorded.

Apparently, Stravinsky was pleased with the Royce Hall concert. Three days later he wrote Vittorio Rieti in New York: "Je viens de donner mon concert de chambre. *Octuor, Soldat, Dumbarton Oaks, Danses Concertantes* avec de très bons musiciens d'ici" (Ricci, pp. 418-19).

Works Consulted

Craft, Robert. *Stravinsky: Chronicle of a Friendship*. 2nd ed. Nashville, TN, and
    London: Vanderbilt University Press, 1994. p. 71 (15 January 1952).
Ricci, Carlo. *Vittorio Rieti*. Naples and Rome: Edizioni scientifiche italiane,
    1987. pp. 418-19.
SD. pp. 39-40.
SD&D. pp. 70-2.
ST&C. pp. 47, 51.
ST&E. pp. 39-40, 45-6.
Stuart, Philip. *Igor Stravinsky – The Composer in the Recording Studio. A Compre-
    hensive Discography*. New York, NY, Westport, CT, London: Greenwood
    Press, 1991. p. 76 (Royce Hall).

90

(1952). Printed **ALL STRAVINSKY PROGRAM, 25.0 × 21.9 cm, three Vancouver newspaper clippings, and two advertisements for a performance, 7 April 1952, of the *Duo Concertant* (1932) by Harry Adaskin (1901-94) and Frances Marr (1900-2001) at UBC and for the Canadian premieres there of the *Concerto for Two Solo Pianos* (1935), played by John Brockington (1929-) and by H. Colin Slim (1929-), and of *Les Noces* (1923), conducted by the latter.**

Acquisition: H. Colin Slim at UBC on 7 April 1952.
Provenance: H. Colin Slim (1952-2002).

Commentary

The program was published by Harry Adaskin thirty years later; undated press clippings are from *The Vancouver Sun* and *The Vancouver Daily Province* April 1952. Adaskin's accounts of the nearly four months of rehearsals for *Les Noces* and of the performance itself – a Canadian premiere – make lively reading. (Almost three decades later at the Royal Opera House in Covent Garden on 2 February 1981, Dr. Slim was delighted to hear the soprano soloist in the UBC performance, Milla Andrew, sing her same part in the Royal Ballet's production of *Les Noces*.) Adaskin sent a copy of Entry 90 from Vancouver to Stravinsky shortly before the concert, this copy now in the Paul Sacher Foundation. As noted in the Introduction, the composer's response to this program ultimately led to him conducting the Vancouver Symphony Orchestra on 5 October 1952 (further, see Entry 91). (For an autograph letter referring to him at rehearsals of *Les Noces* in 1923, see Entry 23; for an autograph letter wherein he thanks the conductor who trained the chorus for the world premiere, see Entry 24; for a page of his player piano sketches for *Les Noces,* see Entry 21; and for an autograph musical quotation from the ballet, see Entry 55.)

Works Consulted

Adaskin, Harry. *A Fiddler's Choice: Memoirs 1938-1980.* Vancouver, BC: November House, 1982. ill. [23] btn pp. 94-5, 132-6.

"Eighteen Drums," *The Vancouver Daily Province.* 2 April 1952.

Royal Opera House Covent Garden. [Program.] "Troy Game, A Month in the Country, Les Noces." Monday, 2 February 1981.

"Stravinsky Program at University." *The Vancouver Sun.* 5 April 1952.

91 (1952). **Photograph, 20.7 × 16.3 cm, on calendered paper, 25.0 × 18.7 cm, taken by Gene Fenn in the Ambassador Hotel, New York, April 1948, with Stravinsky's facsimile signature printed below and on its reverse side a brief biography in French and English, in a red frame; Stravinsky inscribed the photograph in English in black ink on the lower border of its mat, 38.1 × 29.7 cm, 3 October 1952, to Harry Adaskin (1901-94):**

To Harry Adaskin
all best from Igor Stravinsky
Vancouver Oct 3/52

Acquisition: H. Colin Slim in Vancouver on 20 June 1997 by kind gift of Frances Marr Adaskin and her son, Gordon Adaskin. The photograph/biography was separated the following July and August from its mat board backing by Linda K. Ogden; the reverse side of the mat board had been inscribed "Red" by an unknown hand (referring to its future frame). Adhesive from tape had penetrated the paper and was removed as much as possible and the mat was dry-cleaned with a soft vinyl eraser to remove surface dirt; it remains discoloured. At the time of reassembling photograph, mat, glass, and frame, a photocopy of the biography printed on the reverse side of the photograph was inserted in a pocket affixed to the back of the frame.

Provenance: Harry and Frances Marr Adaskin (1952-97).

Commentary

The photograph (slightly cropped) and its mat were published by Adaskin in 1982. A distinguished Canadian violinist and lecturer, Adaskin was among the teachers of H. Colin Slim at the University of British Columbia, 1947-52, where he had been appointed the first professor of Music in 1946 until retiring in 1973. Through Adaskin's initiative during the late spring and summer of 1952, Stravinsky was invited to conduct the Vancouver Symphony Orchestra for the first time. Its program for 5 October contains Adaskin's open letter, which welcomes the composer and mentions the concert at UBC the previous April dedicated to his works (see Entry 90).

Stravinsky probably inscribed the mat of Entry 91 during an evening dinner party given for him, his daughter Milène, and her husband André Marion by the Adaskins on 3 October at their home, an elegantly fitted-out hut erected during the Second World War in Acadia Camp, UBC. At this party, the Adaskins performed his and Dushkin's arrangement for violin and piano of the *Divertimento*. Although Adaskin's memoirs cite several passages from his correspondence with Stravinsky, Mrs. Adaskin reports that her husband never preserved such correspondence. Fortunately, a record of it is in the Paul Sacher Foundation (see the Introduction and entries 90, 92-3).

"Photo Gene Fenne [sic]" is printed in the border below the lower right side of the photograph of Entry 91 above a facsimile of the composer's signature, but both are obscured by the matting. Vera noted in her diary for 12 April 1948, New York: "Betty Bean and photographer Gene Fenn" and on 21 April: "at 11:30 a.m. a photography session with Gene Fenn." A photograph of Stravinsky and Vera taken by Fenn in the Ambassador Hotel is dated variously 9 and 11 April of that year.

Among Fenn's New York photographs from April is one with Stravinsky studying a printed score of his *Orpheus* and its printed first violin part in a hotel room with Vera seated in the background. The background and the clothing he wears show that this photograph was taken at the same time as the one in Entry 91. Identified as a New York photographer, Fenn was presumably engaged by Bean – then head of the New York branch of Boosey and Hawkes, publisher of works by Stravinsky and of its house magazines, *Tempo* and later, *Musik der Zeit* – to take photographs of him at his hotel and at *Orpheus* rehearsals.

The reverse side of the photograph in Entry 91 notes in French and English that *Orpheus* was already published but that the *Mass* was "still in preparation." It includes numerous factual and typographical errors, among the former, for example, "As a child" Stravinsky had "studied the piano under [Anton] Rubinstein" (1829-94) in Russia, whereas he had studied from about 1899 to 1901 with Rubinstein's pupil, Leokadiya Alexandrovna Kashperova (1872-1940). Another mistake was that he had lived in Paris from 1917, but he and his family moved to France only in 1920. The bottom of the page advises the reader to address "All enquiries to: Boosey and Hawkes Ltd.," the main office and its various branches being listed – the one in Los Angeles twice, still another printing error.

Since Stravinsky did not receive the published vocal score of his *Mass* until the beginning of November 1948 (although not yet the full score), the printing of this page on the reverse side of the photograph took place between April and October – that is, between the publication of *Orpheus* (documented no later than 21 April in the above-cited photograph with Vera) and that of the *Mass* the following October. On 28 October, he wrote to Robert Craft in New York: "Enclosed a new nonsense from B. &. H. which they probably call *catalogue*. Even as a proof it is not acceptable."

The double-sided printed page in Entry 91 is indeed a proof – for the first page of a catalogue of his works. The latter was published by Boosey and Hawkes and sent early in April 1949 to him. He complained (not quite accurately) that the revised version that had just arrived was unchanged and had the same mistakes as its 1948 predessesor. A copy of this 1949 catalogue, printed on poor quality paper, is in the Music Library (vertical file) of the University of California at Berkeley. Although it corrects typographical errors, the factual ones in the 1948 proof remain, to which is added a new misstatement: that he became a US citizen in 1946 (it was 1945). He continued to criticize errors in this catalogue in letters of 22 April 1949 and 22 May 1950.

Obviously, Adaskin could not have already owned this proof page of October 1948 in Entry 91 four years before Stravinsky arrived in Vancouver. Even though Stravinsky derided the proof in 1948 as "a new nonsense," nevertheless he used its first page, assembling the image and the mat around it for presentation four years later to Adaskin, further evidence of his frugality. Adaskin had it framed in red, as he did all his celebrity photographs.

Deleting the erroneous factual material on the reverse side of Entry 91, slightly more of Fenn's photograph appeared in Boosey and Hawkes's re-edition in 1952 of the catalogue for the seventieth anniversary of Stravinsky, a copy also preserved in the Music Library (vertical file) at Berkeley. The complete photograph Fenn had taken in 1948 appeared, however, in another Boosey and Hawkes publication in 1952, *Musik der Zeit*. Here the photograph is erroneously dated 1952 because the copy of it reproduced was inscribed by Stravinsky in New York that year (probably in April). The copy of this issue of *Musik der Zeit* he inscribed to the Adaskins in 1952 is also in the present collection (see Entry 93).

During this Vancouver visit, he was presented – after some disgraceful shilly-shallying by the city council – with a key to the city by Mayor Fred Hume on the afternoon of 3 October. Although his acquiescence in this ceremony was surprising because he normally expressed dislike for awards, medals, scrolls, etc., he preserved the key. In 1967 he also accepted the Medal of the Canada Council after he learned that he was the first non-Canadian to receive it ("Dossier").

Between 27 September and 4 October 1952, photographs of Stravinsky appeared many times in Vancouver's three newspapers. He also sat for at least one formal photographic portrait by Eric Skipsey (see Entry 92).

Shortly after returning to Los Angeles, on 10 October, he wrote his son Théodore in Switzerland who had requested money: "I live modestly, and, if comparatively comfortably, this is only because I am still conducting."

Works Consulted

Adaskin, Frances. "The evolution of a musical Vancouver." *The Vancouver Sun*. 24 September 1994. Saturday Review, p. D10.

Adaskin, Harry. *A Fiddler's Choice: Memoirs 1938 to 1980*. Vancouver, BC: November House, 1982. ill. [24] btn pp. 94-5, 136-7.

–. "An Open Letter to Igor Stravinsky." *Vancouver Symphony Orchestra. 1952-1953 First Subscription Concert, Igor Stravinsky Guest Conductor*. [Program.] 5 October 1952. p. 2.

Bois, Mario. *Près de Strawinsky 1959-70*. Paris: Marval, 1996. pl. on p. [98].

Craft, Robert. "Catalog of the Library of Robert Craft." Typescript: Library of Congress, Music Division. IX: Personal Effects, no. 10 on p. 147.

–. *Stravinsky: Glimpses of a Life*. London: Lime Tree, 1992; New York, NY: St. Martin's Press, 1993. p. 131.

"Dossier Stravinsky-Canada 1937-1967." *Les Cahiers canadiens de musique / The Canada Music Book* 4 (Spring/Summer 1972): 23-6, pl. on p. 26, p. 52.

Dykl, Lloyd. "Igor Stravinsky, the five-foot-four-inch giant of contemporary music, visited Vancouver twice." *The Vancouver Sun*. 20-27 July 2000. C31.

"Igor Strawinsky zum siebzigsten Geburtstag." *Musik der Zeit* 1 (1952): pl. facing p. 49.

Lederman, Minna, ed. *Stravinsky in the Theatre*. New York, NY: Dance Index, 1949; repr. Da Capo Press, 1975. pl. facing title page, p. 76.

"Mayor Fred Hume and Igor Stravinsky." *The News-Herald*. 4 October 1952. p. 13 with pl.

"Rehearsals First. City to Give Composer Key – In Afternoon." *The Vancouver Sun*. 2 October 1952. p. 2.

SBu. p. 144 (21 April 1948).

SP&D. pl. on p. 379 [photo by Gene Fenn].

SSC. vol. 1. pp. 348, 361; vol. 3. pp. 323, 328, 331, 342, 360, 366, 368, 370.

Stravinsky, Igor. Papers: Vancouver (1952), Paul Sacher Stiftung, Basle.

"Strawinsky Number." *Tempo* 8 (Summer, 1948): pls. on pp. [11], [21-2].

Taruskin, Richard. *Stravinsky and the Russian Traditions*. Berkeley and Los Angeles, CA: University of California Press, 1996. pp. 96-9.

Tempo 61-2 (Spring/Summer, 1962): pl. on p. [27].

Walsh, Stephen. *Stravinsky, A Creative Spring: Russia and France, 1882-1934*. New York, NY: Alfred A. Knopf, 1999. pp. 52-3.

92 (1952). Rephotograph, uninscribed (slightly cropped at left side and bottom), 23.8 × 18.9 cm, of a photograph taken by Eric Skipsey in Vancouver, 5 October 1952, marked at lower right within a rectangle: SKIPSEY / VANCOUVER. CANADA.

Acquisition: H. Colin Slim on 20 March 1997, by kind gift, Archives, Los Angeles Philharmonic Orchestra.
Provenance: Unknown.

Commentary

On the back of the rephotograph in purple ink by an unknown hand is "Igor Stravinsky" with a stamp "Dec 5 1972." (Another copy in the Philharmonic's Archives is likewise stamped on its reverse side, but has STRAVINSKY, IGOR printed at the lower left.) Marked above in black ink in an unknown (but different) hand is "46% 20-70 / #1." A print of Skipsey's photograph is in the Paul Sacher Foundation.

Eric Skipsey was a well-known and skilful photographer in Vancouver during the late 1940s and 1950s. Subsequently he moved to California where he now lives in retirement at Montecito.

Letters in the Paul Sacher Foundation reveal that Bruce Moss and Eric Skipsey thanked Stravinsky on 21 January 1953 for having graciously posed for the photograph, "taken after the final rehearsal [5 October 1952] with the Vancouver Symphony." He responded on 25 June, congratulating Skipsey on his work: "This portrait of myself is very good and very interesting indeed ... Actually I wonder if you would be willing to let me use it for non-commercial and non-public purposes." On 16 July Skipsey wrote him enclosing several prints of the portrait, one of which he asked him "to autograph and return it at your convenience."

Skipsey's portrait first appeared in *Musical America* for March 1953, illustrating a review of *The Rake's Progress* at the Metropolitan Opera and credited there as: "Skipsey from [Bruce] Moss." Jokingly, George Szell assumed a similar pose in 1956 in front of Skipsey's portrait hanging in the Philadelphia Academy of Music. It appeared (reversed) in a notice of April 1956 about the ensuing summer music festival with Stravinsky and Craft at Ojai, California. At the premiere of the *Canticum sacrum* in Venice, Stravinsky inscribed a smaller (but uncropped) replica, 11.4 × 9.0 cm, on the bottom of its mat: "To Prof. Cesare Frugoni /

sincerely / Igor Stravinsky / Venezia Sept. 13/56." (It sold for 950 Swiss francs in 1996.) The program for his final concert at the Hollywood Bowl in July 1966 also reproduced it. After the composer's death, Skipsey's splendid portrait, so esteemed by Stravinsky, continues to appear in concert programs and in books – often cropped, rarely acknowledged.

Works Consulted

Bois, Mario. *Près de Strawinsky 1959-70*. Paris: Marval, 1996. pl. on p. [98].

Erasmushaus. *Katalog 885. Autographen und Portraits von Musikern*. Basle, December 1996, item 221, pl. on p. 61.

Eyer, Ronald. "Metropolitan Opera Introduces The Rake's Progress to America." *Musical America* 73 (March 1953): pl. on p. 3.

Hollywood Bowl Magazine (5 July 1966): pl. on p. 27.

"Ojai Festivals." *Overture* 36, 1 (April 1956): pl. on p. 33.

Performing Arts. Los Angeles Philharmonic 31, 1 (January 1997): pl. on p. P-2.

Rosenberg, Donald. *The Cleveland Orchestra Story*. Cleveland, OH: Gray and Co, 2000. pl. facing p. 321 (lower).

93 (1952). Autographed periodical, 26.5 × 18.6 cm, MUSIK DER ZEIT / *Eine Schriftenreihe zur zeitgenössischen Musik* / ed. Heinrich Lindlar, 1: IGOR STRAWINSKY/ZUM SIEBZIGSTEN GEBURTSTAG / (Bonn: Boosey and Hawkes, 1952), 80 pp. with 8 pls., inscribed in English in black ink, mailed by Stravinsky in October 1952 to Harry and Frances Adaskin:

To my good friends
the ADASKINS
all best
IStravinsky
1952

Acquisition: H. Colin Slim in Vancouver on 23 May 1999 by kind gift of Frances Marr Adaskin and Gordon Adaskin. Two small tears to the back cover and the final page and the binding were repaired on 10 June 1999 by Linda K. Ogden.

Provenance: Harry and Frances Marr Adaskin (1952-99).

Commentary

Celebrating the composer's seventieth birthday, Entry 93 contains essays in German by Ansermet, Auden, Ballo, Boys, Cocteau, Cortot, Egk, von Einem, Fricsay, Grohmann, Honegger, Karsavina, Malipiero, Markevitch, Mersmann, Sacher, See, Stuart, Stuckenschmidt, White, and Zanetti. Seven of these birthday greetings were, however, recycled from essays in English in *Tempo* n.s. 8 (1948), 10 (1948-49), and 20 (1951), a periodical published in London by Boosey and Hawkes.

The date of donation for both entries 93 and 94 is established by a letter of thanks from Adaskin to Stravinsky of 6 November 1952, now in the Paul Sacher Foundation. In it, Adaskin writes how he and his wife opened Stravinsky's "parcel and found [his] autographed books, inscribed so warmly and generously."

A month later, another letter in the Paul Sacher Foundation to Stravinsky, dated 5 December, by A.E. Lord, Honorary Secretary of the Board of Governors at UBC, tells how the Board "at the last general meeting" was pleased to learn of his donation to the Music Department and it thanked him for his two inscribed volumes: *Poétique Musicale* "in the original French," and *Musik der Zeit*. As shown by their provenance, both these volumes inscribed to the Music Department were retained by Adaskin, then its head and its sole professor. The department's copy of Entry 93 was donated by Gordon Adaskin in May 1999 to the Vancouver Public Library. (The department's copy of the *Poétique Musicale* is Entry 94.)

94

(1952) **Autographed book (with original wrappers), 19.0 × 14.2 cm, "AMOUR DE LA MUSIQUE" / POÉTIQUE / MUSICALE / PAR / IGOR STRAWINSKY /** *avec un portrait de l'auteur par /* ***PICASSO** / Nouvelle édition revue et complétée* **(Paris: Éditions Le Bon Plaisir, Librairie Plon, 1952), 97 pp. with 1 pl., in English in black ink, October 1952, to the Music Department, UBC:**

To the Department of
Music, University of
British Columbia
Vancouver, Oct. 1952
IStravinsky

Acquisition: H. Colin Slim in Vancouver, BC, on 23 May 1999 by kind
gift of Frances Marr Adaskin and Gordon Adaskin. Traces of transparent
tape on the cover were removed and a small hole caused by the tape was
filled by Linda K. Ogden on 10 June 1999.
Provenance: Same as Entry 93.

Commentary

On the *Poétique musicale*, six lectures by Stravinsky at Harvard
University in 1939–40, see entries 64, 78, and 86. Entry 94 is the third
edition (the first complete one in France), printed by Plon in mid–April
1952 and available for sale the following month. Its frontispiece is a
cropped reproduction of Picasso's 1917 drawing of Stravinsky.

A.E. Lord, secretary to the Board of Governors at UBC, thanked
him on 5 December 1952 for Entry 94 (see Entry 93). Its provenance
shows that Adaskin retained Entry 94 for his private library. Lord's
mention of it as "in the original French" perhaps stemmed from a
request by Adaskin to have the board thank him.

Stravinsky also inscribed another copy of Entry 94 for the Adaskins
themselves: "à Frances Marr / et / Harry Adaskin / cordialement /
IStravinsky / 1952." Gordon Adaskin donated it to the Vancouver
Public Library in May 1999.

95 (1953). **Signed typed letter on Stravinsky's printed stationery,
27.9 × 21.6 cm, of 1260 NORTH WETHERLY DRIVE / HOLLYWOOD
46, CALIFORNIA, folded three times, in English in black ink, 27
October 1953, with its air mail envelope, 9.2 × 16.6 cm, its return
address and address as in letter and bearing non-autograph
pencil annotations and a six-cent airmail stamp, postmarked Los
Angeles Oct 27 9 pm 1953, 27 October 1953, to Dylan Thomas
(1914-53):**

October 27, 1953
<u>Air Mail</u>

Dylan Thomas Esq.
c/o J.M. Brinnin
Poetry Center
YM-YWHA
1395 Lexington Avenue
New York 28, N.Y.

Dear Dylan Thomas,
You must be in New York now and I hope everyting is going well for you there.

I have not written you until today because I had no news to give you. I spoke to Aldous Huxley but the agent he knows is in New York and therefore could not do better than yours from overthere.

But we have spoken to some friends and everybody is anxious to see you and hear you here, and we should be able to arrange some private affair from which enough money could be drawn at least to cover your fare to and from California.

You know that you will be my guest here and therefore you do not have to worry about your living expenses.

Do come, the weather is beautiful, too much may be ... we live in short sleeves ...

Please drop me a line.

A bientot,
[in black ink] IStravinsky

Acquisition: H. Colin Slim on 20 May 1997 from La Scala Autographs. *Provenance:* Perhaps Elizabeth Reitell, or Caitlin Thomas (until her death in 1994); Christie's East, *Autographs & Manuscripts Catalog 8001*

(New York, 14 May 1997), lot 132, p. 39 with partial transcription. Entry 95 is framed with its envelope above it.

Commentary

The letter is unpublished; a copy of it is in the Paul Sacher Foundation. In his *Conversations,* Stravinsky incorrectly recalled the date of Entry 95, his fourth – and final – letter to Thomas: "I wrote him October 25 in New York and asked him for word of his arrival plans in Hollywood." Shortly before writing Entry 95, Stravinsky and Huxley had visited each other, 22 and 25 October; on one or the other of these occasions he doubtless "spoke to Aldous Huxley" about Thomas. On the same machine and paper as entries 97-9, Entry 95 was presumably typed by André Marion, the composer's son-in-law, who was his secretary, 1951-54, and who, according to Craft, also collaborated in Entry 95.

An unsigned and mostly erased pencil note on its envelope reads: "John – sending this on / to you because I don't / know whether Strav. should / be written a note or <u>not</u>. / Dylan, I think, wanted me / to write to him for him. – or something." The author of this note is Elizabeth Reitell (1920-), Thomas's lover in New York, who was with him from his arrival in New York on 19 October through his last days. At one time, she owned the Thomas letters to her that were offered in the preceding lots 129 and 130-1 of the above-cited Christie's East sale (several with her annotations and two likewise with their original envelopes).

"J.M. Brinnin" on the envelope of Entry 95 and "John" in Reitell's note written on it is John Malcolm Brinnin (1916-). Brinnin, who had met the Stravinskys at their home during a visit in May 1947, was Thomas's sometime tour manager and Director of the Poetry Center at the Young Men's and Young Women's Hebrew Association in New York. Reitell was Brinnin's assistant. He was away in Cambridge from 25 October until the news of Thomas's hospitalization mandated his return on 5 November. He remained in New York until the poet's death on the 9th, leaving the city thereafter but returning shortly before the memorial service on 13 November.

Among Thomas's "small and motley collection of possessions," which his wife Caitlin Thomas (1913-94) took back to Wales when she sailed from New York that evening, were "letters from Stravinsky" (as noted by Rob Gittins). Their number is unspecified, but perhaps included Entry 95.

Posted airmail from Los Angeles on Tuesday evening 27 October (Thomas's last birthday as it turned out), Entry 95 presumably arrived in New York on Friday or Saturday, 30 or 31 October, and was opened by Thomas and discussed with Reitell. Paul Ferris observed in 1977 – apparently from an interview with Reitell two years previously – that by Thursday evening, 29 October "there was still no definite decision about Stravinsky and the opera." Perhaps poor health caused Thomas to ask Reitell to answer it for him.

Thomas may have evaded replying for another reason. In his letter of 22 September, he had promised to write to Stravinsky as soon as he arrived in New York (19 October) but had failed to do so. Constantine FitzGibbon, to whom Thomas had spoken in London on 15 October about the project, stated: "I sensed a certain trepidation, which was characteristic, towards the unwritten opera ... the libretto [project] not only pleased and flattered but also frightened him." Phillip Burton, another friend who had spent an evening with Thomas a few days before he left for New York, recalled late in 1953: "The setting of the opera was to be the world destroyed by atomic warfare. Almost all life had disappeared. The scene was to be a cave in completely barren surroundings. Miraculously two young people had survived, and they had to find life again in an almost total absence of it."

Stravinsky received, however, no word at all from Thomas, did not know of his subsequent hospitalization, and only learned of his death by telegram on 9 November. In response to a letter of 15 December from the editor of *ADAM,* he wrote on 5 January 1954: "Dylan Thomas' sudden passing away has left me deeply shocked and painfully wounded ... we were both eagerly looking forward to getting better acquainted personally and working on the idea of an opera."

Reitell perhaps wrote her pencil annotation on the envelope of Entry 95 during Thomas's hospitalization but more probably following his death. Whether she actually sent envelope and letter to Brinnin and/or whether it figured among "letters from Stravinsky" which returned to Wales with his widow, Caitlin, remain unknown.

When Thomas died intestate, his widow legally owned Entry 95. It was not put up for sale, as was the case with her unsuccessful attempt to sell her thirty-two letters from Thomas at Sotheby's on 5 December 1975. A decade later all the latter were owned by the Santa Barbara collector and rare book dealer, Maurice F. Neville. In answer to my inquiry, Marcia P. Neville kindly confirmed by letter of 17 July 1997 that the Neville firm never owned Entry 95, although two of the thirty-two Thomas-to-Caitlin letters once owned by Neville figure in the above-mentioned Christie's East sale (lots 126-7).

Introduced to Thomas's poetry by Craft and Auden in 1949-50, the composer met the poet for the first and only time on 22 May 1953 in Boston, the day after Thomas had received a cable from Sarah Caldwell of the Opera Workshop at Boston University enquiring if he would be willing to write a libretto for Stravinsky. Inviting Thomas to come to Hollywood in the fall of 1953, the composer had an extension built at the back of 1260 North Wetherly Drive to house the poet.

Deeply upset by his death, early in 1954 he began composing *In Memoriam Dylan Thomas,* a setting of Thomas's "Do not go gentle into that good night." At the premiere in Los Angeles on 20 September, Aldous Huxley spoke briefly and movingly. Stravinsky treasured a framed photograph of Dylan Thomas. He averred in 1955: "I do not want to let the correspondence I had with Dylan Thomas be published during my lifetime" – letters which included Entry 95 and three others that he wrote to Thomas on 22 June, 26 August, and 26 September 1953 (three originals now in the Harry Ransom Humanities Research Center, University of Texas at Austin). Nevertheless, he published in 1959 two letters of 16 June and 22 September to him from Thomas.

Responding to him in the letter of 22 September, Thomas wrote: "And I *promise* not to tell anyone about it [the opera project] – (though it's very hard not to)." The poet did not let on, however, that he had already discussed it twice: once in Ireland in the latter half of July with the poet, Theodore Roethke, who in turn mentioned it to Auden and Kallman so that Stravinsky learned about it; and again in a letter of 11 September to Thomas's London publisher, E.F. Bozman.

Thomas twice spoke at UBC: 6 April 1950 and 8 April 1952. As an undergraduate there, H. Colin Slim went to his first poetry reading, which he found an unforgettable experience. He well recalled the rich rolling voice while from time to time Thomas hitched up over-sized and beltless trousers. Thomas's letter the next day to his wife reported: "the city of Vancouver is quite a handsome hellhole ... everybody is pious and patriotic, apart from a few people in the university," one in which he also laments the segregation of men and women in beer-parlours; his description perfectly captures the flavour of the city in the early 1950s.

Dr. Slim wishes to thank Dell Anne Hollingsworth, Music Specialist at the Ransom Humanities Research Center, for her assistance.

Works Consulted

Burton, Phillip. "Seventeen further memoirs." *ADAM International Review* 238 (1953): 36-7.

Craft, Robert. *Stravinsky: Chronicle of a Friendship.* 2nd ed. Nashville, TN, and London: Vanderbilt University Press, 1994. pp. 100 (22 May 1953), 105 (9 November 1953).

–. *Stravinsky: Glimpses of a Life.* London: Lime Tree, 1992; New York, NY: St. Martin's Press, 1993. pp. 52-60, 144, 286.

Ferris, Paul. *Dylan Thomas.* London, Sydney, Auckland, Toronto: Hodder and Stoughton, 1977. n. 1 on p. 150, p. 302.

Ferris, Paul, ed. *The Collected Letters of Dylan Thomas.* London and Melbourne: Dent, 1985. pp. xi, 756, 758-9, 782-3, 893-4, 901, 906, 913, 916-17, 944.

FitzGibbon, Constantine. *The Life of Dylan Thomas.* Boston, MA, and Toronto: Little, Brown, 1965. p. 344.

Gittins, Rob. *The Last Days of Dylan Thomas.* London and Sydney: Macdonald, 1986. p. 199.

Grindea, Miron. "For musick's sake." *ADAM* 379-84 (1973-74): n. on p. 8.

Nashold, James, and George Tremlett. *The Death of Dylan Thomas.* Edinburgh and London: Mainstream Publishing Co., 1997. pp. 119-25, 205-6.

Newman, Arnold, and Robert Craft. *Bravo Stravinsky.* Cleveland, OH, and New York, NY: World, 1967. pl. on p. [39] (upper right, Thomas's image unnoted).

SConv. p. 88.

SI&V. pl. 175 and caption on pp. 102-3.

SP&D. pp. 563, n. 110 on p. 652.

SSC. vol. 3. pp. 309, 390.

Stravinsky, Igor. "The Opera that might have been." *ADAM* 238 (1953): 8 (facsimile of Stravinsky letter).

96

(1954). Autographed photograph, 38.1 × 31.3 cm, taken by Douglas Glass (1901-78) between 5 and 23 September 1951 in Venice at the Hotel Bauer-Gruenwald, of Stravinsky leaning on a printed piano/vocal score of *The Rake's Progress* (1951), his wristwatch pointing to 1:10, and inscribed in English in black ink, 1954, to Glass:

To Douglas Glass
Cordially
IStravinsky
1954

Acquisition: H. Colin Slim in New York on 3 November 1995 from Wurlitzer-Bruck.
Provenance: Sotheby's *Continental Manuscripts and Music Sale LN 5294* (London, 18 May 1995), no. 147, lot 283 (1). It and its companion photograph (Entry 107) sold together.

Commentary

The photograph is unpublished. The Paul Sacher Foundation holds correspondence, 1954-62, between Glass and Stravinsky as well as many photographs by Glass. On the occasion for this photograph, taken in 1951 when Stravinsky was in Venice at the Hotel Bauer-Gruenwald, see Entry 107.

On 11 February 1954, Glass wrote from London to Hollywood commiserating over the loss of Dylan Thomas, their mutual friend. He announced that he had tickets for the composer's forthcoming concert at Royal Festival Hall on 27 May. Stravinsky was in London, 22-28 May, to conduct a Royal Philharmonic concert on that date and to receive the orchestra's gold medal. In the same letter Glass acknowledges his own pleasure about his 1951 photographs taken in Venice, but hopes to do even better.

The piano/vocal score on which Stravinsky leans is *The Rake's Progress*, more of which appears in Entry 107, wherein he has the same eyeglasses and wears the same shirt. The time on the wristwatch shows that Glass took Entry 96 more than an hour after Entry 107. On the reverse of Entry 96 in pencil is "Stravinsky – 1954 – " and two stamped addresses: "Copyright / Douglas Glass, / 43, Black Lion Lane, W.6. / Riverside 7522. / [in ink, no.] 3," and: "Douglas Glass / Studio House / Stone-Cum-Ebony, Kent / Wittersham 344." Dimensions of "ca 55 × 45 cm" in the above Sotheby's sale are incorrect.

A well-known London photographer, Glass was famous for his contribution, "Portrait Gallery," run weekly in *The Sunday Times*, 1949-61. Preferring to photograph creative people, his portraits included Shaw, Einstein, Picasso, Max Ernst, André Breton, Sir Thomas Beecham, Auden, and Churchill.

Works Consulted

"Glass, Douglas." *The London Times*. 4 July 1978. p. 18, col. g (obituary). SBu. n. 5 on p. 174.

Stuart, Philip. *Igor Stravinsky – The Composer in the Recording Studio. A Comprehensive Discography*. New York, NY, Westport, CT, London: Greenwood Press, 1991. p. 79 (Royal Festival Hall).

97 (1954). Signed twice-folded typed letter, 27.9 × 21.6 cm, in English in black ink on Stravinsky's printed stationery of 1260 NORTH WETHERLY DRIVE / HOLLYWOOD 46, CALIFORNIA, 23 August 1954, to Arnold Weissberger (1907-81):

Mr L. Arnold Weissberger   August 23, 1954
509 Madison Avenue   Air Mail
New York 22, N.Y.

Dear Mr Weissberger,
I have just received a letter from David Oppenheim to whom I am writing as per copy enclosed.

He disagrees with our suggestion to release in one record SEPTET, OCTET, SYMPHONIES OF WIND INSTRUMENTS, INMEMORIAM and the THREE SONGS FROM SHAKESPEARE and he adds:

"I do not think it is a good idea to mix these various aspects of your work. I think the newer things should remain together on one record and the older pieces on another. It was my idea to put the Suite from L'HISTOIRE DU SOLDAT on one side of the record and the OCTET and the SYMPHONIES OF WIND INSTRUMENTS on the other. The SEPTET, the IN MEMO-RIAM, the Shakespeare Songs, and conceivably some other things we will do can constitute a separate record. I think it is better for sales, reviews, and maybe even art...."

I do not think David Oppenheim is telling me the whole Columbia story on this. I believe that they want mostly to release L'HISTOIRE as soon as they can and before the other or smaller pieces because they have a bigger investment in it. Anyhow, I do not want to jeopardize any of our recording plans and, at this point, I am willing to let off steam.

I hope you had a pleasant journey back home. We all enjoyed immensely seeing you here.

With best wishes,

Cordially,

Encl.

[in black ink] IStravinsky

Acquisition: H. Colin Slim on 21 May 1996, together with the next two letters (entries 98-9), from David Schulson.
Provenance: Public Auction (1996), R.M. Smythe, Inc. (Suite 271 / 26 Broadway / New York).

Commentary

The letter, unpublished, is stamped at the top right: AUG 25 1954, presumably the day Weissberger received it; the envelope is missing. A tear from a staple at the top left probably indicates the above-mentioned enclosure, now lacking. Two circular holes at the left margin were for filing. The stationery of Entry 97 with its printed address differs from that of Entry 85. Eighteen other Stravinsky letters to Weissberger (late

1940s–late 1950s) were offered by Circa of St. Paul, Minnesota, in the fall of 1999 and still another of 1961 by Joyce Muns in 2000.

Entries 97-9 were probably prepared by André Marion whose command of English idioms was by no means perfect, for example, the unidiomatic and inappropriate "I am willing to let off steam" in Entry 97 and "to put up ... performances" in Entry 99 of 25 September (on Marion as secretary, see Entry 102). Without exception, entries 95 and 97-9 employ a capital I for the numeral 1. In letters of this period that Stravinsky certainly typed himself, this usage does not prevail (although it did earlier).

Weissberger, a New York attorney and a friend of Stravinsky from 1949, was also "a photographer of celebrities, represented artists and theatrical personalities such as Igor Stravinsky, Helen Hayes, Laurence Olivier, David O. Selznick, Otto Preminger, Martha Graham, Orson Welles, Placido Domingo, Ruth Gordon and Garson Kanin." Following the dismissal of William Montapert, Stravinsky formally retained him as his personal attorney, first in Los Angeles and then in New York, from July 1969 until his death.

Weissberger published *Close-up: A Collection of Photographs* (New York, NY: Arno Press, 1967) and *Famous Faces: A Photograph Album of Personal Reminiscences* (New York, NY: H.N. Abrams, 1973), the latter including one of Virgil Thomson and Stravinsky on his eightieth birthday and another with Ethel Merman. This book also includes thirteen photos of him taken 1949-70, with an affectionate appreciation by Weissberger. Other pictures by the lawyer are reproduced in the first edition of Craft's *Chronicle of a Friendship*, in *Pictures and Documents*, and in Vera Stravinsky's published diary.

David Oppenheim (1922–), a virtuoso solo clarinettist, was director, 1950-59, of the Masterworks division of Columbia Records. On 1 October 1953, learning that he was again to play clarinet in the *Septet* (1953) – he had played the premiere that very day – Stravinsky wrote: "I am delighted." A photograph taken at the recording session of the *Octet* on 26 January 1954 shows Oppenheim adjusting his mouthpiece. From 1962 Oppenheim took charge of the CBS documentary film portrait of Stravinsky, screened in Paris on 11 June 1966. Dean of the School of the Arts, New York University from 1969, he retired in 1992.

Two days later (25 August) Oppenheim wrote Stravinsky: "I am wondering whether you are planning to conduct at the recording sessions or whether Bob [Craft] will do that. I have not the slightest reservation about the kind of job Bob would do." Craft observes that Stravinsky, who had no "performing experience with either piece [*Three Songs from Shakespeare* and *In Memoriam Dylan Thomas*] wanted me to record them but finally did it himself." Stravinsky thus continued his long series of recordings with much of the preparation having been done by Craft. Oppenheim's suggestion also opened up the later possibility of Craft making recordings under the composer's supervision.

Symphonies of Wind Instruments (recorded 8 October 1951) and the *Octet* and the Suite from *L'Histoire du soldat* (recorded 26-27 January 1954) were, in fact, released by CBS in March 1955 on one LP record. In the latter two works Oppenheim played clarinet.

Works Consulted

Circa. *The Collector's Catalog 19*. St. Paul, MN, October 1999. p. 8.

Craft, Robert. *Stravinsky: Chronicle of a Friendship*. New York, NY: Alfred A. Knopf: 1972. pl. [6]A btn pp. 300-01 (with Vera and Craft). [First edition; not in 2nd ed. Nashville, TN, and London: Vanderbilt University Press, 1994.]

–. *Stravinsky: Glimpses of a Life*. London: Lime Tree, 1992; New York, NY: St. Martin's Press, 1993. n. 4 on p. 18, pp. 166-81.

Muns, J.B. *Musical Autographs List 00-5*. Berkeley, 2000, no. 59.

"Oppenheim, David." *Who's Who in America 2000*. ed. Maurice Brooks, et al. New Providence, NJ: Marquis, 1999. vol. 2. p. 3680.

SBu. pl. 150 on p. 199 (with Aldous Huxley and Vera), p. 216 (8 October 1965).

SP&D. pls. 18 (lower) and 27 (top; both with Vera) btn pp. 400-01.

SSC. vol. 3. p. 378.

"Stravinsky, Igor." *Stravinsky conducts Stravinsky. The Mono Years 1952-1955*. Sony Classical CD, MH2K 63325. 1998. Liner notes booklet, p. 31.

Stuart, Philip. *Igor Stravinsky – The Composer in the Recording Studio. A Comprehensive Discography*. New York, NY, Westport, CT, London: Greenwood Press, 1991. no. 66 on pp. 36-7, nos. 71-2 on p. 59.

"Weissberger, Arnold." *New York Times*. 1 March 1981. p. 36 (obituary).

98   (1954). Signed two-page, twice-folded typed letter; p. 1: 27.9 × 21.6 cm and p. 2: 27.9 × 21.4 cm, in English in black ink, the first page only on the same printed stationery as Entry 97, 2 September 1954, to Arnold Weissberger:

Mr L. Arnold Weissberger   September 2nd, 1954
509 Madison Avenue   Air Mail – Special Delivery
New York 22, N.Y.

Dear Mr. Weissberger,
Thank you for your letter of August 30, 1954.

Now I can see more clearly what is on Columbia' s mind...
it all boils down to a kind of fear to have to swallow more
than they can chew; and there is nothing we can do about it...
Therefore I am in complete agreement with your point of view
concerning the two year option. Let us do without it and sign
the contract as outlined on a straight three year basis starting
in the fall of 1955.

Now, outside of this main contract, and inasmuch as it will
take effect only late in 1955 I would like to secure Columbia's
agreement and what was once called by David Oppenheim the
"smaller works".

Last week David Oppenheim has given me his OK to make
here on September 13th, the recording of "IN MEMORIAM –
DYLAN THOMAS" (8 minutes), and "THREE SONGS FROM
SHAKESPEARE" (7 minutes) for soprano, flute, clarinet,
viola, with the forces at my disposal from the Monday
Evening Concerts organization.

Due to the fact that I have conceded to David Oppenheim to
release on one LP record SOLDAT-OCTET-SYMPHONIES
FOR WIND INSTRUMENTS, the two pieces I am going to
record will have to wait until we can find the complement to
make another LP to include them.

It so happens that Monday Evening Concerts have now settled their programs for the coming season and I am enclosing a folder with these programs for your information.

You will note that after the September 20th concert when IN MEMORIAM – DYLAN THOMAS will be performed there will be several other concerts featuring various so-called "smaller works" of mine and precisely the very ones which should be put together with IN MEMORIAM and THREE SONGS FROM SHAKESPEARE to make one LP.

Here is the list of the other works and the dates of performance:

[typed at top of second page, underscored by a margin-to-margin rule]
Mr L. Arnold Weissberger   page 2 September 2, 1954

October II – FOUR RUSSIAN SONGS for female chorus and 4 horns (5 minutes). (It is a new instrumentation of what was listed on the original list you have as 4 RUSSIAN CHORUSES a capella for female voices.

November 29 – SONGS FOR SOPRANO AND NINE INSTRUMENTS (Two Poems; Three Japanese Lyrics) (I0 minutes). (The Two Poems are a new instrumentation which I made specially to match the one of the Three Japanese Lyrics. Only the JAPANESE SONGS were originally listed and this should replace them).

November 29 – SOUVENIRS DE MON ENFANCE (3 Souvenirs of Childhood) (5 minutes) – (This was originally listed)

February 2I – SONGS FOR SOPRANO, FLUTE, HARP & GUITAR (6 to 7 minutes)– (This is a new instrumentation; it includes more than and it should replace the 2 RUSSIAN SONGS originally listed).

I would like to secure from David Oppenheim his agreement
to let me record here each one of the works myself at the
time of their local performance. It will be a good bargain for
Columbia and an excellent thing from my musical point of
view.

(You may wonder why THREE SONGS FROM SHAKE-
SPEARE is not listed on the enclosed program of Monday Evening Concerts. Indeed it is not being performed in this series
but the Monday Evening Concerts musicians are performing
it for and at a "Museum Concert" here).

If David Oppenheim agrees to do this complete program of
"smaller works" then the time to run from now until the start
of the new contract will be put to very fruitful use at a very
small expense for Columbia.

I hope you can settle all this now without too much trouble.

With best greetings,

Encl.

Cordially

[in black ink] IStr

Acquisition: See Entry 97.
Provenance: See Entry 97.

Commentary

The letter is unpublished, its envelope missing. Entry 98 is stamped at the
upper right corner SEP 3 1954, presumably the day Weissberger received
it. A tear from a staple at the top left of both pages probably indicates the
enclosed program of Monday Evening Concerts, now lacking. Two
circular holes on the left margin were for filing.

The three-year contract mentioned at the beginning of page 1 in
Entry 98 refers to negotiations initiated by Stravinsky in an earlier
four-page letter to Weissberger of 24 June 1954 (auctioned in 1996).
By 1954 the directorate of the Evenings on the Roof had changed from
Peter Yates (1909-76) to Lawrence Morton, who took formal control
in 1954 and who changed the organization's name. Almost a year

earlier, on 23 October 1953, Stravinsky announced that he had just completed his Shakespeare songs and dedicated these works to the Los Angeles concert group called Evenings on the Roof, an organization that pleased him. He especially singled out for high praise its founder, Peter Yates (SSC, vol. 3, p. 378). The 1954-55 programs have been reprinted and the season itself analyzed.

Works Consulted

Crawford, Dorothy Lamb. *Evenings On and Off the Roof: Pioneering Concerts in Los Angeles, 1939-1971*. Berkeley and Los Angeles, CA, and London: University of California Press, 1995. pp. 140-56.

Morton, Arthur, and Herbert Morton. *Monday Evening Concerts 1954-1971: The Lawrence Morton Years*. Los Angeles, CA: A. and H. Morton, 1993. pp. 45-6, 48.

Morton, Lawrence. "Stravinsky in Los Angeles." *Festival of Music Made in Los Angeles*. ed. Orrin Howard. Los Angeles: Philharmonic Association, 1981. p. 79.

Smythe, R.M. *Public Auction [Catalogue]*. New York, 6 June 1996, lot 226.

SSC. vol. 3. p. 378.

99   **(1954). Signed twice-folded typed letter, 27.9 × 21.6 cm, on the same printed stationery as entries 97-8, in English in blue ink, 25 September 1954, to Arnold Weissberger:**

Mr. L. Arnold Weissberger   September 25, 1954
509 Madison Avenue   Air Mail
New York 22, N.Y.

Dear Mr Weissberger,
Thank you for your letter of September 22, 1954.

From David Oppenheim's letter to you it is evident that Columbia cannot do anymore recordings with me until February 21st, 1955.

Therefore I think our answer should be based on the following points:

1/ – I will record in connection with the February 21st performance (and before March 7th, while I will be here) my SONGS FOR SOPRANO, FLUTE, HARP & GUITAR.

2/ – At the same time (in the same session plus a second one) I will re-assemble the performers who will have been playing in the concerts of October 11th and November 29th, and we will record then:

RUSSIAN SONGS FOR FEMALE CHORUS & 4 HORNS
SONGS FOR SOPRANO & NINE INSTRUMENTS
(2 Poems & 3 Japanese Lyrics)
THREE SOUVENIRS OF CHILDHOOD

3/ – All the pieces mentioned above (1 & 2) will be released in one LP with IN MEMORIAM DYLAN THOMAS and THREE SONGS FROM SHAKESPEARE just recorded here two weeks ago. Release to take place in September/October 1955 or March 1956.

4/ – This remains outside of the main 3 year contract terms of which do not seem to require further debating. Therefore I assume the 3 year contract can be signed at once.

(I hope you can convince David Oppenheim that we have to record these pieces <u>then</u>. The possibility of having to record them later is hard to sonsider – in fact we might never be able to do it – because the players are here this season but they may be apart and in other and different places another season. And having to put up entirely new performances here or elsewhere for recording purposes exclusively would not make it easier but only much more difficult and expensive to Columbia).

With all best greetings,

Cordially, [in blue ink] Igor Stravinsky

Acquisition: See Entry 97.
Provenance: See Entry 97.

Commentary

The letter is unpublished, its envelope missing. Entry 99 is stamped at the upper left corner SEP 27 1954, presumably the day Weissberger received it, and has no staple tear. Two circular holes on the left margin are for filing. The *Septet* (recorded in January 1954) and *In Memoriam Dylan Thomas* and *Three Shakespeare Songs* (both recorded 13 September 1954, the former a week before Craft led its public premiere), *Four Songs, Three Japanese Lyrics,* and *Two Balmont Songs* (all recorded 15 February 1955), *Three Little Songs* and *Saucers* (both recorded 28 July 1955) all duly appeared in August 1956 on a single LP record.

Works Consulted

Stuart, Philip. *Igor Stravinsky – The Composer in the Recording Studio. A Comprehensive Discography.* New York, NY, Westport, CT, London: Greenwood Press, 1991. nos. 73-80 on pp. 37-8, p. 59.

100 (1956). Autograph tracing of Stravinsky's right hand in blue ink, on a printed sheet, 25.8 × 19.2 cm, signed in blue ink chiefly within the outline of the back of the hand and wrist, September 1956, perhaps for Hans von Benda (1888-1972):

Igor Strawinsky
Berlin
Sept/56

Acquisition: H. Colin Slim in San Diego, CA, 9 October 1999, from Benedikt and Salmon.
Provenance: Perhaps Hans von Benda, Berlin (1956-72); J.B. Muns, Berkeley (c. 1995); La Scala Autographs (before 1996); Benedikt and Salmon, *Autograph Auction [Catalogue] No. 22* (San Diego, August 1999), lot 227, ill. facing p. 23.

Forget - Me - Not

Your Birthday _Igor Strawinsky_ Date .... 19 .....

Your Name and Address ....

Please put down any thoughts here together with the outline of your hand

Place your left wrist here and trace the outline of your hand with a pencil and afterwards with a pen.

Commentary

Aside from its reduced reproduction in the 1999 auction catalogue, the drawing is unpublished. Its sheet is headed in a Gothic type: "Forget-Me-Not / Your Birthday [leader dots] / Date [leader dots]19 [leader dots] / Your Name and Address [leader dots] / Please put down any thoughts here together with the outline of your hand." Following the above "Your Birthday" section is "Igor Strawinsky" written in pencil, probably in a European hand. At the bottom of the sheet is printed: "Place your left wrist here and trace the outline of your hand with a pencil and afterwards with a pen."

Entry 100 has an irregular left margin from having been torn from an album begun in 1938 and dismembered about 1996. Benedikt and Salmon offered other sheets from this album, described as the "'Hands' Collection," in their 1997-98 catalogues, traced and signed by among others: Richard Strauss (1864-1949), Hidemaro Konoye (1898-1973), Clemens Krauss (1893-1954), and in 1999 they sold one by Wilhelm Furtwängler (1886-1954).

During September 1956 Stravinsky was in Berlin for just five days, arriving from Geneva on the 26th with Erich Winkler, his German concert agent (1951-56), in order to rehearse and then to conduct the West Berlin Radio Orchestra on 2 October. Stravinsky was with Nicolas Nabokov (1903-78) every day. After his arrival they met Craft at Tempelhof airport with Winkler, and Gerhard von Westerman (1894-1963), who had managed the Berlin Philharmonic during the Second World War and resumed this position afterward. On the way to the Kempinsky Hotel, Stravinsky felt ill, but the next day he lunched with George Balanchine (1904-83) to discuss *Agon.* On the 28th he attended Busoni's *Faust,* lunching at the von Westermans on the 29th. On the 30th he lunched with a Senator Bach and with the conductor of West Berlin Radio, Hans Robert Gustav von Benda, and his Finnish wife. He had known this conductor personally since at least early November 1930, when he and Vera Sudeykina had tea in Berlin with the von Bendas. Begun in 1938, the album may have been owned by one or the other of these couples, its original US purchaser, J.B. Muns, suggesting that probably it was the von Benda's. Suffering the first symptoms of a stroke while conducting in Berlin on 2 October, Stravinsky was hospitalized two days later in Munich.

Stravinsky outlined his hand as an autograph on at least three other occasions. At the reception given by a Madame Grossman early in November 1924 (wrongly dated 1926 by Prokofiev's wife) after playing his *Concerto* (1924) in Warsaw, he traced his left hand in her album. Having read a Parisian newspaper's report of Prokofiev's opinions about this hand, he wrote an angry letter on 20 December 1933, to which Prokofiev responded the next day with a conciliatory one.

Craft also reports Stravinsky drawing his hand on a copy of *The Five Fingers* (1921) for Ellis B. Kohs (1916-2000), who had studied with him in 1939-40 at Harvard. Omega's 1949 reprint in New York of this work the year following Kohs's move to California may furnish an approximate date for the drawing.

The third example, which postdates Entry 100, stems from an interview at Toronto in April 1962 with Professor Maryvonne Kendergi of the University of Montreal. With his left hand, he outlined his right one for her at the same time he was photographed doing so.

Entry 100 is the finer of the pair of such outlines for which reproductions are available. Compared with Kendergi's exemplar, the ring on his fourth finger is more carefully delineated, and his fingernails are indicated. Both exemplars should be compared with two photographs: one of just his right hand taken in 1929 by J.-A. Boiffard and the other of both hands, taken at Munich in November 1930 by Eric Schaal (the latter reproduced in Entry 46, final plate).

Finally, the trivia enthusiast will want to know that there is also a tracing of the composer's foot. Stephen Walsh kindly advises that it is in Philadelphia, Rosenbach Archive, Mercedes Acosta collection.

Works Consulted

Benedikt and Salmon. *Autograph/Book Auction Catalogue 19*. San Diego, July 1997, lot 208; *Catalogue 20*. San Diego, January 1998, lot 74.

Brown, Malcolm Hamrick. "Stravinsky and Prokofiev: Sizing Up the Competition." *Confronting Stravinsky: Man, Musician, and Modernist*. ed. Jann Pasler. Berkeley and Los Angeles, CA, and London: University of California Press, 1986. pp. 48-9.

Craft, Robert. *Stravinsky: Chronicle of a Friendship*. 2nd ed. Nashville, TN, and London: Vanderbilt University Press, 1994. pp. 146-47.

Höcker, Karla. *Begegnung mit Furtwängler*. Berlin: C. Bertelsmann, 1956. pp. 34, 36.

Kendergi, Maryvonne. "Stravinsky interrogé (1962)." *Cahiers canadiens/Canada Music Book* 4 (Spring/Summer 1972): pls. on pp. 74-5.

Kroll, Erwin. "Westerman." MGG. p. 14, cols. 524-5.

Rodriguez, Natalia, and Malcolm Herrick Brown. "Prokofiev's Correspondence with Stravinsky and Shostakovich." *Slavonic and Western Music: Essays for Gerald Abraham.* ed. M.H. Brown and Roland John Wiley. Ann Arbor, MI, and Oxford: University of Michigan Press, 1985. nn. 10-11 on pp. 278-9.

Schaeffner, André. *Strawinsky.* Paris: Les Éditions Rieder, 1931. pl. LX.

SBu. pp. 26 (1-7 November 1924), 51 (8 and 28 November 1930), 180 (25-30 September 1956).

SP&D. pp. 310-11, 352.

SSC. vol. 1. p. 214; vol. 2. p. 392.

Stravinsky, Igor. *An Autobiography.* New York, NY: Simon and Schuster, 1936. final plate.

"(von) Benda, Hans Robert Gustav." *Enciclopedia della Musica Ricordi.* Milan: Ricordi, 1963-64. vol. 1. p. 231.

101 (1957). Autograph singly folded letter, 12.7 × 19.4 cm, in English in red ink on blue paper, with typed address on blue envelope, 10.4 × 13.0 cm, 21 June 1957, to Charles Cushing (1905-82):

[envelope]
Mr. C.C.Cushing
2239 Summer Street
Berkeley 9,
Calif.

[stamp] 1260 North Wetherly Drive / Hollywood 46, California
[postmark] Los Angeles Calif/Jun 21/9 PM/1957

[letter in red ink]

Hollywood
June 21/57

Thank you dear Cushing for your good lines.

Hope you liked [crossed out] my what you heard in my
concert the other night

Cordially

IStr

Acquisition: H. Colin Slim in Berkeley, CA, in 1993 by purchase from Cushing's widow, Piquette.
Provenance: Piquette Cushing (Summer Street / Berkeley).

Commentary

The letter is unpublished. Charles Cushing, then professor of Music at the University of California, Berkeley, had heard four days earlier, on 17 June 1957, a Gala Concert at Royce Hall (University of California, Los Angeles), at the Los Angeles Music Festival directed by the movie composer Franz Waxman (1906-67), commemorating the seventy-fifth birthday of Stravinsky, kindly confirmed to Dr. Slim by the late Mrs. Cushing by telephone on 11 November 1994. Whether Cushing – rather conservative in his taste for serial music – was entirely pleased by the premieres of these most recent compositions (1955 and 1957) is unknown.

The program was *Greeting Prelude for the 80th Birthday of Pierre Monteux* (1955) conducted by Franz Waxman, *Symphonies of Wind Instruments* (1920), the American premiere of *Canticum Sacrum* (1955), and the world premiere of *Agon* (1957), led by Craft. Stravinsky concluded by conducting his *J.S. Bach: Chorale and Canonic Variations on "von Himmel Hoch"* (1956), and *Symphony of Psalms* (1930).

The concert opened with the reading of a message from President Dwight Eisenhower (1890-1969) and a speech at intermission by Aldous Huxley (1894-1963). George Balanchine, who was to choreograph the stage premiere of *Agon* in New York, 27 November 1957, was in the audience, as was Christopher Isherwood (1904-86). Isherwood observed that Craft: "pale as a lily and quite beautiful in his exhaustion ... hadn't had enough rehearsals ... Then Igor came on, limp with sweat but wonderfully svelte ... Aldous ... called Igor a 'great genius,' a 'saint of music' and the maker of 'the Stravinsky revolution.' Eisenhower sent an asinine telegram, ... carefully worded so Igor shouldn't be praised *too* highly." *Agon* and the *Canticum* were recorded in Hollywood almost immediately afterward, on 18-19 June.

Letters between Cushing and Stravinsky, 1947–59, are held by the Paul Sacher Foundation. Two others from Stravinsky to Cushing of 11 March 1942 and 11 November 1948 are in the archives of the Berkeley Department of Music. The first one concerns Cushing's arrangement for band of the Stravinsky *Star-Spangled Banner* (1941), which arrangement he approved, and the second concerns his *Mass* (1948). In between, on 10 November 1946, he had lent Cushing the orchestra score of his arrangement (1917) of the *Song of the Volga Boatmen*. Cushing dined at the Stravinskys on 31 October 1947. A year later he was again in Los Angeles, negotiating with Stravinsky about a possible donation of the short score of *Orpheus* (1947) and its sketches to the Berkeley Department of Music; the former arrived in Berkeley early in August 1949.

Yet another letter – an envelope and enclosed annotated calling card – of 9 October 1959 from Stravinsky in Venice to Cushing in Paris turned up in 1998 following his widow's death. Their son, Caleb Cushing, kindly brought it to the attention of Dr. Slim. Cushing had written from Paris on 26 September about a commission from the University of California at Berkeley for a solo or concerted work for organ, but Stravinsky turned it down because of what he described as his heavy work load. A photograph by Walt Lynott survives of Cushing and Stravinsky chatting in May 1968 in Berkeley.

Works Consulted

Craft, Robert. "Catalog of the Library of Robert Craft." Typescript: Library of Congress, Music Division. VI: Parts, no. 12 on p. 90.

Crawford, Dorothy Lamb. *Evenings On and Off the Roof: Pioneering Concerts in Los Angeles, 1939-1971*. Berkeley and Los Angeles, CA, and London: University of California Press, 1995. pp. 170, 255.

Cushing correspondence. Department of Music archives. University of California at Berkeley.

Goldberg, Albert. "Stravinsky at 75." *Musical America* 77 (July 1957): 9-10.

Isherwood, Christopher. *Diaries*. ed. Katherine Bucknell. New York, NY: Harper Collins, 1997. vol. 1., pp. 704-5.

Lynott, Walt (photographer). "Composers Igor Stravinsky and Prof. Charles Cushing." *San Francisco Examiner*. 22 May 1968. ill. on p. 19.

Morton, Arthur, and Herbert Morton. *Monday Evening Concerts 1954-1971: The Lawrence Morton Years*. Los Angeles, CA: A. and H. Morton, 1993. p. 56.

Samson, Valerie Brooks. "Cushing." *The New Grove Dictionary of American Music*. ed. H. Wiley Hitchcock and Stanley Sadie. New York, NY: Macmillan, 1986. vol. 1. p. 558.

SBu. pp. 142, 184.

SScrbk. p. 160 (medical diaries: 14-17 June 1957).

SSC. vol. 3. p. 410.

"Stravinsky, Igor." *San Francisco Examiner*. 6 April 1971. p. 4 (obituary with 1968 Lynott photograph).

Stuart, Philip. *Igor Stravinsky – The Composer in the Recording Studio. A Comprehensive Discography*. New York, NY, Westport, CT, London: Greenwood Press, 1991. nos. 86-7 on p. 39.

102

(1957). **Signed and typed twice-folded letter, 21.8 × 14.0 cm, in French in black ink, 24 June 1957, to Doda Conrad in Paris. Ostensibly from André Marion in Hollywood and with his supposed signature, the letter concludes with a signed forgery by Stravinsky of Marion's name:**

Mr. Doda Conrad
3 rue de Bruxelles
Paris, 1X-eme, France

Hollywood
le 24 juin/57

Monsieur,

Charge de la correspondance de Monsieur Igor Stravinsky dans son absence je reponds a votre lettre du 19 juin.

D'apres mes dernieres conversations telephoniques avec lui il est absolument certain qu'il ne lui sera pas possible d'accepter votre proposition. Il est surcharge de travail cette annee et il ne prend plus d'engagement d'aucune sorte.

Il est en ce moment ci en voyage de concerts (ici, USA et l'Europe) et ne reviendra qu'en decembre.

Veuillez agreer, Monsieur, l'expression de mes sentiments distingues.

[by Stravinsky in black ink] Andre Marion
[typed] Andre Marion,
secretaire de
Mr. Stravinsky

Doda Conrad   Hollywood
Paris   24 June 1957

Sir:

   Entrusted with the correspondence of Mr. Igor Stravinsky in his absence, I am replying to your letter of 19 June.

   According to my recent telephone conversations with him, he is absolutely certain that he will be unable to accept your proposal. He is overwhelmed with work this year and he is no longer undertaking engagements of any kind.

   At this very moment he is on concert tours (here, U.S.A and Europe) and will not return until December.

   Yours sincerely,

   André Marion,

   secretary to Mr. Stravinsky

Acquisition: H. Colin Slim on 10 November 1994 from Wurlitzer-Bruck.

Provenance: Doda Conrad.

Commentary

The letter (presumably sent from 1260 North Wetherly Drive, Hollywood) is unpublished and its envelope missing. A copy is in the Paul Sacher Foundation. A slight tear at the upper left corner of Entry 102 suggests that something was once stapled to it. Typing it himself (absence of all accents suggests a US machine), Stravinsky signed in ink the name of his son-in-law and secretary, André Marion.

   Among the patent falsehoods in Entry 102 are his absence: he had just written Cushing three days earlier from Hollywood (see Entry 101). As Vera's diary reveals, he did not leave California for a concert tour until 7 July. And obviously there was no need for any telephone conversation. Craft notes that, throughout his career, he often protected himself with such deceptions, including one in 1964 wherein he also forged Marion's signature.

   Doda Conrad, son of Marya Freund and himself a distinguished singer, was living in Paris at this time. Entry 102 responds to Conrad's letter of 19 June 1957, held by the Paul Sacher Foundation. It requests the support of Stravinsky in a project to reissue recordings of Monteverdi made by

Boulanger in 1938 as a tribute for her coming seventieth birthday (16 September).

Works Consulted

Craft, Robert. *Stravinsky: Glimpses of a Life*. London: Lime Tree, 1992; New York, NY: St. Martin's Press, 1993. pp. 143-4.

Grindea, Miron. "For musick's sake." *ADAM* 379-84 (1973-74): n. on p. 8.

Rosenstiel, Léonie. *Nadia Boulanger. A Life in Music*. New York, NY: W.W. Norton, 1982. pp. 371, 384-5.

SBu. p. 184.

SP&D. p. 377 (24 October 1945), pp. 440-2.

103

(1957). Signed twice-folded typed letter, 25.9 × 18.4 cm, in English with autograph location and date in red ink, 17 August 1957, to Arnold Weissberger:

Mr. Arnold Weissberger
120 East 56th Street
New York City

Dear friend,

Enclosed a letter which I ask you to answer in my name. PLease find out who the publishers are and what they offer. For your information – My AUTOBIOGRAPHY in Simon & Schuster edition [1936] is out of print for a longue [two letters crossed out in ink] time now and they wanted to reprint it provided I continue the autobiography up to date. This I will never do.

As for Lincoln, I am very disappointed and even not a little humiliated that the Stravinsky Festival has dwindled to nothing. I do not even have a concrete proposition or a date for my ballet. And it appears from Lincoln's last letter that he has canceled the St. Thomas Church concert without so much as advising me first.I do not see how it will bee [one letter crossed out in ink] worth my time to stay in NewYork for a possible single conducting engagement at the ballet. Needless to say I do not blame Lincoln for not beeing able to finde [one letter crossed out in ink] money, but, for his very peculiar actions to ourselfs who are his old and dear friends.

We are very much enjoying our staying in England and we have made many side trips in this beautiful country.

We will be in Venice next week and for the whole September at the Hotel Bauer Gruenwald.

All best

cordially
[in red ink] I Stravinsky
Dartington
Aug 17/57

Acquisition: H. Colin Slim on 5 August 1997 from La Scala Autographs. The final autograph numeral "7" is mostly missing because of a torn lower right corner. Linda K. Ogden mended this corner and some edge tears on 15 September 1997.

Provenance: R.M. Smythe and Co., Inc., *Summer Autograph Auction. "Music: Igor Stravinsky," Public Auction 164* (New York, 12 June 1997), lot 271.

Commentary

The letter is unpublished, its envelope and enclosure missing. A copy is in the Paul Sacher Foundation. Entry 103 is stamped at upper right AUG 21 1957, presumably the date Weissberger received it. Not on the same machine as entries 102 and 104, this letter, with a watermark of "Eaton's corrasable No 5" surmounted by a crown, was surely also typed by Stravinsky himself, as shown by his characteristic contraction "NewYork" (also in entries 104 and 108, and in a typed letter to Craft of 7 October 1949). While visiting south England, he, Vera, and Craft stayed a fortnight in Dartington, 7-21 August 1957, one photograph showing him and Vera in front of Dartington Hall, Totnes.

Presumably the "publishers" cited in Entry 103 are M. and J. Steuer of New York. In 1958 they reprinted the Simon and Schuster edition of the *Autobiography,* unrevised and without its plates (see entries 19, 42-3, 46, and 83).

Stravinsky probably first met Lincoln Kirstein (1907-96) in New York late in 1936 where they were later photographed at a rehearsal of *Jeu de cartes* (see Entry 66). Kirstein invited Stravinsky on 30 August 1950 to conduct his own ballets the following February at the New York City Center, but this venture came to naught. He then proposed a Stravinsky Festival for early February 1956 in letters to Stravinsky of 24 August and 21 December 1954. On 26 August 1954 Stravinsky responded that he supposed it would include the premiere of *Agon.* An approximate date for the premiere of the ballet was set during a luncheon in New York on 12 January 1957 with Kirstein. The stage premiere did not take place, however, until 27 November that year in New York, by which time Stravinsky had returned to Los Angeles (14 November). Kirstein was close to him until the composer's death.

Craft conducted a program at St. Thomas in New York on 2 March 1958 of sacred music – *Symphonies of Wind Instruments, Von Himmel hoch, Mass,* and *Symphony of Psalms.* Stravinsky did not attend these 1957-58 performances, apparently in the case of *Agon,* not anticipating its great stage success.

Works Consulted

Craft, Robert. *Stravinsky: Chronicle of a Friendship.* 2nd ed. Nashville, TN, and London: Vanderbilt University Press, 1994. pp. 172-4; colour pl. [5] (by Edwin Allen, 18 December 1969) btn pp. 462-3.

SP&D. pl. on p. 424.

SScrbk. pl. 136 and caption on p. 64.

SSC. vol. 1. pl. [11, lower] btn pp. 202-3, pp. 278, 289-91.

104   **(1958). Signed twice-folded typed letter, 21.6 × 14.8 cm, in English in red pencil, 30 January 1958, to Deborah Ishlon:**

Miss D.Ishlon
COLUMBIA RECORDS
799, Seventh Ave
NewYork 19, NY

Dear Debbie,
Thank you for your interesting letter of Jan28 What news from
Doubleday? Who comes next? Aldous Huxley suggests
Harcourt Brace – he knows a man there.
Will you kindly send a copy of the Dialogues to T.S.Eliot
(Faber & Faber Ltd , 24 Russel Square, London,
W.1.,England). I wrote to him yesterday promising to send him
them in a few days.
Has Sweeden not yet paid for the 36 Questions?
May be we have to ask A,Weissberger to write them a strong
note.
What is Ocampo's answer about the Dialogues?

    and

Ones more I am obliged to bother you concerning my <u>1911</u>
<u>photo</u> we have lent to S.Spendler. How to get it back?

                    I0000000 best wishes
                    [in red crayon] IStr

Acquisition: H. Colin Slim on 27 April 1996 through Martin A. Silver
from David Schulson.
Provenance: Deborah Ishlon, New York; probably Lion Heart
Autographs, Inc. New York, which in 1997 owned ten such letters to
Ishlon.

Commentary

The letter is unpublished, its envelope missing. A copy is in the Paul
Sacher Foundation. Judging by numerous spelling and hyphenation

errors, Entry 104 was typed at home by Stravinsky on the same machine as Entry 102.

Ishlon, former publicity director for Columbia Records in New York, worked with Stravinsky from at least January 1956 until his death. Recently, she has been selling their correspondence. For example, her letter from him of 27 August 1958, partly printed in 1984 and then again by Craft, was for sale in October 1995; two of his brief notes to her, 20 February 1959 and 21 February 1961, were auctioned at Berlin in March 1997; another one, 25 November 1957, was auctioned at Berlin in July 1998; and two others were auctioned there in November 1999.

On 8 April 1957, Stravinsky had entrusted Ishlon with preliminary editing of a manuscript, variously called in its several manifestations: "Answers to 34" (or "35" or "36") Questions," as for example, Craft in 1957, "Answers to 34 Questions, An Interview with Igor Stravinsky." Swedish Radio (Radiojänst) was involved with "36 Questions," hence the reference to payment from "Sweeden." His inclination in Entry 104 to have Arnold Weissberger "write them a strong note" was fulfilled on 5 March 1958 when he wrote the lawyer to request Ishlon how much she asked for the "Questions," already printed in October 1957 in Sweden, and to request payment. (On Weissberger, see Entry 97.)

Despite the mention of "Dialogues" in Entry 104, their manuscript was eventually entitled *Conversations with Igor Stravinsky*. Published simultaneously by Doubleday (New York) and Faber and Faber (London) in 1959, it was the first of six books of literary collaborations between Craft and Stravinsky (Entry 114 is another exemplar of the same photograph used on the jacket of *Conversations*).

Stravinsky was first introduced to Thomas Stearns Eliot (1888–1965) by Stephen Spender (1909–95) on 8 December 1956. Not "yesterday," but on the same day that he wrote Ishlon, he wrote Eliot. He requested permission to send to Eliot a manuscript he decribed as "short (about 40,000 words)" and entitled *Dialogues*, about which he sought an opinion on how it might be shortened. On 25 March 1958 he wrote Eliot that he had not seen the manuscript sent from New York. There, presumably, Ishlon had imposed on it an order by subject matter. He was to pay a posthumous tribute to Eliot with his *Introitus* (1965).

Stravinsky knew Aldous Huxley from November 1934 when Victoria Ocampo introduced them in London, and afterward during their Hollywood years. He dedicated the orchestral *Variations* (1964) to Huxley posthumously.

Victoria Ocampo, the well-known Argentine writer, and Stravinsky were friends over many years. She was also the publisher in Buenos Aires of *Sur*. He had sent her the "Dialogues," apparently hoping for an Argentine edition to be published by her company. Attending the premiere of the *Rite of Spring* in 1913, she claimed that she had met Stravinsky in 1932. She appears with him in a photograph of July 1934 at London. In 1935-36 she arranged for publication by her company of the Spanish translation of his *Chroniques de ma vie,* prefacing it with a "Letter to Igor Stravinsky." When he and his son Soulima came to Buenos Aires in 1936, both were her house guests and when he conducted *Perséphone* at the Teatro Colón in May she was the narrator. Largely responsible for a second Latin American tour in the summer of 1960 during which he again conducted at the Colón (this time also with Craft), she appears in group photographs with him at her house on 29 August 1960. At this time he reinscribed her short score of *Perséphone*, which he had presented to her in 1936 (now in the Pierpont Morgan Library, New York, MS Cary 516). (On her, see entries 44-5 and 63-4.)

Stravinsky, who first met Stephen Spender at a concert in Rome in 1954, was moving heaven and earth to regain his photo(s). His letter of 19 February 1958 to Nicolas Nabokov, their mutual acquaintance, mentions not one but "two photographs (taken in Monte Carlo with Diaghilev, Nijinsky, Benois, etc. ...) sent to [Spender] a year ago for the illustration of an article." There is no sign of Spender ever having published an article about these figures mentioned by Stravinsky. A series of three additional letters on 8, 10, and 21 March 1958 between Stravinsky and Nabokov contains details about the former's desire to regain his photographs. Apparently Nabokov had to write a strongly worded letter to Spender. Ultimately, on 26 March, Stravinsky wrote Nabokov that Spender had returned one still lacking photograph plus a letter that Stravinsky found unintelligible (SSC, vol. 2, pp. 395-8). Despite this contretemps he and Spender remained friends.

Secure identification of the 1911 photograph he mentions in Entry 104 is not possible, however, because he owned several taken that year. Among Monte Carlo photographs of 1911 is one he took on 17 March of Nijinsky, another by Nikolai Besobrasov on 16 April which includes him, "Diaghilev, Nijinsky, Benois etc" and six other persons, and yet another dated "Spring 1911" of Diaghilev and him.

Works Consulted

Circa. *The Collector's Catalog 19*. St. Paul, MN, October 1999. pl. on p. 8.

Craft, Robert. "Answers to 34 Questions, An Interview with Igor Stravinsky." *Encounter* 9 (July 1957): 3-7.

—. *Stravinsky: Chronicle of a Friendship*. 2nd ed. Nashville, TN, and London: Vanderbilt University Press, 1994. pp. 229-31.

—. *Stravinsky: Glimpses of a Life*. London: Lime Tree, 1992; New York, NY: St. Martin's Press, 1993. p. 68, n. 6 on p. 70.

Meyer, Doris. *Victoria Ocampo. Against the Wind and the Tide*. New York, NY: G. Braziller, 1979. pl. [14] (misdated 1957).

Ocampo, Victoria. "*Perséphone* bajo la batuta de Strawinsky." *Testimonios Octava Serie (1968-1970)*. Buenos Aires: Sur, 1971. p. 231.

Stargardt, J.A. *Katalog 666*. Berlin, 18-19 March 1997, lot 1086c at 412: DM 400, sold at DM 400; *Katalog 670*. Berlin, 7-8 July 1998, lot 998 at 378: DM 400; *Katlog 672*. Berlin, 16-17 November 1999, lots 818-19: DM 600 and DM 350, at 320-21.

SBu. pl. 68 on p. [64].

SP&D. pls. on p. 70, pp. 85, 330-1, 457, 538-9.

SScrbk. pl. 198 on p. 94, pl. 288 on p. 144.

SSC. vol. 2. pp. 395-8, 494.

105   (1958). Unsigned photograph, 23.9 × 17.7 cm, taken by Ingi (professional name of Louis Ingigliardi, 1915-), 1958, Paris.

Acquisition: H. Colin Slim in New York on 3 November 1995 from Wurlitzer-Bruck.

Provenance: An unidentified New York woman who purchased the photograph in November 1994 from the Galerie A l'Image du Grenier sur L'Eau, Paris.

Commentary

This photograph, published in 1994 for an exhibition at the Galerie of Ingi's works, 1955-75, was dated 1958. That year Stravinsky was twice in Paris: 9-20 November and 1 December. Entry 105 was probably taken during his first visit, when he conducted *Threni* (1958) at the Salle Pleyel on 14 November and which he described as the: "unhappiest concert in my life." The back of Entry 105 has in red ink by an unidentified hand "igor strawinsky," and a business stamp: Photo 990-2 / Ingi-Paris / Mention obligatoire / Tous droits réservée.

Louis Ingigliardi, himself a professional cellist in Paris from 1943, began a new career in 1955. Twenty years later he had photographed more than sixty of the most eminent musicians of the third quarter of the twentieth century. Ingi's photographs at the Galerie's 1994 exhibition were priced from 2000 to 8000 francs.

Discussing his ability to delineate a dominant trait of his various subjects' personalities, Jean-Christian Fleury singles out Entry 105 for its "monumentalité d'un Stravinsky vieillissant." The *dossier de presse* of the Galerie notes two photographs of Stravinsky, one, "avec lunettes" and another, "sans lunettes," the latter being Entry 105.

Works Consulted

Ingi. *Photographier la Musique*. ed. Jean-Christian Fleury. Paris: A l'image du Grenier sur l'eau, 1994. pp. 4, 11.

SScrbk. pl. 163 on p. 77, p. 163 (medical diaries: 14 November 1958).

106   (1959). Holograph signed musical quotation, headed THRENI, with inscription, one full side of an unfolded page, 25.6 × 17.8 cm, copied in brown ink on rastrum-drawn staves of four bars (mm. 405-8) from near the close of *Threni* (1958), with pencilled autograph inscription in English at top left, 19 March 1959, to Edward [Elias] Lowinsky (1908-85):

To replace my signatures on my scores
IStr

[music headed] THRENI [and below]
To Edward Lowinsky with sincere and thankful thoughts
IgorStravinsky

Hollywood
March 19, 1956

Acquisition: H. Colin Slim on 29 March 1995 by purchase from Dr. Bonnie J. Blackburn, Oxford, England, widow of Professor Lowinsky. *Provenance:* Edward Elias Lowinsky, Berkeley and Chicago (1959-85); Dr. Bonnie J. Blackburn, Oxford (1985-95).

Commentary

The musical quotation is unpublished as such. Entry 106 has evidently been trimmed at the bottom and perhaps at the sides. Lowinsky's letter of thanks to Stravinsky for it is in the Paul Sacher Foundation.

Stravinsky began composing *Threni* (publ. Boosey and Hawkes, 1958) in a nightclub in the basement of the Bauer-Gruenwald Hotel in Venice on 29 August 1957; a photograph shows him working there on 16 September. About this work (signed on p. 90 of the holograph: "21-III-58"), Lawrence Morton recalls the composer telling many of his friends that "it's a boring piece, *mais très savant.*" The same wording occurs in Morton's papers, in an anecdote dated 17 May 1958. And on 8 May 1958 Morton reports: "After being congratulated by Lawrence Morton on completing Threni, Stravinsky replied: 'I am afraid it is a big bore – but it will be good to bore my enemies'." He was still correcting proofs for *Threni* during August. Photographs survive of him at a *Threni* rehearsal on 2 January 1959 in New York as does one of him and Craft during its rehearsal and another of him following its recording, 5-6 January.

The music quoted in Entry 106 differs in several small respects from pp. 87-8 of the autograph full score copied on sixteen-staved transparencies, which he donated to Oberlin College (24 December 1963); from the second and third sets of proofs donated by Craft to the Library of Congress; and from pp. 68-9 of the 1958 printed edition. On p. 87 of the autograph at Oberlin, Stravinsky numbered mm. 405-7 incorrectly as mm. 390-2, a mistake neither in the edition nor in Entry 106 (which has no measure numbers). The abbreviations for the soloists and their placement at m. 408 above the chorus in Entry 106 correspond to the printed edition (p. 68) rather than to the autograph (p. 88) where he inscribes them on staves below the chorus and above the instruments. Autograph (m. 390 [sic]), proofs, and edition (m. 405) are marked: "Meno mosso," preceding the metronome indication. In Entry 106, however, he omits the former but writes after the latter: "(conclusive chorus)." He also omits the 3/4 metre sign found in both autograph and edition and he reverses note stems in the soprano, m. 406, third beat and in m. 408, first two beats. Diminuendo marks in the chorus are moved between pairs of voices in m. 407 and are entirely lacking at m. 408. The cautionary natural sign within parentheses for the chorus sopranos at m. 408, present both in Entry 106 and in the printed edition, is lacking in the autograph. The "d" of "ad" is missing in both autograph and Entry 106, but is corrected in second and third proofs and, of course, in the edition. Because the first proofs (of 5 May 1958) and the photostat of the autograph corrected by Stravinsky (both also in the Library of Congress) lack the "d" of "ad" and because he added to the photostat in red ink a cautionary natural sign within parentheses for the chorus sopranos at m. 408, it seems probable that the corrected photostat was the source for the music in Entry 106.

Lastly, Stravinsky had to make one correction to an erroneous stemless G he had miscopied in the bass part of the chorus on the first beat of m. 406 (tied from the previous beat) by scraping the G, probably with a razor blade. He drew all the staves with his special stylus, as in entries 7, 48-60, 62, 71, 76, and 115.

Entry 106 testifies to a mutual admiration between him and Lowinsky, the well-known scholar of Renaissance music. At the time, Lowinsky was professor (1956-61) in the Department of Music at the University of California, Berkeley. The circumstances of Stravinsky sending it to Lowinsky in 1959, its correct date rather than his slip of the pen, "1956," and an explanation for the curious pencil annotation at the top of the page about "my signatures on my scores" can be gleaned from five letters in Lowinsky's papers held by the University of Chicago Library. Bonnie J. Blackburn kindly drew the attention of Dr. Slim to them.

On 13 February 1959, Stravinsky thanks Lowinsky for sending him two offprints, and requests a third one. On 21 February Lowinsky sends him the requested offprint, adding: "Should you have a copy to spare of any of your scores I should consider it a real privilege if you wanted to let me have it with you [sic] signature." On 23 February he thanks Lowinsky for a third offprint, writing: "under separate cover I am sending you some of my pocket scores I had at hand." Dating his letter 17 March 1950 (*recte*: 1959), Lowinsky writes: "I thank you warmly for your generous gift of five pocket scores of your compositions. I am only sorry that not a single one of them carried your signature."

But on 31 March 1959, Lowinsky writes Ernst E. Gottlieb in Beverly Hills: "It will please you to hear that Strawinsky after receiving my expression of regret on my not finding his signature on his scores sent me a beautiful leaf containing a chorus from his last work (*Threni*) with a dedication. I am really touched and happy about it." Lowinsky proudly displayed Entry 106 at his home on Spruce Street in Berkeley where Dr. Slim first admired it in the summer of 1961.

In response to Lowinsky's letter of 20 October 1960 concerning his *Tonality and Atonality in Sixteenth-Century Music* (published the following year), Stravinsky wrote a foreword dated "Hollywood, January 27, 1961." It concluded "his method is the only kind of 'writing about music' that I value." (Additional material about this foreword appears in Lowinsky's papers.)

As the Ferdinand Schevill Distinguished Service Professor, Lowinsky was a colleague of Dr. Slim in the Department of Music at the University of Chicago, 1961-65, and again when Dr. Slim returned there as full professor in 1972-73. He was the founder and general editor of the series "Monuments of Renaissance Music." Having edited the first volume of this series, *Musica Nova ... MDXL* (Chicago and London: University of Chicago Press, 1964), Dr. Slim presented it to Stravinsky on 26 January 1966 with a note of appreciation for his music at a break during the final rehearsal in Los Angeles of the Roger Wagner Chorale (which Dr. Slim had just joined) for its concerts with the Los Angeles Philharmonic, led by him and Craft on 27-28 January.

Works Consulted

Brown, Howard Mayer. "Lowinsky." NG. vol. 11. pp. 290-1.

Craft, Robert. "Appendix: Selected Source Material from 'A Catalogue of Books and Music Inscribed to and/or Autographed and Annotated by Igor Stravinsky'." *Confronting Stravinsky: Man, Musician, and Modernist.* ed. Jann Pasler. Berkeley and Los Angeles, CA, and London: University of California Press, 1986. p. 356, nos. 45-6.

—. "Catalog of the Library of Robert Craft." Typescript: Library of Congress, Music Division. IV: Proofs, *Threni*, nos. 26-8.

—. *Stravinsky: Chronicle of a Friendship.* 2nd ed. Nashville, TN, and London: Vanderbilt University Press, 1994. pl. [10, lower] btn pp. 142-3, p. 428.

Lowinsky, Edward E. *Tonality and Atonality in Sixteenth-Century Music.* Berkeley and Los Angeles, CA: University of California Press, 1961; repr. 1962. p. ix.

–. Papers. Box 20. Special Collections. Regenstein Library. The University of Chicago.

Morton, Lawrence. "Stravinsky at Home," *Confronting Stravinsky: Man, Musician, and Modernist*. ed. Jann Pasler. Berkeley and Los Angeles, CA, and London: University of California Press, 1986. p. 345.

–. Papers. Box 85, folder Stravinsky: anecdotes. Special Collections 1522. Charles E. Young Research Library, University of California at Los Angeles.

Stravinsky, Igor. *Threni* autograph. Special Collections. Oberlin College Library, OH.

–. *Threni*. London: Boosey and Hawkes, 1958. p. 68.

SP&D. colour pl. 15 (lower) btn pp. 400-01, pl. on p. 448.

SScrbk. pls. 161-2 on pp. 76-7.

SSC. vol. 3. p. 416.

107

(1959). **Autographed photograph, 37.8 × 29.2 cm, taken by Douglas Glass in Venice, probably in the Hotel Bauer-Gruenwald, 5-23 September 1951, of Stravinsky holding open the piano/vocal score of *The Rake's Progress* at pp. 190-1 and 203, his wristwatch pointing to 11:45, and inscribed in English in brown ink (some fading owing to a faulty pen), 6 November 1959, to Glass:**

To my good friend Douglos Glass
Cordially
I Stravinsky
London Nov. 6/59

Acquisition: H. Colin Slim in New York on 3 November 1995 from Wurlitzer–Bruck.

Provenance: Sotheby's *Continental Manuscripts and Music, Sale LN 5294* (London, 18 May 1995), p. 147, lot 283 (2); it and its companion photograph (Entry 96) sold together.

Commentary

Entry 107 is unpublished. Stravinsky utilizes the tail of *y* in his name to form the *L* of London.

It must have been taken just before or after a virtually identically posed photograph of the composer. This latter photograph, however, lacks his slight smile and reveals less of the turned page 191 of the vocal score than does Entry 107. Lincoln Kirstein attributed this similar photograph in 1957 to "Douglas Glass" and Craft's caption for it in 1972 is "Venice, at the time of *The Rake's Progress,* September 1951. (Photo by Douglas Glass)." Without acknowledging its photographer, Roger Parker captioned this entire image: "Stravinsky at the time of *The Rake's Progress*, leafing through the last act in the vocal score." Here he sits on a settee upholstered in a striped fabric behind which is a curtain, his wristwatch again registering 11:45. The vocal score rests on a highly polished wooden table with scalloped edges. Arriving in Venice on 5 September, he stayed in the Royal Suite of the Hotel Bauer-Gruenwald, departing on the 23rd for Milan.

Glass wrote Stravinsky at Claridge's Hotel in London on 9 December 1958. He had developed films taken that morning and would like him again to visit his studio home for an additional sitting.

The following year Stravinsky was once more in London, this time from 27 October to 9 November to record *Oedipus Rex* with the BBC (broadcast on 9 November). He rehearsed twice on the day that he inscribed Entry 107 for Glass.

In it and in Entry 96 he has the same eyeglasses, wears the same shirt, and holds the piano/vocal score of *The Rake's Progress*. The time on the wristwatch suggests that Glass took Entry 107 in 1951 well over an hour before Entry 96. The reverse side of Entry 107 bears only one business stamp: "Copyright / Douglas Glass, / 43, Black Lion Lane, W.6. / Riverside 7522. / [in ink, no.] 37." Dimensions of c. 55 × 45 cm in Sotheby's sale's catalogue are incorrect.

On 11 December 1959, Glass wrote him in London c/o his publisher, Boosey and Hawkes. Glass hopes the photographs give pleasure, a letter which the composer annotated by hand: "Sent him (Jan 6/60) a visiting card with thanks for his wonderful photos. I.Str."

Works Consulted

Craft, Robert. *Stravinsky: Chronicle of a Friendship*. 2nd ed. Nashville, TN, and London: Vanderbilt University Press, 1994. p. 61; 1st ed. New York: Alfred A. Knopf, 1972. pl. [2]A (cropped at sides and bottom) btn pp. 140-1.

Kirstein, Lincoln. "Pictures from an Album." *High Fidelity* 7 (June, 1957): pl. on p. 36.

Parker, Roger. *The Oxford History of Opera*. Oxford and New York, NY: Oxford University Press, 1994. pl. on p. 322.

SScrbk. p. 166 (medical diaries: November 1959).

SSC. vol. 3. p. 351.

Stuart, Philip. *Igor Stravinsky – The Composer in the Recording Studio. A Comprehensive Discography*. New York, NY, Westport, CT, London: Greenwood Press, 1991. no. L12 on p. 71.

108   (1960). Signed typed singly folded memorandum note, 14.0 × 9.8 cm, in English, printed heading in red: DON'T FORGET, with autograph: 29 April 1960, in red ink, to Broude Brothers:

Dear Sirs,
Under separate cover, I am sending you back KRENEK,E.
Ton[typed over: Mod]al Contrapoint in style of 18th Century.
Your catalogue #270 – Please credit it to me and mail me
KRENEK,E. Mod[typed over Ton]al Countrapoint in style
of 16th Century.
    Yours truly

[in red ink] I Stravinsky
[blue stamp]1260 North Wetherly Drive
Hollywood 46, California
[in red ink] Apr 29 / 60

[typed at lower left]
ALEXANDER BROUDE
130 W. 57 Street
NewYork 19, NY

Acquisition: H. Colin Slim in New York on 23 September 1994 from Wurlitzer-Bruck.
Provenance: Unknown; probably Alexander Broude.

Commentary

The note is unpublished, its envelope missing. The peculiar orthography, corrections, and hyphenation suggest Stravinsky himself at the typewriter rather than a secretary, as does also the consistent and correct use in entries 102 and 104 of "l" for the numeral "1," rather than "I" (as elsewhere), both surely typed by him.

Tonal Counterpoint by Ernst Krenek (1900–91) was published in 1958, his *Modal Counterpoint* the following year, both by Boosey and Hawkes. Evidently the desired volume arrived quickly, for he signed and dated his requested copy of *Modal Counterpoint*: "I Str May 1960." He had studied counterpoint with pleasure from about 1900, as he observed in *Chroniques de ma vie*.

First meeting Krenek at Nice in 1925, Stravinsky renewed the friendship around 1950, Craft noting that Krenek was the sole Los Angeles composer who interested him (but see Entry 77: Tansman in 1946). In 1962, Stravinsky acknowledged that "Krenek's [*Studies in Counterpoint Based on the Twelve-Tone Technique* (New York, NY: G. Schirmer, 1940)] was the first work I read on that subject."

Works Consulted

Craft, Robert. "Appendix: Selected Source Material from 'A Catalogue of Books and Music Inscribed to and/or Autographed and Annotated by Igor Stravinsky'." *Confronting Stravinsky: Man, Musician, and Modernist*. ed. Jann Pasler. Berkeley and Los Angeles, CA, and London: University of California Press, 1986. p. 355, no. 34.

Stravinsky, Igor, and Robert Craft. "Some Composers." *Musical America* 82, 6 (June 1962): p. 8.

SChron. vol. 1. pp. 33-4.

SD. p. 103.

SD&D. p. 52.

SSC. vol. 2. pp. 325-46.

109

(1960). **Autographed first edition of miniature score, 18.8 × 13.6 cm, IGOR STRAVINSKY / MONUMENTUM / pro / Gesualdo di Venosa / ad CD annum / *Three Madrigals* / *recomposed for instruments* / (London, Paris, Bonn, Capetown, Sydney, Toronto, Buenos Aires, New York: Boosey and Hawkes, 1960), 15 pp., inscribed in blue ink, October 1960, to Virgil Thomson (1896-1989). The score's cover bears an embossed stamp: Virgil Thomson Collections [surrounding] RVTI.**

To Vergil Thomson
with my affectionate thoughts

I Stravinsky
[wavy underscoring] Venezia
Oct/60

Acquisition: H. Colin Slim in Los Angeles on 26 September 1999 from La Scala Autographs.
Provenance: Unidentified collector, summer 1999.

Commentary

After Stravinsky conducted the premiere of *Monumentum* in the voting hall of the ducal palace on 27 September 1960, he and his wife remained in Venice at the Hotel Bauer-Gruenwald during October and early November. Thomson's review of 2 October in the *New York Times,* "Stravinsky – Gesualdo," observes that "these madrigals have come alive more vividly than they could ever possibly do in their vocal form." Thomson's diary (now at Yale's Gilmore Music Library) shows that he left Venice the day after the premiere for Paris where he apparently stayed through December. Stravinsky may have mailed the inscribed score to him there, perhaps after having been apprised of or having seen the *Times* review.

Thomson could first have met him in Paris during the 1920s, perhaps through Cocteau, Boulanger, Antheil, or the Princesse de Polignac, even though the editors of Thomson's letters do not mention Stravinsky as then in his "musical orbit." Early in 1925, before moving to Paris that September, Thomson had written about Stravinsky, Schoenberg, and Satie for *Vanity Fair*.

With the rapid advance of the Germans on Paris, Thomson left for New York in mid-August 1940, returning five years later. During the war Stravinsky saw him in New York and Los Angeles. Upon the death of Thomson's father in April 1943, Stravinsky (recalling the centenary of his own father) sent a note of consolation to Thomson, who visited his colleague in Los Angeles in July 1943. Stravinsky lunched with him in New York near the end of February 1945 and just a month before returning to France, Thomson twice visited Stravinsky in California.

Although he observed in 1947 that: "Thomson is the only critic clever enough always to avoid discussing music" (an inaccurate evaluation), they remained friends, Thomson writing in 1966: "for twenty years we saw each other joyfully – in New York, Hollywood, Venice, wherever we were." For instance, Stravinsky rightly intervened on Craft's behalf with a letter to Thomson on 12 April 1948 (published thereafter in the *New York Herald Tribune*), attended a performance in Denver on 24 July 1948 of Thomson's opera, *The Mother of Us All*, invited Thomson to a post-concert reception on 19 February 1949, and first met Pierre Boulez at Thomson's New York apartment in December 1952. During the period in which Thomson reviewed for the *New York Herald Tribune* (1940-54), he often wrote about works by Stravinsky, many of these reviews and later ones being reprinted in Thomson's books. In March 1960 Stravinsky lunched at home with the loquacious Thomson, whom Vera described as "very brilliant, but ... like a lecture." Arnold Weissberger, lawyer to both composers, photographed them together at his apartment in New York in the summer of 1962 on the occasion of eightieth birthday celebrations for Stravinsky.

The small initials RI flanking VT in Thomson's library stamp in Entry 109 are those of the artist, Robert Indiana (1928-). Subject of a piano portrait by Thomson in 1966, he designed productions for *The Mother of Us All* at Minneapolis in 1971 and at Santa Fe in 1976.

"Rehearsal here of Gesualdo madrigals": so wrote Vera in her diary for 6 September 1954, with a similar notation on the 18th. Both were Craft's rehearsals for a Monday Evening Concert two days later, which included a group of madrigals conducted by him. Stimulated by studying and hearing these works, Stravinsky completed three motets by Gesualdo between 1957 and 1959, also visiting in the latter year the composer's castle in Gesualdo. In 1962 he noted: "The idea of composing instrumental translations of Gesualdo madrigals occurred to me as far back as 1954." By February 1960 he had chosen three, on 1 March he told Craft he had completed a *Gesualdo Monumentum,* and on 28 March he wrote his publisher: "I just finished to recompose three Gesualdo madrigals for instruments." He also told Craft that "it's the most difficult thing he ever did." Shortly after recording them on 9 June, he received the first proofs for their edition. Craft's crucial role in the *Monumentum* is emphasized by the manuscript dedication in the first edition to him.

The final page of Entry 109 is dated by its engraver: "8 60," whereas the same page of Dr. Slim's copy (bought in Chicago, September 1962) reads: "12 61" and replaces "Capetown" on the title page of Entry 109 by "Johannesburg." Between the two editions, however, there are no changes in musical content.

Richard Boursy, archivist of the Gilmore Music Library at Yale University, kindly provided information concerning Thomson's whereabouts in the fall of 1960.

Works Consulted

Craft, Robert. *Stravinsky: Chronicle of a Friendship.* 2nd ed. Nashville, TN, and London: Vanderbilt University Press, 1994. p. 233 (27 September 1960).

–. *Prejudices in Disguise.* New York, NY: Alfred A. Knopf, 1974. p. 209.

Crawford, Dorothy Lamb. *Evenings On and Off the Roof: Pioneering Concerts in Los Angeles, 1939-1971.* Berkeley and Los Angeles, CA, and London: University of California Press, 1995. pl. 6 btn pp. 92-3, pp. 149-50, 158-9.

Heyworth, Peter. "Profiles (Pierre Boulez – II)." *The New Yorker* 49 (31 March 1973): 45.

Page, Tim, and Vanessa Weeks Page, ed. *Selected Letters of Virgil Thomson.* New York, London, Toronto, Sydney, Tokyo: Summit Books, 1988. pp. 51, 67-8, n. on p. 350, 354, 390 (14 May 1982).

SBu. pp. 128 (18 July 1943), 132 (24 February 1945), 133 (28 June and 4 July 1945), 175, 194 (22 March 1960), 201.

SE&D. pp. 118-20.

SP&D. pp. 391, 457.

SScrbk. pls. 126-33 on pp. 60-3, pls. 185-6 on pp. 88-9.

SSC. vol. 1. pp. 340, 343; vol. 3. pp. 326, 423-5.

Stuart, Philip. *Igor Stravinsky – The Composer in the Recording Studio. A Comprehensive Discography*. New York, NY, Westport, CT, London: Greenwood Press, 1991. p. 41, no. 94.

Thomson, Virgil. *The Art of Judging Music*. New York, NY: Alfred A. Knopf, 1948. passim.

–. "How Modern Music Gets That Way: Some Notes on Stravinsky, Schoenberg, and Satie, as Representative Moderns." *Vanity Fair* 24, 2 (April 1925): 46, 102.

–. *Music Right and Left*. New York, NY: Holt, 1951. passim, but esp. pp. 139-42.

–. *The Musical Scene*. New York, NY: Alfred A. Knopf, 1945. passim.

–. "Stravinsky-Gesualdo." *New York Times*. 2 October 1960. section 2, p. 11X.

–. *Virgil Thomson*. New York, NY: Alfred A. Knopf, 1966. pp. 356-7, 384, 402-4, pl. facing p. [407].

Tommasini, Anthony. *Virgil Thomson: Composer on the Aisle*. New York and London: W.W. Norton, 1997. p. 518.

Watkins, Glenn. "The Canon and Stravinsky's Late Style." *Confronting Stravinsky: Man, Musician, and Modernist*. ed. Jann Pasler. Berkeley and Los Angeles, CA, and London: University of California Press, 1986. n. 12 on p. 235.

Weissberger, L. Arnold. *Famous Faces: A Photograph Album of Personal Reminiscences*. New York, NY: H.N. Abrams, 1973. colour pl. c on p. 84.

110   (1962). Customer or file copy of a Western Union Telegram, 15.4 × 21.0 cm, from Stravinsky in Hamburg, [18 June 1962], to the editor of the now defunct *New York Herald Tribune*:

RCA POSN 6l
TRIBUNE 224352

HBL 88
HAMBURG 57 l8 0219

EDITOR NEWYORK HERALD TRIBUNE NEWYORK

LETTERS TO EDITOR OF HUNDREDS OF REVIEWS OF
MY NEW WORK MOST OF THEM LIKE EVERY OPUS
SINCE l905 GRATIFYINGLY UNFAVORABLE I FIND

ONLY YOURS ENTIRELY STUPID AND SUPPURATING
WITH GRATUITOUS MALICE THE ONLY BLIGHT ON
MY EIGHTIETH BIRTHDAY IS REALIZATION MY AGE
WILL PROBABLY KEEP ME FROM CELEBRATING THE
FUNERAL OF YOUR SENILE MUSIC COLUMNIST

Igor Stravinsky

COL 1905
FX 1155P

Acquisition: by kind gift to H. Colin Slim on 1 March 1995 from Marianne Wurlitzer and Gene Bruck on the occasion of their visit to Laguna Beach.
Provenance: Unknown.

Commentary

An almost identical version was published in the *New York Herald Tribune* on 24 June 1962. Stravinsky's "NEW WORK" was *The Flood* (1962) at its CBS television premiere, 14 June 1962. Interviewed a year later for *The Irish Times*, Stravinsky paraphrased Entry 110.

Though hardly "SENILE," the "MUSIC COLUMNIST" was Paul Henry Lang (1901-91), who in fact did outlive him by two decades. One of three critics, Lang had reviewed its score on 15 June 1962 for the same newspaper. Among Lang's remarks that presumably irritated Stravinsky were:

'Noah' is far from being a major, or even a significant, work. In his patriarchal old age Mr. Stravinsky's once flaming temperament expunges all emotional violence and almost all uninhibited movement from his music and softens even his solemnity into a mood that, in the vocal pieces, I suppose represents Christian musing. Mr. Stravinsky is not a dour decaphonist by nature, nor indeed by grace; compared to other living practitioners of the 'system' he is a Bohemian, and though reformed and under discipline, his glorious past is there.

Lang then implies that the *Flood*'s music cannot match that found in such mystery plays as *The Play of Daniel*. He observes that any comparison of him with Monteverdi as theatre composers in their old ages cannot be sustained.

The review is also condescending in tone: "The best numbers are the tiny overture, and such self-contained pieces as 'the Building of the Ark'. The opening Te Deum is also impressive, as is the very short closing Sanctus, and the two–part vocal interludes are vaguely medieval-sounding but monotonous." These remarks followed the preceding day's issue of a full-page advertisement for the premiere of *The Flood,* its upper photograph showing Stravinsky conducting and a lower one Balanchine's dancers.

Lillian Libman (1912-92), then Stravinsky's personal manager and press representative from 1959 until his death, chronicled his anger in Hamburg and posited Craft's role in the telegram. *The New York Herald Tribune* printed Entry 110 (though not in upper case) in the middle of Lang's remarks: "Stravinsky Aims, Fires." Several editorial changes were made to Entry 110: "York" was inserted between "NEW" and "WORK"; "were" was added to precede "GRATIFYINGLY"; a period followed "UNFAVORABLE"; and "found" replaced "FIND." Lang also continued his attack: "The Flood was nothing but a slight *pièce d'occasion* imbedded in a television medley both silly and artificial."

Lang's essay published two weeks later, "Stravinsky: A New Appraisal of his Work," could hardly have altered the judgement expressed in Entry 110. Stravinsky had already castigated Lang as "H.P. Langweilich" in a scathing analytical essay written in 1960: "Slightly More of a Plague on One of Their Houses (A Comparison of Two Critics)."

Works Consulted

Iams, Jack, Paul Henry Lang, and Walter Terry. "'Noah and the Flood' – Story, Music and Dance." *New York Herald Tribune*. 15 June 1962. p. 15.

Lang, Paul Henry. "Stravinsky: A New Appraisal of his Work." *The Musical Quarterly* 48 (1962): 362-91.

Libman, Lillian. *And Music at the Close: Stravinsky's Last Years, A Personal Memoir*. New York, NY: W.W. Norton, 1972. pp. 172-3.

New York Herald Tribune. 14 June 1962. p. 22 (full-page advertisement for *The Flood*).

SE&D. (1962) pp. 170-9.

SI&V. caption to pl. 243 on p. [136].

111 (1962). **Twelve unsigned photographs, each 17.0 × 12.1 cm, taken within the orchestra by Fred Fehl (1906-95) from 10 a.m. on 11 (or 12) July 1962, of Stravinsky rehearsing his** *Firebird Suite* **outdoors with members of the New York Philharmonic at Lewisohn Stadium, New York.**

Acquisition: H. Colin Slim on 5 June 1995 from Wurlitzer-Bruck.
Provenance: Mr. and Mrs. Fred Fehl, 415 West 115th Street, New York (1962-95).

Commentary
Fred Fehl's unpublished photographs in Entry 111 are framed in the numerical (and presumably chronological) order in which he took them. His pencilled numbers on the back of the twelve photographs are: 6230; 6320-22; 6324-26; 6329-30; 6332; and 6337-38.

Four photographs taken from the left side of Stravinsky have Fehl's pencilled numbers and his dates on their reverse sides: 6230 (1962), 6329-30 (1960), and 6332 (1960). Eight others taken from his right side bear pencilled numbers and dates on their reverse sides: 6320 (1960), 6321 (1962), 6322 (1960), 6324-25 (1960), 6326 (1962), and 6337-38 (1960), the latter pair also including a standing Craft and Libman. Reports about the four-hour rehearsal and subsequent concert on 12 July note that Libman was present.

Although Fehl obviously took them all on the same occasion, his several later(?) pencilled dates of 1960 reveal confusion. Stravinsky did not conduct at Lewisohn Stadium in 1960. Unfortunately, illness and then death prevented Fehl from clarifying this matter, but his widow and Marianne Wurlitzer and Gene Bruck have provided helpful information as to locale and date.

The program for 12 July 1962 was *Fireworks* led by Craft, and *Scherzo à la Russe*, *Scherzo fantastique*, and *The Firebird Suite*. Stravinsky conducted the latter three; after intermission Craft led the *The Rite of Spring*. An estimated 11 000 persons heard this concert. A photograph by Allyn Baum of the composer in white jacket conducting *The Firebird Suite* is included in a review by Raymond Ericson who reported: "He got the Stadium Symphony to play with the kind of precision and clarity of ensemble that gave the music an unaccustomed dryness that points up all the beautiful details of the scoring."

The music for violin 1 on the stand in photograph 6332 (decipherable by enlarging that area of the photograph) is the opening page of *The Firebird Suite*, one measure before rehearsal **3** in the 1919 and 1945 editions. Probably Stravinsky used the latter because a letter to his lawyer, Arnold Weissberger, in 1961 concerning royalties due him states in part: "I have myself played *The Firebird Suite* many times

(I never play the old version)." A photograph shows him studying a score at Lewisohn Stadium on 11 July (probably listening to Craft rehearse) and an account reveals what he owed the younger man for his share in conducting.

Born in Vienna 21 January 1906, Fehl was photographing by 1935 such conductors at Salzburg as Furtwängler, Walter, Klemperer, and Toscanini. Fehl fled Austria in 1938, lived briefly in London early in 1939, and then emigrated to New York that September. There he was a photographer, 1940-80, of professional musicians, dancers, and actors. One of his photographs, signed "Fehl," of the 1970 New York City Ballet production of *The Firebird* choreographed by Balanchine is in Paris, at the Bibliothèque Nationale, Opéra. Fehl died on 5 October 1995. Mary Clarke's obituary calls him: "the outstanding theater photographer of his time and a pioneer, above all, of what he called 'performance photography'."

He published four books of his photographs: *On Broadway* (Austin, TX: University of Texas Press, 1978); *Giselle & Albrecht* (New York, NY: Dance Horizons, 1981); *Stars of the Broadway Stage 1940-1967* (New York, NY: Dover, 1983); and *Stars of the American Ballet Theatre* (New York, NY: Dover, 1984), the first two containing extensive biographical information about him. From Fehl's archive of more than 100 000 photographs the Library of the Performing Arts in Lincoln Center honoured him in 1976 with an exhibition of 450 images and again in 1991.

Apart from such compelling visual evidence as Entry 111, the finest evocation of Stravinsky conducting at this period is a description by Paul Horgan of a rehearsal in Houston on Friday morning, 3 January 1958.

Works Consulted

Anderson, Jack. "Fred Fehl, 89, Whose Camera Captured Broadway and Ballet." *New York Times*. 6 October 1995. p. A21 with photograph of Fehl in 1977.

Clarke, Mary. "Fred Fehl. Capturing the Moment." *Manchester Guardian*. 7 October 1995. p. 32 with photograph.

Craft, Robert. *Stravinsky: Chronicle of a Friendship*. New York, NY: Alfred A. Knopf, 1972. pl. [1]A facing p. 300. [First edition; not in 2nd ed. Nashville, TN, and London: Vanderbilt University Press, 1994.]

Ericson, Raymond. "Stravinsky at the Stadium." *New York Times*. 13 July 1962. ill. on p. 11.

Horgan, Paul. *Encounters with Stravinsky: A Personal Record*. New York, NY: Farrar, Straus and Giroux. 1972. pp. 104-9.

Lesure, François. *Igor Stravinsky. La carrière européenne*. Paris: Musée d'Art Moderne, 1980. p. 29, no. 76.

Muns, J.B. *Musical Autographs List 00-5*. Berkeley, 2000, no. 59.

SBu. p. 210 (12 July 1962).

SScrbk. pl. 233 (item 6) on p. 113.

112

(1963). Autographed book (with original wrappers), 21.3 × 15.2 cm, IGOR STRAWINSKY / Eine Sendereihe des Westdeutschen Rundfunks zum 80. Geburtstag / mit [13] Beiträgen von / Pierre Boulez Jean Cocteau /... / Pierre Souvtchinsky Roman Vlad / Herausgegeben von Otto Tomek / (Cologne: Westdeutscher Rundfunk, 1963), 86 pp. with 10 pls., inscribed on the front free endpaper in English in blue ink, 1963, to Dr. Max[imilian] Edel (1906-91):

To Dr Max Edel
affectionately
IStravinsky
1963

Acquisition: H. Colin Slim at Goleta on 5 March 1997 through Martin A. Silver from Kenneth Karmiole Books.

Provenance: Unknown; possibly Mrs. Edel (417 S. Holt Avenue / Los Angeles) who died in 1998.

Commentary

Celebrating the composer's eightieth birthday the previous year, Entry 112 contains essays in German by Cocteau, Curjel, Kirchmeyer, Lindlar, von Milloss, Ruppel, Schrade, Schubert, Souvtchinsky, and Vlad. It concludes with a three-way discussion among Boulez, Sacher, and Schuh.

Arriving in New York in 1939, Dr. Maximilian Edel was licensed in 1945 to practise medicine in California. He was physician to Stravinsky and Vera from 1947 until dismissed by her on 27 December 1967. Introduced to them by their neighbour, Baroness Catherine d'Erlanger (c.1880-1959) on North Wetherly Drive, Edel – whose office was at 360 North Bedford Street, Beverly Hills – sometimes travelled with them. Craft noted that of some eighty-four visits Edel made to their home: "more than a third were social." Even after their rupture, Stravinsky was moved on 25 August 1968 to shake hands with him:

> The doctor was Viennese, and five minutes with him exposed a brilliant and cultured mind, which thoroughly encompassed fields of study other than medicine. He spoke fluent French and English as well as German, using the latter language frequently in his talks with Stravinsky, who regarded him, as did Mrs. Stravinsky, with great affection. His conversations dealt with music, art, literature, psychology; and in this last field he excelled in handling his patient, for he recognized and understood the complete hypochondria of the man, and did not treat it lightly. In my opinion, he was far and away the best of the doctors who treated Stravinsky, at least during my association [1959-71] with the composer. And like the greatest of his professional brethren, he was human.

So stated Libman, whose knowledge of Edel, however, Craft disputes.

Also a capable sculptor, Edel began sketching the composer on 24 April 1960 for a bronze head completed in 1961 which Stravinsky eventually placed on top of a glass-enclosed book cabinet in his studio. Photographs were taken of it there in 1966 and it is also illustrated on CBS recordings made in honour of the composer's eightieth birthday. Surviving Stravinsky by some twenty years, Edel died 3 September 1991, although, confusingly enough, the 1992 and the 1994 AMA *Directory* still report him those years as in practice and inactive, respectively.

Works Consulted

Directory of Physicians in the United States. 33rd ed. Chicago: American Medical Association, 1992. vol. 2. p. 2274; 34th ed. 1994. vol. 2. p. 2261.

"Edel, Dr. Maximilian." *Los Angeles Times.* 9 September 1991. p. A22 (death notice).

Howell, Betje. "Twelve California Sculptors." *American Artist* 32 (May 1968): 27 (photograph of Edel), 73.

Libman, Lillian. *And Music at the Close: Stravinsky's Last Years, A Personal Memoir.* New York, NY: W.W. Norton, 1972. p. 312.

Newman, Arnold, and Robert Craft. *Bravo Stravinsky.* Cleveland, OH, and New York, NY: World, 1967. pls. on pp. [5], 49.

SBu. pp. 142 (2 October 1947), 194 (31 December 1959), n. 7 on p. 225, n. 5 on p. 227.

SP&D. pp. 578-9.

SScrbk. p. 156 (medical diaries).

ST&C. p. 300.

Stravinsky and the Theatre. New York, NY: Public Library, 1963, item 36 (Edel's bronze head) ill. on p. 48, p. 51.

Stuart, Philip. *Igor Stravinsky – The Composer in the Recording Studio. A Comprehensive Discography.* New York, NY, Westport, CT, London: Greenwood Press, 1991. p. 18.

113

(1964). Signed carbon typescript, 27.8 × 21.6 cm, in English in blue ink, of a legal agreement with Paul Kohner, Inc. of Los Angeles drawn up 27 April 1964 for Stravinsky by William D. Montapert (1930-):

April 27, 1964

Paul Kohner, Inc.,
9169 Sunset Boulevard
Los Angeles, California

Gentlemen:

This will confirm our understanding with reference to the matters herein contained.

IT IS HEREBY AGREED AS FOLLOWS:

1. I hereby represent that you acted as my exclusive agent in procuring employment for me with Dino De Laurentiis

Cinematografica, SPA, covering my services as composer and conductor of music in the motion picture (hereinbelow called "motion picture"), entitled "The Bible".

2. In consideration of your services as set forth above, I agree to pay to you a sum equal to ten percent (10%) of all salary ~~and other compensation~~ [crossed out in blue ink] received by me for my services in said motion picture, the same to be paid to you as and when said salary and other compensation is paid to me.

[initialled by hand in right margin] IS PK

If the foregoing is in accordance with our understanding please indicate your approval and consent thereto by signing the copy of this letter.

Very truly yours,
[in blue ink] Igor Stravinsky
[rule added by hand above typed] IGOR STRAVINSKY

APPROVED AND CONSENTED TO:
PAUL KOHNER, INC.
By [in blue ink on typed rule] Paul Kohner

Acquisition: H. Colin Slim on 16 January 1997 from Kenneth W. Rendell Gallery, New York.
Provenance: Unknown; perhaps either from the files of Kohner (1902-88) and Dr. Felix Guggenheim in Los Angeles after Kohner's death, or from the Newport Beach investment office of lawyer William David Montapert, the latter a self-styled "recognized expert in the field of art and collectibles." Entry 113, bearing some now illegible erased pencil markings at the upper left, was framed not earlier than c. 1989 by Rendell together with an early photograph of Stravinsky. The original mat had at the top: "~~O'Brien~~ Stravinsky" and below it: "8510 ~~O'Brien~~ Stravinsky," possibly a previous owner's or a dealer's mark.

Commentary

The document is unpublished, its paper watermarked: Erasable Bond. Entry 113 was originally framed with a slightly enlarged copy, 14.7 × 9.5 cm, made c. 1989 by Crossing Cards from the New York Public Library exemplar of the same photograph from 1911 cited in Entry 2.

Stravinsky signed Entry 113 in Hollywood, Kohner later dining with him and Vera there on 14 July 1964. A well-known Hollywood theatrical and film agent, Kohner had hanging on his office wall, c. 1975, an inscribed photograph of Stravinsky.

Although Libman states she was involved in these negotiations, Craft denied it in 1978. According to him, Stravinsky was interested by Kohner and [Dr. Felix] Guggenheim for two reasons: the project would be non-taxable and he need write no new music. Lawyer Montapert (employed 1959–mid-1969) did draw up a contract, which surprised de Laurentiis who apparently had made no proposal.

Craft's account is amplified by two letters Stravinsky sent from Hollywood and Craft's own footnote in his edition of them. Stravinsky wrote on 5 August 1964 from Hollywood to Rufina Vsevolodovna Ampenoff, his representative at and a member of the board of directors at Boosey and Hawkes in London, of an offer made to him in Rome to write music for a film. Two days later he wrote to her that he had turned down the project because he knew that it would only cause him distress, musical and otherwise. Craft's footnote to the former letter relates that de Laurentiis wanted his music for *The Bible*.

Entry 113 thus documents the last of his many failed attempts to make the Hollywood film industry come to terms with him, beginning with his first visits there in 1935 and 1937.

Works Consulted

Craft, Robert. *Stravinsky: Glimpses of a Life*. London: Lime Tree, 1992; New York, NY: St. Martin's Press, 1993. p. 145, n. 38 on pp. 190-1.

Dahl, Ingolf. "Stravinsky on Film Music." *Cinema* 1 (June 1947): 7-8, 21.

Kohner, Frederick. *The Magician of Sunset Boulevard: The Improbable Life of Paul Kohner, Hollywood Agent*. Palos Verdes, CA: Morgan Press, 1977. pl. [12] btn pp. 86-7.

"Kohner, Frederick." *Los Angeles Times*. 18 March 1988. pt. 1, p. 26 (obituary).

"Kohner, Frederick." *New York Times*. 19 March 1988. pt. 1, p. 13 (obituary).

Libman, Lillian. *And Music at the Close: Stravinsky's Last Years, A Personal Memoir*. New York, NY: W.W. Norton, 1972. pp. 177–8.

Montapert, William David. *The Omega Strategy: How You Can Retire Rich by 1986*. Santa Barbara: Capra Press, 1982. p. 255.

Morton, L. "Stravinsky in Los Angeles." *Festival of Music Made in Los Angeles*. ed. Orrin Howard. Los Angeles: Philharmonic Association, 1981. p 80.

Rosar, William H. "Stravinsky and MGM." *Film Music 1*. ed. Clifford McCarty. New York, NY, and London: Garland, 1989. pp. 108–22, esp. n. 20.

SP&D. p. 591.

SScrbk. p. 163 (medical diaries: 17 February 1959).

SSC. vol. 3. p. 449 and n. 57.

114

(1965). Autographed photograph, 10.0 × 15.2 cm (including margins), taken by Don Hunstein for Columbia Records in 1957 (probably January), of Stravinsky in a recording studio studying music, inscribed in English in black ink on lower margin, 1965, to Marshall E. Bean:

To Marshall E. Bean
Igor Stravinsky
1965

Acquisition: H. Colin Slim in New York on 23 September 1994 from Wurlitzer-Bruck.
Provenance: Unknown.

Commentary

By the time Stravinsky inscribed Entry 114, he had moved (in September 1964) from 1260 to 1218 North Wetherly Drive, Hollywood. A copy of the photograph is in the Paul Sacher Foundation, attributed there to Don Hunstein, 1957. Entry 114, which has been cropped at the left, is identical to a photograph on the cover of a seventy-fifth birthday tribute in the June 1957 issue of *High Fidelity*. It appears two years later on the front dust jacket of the Stravinsky-Craft *Conversations*, credited on its back dust jacket, "Courtesy Columbia Records." (On the marketing of this book, see Entry 104.)

Entry 114 is also the same image in a photograph he inscribed in Russian, c. 1962, to his niece Kseniya Yuryevna and, in yet another one, he signed and dated 1965 (listed by Gary Combs in his 1995 catalogue). An uncropped reproduction of the photograph, which depicts at the left a young woman looking upward, is in the booklet to the compact disc edition of Stravinsky recordings. The recording studio in Entry 114 is probably that of CBS on East 30th Street, New York, an extant photograph depicting him emerging from it on 5 January 1959 (although the photographer on this occasion was not Hunstein).

Another photograph of Stravinsky is credited to Don Hunstein and reproduced on the back cover of the LP recording of *Perséphone* made on 14 January 1957 (issued the following October). It shows him in the same jacket, wearing the same glasses, and the background has the same studio equipment, its light switches identically activated.

The brevity of the inscription in Entry 114 does not suggest any personal acquaintance. The dedicatee remains unidentified, perhaps related to Hugh Bean, concertmaster of London's Philharmonia Orchestra and of the New Philharmonia, c. 1963-73, or to Miss Betty Bean of Boosey and Hawkes's New York office, often corresponding, 1946-52, with Stravinsky.

Works Consulted

Combs, Gary E. *Catalogue.* New York, 1995, item 122 on p. 45.

Sony Records. *Igor Stravinsky 1882-1971. The Edition* (c. 1992), pl. on p. 191 in booklet.

Stravinskaya, Kseniya Yuryevna. *O I.F. Stravinskom i evo blizkikh.* [I.F. Stravinsky and his intimates.] Leningrad: Muzïka, 1978. pl. on p. 94.

"Stravinsky 75th birthday issue." *High Fidelity* 7 (June 1957): photo on cover.

SConv. photo on front dust jacket.

SP&D. pl. on p. 448.

SSC. vol. 3. pp. 312-64.

Stuart, Philip. *Igor Stravinsky – The Composer in the Recording Studio. A Comprehensive Discography.* New York, NY, Westport, CT, London: Greenwood Press, 1991. p. 39 (CBS Studio).

115 (1966). Autograph signed untitled musical quotation on cardboard of the first six notes from the "Introduction" to *The Firebird* using his rastrum for the stave, with an inscription in English in black ink below a likeness of Stravinsky's head in pencil, red Conté crayon and black ink, signed "B," overall 33.2 × 24.7 cm, inscribed October 1966 for E. Maurice Bloch (1915-89):

with best wishes
to E. Maurice Bloch
Igor Stravinsky
Oct/66

Acquisition: On 10 June 1996 from Lisa Cox, bidding for H. Colin Slim at Sotheby's, *Important Printed and Manuscript Music, Books on Music and Continental Manuscripts Sale LN6286* (London, 15 May 1996), lot 511. *Provenance*: E. Maurice Bloch, 1966-89.

Commentary

The painting by Bloch, who twice initialled "B" in pencil and then erased these initials below the present "B," is unpublished. A distinguished art historian and collector, Bloch was professor, 1956-83, and curator of the Grunwald Center for Graphics, University of California, Los Angeles. An auction by Christie's at New York in 1990 included two pencil-watercolors on paper signed by him and the preface to Christie's catalogue contains a fine memorial by Bloch's student, Joyce Treiman.

Bloch himself, interviewed in 1987 at the University by Bernard Galm, recalled that already as a high-school student: "I also began to do drawings of celebrities, most of them based on secondary materials I could find and bring together and create from that original portraits. I would then send them to them, or try to meet them, and have them autograph or approve them." He then mentioned portraits he did of writers and musicians:

[Bloch:] – those are among the literary people. Some of these are still in this collection I still have. Where it will go I don't know. It's become a rather valuable collection, but a rather private thing. We have never exhibited any of it. And then in music, beginning with people like Rachmaninoff, Paderewski, Toscanini, Stokowski – I could go right on.

[Galm:] Did they also sign them?

[Bloch:] Oh, absolutely. Arnold Schoenberg [1874-1951] (whose name, really I only came in closer contact with when I came here [in 1956 to Los Angeles] because I know people related to him here) with a great big bar of music, rather stunning. And Stravinsky more than once.

For example, Bloch's drawing of Arturo Toscanini (1867-1957) signed by the conductor was offered for sale by David Schulson in 1996.

Although the 1990 appraisal report of Bloch's estate does not identify Entry 115, it notes: "With the ephemera and autograph collection Mr. Bloch was breaking new ground. Clearly he was an autograph collector in the traditional sense and his own artwork of portraits of artists and statesmen bears this out ... and many of the autographs are personally inscribed to Bloch."

Whether Bloch was acquainted with Stravinsky remains unknown as does the precise day in October that he inscribed Entry 115 for Bloch. Perhaps he did so after returning to Los Angeles on the 12th from New York and after his recovery from influenza, which struck him the following day. On 20 October, for instance, he inscribed the beginning of *The Rite of Spring* for Craft's birthday.

When autographing, he often penned the opening notes of *The Firebird*, for example: in 1933 below his photograph, offered at a Sotheby's auction, London, 1 December 1995, lot 354; on a 1935 photograph of him by Edward Weston offered by Kenneth W. Rendell in May 1996 and again in July and December 1998; and in the celebrated example of 1921 for Vera Sudeykina, later "decorated" by her husband (about which see Entry 18).

Works Consulted

Ars Libri Ltd. *Kindred Spirits. The E. Maurice Bloch Collection of Manuscripts, Letters and Sketchbooks of American Artists ... Catalogue 87.* Boston, 1992.

Christie's. *American and European Works on Paper From the Estate of E. Maurice Bloch, Part 1.* New York, 19 June 1990. preface and lots 253-4.

Craft, Robert. *Stravinsky: Chronicle of a Friendship.* 2nd ed. Nashville, TN, and London: Vanderbilt University Press, 1994. pl. [9] btn pp. 302-3.

Escher, Nancy, ed. *The estate of E. Maurice Bloch appraisal report: Collection of books, ephemera, files; date of evaluation: November 29, 1990.* Beverly Hills, CA: Nancy Escher, 1990. pp. 3, 6.

Galm, Bernard. *Collector and Connoisseur E. Maurice Bloch.* University of California at Los Angeles, CA. 1991. vol. 1. pp. 12-14.

Schulson, David. *Catalog 87.* New York, November 1996, item 129 on p. 57.

SBu. p. 222 (13 October 1966).

116   (1966). Autographed photograph, 23.9 × 13.8 cm, taken in 1965 by Roddy McDowall (1928-98), in English in black ink, 1966, to Arthur Mourcale. The back of the photograph is stamped: "Photo by Roddy McDowall 300 Central Park West New York 24, New York."

To Arthur Mourcale
Sincerely
IStravinsky
1966

Acquisition: H. Colin Slim on 1 May 1995 from J. and J. Lubrano.
Provenance: "Bill" (16 November 1966); an unidentified female dealer in Connecticut (c. 1993).

Commentary

The photograph and its accompanying letter are unpublished. The dedicatee remains unidentified – his name might also be read as "Morncale" or even "Monreale" – as does the day and month Stravinsky wrote the inscription. Although there is no compelling reason to assume he inscribed Entry 116 in Los Angeles, perhaps he did so shortly before departing for Honolulu on 12 November 1966.

The photograph is accompanied by a folded typed letter on embossed stationery, 19.8 × 12.3 cm, lettered in red at the upper right: "RODDY Mc DOWALL." Dated November 16, 1966, it reads "Dear Bill: / Enclosed is the picture of Stravinsky that you requested. I hope it is okay. / Best, [signed] Rod."

Actor-photographer Roddy McDowall, a Hollywood child star and later noted for his celebrity portraits, included this photograph in 1966 (but solely of Stravinsky's head) in his book, *Double Exposure*, noting therein that he took the photograph in 1965 at Hollywood. This was at the composer's last California address, 1218 North Wetherly Drive. He wears the same shirt with its pocket revealing the same pen and tip of eyeglasses as in a double portrait with Vera. Additional McDowall photographs of 1965 are dated 1967 and 1968 by Craft. Four of these are assigned to 1967 in the Paul Sacher Foundation.

In response to a letter of enquiry as to the identity of "Bill," the late Mr. McDowall kindly informed Dr. Slim by postcard of 8 October 1995: "It is awful I know – BUT – I have no[t] one iota of a memory about 'Bill' or that photograph. All I know is that I was thrilled and priviledged [sic] to have taken Stravinsky's picture and most delighted that he loved it!"

William Theophilus Brown, a close friend during the 1960s of both Stravinsky and Vera, kindly advises that the: "Bill is not he" (letter of 15 March 1997) and also that the dedicatee, unknown to him: "cannot have been close to Stravinsky" because of the impersonal nature of the inscription in Entry 116. Nor is the "Bill" in McDowall's letter likely to have been the painter William Congdon (1912-98), a friend of both Stravinskys from March 1955, who lived mostly in Italy, or the playwright William Inge (1913-73), who first met them in 1966, only two months before Entry 116 was sent to "Bill." Another possible "Bill" at this period might be William Vanderhoef (Lawrence Morton's companion). Composer William Kraft (1923-), then percussionist of the Los Angeles Philharmonic, advises it was not he.

Perhaps, however, "Bill" is William Bernal, an authority on film music, or William Claxton, a photographer of musicians and actors in the 1950s–60s. Both men were associated in one way or another with the composer at this period.

In October and November 1966, Bernal fitted music by Stravinsky to an already completed United Airlines Film, a commercial travelogue for United Airlines called "Discover America." Craft recorded the musical excerpts for it in Hollywood on 15 December. Bernal then completed the splicing at Chicago in December, and the Stravinskys dined with Bernal and others there on 29 December. Dr. Slim could discover no photographs, however, by Bernal, Congdon, and Inge in the Paul Sacher Foundation.

William Claxton photographed Stravinsky and Vera in Beverly Hills in the 1960s. On an envelope giving Claxton's address in Beverly Hills, Stravinsky notated: "Hollywood Juin 1961." At least two sets of nine photos each by Claxton taken in Beverly Hills, some of them cited in Craft's manuscript "Catalog" as from 1953, 1958, and 1965, are in the Paul Sacher Foundation.

Works Consulted

Craft, Robert. "Catalog of the Library of Robert Craft." Typescript: Library of Congress, Music Division. VIII: Robert Craft's Stravinskiana, no. 4 on p. 140; XII: Photographs, no. 88 on p. 192, nos. 218-31 on p. 210, and no. 360 on p. 211.

—. *Stravinsky: Chronicle of a Friendship*. New York, NY: Alfred A. Knopf, 1972. pl. [4]A btn pp. 300-01; 2nd ed. Nashville, TN, and London: Vanderbilt University Press, 1994. pp. 444-6, 565 (5 October 1971).

Crawford, Dorothy Lamb. *Evenings On and Off the Roof: Pioneering Concerts in Los Angeles, 1939-1971*. Berkeley and Los Angeles, CA, and London: University of California Press, 1995. p. 168, n. 25 on p. 327.

McDowall, Roddy. *Double Exposure*. New York, NY: Delacorte Press, 1966; rev. ed., New York, NY: Morrow, 1990. pl. on p. 63, p. 253.

"McDowall, Roddy." *Los Angeles Times*, 4 October 1998, A3 (obituary).

Newman, Arnold, and Robert Craft. *Bravo Stravinsky*. Cleveland, OH, and New York, NY: World, 1967. pp. [44-5].

SBu. pl. 152 on p. 200, pl. 167 on p. [217], nn. 5 and 9 on p. 222.

SScrbk. pl. 279 on p. 138, pl. 283 on p. 140.

117 (1967). Signed twice-folded typed letter, 27.9 × 21.6 cm, in English in black ink, 28 February 1967, to John McClure (1932-):

[typed above margin-to-margin rule] 1218 North Wetherly Drive
Hollywood, California 90069

28 February 1967

Mr. John McClure
COLUMBIA RECORDS
51 West 52nd Street
New York, New York

Dear John,

Several of my friends whose musical judgment I respect have told me, after the Oppenheimer memorial concert, that the LIBERA ME movement in the <u>Requiem Canticles</u> sounded like chaos and therefore I don't want that record to be released. The contralto and bass solos are faulty in intonation, and there are a number of wrong notes and other errors. Certainly this is not a fault of yours, but only an immature performance: you are quite right in opposing any recording of any new piece on its trial run. But the performance is bad, and would only do us injury by being released, because, of course, DGG or London will record it at Edinburgh with a first rate chorus and good soloists. I know that you have gone out on a limb because of that recording session, and I would, therefore, be glad to send a copy of this letter or write another letter to Goddard absolving you of blame.

Very cordially,
[in black ink] Igor Stravinsky
Igor Stravinsky

IS:ms

Acquisition: H. Colin Slim on 27 August 1997 from La Scala Autographs. *Provenance:* New York, Swann Auction of Stravinsky business correspondence (c. 1996); James Lowe, New York (until 25 August 1997).

Commentary

The letter is unpublished, its envelope missing. A copy of the letter is in the Paul Sacher Foundation. Entry 117 was typed by Marilyn Stalvey, part-time secretary, 1962-66, of Stravinsky and Craft, and full-time, 1966-69. (Apparently on Craft's instructions, she saved certain Stravinsky documents from the wastebasket, a task also performed at this period with Vera's approval by Edwin Allen.) Brief excerpts from Entry 117 (dated as 27 February) were published by Craft in his *Stravinsky: Glimpses of a Life*.

John McClure succeeded David Oppenheim in 1959 as producer of Stravinsky recordings for Columbia (see entries 97-9). He appears with the composer in several photographs, one reproduced in a 1962 eightieth birthday tribute, the others taken on 20 July 1964 when recording *Orpheus* with the Chicago Symphony. Afterward that same day Stravinsky flew with McClure to Los Angeles. He is heard in conversation with Stravinsky in rehearsals for recordings in 1962 and 1964-65. Late in 1971, as director of Columbia Records Masterworks Division, he spoke at a colloquium in remembrance of Stravinsky held at the University of Toronto.

Goddard Lieberson (1911-77), composer and critic, was for a decade producer of Stravinsky recordings for Columbia from April 1940, succeeding to the presidency of Columbia Records in 1956. For the record company Lieberson wrote a tribute on his eightieth birthday and a memorial in 1971.

J. Robert Oppenheimer (1904-67) first met Stravinsky at Princeton on 28 August 1959. The great physicist and director (1947-66) of the Institute for Advanced Study admired the *Requiem Canticles* at its premiere there on 8 October 1966, leaving a request that it be played at his funeral. The recording used for the Oppenheimer memorial concert on 25 February 1967 was either a tape made at Princeton or one made in New York the previous 11 October. The latter was not released commercially until March 1970.

Stravinsky first heard this recording in New York on 7 January 1967, at which time he deplored its many errors. As to the unidentified informants mentioned in Entry 117, in addition of course to Craft, several musically knowledgeable "friends" pictured at rehearsals in New York and Princeton in October 1966 attended the memorial concert for Oppenheimer, some of them surely including Claudio Spies. Late in 1966 and the ensuing 19 January, Spies had written Stravinsky about various "mistakes" in the *Requiem Canticles*.

On 28 March 1970 Stravinsky commented: "A recording of the [*Requiem*] *Canticles* has finally been released, by the way, but nearly four years after it was made, for which reason, standards of live performance having long since overtaken it, I am inclined to say better never than this late." Libman refers to another 1967 letter by Stravinsky shown to her by Craft which concerns the recording.

Even before the premiere of the *Requiem Canticles* at Princeton, he (or Craft) had planned to conduct a European premiere the following spring. Although Entry 117 suggests that this would be delayed until the Edinburgh Festival in September, by 10 December 1966 Edinburgh had already been informed that he would not be going there to conduct the work, nor did Craft do so. By 17 May 1967 he had promised the European premiere to Paris for the coming December. In the event, it took place at Edinburgh on 2 September 1967, led by Pierre Boulez.

Entry 117 and the subsequent issue of the *Requiem Canticles* in 1970 against his wishes illustrate the degree of disillusionment with the record industry that he experienced during his final years.

Works Consulted

Allen, Edwin. "The Genius and the Goddess," *Confronting Stravinsky: Man, Musician, and Modernist.* ed. Jann Pasler. Berkeley and Los Angeles, CA, and London: University of California Press, 1986. p. 329.

Craft, Robert. *Stravinsky: Chronicle of a Friendship.* 2nd ed. Nashville, TN, and London: Vanderbilt University Press, 1994. p. 448 (7 January 1967).

–. *Stravinsky: Glimpses of a Life.* London: Lime Tree, 1992; New York, NY: St. Martin's Press, 1993. n. 5 on p. 18.

Crawford, Dorothy Lamb. *Evenings On and Off the Roof: Pioneering Concerts in Los Angeles, 1939-1971.* Berkeley and Los Angeles, CA, and London: University of California Press, 1995. pp. 284-5.

Libman, Lillian. *And Music at the Close: Stravinsky's Last Years, A Personal Memoir*. New York, NY: W.W. Norton, 1972. pp. 224, 280, 299-300, 330, 360-2.

Lieberson, Goddard. "Igor Stravinsky. A Tribute." *The Gramophone* 49 (June 1971): 19.

"Lieberson, Goddard." *Current Biography Yearbook 1976*. ed. Charles Moritz. New York, NY: H.W. Wilson, 1977. pp. 233-6.

McClure, John. "Igor Stravinsky at Eighty." *The Gramophone* 40, no. 469 (June 1962): 1-3, with pl. on p. 1.

Meyer, Felix, ed. *Settling New Scores. Music Manuscripts from the Paul Sacher Foundation*. Mainz: Schott, 1998. pp. 74-5, nos. 32-3.

Miller, Eileen. *The Edinburgh International Festival 1947-1996*. Louth: Scolar Press, 1996. pp. 69, 220.

Newman, Arnold, and Robert Craft. *Bravo Stravinsky*. Cleveland, OH, and New York, NY: World, 1967. pls. on pp. [48-61], [84], [88-91], [96-100], [108].

"Regards en arrière/Looking back." *Les Cahiers canadiens/The Canada Music Book* 4 (1972): 29-30.

Straus, Joseph N. "Stravinsky's Serial 'Mistakes'." *The Journal of Musicology* 17 (1999): 238-41.

SP&D. p. 584.

SScrbk. p. 175 (medical diaries: 20 July 1964).

SSC. vol. 2. n. 90 on p. 419; vol. 3. pp. 456-7.

ST&C. p. 293.

Stuart, Philip. *Igor Stravinsky — The Composer in the Recording Studio. A Comprehensive Discography*. New York, NY, Westport, CT, and London: Greenwood Press, 1991. pp. 10-11, 18-23, T3 on p. 56, 179c on p. 61.

Wagner, Denise. "A Stravinsky Scrapbook from the Chicago Symphony Archives." *Notebook. The Program of the Chicago Symphony Orchestra* (24-26 and 29 October 1996), pls. on pp. 17, 26.

118

(1967). **Autographed unsealed first day cover, 9.3 × 16.4 cm, commemorating a 25th anniversary issue of Voice of America five-cent US stamps, all four of which are cancelled, and mailed from Washington, DC, 1 August 1967. Stravinsky wrote sideways in English in green ink on the envelope:**

Igor Stravinsky
August
1967

Acquisition: H. Colin Slim on 20 January 1995 from Wurlitzer-Bruck.
Provenance: Unknown.

Commentary

This first day cover is neither published, nor its sender from Washington
known. Stravinsky had often taped interviews for future broadcasting
by the Voice of America. The sender of Entry 118 might have been
Harold Box for whom he had taped many interviews or his longtime
New York friend, Natasha Nabokov, both employees of the Voice of
America.

The strength of Stravinsky's handwriting in Entry 118 suggests,
however, a date before 21 August 1967. From that date until 4
September, he was hospitalized with a bleeding ulcer at Cedars of
Lebanon in Los Angeles. His medical diary for 1967 has not been
located. (Entries 118 and 123 are framed together.)

Works Consulted

Craft, Robert. *Stravinsky: Chronicle of a Friendship*. 2nd ed. Nashville, TN, and
    London: Vanderbilt University Press, 1994. pp. 459-60.
SBu. p. 223 (September 1967).
SP&D. p. 248, n. 143 on p. 654.
SScrbk. p. 155 (preface to medical diaries).

119

(1967). **Autograph untitled musical quotations in black ballpoint ink, one on each side of a single sheet of twelve-staved
com-mercial music paper, 31.9 × 24.3 cm (Pacific Music Papers,
Hollywood Calif., no. 703-W), from the "Russian Dance" in
Petrushka (1911) with an inscription in English on one side. The
first quotation on the third stave has thirteen notes, cancelled
by Stravinsky. The second one on the other side of the sheet on
the fourth stave with twenty notes he inscribed to an unknown
recipient, 10 November 1967, perhaps a nurse:**

Every kooky
note, I hope,
[of] this music

Igor Stravinsky
Sinai Hospital
Los Angeles
1967, Nov 10

Acquisition: H. Colin Slim on 1 May 1995 from J. and J. Lubrano.
Provenance: Probably someone on the Mount Sinai Hospital staff, Los Angeles (November 1967); an unidentified collector in the United States (c. 1990-95).

Commentary

The quotations are not published as such. Both passages in Entry 119 lack (treble) clefs, bar lines, and are not quite accurate in respect to rhythm. Evidently dissatisfied with his first and incomplete attempt, he turned over the music sheet and wrote notes and inscription.

After finishing *The Owl and the Pussycat* (1966), he was unable to compose any more. Hospitalized 2-28 November 1967, this time in Mount Sinai with a gangrenous left hand, Stravinsky, as Craft noted, granted autographs for nurses, some including music, on the morning he left the hospital. Even though executed in a shaky hand, the notations on Entry 119 are little short of miraculous from an eighty-five-year-old in great pain and frequently under heavy sedation during much of his stay in the hospital. His fascination with the "Russian Dance" is also demonstrated in the counterpoint he wrote in red and green inks to the same theme two years previously. (La Scala Autographs offered in December 1998 a signed 1955 quotation of the opening of the Russian dance.)

Works Consulted

Craft, Robert. *Stravinsky: Chronicle of a Friendship*. 2nd ed. Nashville, TN, and London: Vanderbilt University Press, 1994. p. 471 (28 November 1967).

La Scala Autographs, Inc. *1998 Holiday Catalogue*. Pennington, NJ: 1998. p. 24, no. 127.

SP&D. uppermost colour pl. 2 btn pp. 144-5.

120 (1970). Signed twice-folded typed letter, 27.7 × 21.5 cm, in English in black ink, 30 September 1970, to George Rizza:

Essex House
160 Central Park South
New York, N.Y. 10019

Mr. George Rizza   September 30, 1970
J. & W. Chester Ltd.
Eagle Court
London, E.C. 1
England

Dear Mr. Rizza:

Since I moved to New York a year ago my files have not yet been put completely in order, and I am unable at present to find a copy of my contract with Chester. Would you be kind enough to send a copy to my attorney at the following address?:

> Mr. Arnold Weissberger
> Weissberger & Frosch
> 120 East 56th Street
> New York, New York 10022

Thank you very much for your cooperation.

Sincerely yours
[signed in black ink] Igor Strawinsky
[typed] Igor Strawinsky

IS:pa
[in blue ink, not by Stravinsky] CC: Mr. A.W.

Acquisition: H. Colin Slim on 2 May 1999 from David Schulson, his catalogue, *David Schulson Autographs 100* (New York, Spring 1999), 46, item 102.

Provenance: Unidentified dealer in England; at the top left margin by an unknown hand (presumably a dealer) in pencil is: "Died April 6,71"; and at the bottom: "He was already quite ill hence poor signature."

Commentary

The letter is unpublished, its envelope missing. The former is watermarked: Eaton's Corrasable, surmounted by a crown; the typist, "pa," remains unidentified. The statement in Schulson's catalogue that Stravinsky "conducted his last symphony" at "New York in 1969" is incorrect. He last conducted on 17 May 1967, at Toronto's Massey Hall.

The extremely shaky signature of the eighty-nine-year-old composer is to be compared with the already wobbly one in Entry 119, almost three years earlier. In Entry 120 he has reverted to his first mode of signing his name with "w" rather than "v."

Both signatures testify eloquently to the medical attention he required and which was provided in his last years by doctors in New York. He and Vera moved there permanently from Los Angeles on 15 September 1969, living first at the Plaza Hotel and then at Essex House from 14 October. On the following 11 June, they flew to Evian on Lake Geneva, dining two days later in the Hôtel Royale's restaurant with their lawyer Arnold Weissberger and his friend Milton Goldman. The day after Lord Snowdon took his celebrated portraits of the composer, they returned to Essex House, on 26 August, until they moved to their apartment at 920 5th Avenue on 29 March 1971, just a week before he died, on 6 April.

Although by 1915, J. and W. Chester represented his Russian publishers abroad, he first published with the English firm early in the 1920s when they took over five works which Adolphe Henn had issued in 1917 (see Entry 13). At this time the Chester firm published such important works as *Renard* (in 1920), *Les Noces* (in 1922-23), *The Soldier's Tale* (in 1920-24), and the piano reduction of *Pulcinella* (in 1920). Often stormy, their relationship was soured by a lawsuit in 1926-27 about the 1919 *Firebird Suite* and by the firm's often dilatory publishing practices. For example, in 1929 Stravinsky complained to Willy Strecker of Schott & Sons that the *Four Russian Peasant Songs*, finished in 1917, had been with J. & W. Chester Ltd. and neglected by them for over a decade (SSC, vol. 3, p. 222), and indeed, they were not published until 1930. Two years later he again wrote Strecker in Wiesbaden, calling Chester "bandits" and styling himself a thirteen-year martyr of that firm (SSC, vol. 2, p. 249).

Owing to his addition of four French horns to and the revision in 1954 of the already-mentioned *Four Russian Peasant Songs* (publ. Chester 1958) and to his creation in 1962 of *Eight Instrumental Miniatures* (publ. 1963) from *The Five Fingers* (1922), he once again signed contracts with J. and W. Chester. It is probably to one or the other of these works that "my contract with Chester" in Entry 120 refers. (A photostatic copy of the *Four Russian Peasant Songs* of 28 July 1955 with corrections and annotations by Stravinsky was auctioned in October 1999.)

Works Consulted

Bois, Mario. *Près de Strawinsky 1959-70*. Paris: Marval, 1996. pls. on pp. [100], [128].

Craft, Robert. *Stravinsky: Chronicle of a Friendship*. New York, NY: Alfred A. Knopf, 1972. pls.[6-7]B and C, btn pp. 300-01. [First edition; not in 2nd ed. Nashville, TN, and London: Vanderbilt University Press, 1994.]

Horgan, Paul. *Encounters with Stravinsky: A Personal Record*. New York, NY: Farrar, Straus and Giroux. 1972. pp. 253-70.

Libman, Lillian. *And Music at the Close: Stravinsky's Last Years, A Personal Memoir*. New York, NY: W.W. Norton, 1972. pp. 353-84; captions are reversed in two 1969 photographs by Miriam Pollack, pl. [7] btn pp. 208-9.

SBu. pp. 230-7.

SI&V. pls. 251-4 on p. 141.

SP&D. p. 494, pl. on p. 497.

SScrbk. pl. 282 on p. 140.

SSC. vol. 2. pp. 227-49; vol. 3. p. 222.

Strawinsky. Sein Nachlass. Sein Bild [with] *Katalog der ausgestellten Bildnisse und Entwürfe für die Ausstattung seiner Bühnenwerke*. Basle: Kunstmuseum and Paul Sacher Stiftung, 1984. pl. on p. 283 and *Katalog* 237 (both miscaptioned "September").

Swann Galleries. *Autographs, Public Auction Sale 1836*. New York, 14 October 1999, lot 139.

121 (1971). Poster printed in blue and black, 92.7 × 63.5 cm, in Italian announcing funeral arrangements, 14-15 April 1971, at Venice:

La città di Venezia rende omaggio alle spoglie del grande
musicista IGOR STRAVINSKY che con gesto di squisita
amicizia desiderò in vita di essere sepolto nella città che amò
sopra ogni altra

The city of Venice pays homage to the remains of the great composer IGOR STRAVINSKY, who, with a gesture of exquisite friendship, desired while living to be buried in the city that he loved above all others.

Acquisition: by kind gift to H. Colin Slim on 9 April 1979, from William C. Holmes (1928-99) and Frank A. D'Accone (1931-). Attending the funeral in 1971, the late Professor Holmes afterward removed the poster from a wall.
Provenance: William C. Holmes, Laguna Beach (1971-79).

Commentary
Colour reproductions of three such posters on a Venetian wall, 13 April 1971, are in Craft's *Chronicle of a Friendship* and in *Pictures and Documents*. Libman gives an account of the funeral and supplies photographs of the family at it, of the grave at San Michele (before placement of its headstone), and of a tattered poster on the facade of San Zanipolo, three months after the funeral.

Concerning the choice of Venice itself, Craft observes that, contrary to Entry 121, Stravinsky: "never expressed any desire to be buried here," that the decision was taken by him and by Vera, and that St. Petersburg was the composer's favourite city. According to Nicolas Nabokov, he once observed: "I will someday lie there [St. Petersburg] next to my father" (Libman, p. 32). Indeed, he remarked in 1962: "it is dearer to my heart than any other city in the world" (SE&D, p. 37).

Works Consulted

Craft, Robert. *Stravinsky: Chronicle of a Friendship*. 2nd ed. Nashville, TN, and London: Vanderbilt University Press, 1994. colour pl. [6] btn pp. 462-3, pp. 550-4.

Libman, Lillian. *And Music at the Close: Stravinsky's Last Years, A Personal Memoir*. New York, NY: W.W. Norton, 1972. pp. 17-50 and pl. [8] facing p. 209.

SE&D. (1962) p. 37; (1981) p. 35.

SP&D. colour pl. 28 facing p. 496.

122

(1972). Round bronze medal, 3.8 cm in diameter, struck for the New York City Ballet 18 June 1972, commemorating the Stravinsky Festival by George Balanchine and given by Vera Stravinsky to Olga Maynard (1914-94) at the festival. Its face has on a five-line stave: "iS" (the second letter shaped as a treble clef), and is circumscribed: IGOR STRAVINSKY 1882 1971 NEW YORK CITY BALLET JUNE 18 1972; its obverse reproduces a Greek lyre.

Acquisition: by kind gift to H. Colin Slim in 1989 from Professor Maynard.

Provenance: Vera Stravinsky, New York (1972), to Olga Maynard (1972-89).

Commentary

Olga Maynard was Professor in the Department of Dance, University of California at Irvine, from 1969 until her retirement in 1989. Craft provides a close critique of this festival. The medal's obverse perhaps refers to Stravinsky's *Orpheus*.

Works Consulted

Craft, Robert. *Stravinsky: Glimpses of a Life*. London: Lime Tree, 1992; New York, NY: St. Martin's Press, 1993. pp. 270-5.

123

(1982). Mint sheet, 26.0 × 23.0 cm, of 100 definitive two-cent US stamps commemorating Stravinsky's one-hundredth birthday, issued by the United States Postal Service late in 1982.

Acquisition: H. Colin Slim on 17 October 1994 from Champion Stamp Co. Inc. (430 West 54th Street / 2nd floor / New York).
Provenance: Champion Stamp Co. (1982-94).

Commentary

Lawrence Morton was the principle instigator of the project to have this stamp issued. The same year the principality of Monaco also issued its own commemorative stamp. (Entry 123 is framed with Entry 118.)

Works Consulted

Morton, Lawrence. Papers, Box 5. Special Collections 1522. Charles E. Young Research Library. University of California at Los Angeles.

Tower, Samuel A. "Newest Addition to the Great American Series." *New York Times.* 21 November 1982. "Stamps."

INDEX

quotations (1937, 1966), 10, 187, 334-6; translation of program notes, 37

The Firebird Suite (1919): at Hollywood Bowl (1940), 220-1; lawsuit concerning, 346; photographs of S and NY Philharmonic (1962), 324-7; planned concert in London (1915), 40, 42; signed concert program, 10, 194-6; in Vancouver 1952, 7

The Five Fingers (1922), 347

Flonzaley Quartet, 40, 41

The Flood (1962), 321-4

Foetisch Frères (publishers), 58

Forbes, Edward Waldo, 158, 225, 228, 262

Four Russian Peasant Songs (1914-17), 113, 290, 293, 347

Fraser, C. Lovat, 87-8

Freistadt, Harry, 256-8

Freund, Marya: postcards from S (1915, 1921), 44-7, 50-5, 92; singing voice, 46, 51, 52-3, 53-4

Fruhauf, Aline, 152-4

Galm, Bernard, 334-5

Garbat, Abraham Leon, 128-9

German Institute for Musical Performing Rights, 14, 63-6

Gershwin, George, 127, 129, 141, 155

Gesualdo madrigals, 318-20

Glass, Douglas, 284-5, 314-16

Gollancz, Victor, 165

Golubeff, Gregory, 215

Goth, Trudy, 263-5

Gui, Vittorio, 197-200

Halpern, Ida, 7

Hammond, Richard, 235

Handschin, Jacques, 71

Henn, Adolfe, 64, 65-6

Hessenland, Werner, 265-8

Hill, Ginny Carpenter Hill, 91, 139

Hindemith, Paul, 12, 123-5

L'Histoire du soldat (*Story of a Soldier / The Soldier's Tale*, 1918), 114-16, 189, 288, 289, 346

Hollywood Bowl (1940), 219-21, 231-2

Hopper, Dorothy Ellis McQuoid. *See* McQuoid, Dorothy Ellis

Hoyningen-Huené, George, 12, 222-4

Hunstein, Don, 332-3

Huxley, Aldous, 279, 280, 299, 306, 307-8

In Memoriam Dylan Thomas (1954), 282, 289, 290, 293-4

Indiana, Robert, 319

Ingi (Louis Ingigliardi), 309-10

Isherwood, Christopher, 299

Ishlon, Deborah, 14, 91, 305-9

Janacopulos-Staal, Vera: career, 105-8, 119, 122-3; inscription from S (1920), 107; letters (1923, 1924), 14, 102-10, 116-20, 120-3; photograph with S (1926), 122

Japanese Lyrics, 37, 107, 118, 122

Jeu de cartes (*Card Game*, 1936), 206-7, 209-11, 305

Johnston, Richard, 250

Jurgenson, B.P., 42

Kall, Alexis Fyodorovich: letter from S re tuberculosis (1939), 198-9; photograph with S and Robinson (1935), 4, 12, 154-60; relationship with S, 3-4, 155, 156-8; translator and secretary to S, 158, 199, 206, 215

Kashperova, Leokadiya Alexandrovna, 156

Khovanshchina (1913), 25

Kibalchich, Vasily Fyodorovich, 110-13

Kirstein, Lincoln, 303-5, 315

Kochanski: Paul, 127, 129, 140-4; Zosia, 127, 142

Kochno, Boris, 53, 77-8, 88-9

Kohner, Paul, 329-32

Koussevitsky, Serge, 107, 145, 210

Krenek, Ernst, 316-17

Laffitte, Paul, 14, 66-9

Lang, Paul Henry, 322-3

Larmanjat, Jacques, 94, 95, 203-4

Letters, autograph: to Brodetsky re *Apollo* score (1942), 239-41; to Calvocoressi, mentioning Rimsky-Korsakov, 22-7; to Charles Cushing (1957), 298-301; to Clara Bickford (1937), 180-3; to Dr. Garbat (1925), 128-9; to E. Mounez (1936), 161-3; to Jacques Rouché about Colette

(1916), 56-9; to Kall re tuberculosis (1939), 198-9; to Kibalchich re contribution to *Les Noces* (1923), 110-13; love letters to VS (1921), 13, 76-83, 83-90; to McQuoids (1940, 1941), 7, 218-22, 226-8; overview of correspondence, 12-14; to Paul Laffite re publishing contract (1918), 14, 66-9; to Rabeneck re *Chant du Rossignol* (1927), 14, 144-7; to Robert Lyon re illness (1920), 72-3; to Roland-Manuel for Diaghilev (1920), 74-5; to Sakharoff re neuralgia (1916), 59-63; to Steinway and Sons (1925), 129-31; to unnamed friends re chauffeur (1925), 131-5; to VJ re loan (1923), 102-10

Letters, typed and signed: to Bottenheim re Brussels festival (1930), 148-52; to Brodetsky re chamber music ensemble (1942), 235-8; to Broude Brothers re book (1960), 316-17; to Deborah Ishlon, re publishers (1958), 14, 305-9; to Doda Conrad, with forged signature (1957), 301-3; to Dylan Thomas re California (1953), 278-83; to George Rizza re contract (1970), 14, 345-7; to German Institute for Musical Performing Rights (1917), 14, 63-6; to J. Nizon re music and feelings (1945), 254-6; to John McClure re *Requiem Canticles* (1967), 17, 339-42; overview of correspondence, 12-14; to Paul Kohner re his acting as agent (1964), 14, 329-32; to Pierre Monteux re rehearsals (1939), 4, 204-9; to Roland-Manuel re Jean Marx (1939), 200-4; to van Patten re *Danses concertantes* manuscript (1947), 258-60; to VJ re concerts (1923, 1924), 116-20, 120-3; to Walter de Bourg re delivering score (1944), 252-4; to Weissberger re Columbia Records (1954), 14, 285-8, 289-92, 292-4; to Weissberger re Stravinsky Festival (1957), 14, 303-5

Libman, Lillian, 323, 325, 341, 348

Lifar, Serge, 95, 148

Lieberson, Goddard, 340

Los Angeles Chamber Symphony Orchestra, 268-9

Los Angeles Festival Symphony Orchestra, 298-300

Los Angeles Philharmonic, 9, 158, 179

Lowinsky, Edward, 310-14

Lyon, Robert, 72-3, 96

McClure, John, 339-42

McDowall, Roddy, 12, 336-8

McQuoid, Cary Ellis, 10, 211-12 (photographed with S)

McQuoid, Dorothy Ellis: autographed 1934 photograph of S (1940), 12, 222-4; "Firebird" hat, 10, 221; first edition of *The Star-Spangled Banner* (1941), 228-33; letter, with untitled musical quotations (1940), 7, 218-22; notes and postcards from S (1939, 1940, 1941), 11, 211, 212, 215-18, 226-8; photograph of her, Edwin McQuoid, and VS, 11, 217; piano teacher, Alexis Kall, 10, 157, 158; relationship with S, 10-11, 158, 211-29; score of *Petrushka* (1939), 213-14

McQuoid, Edwin, 10, 212, 224-6, 227-8. *See also* McQuoid, Dorothy Ellis

Maggio Musicale festival, Florence, 198, 199

Mandelstamm, Yury Vladimirovich, 207-8

Marcus, Adele, 158

Marion, André (son-in-law of S), 4, 7, 280, 287, 301-3

Marx, Jean, 203

Mastrazzi, Aída Victoria, 165-9

Matharel, Guy de, Count, 134

Mavra (1922), 71, 78, 81, 190

Mayakovsky, Vladimir, 94

Maynard, Olga, 349

Medals, commemorative, 349

Mercury Music Corporation, 229-31

Merritt, Arthur Tillman, 8

Milhaud, Darius, 107, 108

Montapert, William, 329-31

Monteux, Pierre, 4, 41, 204-9

Monumentum (1960), 318-21

Morton, Lawrence, 4, 291-2, 350

Mounez, E. , 161-3

Murphy, Gerald and Sara, 134

Music, autograph: *Apollo* (1937), 193; Christmas card, with musical quotation (1941), 233-5; *Concerto in D for violin and orchestra* (1937), 194; *Deux poèmes*, 3, 15; *Divertimento* (1936), 10, 14-15, 169-78; *The Firebird* (1937, 1966), 10, 187, 334-6; *Jeu de cartes* (1939), 209-11; *Le Chant du Rossignol* (1937, 1939), 189, 196-7; *Les Noces*, 14, 92-9; letter to McQuoids, with untitled musical quotations (1940), 7, 218-22; *L'Histoire du soldat* (1937), 189; *Mavra* (1937), 190; *Octet* (1937), 192; *Oedipus Rex* (1937), 192; *Petrushka* (1937, 1967), 187-8, 343-4; *Pulcinella* (1937), 190; *The Rite of Spring* (1937), 188; *Scherzo à la Russe* (1943-44), 2, 15, 241-9; song, "Myosotis," 28-32; *Symphony of Psalms* (1937), 193-4; *Threni* (1959), 310-14; undated quotations, Bickford collection, remarks, 183-7; *The Wedding* (1937), 191-2

Musica nova 1540, 9

Musical America, 152-4, 275

Musical Courier, 152

Musical quotations. *See* Music, autograph

The Musical Times, 24, 25

Musik der Zeit, 276-7

Mussolini, Benito, 199, 203

"Myosotis" ["Forget-me-not"], 28-32

Nabokov, Nicholas, 15, 296, 308

New York City Ballet, commemorative medal, 349

New York Herald Tribune, 321-4

New York Philharmonic Orchestra, 5, 220, 324-7

Nightingale. See Le Rossignol

Nijinska, Bronislava, 134, 167, 176

Nizon, J., 254-6

Les Noces (The Wedding, 1923): autograph sketches, 14, 92-9; Canadian premiere (1952), 6, 269-70; "Choeurs russes" of Kibalchich, 112; collection of items, 5, 6, 9-10; for player piano, 94, 95; premieres, 94, 95, 101; published by Chester, 346; set painting, 134; souvenir program (1923), 94

Nouvel, Walter ("Valechka"), 89, 157, 165

Ocampo, Victoria, 167, 176, 199, 201-2, 308

Octet (1923), 9, 146, 192, 288, 289

Oedipus Rex (1926), 141, 145, 192, 265-8

Oppenheim, David, 285-8, 289-93, 340

Oppenheimer, J. Robert, 339, 340

Orpheus (1947), 8, 272, 349

Païchadze, Gavriyil Gregorievich, 145

Pastorale (1907), 119

Pater Noster (1932), 145

Perséphone, 168, 198-9, 308, 333

Petrushka: composition, 25-6; conducted by Casella (1915), 40, 41, 45-6, 48, 49; conducted by S (1926), 137-8; danced by Mastrazzi, Bolm, 167, 220; inscribed edition (1939), 213-14; letter re premiere, 23, 26; musical quotations (1937, 1967), 187-8, 343-4; revised edition (1914), unpublished, 36, 37

Photographs: autographed 1934 photograph of S, by Hoyningen-Huené (1940), 12, 222-4; McQuoids and VS, 11, 217; photograph of Buenos Aires, by Lazaro Sudak (1936), 165-8; S, by Edward Weston (1935), 212; S, by Edwin McQuoid (1940), 224-6, 227-8; S, by Ingi (1958), 309-10; S, by Paola Foa (1946); S by Roddy McDowall (1966), 336-8; S, Cocteau, Picasso, and Olga (1925, 1926, or 1927), 133; S, inscribed to Douglas Glass (1954, 1959), 284-5, 314-16; S, inscribed to Georges Auric (1923), 12, 99-102; S, inscribed to Harry Adaskin (1952), 7, 270-4; S, inscribed to Marshall Bean (1965), 332-4; S, inscribed to Werner Hessenland (1951), 265-8; S, Kall, and Robinson (1935), 4, 12, 154-60; S, Paul Hindemith, and Amar Quartet (1924), 12, 123-5; S, rephotograph of Eric Skipsey's (1952), 7, 12, 275-6; S, VJ, and husband (1926), 122; S and Ansermet in Villa Rogivue (1915 or 1916), 52; S and Cary McQuoid (1939), 211-13; S and Debussy, by Eric Satie, 12; S and J. Castro (1960), 176; S and NY Philharmonic (1962), 324-7; S and Robinson (1935), 4, 12, 154-60, 212; S and VS (1940), 4, 214-15; S at Aeolian Hall, NY (1925), 126-7; S at Carantec, France (1920), 121; S at piano, inscribed to Bottenheim (1924), 151; S conducting *Rake's Progress* (1951), 263-5; villa at Ustilug (1911), 28-9, 31

Piano Concerto, 124

Picasso, Pablo, 68, 107, 132-3, 164-5, 178, 179

Piccagliani, Erio, 263-5

Player piano transcriptions: enthusiasm of S for, 94, 95-6, 98; *Le Faune et la bergère*, 116-18; *Les Noces* sketches, 14, 92-9; Pleyel contracts, 94, 203

Weissberger, Arnold: comment about his enforcing payment, 306, 307; letter re autobiography of S, 14, 303-5; letters re Columbia Records (1954), 14, 285-8, 289-92, 292-4
Whiteman, Paul, 249

Wiborg, Mary Hoyt "Hoytie," 134
Wise, C. Stanley, 52, 134

Zay, Jean, 202-3
Zvezdolikiy [Star-Faced One] (1911), 9, 30